From Deluge to Discourse

SUNY Series in Chinese Philosophy and Culture
David L. Hall and Roger T. Ames, Editors

From Deluge to Discourse

Myth, History, and the Generation of Chinese Fiction

Deborah Lynn Porter

State University of New York Press

Published by
State University of New York Press, Albany

Printed in the United States of America

For information, address State University of New York
Press, State University Plaza, Albany, N.Y., 12246

Production by E. Moore
Marketing by Nancy Farrell

Library of Congress Cataloging-in-Publication Data
Porter, Deborah Lynn.
From deluge to discourse: myth, history, and the generation of
Chinese fiction / Deborah Lynn Porter.
p. cm.—(Suny series in Chinese philosophy and culture)
Includes bibliographical references and index.
ISBN 0-7914-3033-2 (alk. paper).—ISBN 0-7914-3034-0 (pbk.: alk.
paper)
1. Mythology, Chinese. 2. Legends—China. 3. Chinese fiction—
History and criticism. I. Title. II. Series.
BL1825.P37 1996
895.1'31—dc20

95-41456
CIP

10 9 8 7 6 5 4 3 2 1

In Memory of Stephen S. and Carol R. Porter

CONTENTS

Acknowledgments

A journey of intellectual pursuit is never completed single-handedly. I would like to express my appreciation to those who accompanied me at various points along the way. Professor Edward Shaughnessy's impassioned teaching ignited in me the enthusiasm for and interest in Early China; to him I also am indebted for the initial idea of examining the *Mu T'ien-tzu chuan* from a literary perspective. The Committee of Scholarly Communication with the People's Republic of China granted me support in 1989–1990, to begin work on the project. While in China I greatly benefitted from the generous and gracious help of Professor Li Xueqin of the History Institute of the Academy of Social Sciences, and Hu Pingsheng, of the Cultural Relics Bureau in Beijing. As the project began to take shape, the stimulating comments from Professors Anthony Yu, Esther Rashkin, Jerry Root and Joan Judge nourished my critical development and ensured that I was always in great supply of intellectual fare. Professor David Pankenier, whose own scholarship served in part as a figurative map for my journey, tirelessly contributed his erudition, enthusiasm and critical perspective. A generous and consummate scholar, Professor Pankenier supremely enriched the process of my intellectual growth. Laura Anne Skosey, the ideal travelling companion, gave me her most valuable gift: her genuine excitement over my project and her time. Often engaging with me in hours long discussions as I struggled with the conceptual countours of the project's evolving geography, she would inevitably offer incisive, constructive comments which enabled me to negotiate the rough terrain that I was forging. I am so very thankful for her warm and stimulating companionship. A Dolores Eccles Fellowship from the University of Utah Humanities Center enabled me to complete the writing of the manuscript during the year of 1993–1994. I am extremely grateful to my department, the Department of Languages and Literature at the University of Utah, for allowing me to take this time off, and to Dr. Lowell Durham, the director of the Center, and Lynne Rasmussen, the Executive Secretary, whose interest, support and general mirth made my year at the Center both productive and extremely enjoyable. Thanks are also due to Ilene Cohen for her helpful editorial comments; and to my student Emmy Ebanks, who helped compile the index. The editors at SUNY Press, Carola Sautter and Elizabeth Moore, have been extremely helpful and enjoyable to work with. I am thankful for how smooth they have made the publication process.

Finally, my family, Dan, Laura, Kelly, Kevin and Tamara, all played integral roles along the way. Like beacons guiding the passage of boats along a rough sea, they have consistently provided me with the means to anchor the coordinates of my travel in a larger, denser and immensely richer context. To A.A.Y., who initially questioned the appropriateness of my journey's direction, I can only vaguely express my inexpressable sentiments of appreciation; the arrival at the destination of this intellectual pursuit was made to be so much more personally significant because of my involvement with you. The successful transcendence of barriers separating these two realms—intellectual and personal—is indeed for me the most precious outcome of this project.

Introduction

This book is a study of the interrelations between myth, history, and the emergence of fictional narrative in China. Its aim specifically is to provide an aesthetic theory that accounts for the distinction between the genres of historiography and fiction in Chinese narrative. In this it is very much in line with other recent work on Chinese narrative, and it owes a debt to the innovations of these critical predecessors. Nonetheless, it also advances a new line of inquiry, both theoretical and methodological. It is an approach premised on the belief that early myths can be employed as heuristic devices to shed light on the discursive features that distinguish Chinese fiction as a distinct form of representation.

My use of the term "fiction" in this study is qualified; as used here, the term is connected to the word's conventional meaning *only* in the sense that it is a form of literary expression distinct from history. Thus, notions of truth, falsity, authorial intention, plot, or even storytelling are not relevant qualities for determining what I call fiction. I choose nevertheless to use the term rather than discard it, for the sake of continuity with previous studies of the same literary phenomenon. This does not, I rush to add, signify any adherence on my part to the underlying assumptions that have colored its use in those studies. In fact, the present study can be construed as an endeavor to offer a new definition of the term that is appropriate for the Chinese context.

With its interest in analyzing mythic discourse to illuminate the discursive strategies organizing fictional forms of expression, this study shares Andrew Plaks' premise that the two forms are connected by rhetorical principles of coherence.[1] We are both alert to an array of rhetorical techniques that camouflage, transform, and disarray meaning and cultural codes. By contrast, however, my study does not privilege structuralism, with its reliance on establishing underlying formal systems of oppositions for evaluating the text's conformity to predetermined cultural and literary expectations, conventions, and modes of organization (Plaks' "archetypes"). Rather, I am interested in going beyond surface meaning of a text to identify those rhetorical strategies that challenge or displace meaning. More than elaborating *how* meaning is rendered indeterminable in a text, I attempt to explain *why* that meaning of the text is unattainable. The source responsible for the deferment of meaning is, I demonstrate, implicitly contained within the texts.

The conceptual configuration of symbol articulated by the psychoanalyst and philosopher Nicolas Abraham has been an important tool in my attempt to unveil these linguistic and literary processes in myth and fiction. His elucidation of the ontological implications of the processes leading to the creation of symbols has profoundly influenced my exploration of the theoretical and interpretive implications of the symbol for the study of fictional discourse in traditional China.

My understanding of discourse has profited from the recent theoretical work on the subject, even if it does not accept that work in toto. Thus, I find Seymour Chatman's distinction between story and discourse helpful in distinguishing between various levels of signification, but am not persuaded that his formalist model is the best way to account for the complexity of the literary effects produced by the differing levels.[2] In the same vein, Michel Foucault's notion of discourse as practice, as a discontinuous activity that can only be understood from the perspective of its "external conditions of existence," is helpful for its emphasis on "restoring to discourse its character as an event," but it, too, falls short as a critical tool for literary analysis because it negates the value of burrowing to the hidden core of discourse.[3] It denies the validity of seeking within discourse the traces of its own origins.

For my part, I construe discourse as the expression of an attitude manifested through the strategic manipulation of signs. The types of signs that are relevant here, are of course linguistic (though they need not be) and are manifested in a form that can be called texts. In elucidating the difference between the notion of text and discourse the work of linguists has been especially helpful.

Willis Edmondson distinguishes between text and discourse in terms of how each deploys language. "A text," he states, "is a structured sequence of linguistic expressions forming a unitary whole, and a discourse is a structured event manifest in linguistic behavior."[4] In recognizing the intimate connection between discourse and the notion of event, Edmondson is able to locate more clearly the operative force underlying discursive expression. Discourse would thus imply a specific rhetorical intent that is determined by the event that it linguistically manifests. A text is not so clearly determined, however, although there is nothing to preclude its being connected to the discursive act. Indeed, M. A. K. Halliday has argued that a text is in fact a product of some discursive process.[5] Taken in the Foucauldian sense of every linguistic expression being inextricably connected to a certain discursive practice, such a statement is not all that revealing. However, if we narrow the paramaters of the statement to suggest that certain events, or certain types of events, are apt to produce certain types of texts, then the notion of discourse becomes a critical site of interaction that mediates between the text's source (the event) and the means of its expression. Russel S. Tomlin looks at this connection from a linguistic perspective:

> Discourse represents the entire spectrum of linguistic, cognitive, and social processes involved in the cooperative enterprise of speech communication. Text represents the specific artifact produced during the process of discourse creation. Thus, the text artifact, or simply text, is the product of a larger set of active processes grounded in the pyscholinguistic makeup of the discourse participants and the sociolinguistic conventions under which they interact. . . . Text analyses seek to understand the organization of the text artifact through the description of semantic and pragmatic parameters revealed by the linguistic structure of the artifact itself. Discourse analysis, on the other hand, seeks to identify and explain those linguistic, cognitive and social processes through which communication is effected and the text artifact produced and comprehended.[6]

At the root of my examination of Chinese fiction, then, is the belief that it is constituted by a specific and distinct source of production, and not by the falsity of the object of its expression or by its particular mode of characterization or emplotment. This source of production can be gleaned only by analyzing the rhetorical strategies of a fictional text. Each fictional text necessarily represents a unique and distinct "event manifest in linguistic behavior" and can be critically appreciated only on the basis of its own specific linguistic elements, but, I will further argue, fictional works are also more generally connected by the similarity of the nature of the event that is the source of their production and by the discursive strategies that effect their manifestation. The thrust of this book is thus to articulate the nature of the events that lead to the production of fiction and to delineate the discursive operations that create the aesthetic of fiction.

In endeavoring to represent the specific features of this aesthetic, I focus on the interpretation of a single Chinese narrative work, the *Mu T'ien-tzu chuan* 穆天子傳 (*Narrative of the Son of Heaven, King Mu*). The *Mu T'ien-tzu chuan* recounts a journey undertaken by the sixth king of the Chou dynasty (1045–221 B.C.), King Mu (956?–918? B.C.), to the western regions of China. Beginning as it does with a description of King Mu's daily itinerary, the text appears, at first glance, to be nothing more than a record of the king's travels. However, with his arrival at a location called Yang-yü 陽紆, the nature of the narrative changes, in terms of both content and style. The king is greeted by Ho-tsung Po-yao 河宗伯夭, who, we are told, is the River God's (Ho-tsung) descendant. The land he lives in had been enfeoffed to the River God by King Mu's ancestors. King Mu commands Ho-tsung Po-yao to perform a sacrifice to the River God, in part to acknowledge the fine service shown to the Chou Kings. During the sacrifice, God on High (*ti* 帝) speaks to King Mu and urges him to make "timely use" of his privilege as king by going to K'un-lun 昆侖 mountain.

Since King Mu does as ordered, heading westward in search of K'un-lun mountain with Ho-tsung Po-yao as a guide, God on High's command is the underlying impetus driving much of the journey. Indeed, the numinous tone of the journey's beginning pervades the narrative of the trip: the king passes through strange new lands full of exotic resources, many of which he decides to bring home; and he is entertained by the various rulers he encounters, many of whom he learns have ancestral ties to his own Chou ancestors. King Mu then visits Hsi-wang-mu 西王母, the Queen Mother of the West, who lives right by K'un-lun mountain.

The first chapter of this study begins with a description of the details pertaining to the discovery and transcription of the *Mu T'ien-tzu chuan*. It then discusses the textual issues that ultimately informed the critical scholarship on the text. By far the most significant issue for the criticism is that the date of the text's composition is unknown; we know only that it was discovered in a tomb in A.D. 279. Structured as a day-by-day record of events, the *Mu T'ien-tzu chuan* at first appears to be an actual account of King Mu's journey. This annalistic mode, a form that predominated in early Chinese historiography, was often taken as proof of the text's historicity, and this has led many scholars to conclude that the *Mu T'ien-tzu chuan* is an account of actual events. Others questioned the text's historical authenticity because of the fantastical nature of some of the events narrated; they judged the text to be a "forged" rendition of historical events and hence unworthy of critical or literary analysis. My evaluation of the corpus of scholarship on the *Mu T'ien-tzu chuan* leads me to conclude that indeed the text is not a contemporary record of King Mu's activities but rather represents a fictional, fourth-century B.C. account of a symbolic journey undertaken by King Mu.

The point of departure for my literary analysis is the unchallenged assumption that the places visited by King Mu in the text have verifiable geographical referents. Whereas even modern scholars who recognize the importance of exploring the literary significance of the *Mu T'ien-tzu chuan* have accepted this premise, I hold that many of the place-names in the text should be read as having mythical referents rather than geographical ones. In particular, the concurrence of place-names such as Yang-yü, K'un-lun, and Yen 弇 Mountain in the *Mu T'ien-tzu chuan* and in cosmogonic myths, especially those related to the Chinese flood myths, has led me to question the regnant view. In positing a mythic origin for many of these place-names, I then argue for the need to evaluate the meaning of the *Mu T'ien-tzu chuan* from a different theoretical framework.

Such a framework is provided by an extensive analysis of the cosmogonic intentions underlying the flood myths. My analysis, presented in the second chapter of this book, shows that the myths can be read as referring to astronomical phenomena that occurred within a specific celestial territory. That territory, according to scholars of Chinese astronomy, symbolically marked for the ancient Chinese the point of transition between the primal forces of life and death. I argue that its significance derives from the effects of the gradual shift of the position of the equinoxes, a phenomenon called the "precession" of the equinoxes. I then postulate that the Chinese associated this shift with a change in the world order, that is, the death of one age and the birth of another.

My ability to reconstitute the cosmogonic intentions underlying the Yü flood myths derives from a specific form of reading that allows me to uncover traces of the cosmogonic discourse inscribed in the myths. These textual traces, described by Nicolas Abraham as "symbols," are generated by the act of transcending an "obstacle to being" or, more simply, a traumatic crisis. According to Abraham, the process of transcendence is effected by silencing discourse related to a traumatic crisis that threatens the existence of a subject. Critical to the interpretation of a symbol is the notion of an "absent text" that must be reconstructed if the symbolic elements of a text are to be understood. More than just textual elements with external reference, symbols are "traces that give voice to their founding silence," a silence that must be made audible if the symbolic meaning of a text is to be revealed. The silence is necessary for interpretation because it signifies the obstacle to being that stimulated the generation of the symbolic process in the first place.

Chapter 3 introduces Abraham's theory of the "symbol." Symbolization, I suggest, accounts for the way that the Yü myths both conceal and reveal their cosmogonic intentions. The symbolic mode of the myths thus emerges as having been a response to the "obstacle to being" presented by the astronomical phenomenon of precession, which I identify as the source for the cosmgonic intentions themselves.

I also link Abraham's conceptual configuration to traditional Chinese notions of the term most frequently translated as "symbol," *hsiang* 象. From the early appropriation of the term by the philosophical texts of Taoism and by the commentary to the divinatory *Book of Changes* (*I ching* 易經) we see how the term *hsiang* was traditionally construed by the Chinese to represent the force underlying the generation of symbols, which, by their very nature must conceal the very event that led to their production. In this second part of the chapter, I recapitulate and expand upon aspects of symbolic production that are mirrored in the Chinese conception of the function and essence of *hsiang*. The chapter as a whole offers a new vantage point from which to consider the shared cosmogonic concerns of the Yü flood myths, early Taoist thought, and the *Book of Changes*. It becomes clear that each of these textual systems, while always enigmatic and mysterious to readers, nonetheless also shared with the others the same means to unravel its own particular mysteries. The obvious appropriation of fragments of cosmogonic myths in the *Mu T'ien-tzu chuan* suggests that a similar symbolic operation is at work there as well, which opens the way to a literary reading of the *Mu T'ien-tzu chuan*.

In the fourth chapter of this study I examine the mythic provenance of three of the most crucial elements of the *Mu T'ien-tzu chuan*, K'un-lun mountain, Ho-tsung, and Hsi-wang-mu, each of which constitutes the center of its own substantial mythic tradition. As these elements are also symbols of the same astronomical circumstances that informed the generation of the Yü flood myths, they should be understood as symbols of the same cosmogonic transition implied in the Yü myths, that is, as symbols invested with regenerative significance. King Mu's trip to K'un-lun, the ultimate destination of his westward journey, can then be interpreted not as a historical narrative but as a literary articulation of a symbolic journey involving his rebirth—that is, the emergence of a new identity.

The fifth chapter of this book provides an in-depth literary analysis of the *Mu T'ien-tzu chuan*. In addition to reading the journey as a narration of the emergence of an individual's new identity, we have also to read it as a reflection or representation of the emergence of a new collective identity: that of the Chou dynasty. The textual evidence as I interpret it leads to a reading of King Mu's journey as a journey of redefinition and in turn as a sign of the desire of the Chou dynasty to redefine itself and thereby define the king's posthumous reputation.

Why the Chou would need to redefine itself is, I argue, connected to the question of legitimacy and to the maintenance of political control that preoccupied the dynasty's rulers. More specifically, I identify the crisis presented by the drowning of King Chao, King Mu's father, as an obstacle to being, the transcendence of which is manifested symbolically in the *Mu T'ien-tzu chuan*. I examine in detail how the Chou need to suppress the details surrounding this catastrophic event, which is intimated by at least two historical texts, in effect propelled the production of the *Mu T'ien-tzu chuan*, in all its symbolic richness. The persistent references to elements of the cosmogonic myths are the key to deciphering the text's own underlying source of signification. Thus, the hidden discourse—encrypted within the text—of King Chao's drowning can be uncovered by a close examination of this rhetorical strategy. The *Mu T'ien-tzu chuan* then presents both a symbolic, literary articulation of this crisis and a resolution for it.

I also analyze how the various discursive modes deployed in the text reflect two discordant views of legitimacy, represented, respectively, by the annalistic form and by the references to cosmogonic myths. Their distinct literary functions overlap to yield a new form for representing experience in narrative. The specificity of the references to the cosmogonic myths functions to call attention to the motivations underlying the action. King Mu's trip to K'un-lun and his obsession with posterity are symptoms of the underlying crisis that motivates the narrative that represents him.

The final chapter of this book presents in metacritical terms an analysis of the literary and cultural implications of this new form of narrative representation embodied in the *Mu T'ien-tzu chuan*. I suggest that this literary development constitutes an initial stage of fictional representation in the Chinese narrative tradition, a tradition that came to be distinguished by its particular symbolic and figurative mode of articulation. By dissecting the discursive features of this mode of articulation, I find that the very mode itself can be construed as deriving from a specific traumatic source: the breakdown of order during the Warring States period. I thus argue for a rereading of Chinese fiction from the perspective of symbol formation, and in turn reconsider the status of the aesthetic in fictional works. The result is an elaboration of a new way of interpreting mainstays of Chinese fiction such as fantastical and supernatural elements as well as the ever-present trace of orality, whereby the representational mode itself symbolizes an initial collective crisis of representation. Finally, I conclude that Chinese fiction is best understood as a discursive, wholly symbolic form. By reading fictional texts symbolically, we see what they have to tell us about the specific context of their production. Interpretation of these texts has significant implications for the wider realm of the interconnections between history, discourse, literature, and culture.

ONE

Contextualizing the Text: The Discovery, Compilation, Transmission, and Traditional Appreciation of the *Mu T'ien-tzu chuan*

In the tenth month of the fifth year of the Hsien-ning 咸寧 era of the Chin emperor Wu-ti 武帝 (A.D. 279), the scholarly tradition met with the startling discovery of what appears to have been a personal library of texts—some theretofore unknown—written in ancient script on bamboo strips.[1] The vault containing the texts and various objects of jade and precious metal is generally believed to have been the tomb of King Hsiang of Wei 魏襄王, who died in 296 B.C.; this means that the texts could not have been written any later than that date.[2] Antedating as they do the later intellectual trends of the Han dynasty (206 B.C.–A.D. 219), these texts offer a record of how pre–Han dynasty writers viewed their world and their cultural tradition.

The process of transcribing the ancient script (*ku-wen* 古文) into clerical script (*li-shu* 隸書) and the editorial work of transforming into texts the great mass of bamboo strips discovered in Chi 汲 district constitutes one of the first great paleographical enterprises in Chinese history. According to Li Xueqin 李學勤, the work of the scholars who contributed their efforts to the project serves even today as a model for paleographers.[3] The story of this process is fascinating in its own right, but it is also critical for this particular study, because only when issues surrounding the provenance, the redaction, and the exegetical tradition of the text are elucidated can one begin to appreciate the literary nature of the *Mu T'ien-tzu chuan*, one of only two of the fifteen discovered texts that has survived to the present. This chapter summarizes the pertinent facts of the discovery, transcription, and transmission of the *Mu T'ien-tzu chuan* and so sets the context for the literary analysis that follows. Indeed, the analytical point of departure stems in part from "clues" provided by the comments and analyses of the earliest redactors of the text.

1

The first issue to be examined concerns the provenance of the texts. As noted above, the vault containing the texts and various objects of jade and precious metal is generally believed to have been the tomb of King Hsiang of Wei, who died in 296 B.C. Notwithstanding the antiquity of this view, however, there are several problems with the identification. As Chu Hsi-tsu's analysis of these problems is the most lucid and illuminating, it bears citing in full.

> As for those [texts] that claim the Chi vault was the tomb of King Hsiang of Wei, there is the Annals of Emperor Wu in the *Chin shu*, and the *Calendrical Treatises* ("Lü-li chih" 律曆志) which is in the sixteenth *chüan* of the *Chin shu*; Hsün Hsü's preface to the *Mu T'ien-tzu chuan*; Wei Heng's *Ssu-t'i shu-shih* 四體書勢. As for those texts that claim the vault was the tomb of King An-li 安釐 of Wei, there is the biography of Su Hsi 束晳 by Wang Yin 王隱. As for that text which claims the vault was the tomb of either King Hsiang or King An-li of Wei, but which never cites a source for this information, there is Su Hsi's biography in the T'ang revised edition of the *Chin shu*. All of these claims lack concrete evidence. For those who claim that the vault was the tomb of King Hsiang of Wei, [the claim] is based on the fact that the *Annals* [discovered in the vault] terminates in the twentieth year of the "present king" of the Wei state. Hsün Hsü, in his preface to the *Mu T'ien-tzu chuan*, states: "Based on the *Annals* that were obtained [from the vault] it is probable that the vault is the tomb of the 'present

king,' the son of King Hui-ch'eng 惠成 of Wei. According to the *Shih-pen* 世本, this was King Hsiang. . . ." If we search in the *Shih chi* 史記 under King Ai 哀, we will find that he is referred to as King Hsiang in the *Shih pen*.[4] King Ai died in the twenty-third year of his reign, therefore he is referred to as the "present king" in his twentieth year. Yet, if in his twenty-first year the king had not yet died, how could these *Annals* be used to accompany his burial? Therefore, it must be that the years noted by Hsün Hsü more likely referred to the years after the recording of the *Annals* was terminated. Later scholars misunderstood his reference to indicate the year that the text was itself entombed; hence no one was clear about [the significance of the dates]. Given these circumstances, there were also scholars who claimed that King Ai's death was in his twentieth year, in order to defend their original identification [of the vault as King Hsiang's tomb]. The *Suo-yin* 索隱 commentary to the 44th *chüan* of the *Shih chi*, the "Hereditary Houses of Wei" 魏世家, states: "The *Annals* from the Chi vault terminate in King Ai's twentieth year. King Chao 昭 mourned for three years and only then established the first year of his own reign."[5] The intended meaning of this commentary is to suggest that although King Ai died in his twentieth year, the *Shih chi* refers to a twenty-third year of his reign because it was only until the end of that third year that King Chao established his own reign title. Rare are those cases when during the Warring States era a mourning period of three years was observed. There were cases when a year was skipped before a new reign title was established, but I have never heard of skipping three years. Moreover, if King Ai had died, why was he referred to as the "present king"? It does not make any sense. . . . [F]rom ancient times to the present I have never heard of a ruler being buried with his state's history, and I have never heard that a state history destined to accompany a ruler's entombment must terminate with the last year of the said ruler. [Previous scholars] simply did not know that the *Annals* were a comprehensive history and not the official annals of any one state; they represent the private record of a citizen of Wei, and do not represent the records of Wei officials. For this reason every explanation [of the provenance of the tomb] has been far-fetched. . . . [T]hose theories claiming the vault was the tomb of King Hsiang or King An-li of Wei are nothing more than nonsense.[6]

Chu Hsi-tsu contends that the problem of deciding which Wei king was buried in the tomb derives solely from the assumption that the *Bamboo Annals* was the official history of Wei.[7] This observation must be qualified, however, because Chu himself never questions the assumption that the tomb is a royal tomb. Whereas he takes the discovery of a jade pitch pipe, bells, and a *ch'ing* 磬 to be proof of a royal provenance,[8] we now know from the discovery of the Warring States tomb of the Marquis I of Tseng 曾 in Sui 隨 county, Hupei, that access to riches was not restricted to kings. The stunning set of bells and other bronze and jade objects found in this tomb, as well as in the much later Ma-wang-tui 馬王堆 tomb, attests to the level of grandeur enjoyed by people of "lesser rank" than a king.[9] Moreover, even in the case of lesser officials, texts were frequently among the mortuary objects, which qualifies any premise that the presence of bamboo strips must point to royal provenance.[10] Given this archaeological evidence, Chu Hsi-tsu's suggestion that the *Annals* constitute a comphrensive history, the product of a private scholar and not a public state offical, in fact contains a clue about how to identify who was entombed in the vault: even if the last year entered refers to the reign of King Hsiang, it does not necessarily follow that King Hsiang was the "tomb master." The discovery of a set of *Annals* (*nien-piao* 年表) in the tomb of the Marquis of Ju-yin 汝陰 in Fu-yang 阜陽 in 1977 reveals that records of historical events were accessible to and preserved by people outside the immediate royal domain.[11] The case of the almost personalized *Annals* (*ta-shih-chi* 大事紀) of a local official, Hsi 喜, which were discovered in the latter's tomb at Shui-hu ti 睡虎地 and which begin with the first year of King Chao of Ch'in 秦肇王 (306 B.C.) and end (abruptly) in the thirtieth year of the First Emperor's reign (217 B.C.), points to a similar conclusion.[12] The fact that the last date of the *Annals* is the year in which the deceased died offers perhaps a more realistic and logical explanation of the significance of the closing year of the Chi vault *Bamboo Annals*.

Wei T'ing-sheng offers a different hypothesis about the provenance of the tomb. He argues that the absence of any mention of a corpse or of any other mortuary items suggests that the vault was not a tomb at all.[13] Instead, he postulates, the objects retrieved from the vault were a part of a corpus of treasures belonging to the royal family of Wei that were buried in the mound to hide them from enemy states or to protect them from the floodwaters of the Yellow River. As evidence that the vault was used for storage and not burial, Wei cites the presence of a text entitled *Treasures of Liang Hill*

(*Liang-ch'iu tsang* 梁丘藏) among the discovered bamboo strips. This text recorded "Wei's hereditary houses along with a list of gold and jade objects kept hidden in the mound."[14] The mound, that is, must have been the said Liang Hill.

The thesis is intriguing, especially in light of the absence of any mortuary evidence. Nonetheless, as Wei concedes, it is possible that the thief Pu-chun took those items before officials were alerted to his thievery. Moreover, if the vault were indeed just a cache of royal treasures, one would expect the number of texts, presumably belonging to the Wei library, to be more representative of the vast number in circulation at the time. As it is, because many of the texts discovered seem connected thematically, it is more likely that the cache represents a personal rather than a royal library.

While we may never know the true provenance of the Chi vault, or whether or not it ever had a "tomb master," certain conclusions based on the texts can be drawn and can shed at least some light on the significance of the corpus as a whole, and more specifically on the literary significance of the *Mu T'ien-tzu chuan*.[15] Wei T'ing-sheng observes that the texts found in the vault have much in common with the thought of the philosopher Tsou Yen 鄒衍 (305–240 B.C.), who was said to have spent several years as an adviser and teacher of King Hui of Liang 梁惠王.[16] Although one would be hard pressed to accept Wei's argument that all the texts were penned by Tsou Yen for the king in appreciation of the latter's patronage, the fact that many of them seem connected thematically, and that the themes concern major tenets of Tsou Yen's philosophy—the relationship between history and the workings of the cosmos—deserves attention.

The best description of the texts discovered at Chi is found in the biography of Su Hsi, one of the redactors of the texts. This important passage, recorded in the *Chin shu*, warrants citation in full:

> Previously, in the second year of the T'ai-k'ang 太康 reign (A.D. 281),[17] a bandit named Pu-chun 不準 from Chi prefecture, broke into the tomb of King Hsiang of Wei, or, as some claim, the tomb of King An-li of Wei.[18] From this tomb were recovered ten cartloads of texts written on bamboo strips. Amongst them the *Annals* (*Chi-nien* 紀年) of thirteen sections recorded events beginning with the Hsia 夏 dynasty down through the time when King Yu 幽 of Chou was exterminated by the Ch'üan-jung 犬戎 barbarians; from there the events recorded

all concerned the state of Chin.[19] The *Annals* focused on events concerning the state of Wei after Chin was separated into three states (i.e., ca. 376 B.C.); it records these events up till the twentieth year of King An-li's reign. The *Annals* probably constitute a Wei history. For the most part it accords with the records of the *Spring and Autumn Annals* (*Ch'un-ch'iu* 春秋), although there are places that differ significantly from it and the *Tso Commentary* (*Tso chuan* 左傳). For example, the years ascribed to the Hsia dynasty outnumber those of the Yin dynasty . . . [the number of years that passed] from the time that the Chou received Heaven's Mandate until King Mu ascended the throne [is given in the *Annals* as] one hundred years; it was not [as is traditionally recorded in other texts] that King Mu [himself] lived to be one hundred years old. When King Yu had fled, there was one Earl Ho of Kung 共和伯 who usurped the king's power, it was not that there were two ministers called Kung and Ho. As for the *Book of Changes* comprised of two sections, it is similar to the *Chou-i* 周易. A text of two sections entitled *I Line Statements and Yin-yang Hexagrams* 易繇陰陽卦 is somewhat similar to the *Chou-i*, although the line statements are different. There is a text, the *Classic of I Below the Hexagrams* 卦下易經 of one section that is similar to the *Explanation of Hexagrams* (*Shuo-kua* 說卦), yet also different. A text called the *Kung-sun Tuan* 公孫段 of two sections comprises a dialogue between Kung-sun Tuan and Shao Chih 邵陟 on topics concerning the *Book of Changes*. Three sections of the *Kuo-yü* 國語 deal with events of the Chin and Ch'u 楚 states. A text entitled *Names* (*Ming* 名) of three sections resembles the *Book of Rituals* (*Li chi* 禮記) yet also resembles the *Erh-ya* 爾雅 and the *Lun-yü* 論語. The *Shih Ch'un* 師春, comprising one section, deals with divinations that occur in the *Tso Commentary*; Shih Ch'un appears to be the family and given name of the author of this text. The *Fragmented Dialogues* (*Suo-yü* 瑣語), made up of eleven sections, is a book that deals with prognostications, dreams and strange events that occurred in many different states. A text of one section called the *Treasures of Liang Vault* (*Liang-ch'iu tsang*) first narrates the hereditary houses of the state of Wei and then speaks of the metal and jade objects related to the vault. The *Chiao-shu* 繳書 of two sections contains discourses on methods of archery. The *Sheng-feng* 生封 of one section relates the fiefdoms established by various kings. The *Great*

> *Calendar* (*Ta li* 大曆) of two sections is similar to those texts of Tsou Yen's cosmology. The *Narrative of the Son of Heaven, King Mu*, of five sections, relates the journey of King Mu of Chou to the four seas and his visits to Ti T'ai 帝臺 and Hsi-wang-mu. The *T'u-shih* 圖時 of one section belongs to the genre of paintings with colophons. There are in addition nineteen sections of miscellaneous texts referred to as *Tsa-shu* 雜書: *Procedures of Enfeoffment of the Chou* (*Chou shih t'ien-fa* 周食田法); the *Book of Chou* (*Chou-shu* 周書) in which affairs of Ch'u are discussed; and a piece which concerns the death of King Mu of Chou's concubine, Sheng Chi. In all there are about seventy-five sections. Of them seven were ripped so that the original title could not be discerned. . . . The texts of the bamboo strips were written in tadpole script. The first one who discovered the vault burned the strips to provide light to pilfer the objects. When the officials finally collected them, there were many burnt strips that were broken and fragmented. The texts had decomposed, and the strips were not in their correct order. Emperor Wu-ti ordered that the books be added to the Palace Library and that the strips be arranged according to their proper order, organized and transcribed with the [clerical] script used today.[20]

Notwithstanding the likelihood that these texts do not constitute the entirety of what was originally entombed, the texts as a corpus nonetheless lend themselves to interpretation. If we accept the hypothesis that the texts found in recently excavated tombs at Yin-ch'üeh shan 銀雀山, Shui-hu ti, and Pao-shan 包山, for example, represent those that would have had the greatest value to the deceased while he was alive and thus were buried with him to provide reference in the afterlife as well, then what are we to make of the significance of the Chi vault corpus?[21]

Consider first the obvious pragmatic bent to the corpus: not only are histories such as the *Chou-yü* and the *Bamboo Annals* represented, but there is also an evident interest in enfeoffment procedures and in other ritualistic practices.[22] Of significance as well are calendrical or perhaps more accurately astonomical and cosmological issues along with the proper elucidation of terms.[23] Presumably these texts had a practical function: replete with historical precedents, they would have been an important resource for a reader looking to implement his own affairs properly.[24]

But the texts concern more than just political history or ritualistic and bureaucratic statutes; almost half of the corpus deals with topics of divination, dreams, and "strange" events.[25] Noteworthy, too, is the apparent historical context—and a textually derived context at that—within which the supranatural events are anchored. For example, the topic of the *Shih Ch'un* is divination, but specifically those divinations that take place during the Spring and Autumn era as recorded in the *Tso chuan*. Likewise, the *Fragmented Dialogues* record dreams, divinations, and strange events that are placed in a historical setting. The mix of the historical and the supranatural also characterizes the *Mu T'ien-tzu chuan*. While the narrative at first appears to be a historical account of King Mu's journey to the western region of China, the nature of the narrative, in terms of both content and style, changes when King Mu arrives at a location called Yang-yü. Indeed, it was probably its numinous tone that prompted one of its redactors, Hsün Hsü, to comment "Although its content is not canonical, it is [truly] an ancient book."

There is, then, a unifying theme to the corpus of texts unearthed at Chi, aptly characterized by Benjamin Schwartz as "a strain toward transcendence." Schwartz so describes the nature of philosophies emerging late in the first millennium B.C., which he identifies as China's "axial age."[26] In speaking of the admittedly polysemous term "transcendence," Schwartz writes: "What I refer to here is something close to the etymological meaning of the word—a kind of standing back and looking beyond—a kind of critical, reflective questioning of the actual and a new vision of what lies beyond."[27]

The "strain toward transcendence" reflected in the texts discovered in the Chi vault involves a revalorization of the meaning and significance of human action. The combination of texts represents human action from at least two different perspectives. On the one hand, the historical representation, often using the literary form of the annal, organizes human experience in a framework that emphasizes relationships among events and people. On the other hand, the texts centering on divination, dreams, and strange events focus on conveying particular nuances of various personalities (mostly rulers) and of the circumstances in which they find themselves. The main focus is not action itself but rather motivations and facets of personality that contribute to the actualization of action. The supranatural texts thus emphasize the particularity of each individual's experience and in this way complement the one-dimensionality of annalistic history, which is much more of an abstract conceptual framework.

The Chi vault corpus of texts, therefore, reflects an interest in "transcending" ways of representing and evaluating experience that presumably can lead to a new understanding of the significance of human action. The interplay of perspectives reflected in the various texts seems to emphasize the idea of man as agent; they reveal a sensitivity to how man's actions can be evaluated and how this evaluation may be conveyed by subtle manners of verbalization.

To appreciate the literary value of the *Mu T'ien-tzu chuan,* one must really understand the context of the Chi vault corpus as a whole. A. F. P. Hulsewé also recognized this and suggested that given the strong representation of supranatural texts accompanying the *Mu T'ien-tzu chuan,* the latter text may perhaps be a religious text similar in function to the Egyptian *Journey of the Dead* texts.[28] David Hawkes has argued that the journey of King Mu is similar to other magical journeys in Chinese literature that affirm the value of acquiring power, usually over the cosmos.[29] King Mu's travels, then, can be understood as an allegory for the legitimization of a divine right to rule. Both observations were made without the benefit of an in-depth study of the *Mu T'ien-tzu chuan,* yet are remarkably apt. I would qualify these comments modestly, by suggesting that rather than see the text as a literal "guide" to the underworld, or as an affirmation of King Mu's power, it seems more in line with the theme of transcendence that permeates the corpus to view the *Mu T'ien-tzu chuan* as a symbolic narrative of a personal journey in search of a new identity. King Mu's excursions, like the texts that accompanied the *Mu T'ien-tzu chuan,* may have served as a medium for introducing the question of the role of the individual in social transformation. Indeed, my analysis of the literary significance of the *Mu T'ien-tzu chuan* bears out this interpretation.

Before proceeding to these issues, however, it is necessary to review the textual history, including the initial compilation of the *Mu T'ien-tzu chuan,* the transmission of the narrative throughout the centuries, and the way the text was appreciated by readers and bibliophiles. Consideration of these issues should enable us to establish a "definitive" text upon which to base a literary analysis.

2

Almost one and a half years had elapsed after the initial discovery of the texts in the Chi vault before work began on the transcription and collation of the strips. The delay was due to the understandably difficult logistics of transporting ten cartloads of strips to the Palace Library (*pi-shu chien* 秘書監), a problem compounded by the fact that many officials were engaged at that time in an attack against Sun Hao 孫皓, the emperor of Eastern Wu 東吳, and thus could not assist with the management and organization of the strips.[30] Emperor Wu Ti conquered Sun Hao and exterminated the Eastern Wu in the third month of the following year, the first of the T'ai-k'ang reign (A.D. 280). It was still some time, however, before bureaucratic affairs once again took precedence over military concerns and it was not until the spring of the next year, the second of T'ai-k'ang's reign (A.D. 281), that Hsün Hsü was finally commissioned to begin transcibing the ancient graphs into clerical script.[31]

Just what those ancient graphs looked like has been a source of some confusion and dispute. Chu Hsi-tsu lists three different opinions: (1) one view holds the graphs were written in small seal form; (2) another claims that the graphs were written in a "tadpole" form; (3) and yet another holds that the graphs were written in what is simply called an "ancient script" (*ku-wen*).[32] According to Chu Hsi-tsu, the graphs could not have been written in the small seal script, which was recognizable by most scholars of ancient texts; he concludes that the texts were written in the "ancient script," that is, the "script that was used during the Chou era"; "tadpole script" was simply a popular way of referring to the "ancient script of the Chou period."[33]

Although most scholars of the Chin dynasty were not familiar with ancient script, they had at their disposal a set of thirty five steles, the *Stone Classics of Three Graph Forms* (*San-t'i shih-ching* 三體石經) to aid them. Inscribed in the middle of the Cheng-shih reign (ca. A.D. 240–48) of the Wei dynasty, these stelae preserved the *Book of History* (*Shang shu* 尚書), the *Spring and Autumn Annals* and a section of the *Tso chuan* in three different scripts: ancient script, seal script (*chuan* 篆), and clerical script.[34] Since the graphs comprising the text of the *Bamboo Annals* were for the most part used in the classics, it was fairly easy for the compilers to complete the transcription of that work. The *Mu T'ien-tzu chuan* posed a greater challenge, because many of the graphs, such as the names of the steeds that King Mu used to draw his chariot, not only were unfamiliar but also were not written consistently throughout the text.[35] Nonetheless, within the remarkably short span of one year, Hsün Hsü and his colleague Ho Chiao finished the transcription and compilation of the *Mu T'ien-tzu chuan*.[36]

This edition of the *Mu T'ien-tzu chuan* was not the only one, however. After it had been in circulation for almost ten years, another edition appeared under a different title and, it seems, with different content in several places. This second edition was the work of Su Hsi, who had replaced the scholar Wei Heng as an editorial director (*chu-tso lang* 著作郎) of the Palace Library when the latter was killed in A.D. 291.[37] As we noted above, according to Wang Yin's biography of Su Hsi, the latter edited a text called *The Travels of a Chou King* (*Chou-wang yu-hsing*), which "relates King Mu's travels to the four seas and his visits to Ti T'ai 帝臺 and Hsi-wang-mu."[38] The edition of the *Mu T'ien-tzu chuan* that has survived until the present contains no mention of a visit to Ti T'ai, however; nor does the edition that had been annotated by Kuo P'u 郭璞 (276–324) in the latter part of the Chin dynasty. This is adduced by Chu Hsi-tsu from the fact that Kuo P'u did not cite the *Mu T'ien-tzu chuan* as a reference in his annotation to the "Central Mountain Classic" (*chung-shan ching* 中山經) chapter of the *Classic of Mountains and Oceans* (*Shan-hai-ching* 山海經), where Ti T'ai is mentioned.[39] Since Kuo cites the *Mu T'ien-tzu chuan* in many other annotations to the *Shan-hai-ching*, his failure to do so here indicates that he was not aware of any visit by King Mu to Ti T'ai.[40]

Obviously, however, there were readers familiar with Su Hsi's edition; as Chu Hsi-tsu points out, the visit to Ti T'ai is referred to in a rhyme-prose (*fu* 賦) written by Yen Yen-chih 顏延之.[41] Although we will never know the exact nature of Su Hsi's text, Chu Hsi-tsu makes the case that Su Hsi's text more accurately reflected the composition of the original text than did Hsün Hsü's. Hsün Hsü's edition had six *chüan* and included the story of King Mu's concubine Sheng Chi, whereas Su Hsi's edition had only five *chüan* because he considered the Sheng Chi story to be one of the "miscellaneous" texts of the corpus. And indeed, while the story exhibits some connection with the themes and style of the text of King Mu's travels, it seems to be more of a self-contained unit. Chu Hsi-tsu thus concludes that Su Hsi's edition was the more accurate representation of the original text.[42]

Second, Su Hsi's title, which represents a deliberate alteration of the title given to the text by Hsün Hsü, better reflects the content of the text. Indeed, even the description of the content of the *Mu T'ien-tzu chuan* given by Hsün Hsü in his preface employs the expression "the travels of King Mu" (*Chou Mu-wang yu-hsing* 周穆王遊行). This description is very similar to the title of Su Hsi's edition. Chu points out that this phrase, like the titles of all of the other texts found in the vault, refers to the content of the text.[43] Hsün Hsü's addition of the term *chuan* 傳, which I have loosely translated as "narrative," designates the style and form of the text, rather than the content, and thus is not in keeping with the other examples. Su Hsi, Chu argues, did nothing more than substitute a more appropriate title for Hsün Hsü's misleading one; he changed the title because the text deals only with a few events in King Mu's life, whereas the term *chuan*—the same term used for biographies, especially in the official dynastic histories—has connotations that do not really reflect the true content of the text.[44]

Kuo P'u's ignorance of Su Hsi's edition attests to its short-lived transmission. There is no record of any text by that name in any bibliographic treatises from the Sui dynasty onward. With the disappearance of Su Hsi's text, Hsün Hsü's text was the only one in circulation, which had ramifications for how the *Mu T'ien-tzu chuan* was read and appreciated in subsequent centuries: in particular, Hsün Hsü's perhaps inadvertent use of the term *chuan* established for the *Mu T'ien-tzu chuan* a historical premise that greatly informed the way the text was categorized in bibliographies.

Citations of the *Mu T'ien-tzu chuan* in bibliographies of the dynastic histories and in private collections from the Sui dynasty through the Ch'ing dynasty will reinforce this point. The work is classified as a history, under the subcategory of "Diaries of Activity and Repose" (*ch'i-chü chu* 起居注) in seven bibliographies;[45] as a "nonofficial history" (*pieh-shih* 別史) or a "miscellaneous history" (*tsa-shih* 雜史) in three bibliographies; and as a biography in five bibliographies; finally, only in the Ch'ing dynasty is the text classified as fiction (*hsiao-shuo* 小說).[46] As these statistics indicate, for more than a thousand years the text was taken to be a historical work, although the shift to "miscellaneous history" suggests at least some reevaluation of the classification.

The establishment of the historical identification is, however, based on more than the use of the term *chuan* by Hsün Hsü in his title. The large number of bibliographies that list the *Mu T'ien-tzu chuan* under the subcategory of "Diaries of Activity and Repose" suggests that the very annalistic form used in the text, whereby the king's activities are recorded according to days of the sexegenary cycle and seasons (although never according to the reign year) was also a factor.[47] This annalistic mode, a form that predominates in early Chinese histories, was taken by many bibliophiles as proof of the text's historicity. This assumption held sway until the great bibliophile Chi Yün 紀韻 compiled his *Ssu-k'u ch'üan shu tsung-mu* 四庫全書總目 and relegated the *Mu T'ien-tzu chuan* to the category of fiction. He advanced the following for his decision:

> The *Mu T'ien-tzu chuan* was traditionally listed under the category of "Diaries of Activity and Repose" only because it employed the method of using years and dates to narrate [King Mu's] travels to the west. In fact [this premise] is absurd and without substance; [the text] is also not comparable with texts such as the *I Chou-shu* 逸周書. To consider [the *Mu T'ien-tzu chuan*] as an ancient text and thus preserve it is permissible. But to consider and record it as a veritable history [is not, for] the form is motley and the historical examples (i.e., the events of the narrative that might constitute history) are exposed [as invalid]. Today my intent in categorizing the text as fiction is to conform with what is appropriate, and not reward those who transform what is ancient into [something worthy of] suspicion.[48]

Chi Yün's comments touch upon issues that eventually became central to the scholarly work on the *Mu T'ien-tzu chuan* and then evolved into a polemical dispute. This polemic in part grew out of pan-Sumerian diffusionist theories of the origin of civilization.[49] These theories stimulated Chinese and Japanese scholars to reexamine ancient texts such as the *Mu T'ien-tzu chuan*, which contain information pertaining to early Chinese contact with the West.[50] To support the pan-Sumerian theories, two scholars, Liu Shih-p'ei (1884–1919) and Ting Ch'ien (1843–1919), produced extensive commentaries and annotations of the narrative of King Mu's westward journey, especially the references to geographical locations.[51]

Liu Shih-p'ei's and Ting Ch'ien's use of the *Mu T'ien-tzu chuan* to argue for the Western origins of Chinese civilization in turn stimulated a renewed interest in the question of whether the text was in fact history. At stake was not only the historical reputation of an ancient text but also the antiquity and uniqueness of Chinese civilization itself.[52] Even with the development of more sophisticated theories of the emergence of civilizations, which eventually vitiated the theories of pan-Sumerian diffusionism and in turn reaffirmed the uniqueness of Chinese civilization, the scholarly division over the true nature of the *Mu T'ien-tzu chuan* did not abate.

Despite the text's annalistic mode, which was taken as the sign of its historicity, there were scholars who questioned this judgment because of the fantastic nature of some of the narration or because of apparent anachronistic references.[53] They concluded that the text was a "forged" rendition of historical events (*wei-shu* 偽書).[54] The debate over the "historicity" of the text, then, was in fact a debate over the date of composition of the text.[55]

Advocates of the text's historicity based their arguments on evidence derived mainly from calendrical and geographical considerations. Some scholars including the Ming dynasty bibliophile Hu Ying-lin 胡應麟 (1551–1602) and two modern experts, Wei T'ing-sheng and Ku Shih,[56] argue that the use of the Chou calendrical system supports a Western Chou dynasty date of composition. Both scholars contend that the use of the seasonal divisions "first month of" (*meng* 孟), "second month of" (*chung* 仲), and "third month of" (*chi* 季), which appear frequently in the text, reflects adjustments made to the Hsia calendar by the Chou court.[57] Others argue the opposite, however, that references to the seasonal divisions in fact suggest a late date of composition. Huang P'ei-jung, for example, has argued that these divisions appear to be a late (Warring States) invention.[58] Indeed, recent scholarship on the dating system used in Western Chou bronze inscriptions has documented the use of the Hsia calendrical system, one that begins the year at the spring equinox, that is, on the second month after the month of the winter solstice, as a basis for the civil calendar.[59] Finally, it is clear from Chin and Wei bronze inscriptions, as well as from the *Bamboo Annals*, that the Hsia calendar was used by these states. It is thus likely that the calendrical system used in the *Mu T'ien-tzu chuan* also accords with the Hsia system.[60]

King Mu's travel itinerary itself has also been taken by some as an affirmation of the "authenticity" of the *Mu T'ien-tzu chuan*. By identifying all of the place-names in the narrative with real locations, scholars offer what they believe to be geographical evidence supporting a Western Chou date of composition.[61] Wei T'ing-sheng, for example, argues that the reference to Tsung-chou 宗周 indicates that the text could only have been written during the Western Chou, for this was the appellation used by the Chou to refer to their capital, where the king resided and conducted governmental affairs.[62] Nonetheless, Ku Chieh-kang and Wang Kuo-wei cite the same reference to Tsung-chou to argue that the text was written later than the Western Chou.[63] As Ku argues, a geographical reading of the text indicates that Tsung-chou refers to the Eastern Chou capital Lo-yang 洛陽, and thus must be read as an anachronistic reference to the Chou capital. Wei T'ing-sheng acknowledges that the geography of King Mu's itinerary in the *Mu T'ien-tzu chuan* makes it impossible to locate Tsung-chou in any place other than Lo-yang, but he postulates a relocation of the capital to Lo-yang in the first year of King Mu's reign. The appellation Tsung-chou was then used, in Wei's reckoning, to refer to Lo-yang (originally called Ch'eng-chou 成周), while the appellation of the former capital was changed to Fang 芳.[64] He cites several bronze inscriptions that speak of King Mu engaging in recreational activities at Fang to argue that Fang was not a governmental center during King Mu's reign, but only a place for leisure.[65]

Wei is unconvincing. His interpretation of several inscriptions is problematic, and these problems are compounded by the imprecise criteria used to date the bronzes. For example, he dates the *Shih shang ho* 士上盉 and *Shih shang yu* 卣 vessels to King Mu's reign, even though the inscriptions on these vessels connect them to that of the Ling 令 vessels, which are dated by most specialists (including Wei himself) to the reign of King Chao 昭王.[66] Moreover, he misreads the sacrificial term 𥧹 for a word meaning "to reside in" (*kuan* 館) and thus reads the first line of the inscription as, "It was in the year when King [Mu] performed the Yüeh sacrifice at Tsung chou and then went to reside [to escape the heat] in Fang."[67] Wei's thesis is further compromised by his failure to deal adequately with the indisputable absence of textual evidence pointing to a possible eastern relocation of capitals by King Mu. He argues only that this merely reveals a negative bias against King Mu.[68]

Besides the aforementioned geographical considerations, other evidence based more on content was also adduced to prove a late date of composition. In his extensive study of the *Mu T'ien-tzu chuan,* for example, Wei Chü-hsien cites Wang Kuo-wei's study on the continual attacks made by the western "barbarian tribes," the K'un-yi 昆夷 and the Hsien-yün 玁狁, which sparked quite a bit of unrest within the Western Chou court.[69] Wei argues that given this historical context, the premise underlying the *Mu T'ien-tzu chuan* is unrealistic: King Mu could not have been presented repeatedly with grand tribute by the various tribes he met on his trip across the western steppes of China.[70] This view is corroborated by recent studies indicating that the nature of the political and cultural control exerted by the Chou court over the inhabitants of the Yellow River basin and beyond was not as far-reaching or stable as had been traditionally believed. King Mu's own father, King Chao, was killed along with his entire army in a battle with the southern Ch'u, a catastrophe that had disastrous and enduring political ramifications for the Chou court and for King Mu.[71] Thus, the image of the revered and benevolent monarch presented in the *Mu T'ien-tzu chuan* may not reflect the reality of King Mu's reign.

The apparent influence of other texts, most notably the *Book of Odes* (*Shih ching* 詩經) and the "Tributaries of Yü" ("Yü kung" 禹貢) chapter of the *Shang shu* has also been adduced as proof of the late date of composition of the text.[72] Not only is the poem "Nan shan yu t'ai" 南山有臺, poem 171 of the "Lesser Elegies" ("Hsiao ya" 小雅) section of the *Shih ching* referred to in the *Mu T'ien-tzu chuan*,[73] but in at least one instance a strophe of another poem is identical to that of poem 161, "Lu ming" 鹿鳴, also of the "Hsiao ya".[74] Rémi Mathieu also sees a connection between an anecdote about the capture of a tiger in the *Mu T'ien-tzu chuan* and poem 195 "Hsiao min" 小旻.[75] As for the relationship between the "Yü kung" and the *Mu T'ien-tzu chuan*, the obvious textual overlap of the places visited by both King Mu and Yü and the emphasis on receiving tribute from natives of these places suggests that the latter text was influenced, if not written in imitation of, the former text. Since most scholars agree on a Warring States date of composition for the "Yü kung," the composition of the *Mu T'ien-tzu chuan* must also have occurred during or after this time.[76]

In addition to issues of content, linguistic factors are also brought to bear on dating the composition of the text. Wei Chü-hsien argues that the prevalence of the prepositions *yü* 於 (Wei counts thirty occurrences within the text) and *yi* 以, especially the use of the latter in constructions denoting the arrival of a subject at a place, bespeaks a late Warring States date of composition because that is when these constructions were first used used consistently and frequently.[77] The same can be said for the way the final particle *yeh* 也 and the referential *shih* 是 (this) are used in the text.[78] Bernhard Karlgren's conclusion regarding the date of composition of the *Tso chuan* was also based in part on the use of the particle *yü*.[79] His Warring States date of composition corroborates Wei's findings.

Finally, Rémi Mathieu brings another interesting issue, that of the unique literary nature of the *Mu T'ien-tzu chuan*, to bear on the question of the date of its composition. He points out that the *Mu T'ien-tzu chuan* is the earliest extant narrative that recounts the adventures of a man rather than those of a demiurge, and in this way it differs from the "Yü kung."[80] He adds that the human element of the text is what marks it as "fiction" (albeit historical fiction) as opposed to "mythology," and that this most likely reflects a late stage in the development of Chinese narrative modes. While Mathieu's definitions of fiction and mythology are too amorphous to be critically useful, his insight vis-à-vis the relevance of the literary mode to the problem of dating the text is important. One might add that the incorporation of a series of forms or styles, such as poetry and the *ch'i-chü* annalistic form, to create a hybrid medium, is also especially significant, for this eventually becomes a generic feature of (vernacular) fiction.

Before examining issues of textual filiation and transmission, a word should be said about the seemingly oral provenance of much of the content of the *Mu T'ien-tzu chuan*. The consistent use of the phrase "it is said" (*yüeh* 曰) suggests an oral dimension; it signals information provided by the implied narrator to illuminate the significance of King Mu's actions or even just to impart narrative information concerning the voyage. This is not to say that the *Mu T'ien-tzu chuan* was exclusively an oral composition, but merely that elements of the text derive from the "storehouse of cultual information" that is preserved orally by a society.[81] I suggest below that these elements are the product of a specific form of symbolic production and that their incorporation into a written text was to a large part determined by certain social and cultural trends prominent during the Warring States period.

Thus, I believe that historical, linguistic, and stylistic factors rule out the possibility that *Mu T'ien-tzu chuan* is an accurate detailing of the daily actions of King Mu as he traveled to the western sphere of his domain. In this I concur with the conclusions of Wei Chü-hsien, Rémi Mathieu, and other Western scholars[82] that the text is the product of the Warring States era. But what does this mean for our understanding of the text? The absence of any Chinese studies that address this question reveals the scholarly ramifications of the polemical debate over the text's date of composition: they set the parameters for the way the text was read and appreciated. Scholars who believed the text was composed during King Mu's reign, directed their study toward substantiating the historicity of the events narrated; those who believed that the text was composed later than King Mu's reign and thus constituted only a rendition of events that (may have) occurred, deemed it unworthy of vigorous analysis. Thus while scholars such as Wei Chü-hsien negated the historicity of the text by arguing for a Warring States date of compositon, they never troubled to examine the significance of the text from other (that is, literary, religious) perspectives.[83]

Several Western scholars had intimated at the rich possibilities of such studies, but never seriously pursued them.[84] Only with Rémi Mathieu was the text analyzed from literary, sociological, and mythological perspectives. While Mathieu's study, as one reviewer has observed, is "by far the best study of this book in a Western language, Mathieu's efforts fail in three areas: (1) establishment of the text, (2) scholarly methodology, and (3) bibliography."[85] Regrettably, many of the commentaries that address issues surrounding textual variants were neither consulted nor mentioned by Mathieu. Nor does he establish a "definitive text" upon which to base an in-depth literary analysis. These are issues of great significance to a literary appreciation of the text, and bear some discussion of them here.

Both Ku Shih and Wei T'ing-sheng list over thirty different editions of the *Mu T'ien-tzu chuan* including two Yüan 元 dynasty printed editions (*k'an-pen* 刊本), ten printed editions, five hand-copied editions (*ch'ao-pen* 抄本), and two collated and revised editions (*chiao-pen* 校本) from the Ming 明 dynasty; two hand-copied, and six collated and revised editions from the Ch'ing 清 dynasty.[86] Of the last type of edition, Hung I-hsüan's 洪頤宣 (1765–1837) collated and revised edition is by far the most famous for it is the one preserved in the *Ssu-pu pei-yao* collection.[87] Based on the *Han-wei ts'ung-shu* edition of the text, Hung compared this edition with the editions of Ch'eng Jung, Wu Kuan, Wang Ming-chi, as well as the *Cheng-t'ung Taoist Canon* editions. He also incorporated annotations of the *Shih chi* and the *Han shu* 漢書 that cite the *Mu T'ien-tzu chuan,* as well as citations preserved in T'ang and Sung encyclopedias.[88]

In addition to the aforementioned collated editions there are several others that have extensive comments and annotations. Ch'en Feng-heng's 陳逢衡 *Mu T'ien-tzu chuan-chu pu-cheng* 穆天子傳注補正[89] incorporates several texts that were not considered by Hung I-hsüan and the outstanding precision of his annotations, to quote Ku Shih, "goes far beyond those of Hung [I-hsüan] and Ti [Yün-sheng]."[90] T'an Ts'ui's 檀萃 voluminous *Mu T'ien-tzu chuan chu-shu* 穆天子傳注疏, although often criticized for containing far-fetched interpretations of the text, nonetheless is valuable for the sometimes more literary tenor of his comments.[91] T'an also provides appendices that contain a wealth of information on traditions surrounding Hsi-wang-mu and K'un-lun 崑崙 mountain.

While variants of specific Chinese characters distinguish many of the editions of the texts, the major distinction derives from differences in the content and placement of the third poem of a sequence of exchanges between King Mu and Hsi-wang-mu in the third *chüan* of the text. In the recension preserved in the *Han-wei ts'ung-shu* (which served as the basis for the Ch'ing scholar Hung I-hsüan's collated and revised edition), the poems are presented in the context of a dialogue initiated by Hsi-wang-mu. King Mu responds and the third poem is then cast in the voice of Hsi-wang-mu responding once again to the king. In the recension preserved in the *Taoist Canon* and in Fan Ch'in's edition, however, the third poem is not in the voice of Hsi-wang-mu but in the voice of King Mu as he leaves Hsi-wang-mu and laments his neglect of his subjects.[92] Furthermore, the latter recension includes four lines that do not appear in the former, while the former text contains two lines that do not appear in the latter. In establishing a text upon which to base my own literary analysis, it was necessary to examine the reasons adduced by commentators and editors to support the authority of one recension over another.

The poems as they appear in both recensions are as follows:

Tao tsang Recension	*Han-wei ts'ung-shu* Recension
He thought of the people distressed and created a poem:	Hsi-wang-mu responded again with a poem:
Toward that western land [I traveled];	To the western lands [you came]
To reside in its wilds.	And resided [with me] in the wilds.
[With] tigers and leopards [I] formed a pack;	[With] tigers and leopards [you] formed a pack
[With] the black magpies [I] interacted.	[With] black magpies [you] interacted.
The glorious mandate cannot be changed;	The glorious mandate cannot be changed
I am God on High's Son of Heaven.	I am the daughter of God on High.
There is a great mandate but I do not measure up.	What are those people of the world,
When I consider the favor [given me by] the people	That you should prepare to leave me again?[93]
My tears fall profusely.	I blow the flutes and vibrate the reeds

[Although] flutes pipe and
reeds vibrate;
The depths of my heart
flutters [with anxiety]
A child of the people of the
world,
[In me] Heaven places its
hopes.

The depths of my heart
flutters;
A child of the people of the
world,
[In you] Heaven places its
hopes.

其念世民作憂以吟曰
徂彼西土
爰居其野
虎豹為羣
於鵲與處
嘉命不遷
我惟帝天子
大命而不可稱
顧世民之恩
流涕芔隕
吹笙鼓簧
中心翔翔
世民之子
惟天之望

西王母又為天子作吟曰
徂彼西土
爰居其野
虎豹為羣
於鵲與處
嘉命不遷
我惟帝女
彼何世民
又將去予
吹笙鼓簧
中心翔翔
世民之子
惟天之望

Both versions of the poem were known to most commentators. Hung I-hsüan, for example, notes that in another "contemporary edition" of the *Mu T'ien-tzu chuan* the poem appears later in the text, but he argues that the text is corrupt.[94] His decision to disregard this alternative reading was informed by his belief in the authority of an excerpt of the *Mu T'ien-tzu chuan*, cited by Kuo P'u in an annotation of the *Shan-hai-ching*, which attributes authorship of the third poem to Hsi-wang-mu.[95] Hung argues that Kuo's annotation must have been based on one of the earliest editions of the text and thus represents a text devoid of the corruptions that accrued as the text was transmitted over the centuries. Hung also believes that Kuo's rendition preserves a narrative logic that is lacking in the alternative recension.[96] Notwithstanding Hung's considerable accomplishment in providing a collated and well-informed annotated edition of the *Mu T'ien-tzu chuan*, his reasoning for rejecting the alternative recension is not convincing. As for Kuo P'u's "authoritative" annotation upon which Hung's recension is based, it does not preclude the possibility of an equally early but different textual tradition. As we noted above, Kuo P'u was not even familiar with Su

Hsi's recension of the text. Hung's argument that the text cited in Kuo's annotation is the most lucid is also not compelling. Indeed, rather than rely on what appears to be circumstantial evidence of precedence to establish the authority of Hung's recension, one can advance a strong case for the authority of the *Tao tsang* recension by closely examining the poems themselves and their relation to the rest of the text.

Consider, for example, that the diction of the poem unambiguously reflects the perspective of King Mu even though the poem is attributed to different speakers in the two recensions. The first two lines represent the perspective of one who has "gone over" (*ts'u*) to "those" (*pi*) "western lands" (*hsi-t'u*), such as King Mu, as opposed to the perspective of someone who lives there permanently as Hsi-wang-mu does.[97] In addition, the term "wilds" was already used by King Mu in the second poem of the sequence to refer to Hsi-wang-mu's home.[98] Likewise, rather than interpreting the phrases "forming a pack with leopards and tigers" and "interacting with black magpies" as Hsi-wang-mu's description of King Mu's visit to the west, they are better understood as metaphorical descriptions of King Mu's interaction with Hsi-wang-mu, who has traditionally been associated with these animals.[99]

The following two lines also contain clues that point in the same direction. Mathieu, following Kuo P'u's commentary, interprets the phrase "glorious mandate" (*chia-ming*) as a reference to a decree given by King Mu ordering Hsi-wang-mu to govern and protect her region. As such he reads the reference to *ti* 帝 as a reference to King Mu; the line *wo wei ti nü* (我惟帝女) is thus translated by Mathieu as "Je pense à vous, divin empéreur," although William Nienhauser's "I recognize only you as emperor (since I am your vassal)" seems closer to Mathieu's sense.[100] Ku Shih, in his zeal to prove the historicity of the *Mu T'ien-tzu chuan*, reads this line literally, as an affirmation of familial ties between King Mu and Hsi-wang-mu: he argues that they are father and daughter![101] It is noteworthy that both Mathieu and Ku ignore Kuo P'u's note that *ti* should be read as "God on High" (*t'ien-ti* 天帝), a reading that is more in keeping with the reference to "God on High" in the first *chüan* of the text. Although the use of *ti* to refer to mortal "emperors" as opposed to one supreme deity developed quite late,[102] Ku Shih and Mathieu opt for this anachronistic reading because it makes sense of what would otherwise be a puzzling if not unintelligible strophe.

Ch'en Feng-heng offers a different solution. First, he reads the phrase *chia-ming* as a reference to Heaven's Mandate and not to a decree given by King Mu. Given the reference to King Mu's "greatly receiving the Mandate" (*ta shou ming* 大受命), which occurs in *chüan* five, in addition to the even clearer reference of King Mu "receiving [God on High's] mandate" (*shou ming*) in the first *chüan*, Ch'en's reading is consistent with other usages of the word *ming* in the text.[103] Second, accepting the authority of the *Tao tsang* recension and the added four lines, Ch'en eliminates the character *nü*, seeing it as a corruption of the text, and appends the phrase "Son of Heaven" (*t'ien-tzu*), to the preceding phrase "I am God on High's." His text thus reads, "[As for me] I am God on High's Son of Heaven." The next line continues smoothly, "[I have received] the great mandate but I do not measure up."[104] This realization of King Mu coupled with his consideration of the favor bestowed on him by the people of the world, stirs him to "cry profusely."

Acceptance of Ch'en Feng-heng's revisions eliminates the problem generated by the apparent switch of subjects from the speaker to "the people of the world" in the two lines that follow the line "I recognize only you as Emperor" of the *Han-wei ts'ung-shu* recension. The lines, "What are the people of the world/ that you should prepare to leave me again" seem strangely outside the general cadence of the poem, and they seem to conflict with the general perspective of Hsi-wang-mu as a diety that can and will help "these people of the world."[105] Mathieu's translation, "De nouveau, vous allez nous quitter," is in line with Thomas Smith's translation but he too does not provide any literary evidence that might contextualize the intended meaning.[106] By contrast, the four "additional" lines of Ch'en's edition resonate with the context of the poem as a whole.

The context of King Mu's self-reflection is established by his acknowledgment of his "God on High"–given responsibility to serve as the Son of Heaven. Since he will not abandon (*ch'ien*) this responsibility he must provide for his subjects adequately. This is the sense of the final four strophes of the poem: although he delighted in pleasing Hsi-wang-mu, his heart is anxious for he knows that the people of the world expect him to act according to Heaven.[107] King Mu fears that his travels will be perceived as inauspicious; the key lies in the word *wang* 望, which appears in the name of the twenty-fifth hexagram of the *Book of Changes* and is associated with the inauspicious results of travel.[108] Not only do these lines accord perfectly with the context of this poem, but the tone is also consistent with the king's other poetic expressions which occur in at least three other places in the narrative.[109] Most striking is the sense of anxiety that pervades all four examples, and the fact that the anxiety stems from what appears to be a conflict of interests: King Mu's prerogative to travel and his need to be a conscientious ruler.[110] Rather than merely "reflect Confucian sentiments"[111] the poem is reflective of a genuine concern for preserving dynastic legitimacy, an issue that was of utmost urgency for the Chou. We will have chance to return to this issue in great detail in chapter 5 below. We can conclude, then, that the context of the poem as it is preserved in the *Tao tsang* recension is more consistent with both the established context of expression and the overall development and representation of King Mu's character in the text than it is in the *Han-wei ts'ung-shu* recension. The literary analysis of the text is based on the former recension.[112]

There is one other textual issue to be addressed in establishing a "definitive text," the status of the fifth *chüan*. Several scholars have noted both the incongruity of the narration of events within the *chüan* itself and the amorphous quality of its narrative in comparison with the first four *chüan,* which take as their theme King Mu's trip to K'un-lun.

The amorphous quality of the *chüan* derives in part from the plethora of events that have more to do with unrelated affairs concerning King Mu's governance (military expeditions, the construction of palaces, and so on), than with his trip to K'un-lun, although there are also not a few depictions of the kind of events portrayed in the first four *chüan*. A political or historical tone seems to permeate the narrative of *chüan* five. This may have something to do with the high percentage of narrated events that are also recorded in the *Bamboo Annals*. According to Mathieu's tabulations, out of twenty-five events recorded both in the *Mu T'ien-tzu chuan* and in the *Bamboo Annals,* fourteen of them occur in the fifth *chüan*.[113] This fact combined with his quantitative analysis of the number of particles used and the manner of their use in the fifth *chüan* as opposed to the other four *chüan,* led him to conclude that the former was composed later than the others.[114]

Wei T'ing-sheng, Ting Ch'ien, and Cheng Te-k'un have all identified chronological inconsistencies in *chüan* five.[115] The most glaring is the obvious incongruity of the text's first narrating that a tribal chieftain named "Ling Ti 陵翟 offered concessions of one hundred teams of four fine horses each and returned the precious vessels of Pi 畢," only to narrate later that "messages came from the people of Pi reporting the invasion of their country by the people of

Ling Ti; the Son of Heaven ordered Meng Yü 孟悆 to set out for the border to conduct a campaign against the barbarians."[116] Unlike Cheng Te-k'un, who simply transposes the latter entry so that it precedes the former, Wei regards the entire second half of the *chüan* as misplaced and reorganizes it accordingly. In addition, by matching events narrated in the fifth *chüan* to events recorded in the *Bamboo Annals,* Wei posits a specific chronology commencing in the first month of autumn of the tenth year of King Mu's reign. He then calculates, according to the *kan-chih* days presented in the text, that the traditional beginning of the text—which admittedly is abrupt due to corruption—records events that "occurred" in King Mu's twelfth year. For this reason, Wei places the newly reorganized fifth *chüan* at the beginning of the text.[117]

Wei's revisions constitute a laudable attempt to restore order in an incomplete and corrupt text. But because his work was based on the a priori assumption that the entire narrative is an accurate record of King Mu's activitities, he does not acknowledge any qualitative difference between the narrative style of the fifth *chüan* and the narrative style of the others in the *Mu T'ien-tzu chuan*. This cannot be ignored, however.

The chronological mixup noticed by Wei and others is indicative of the fragmentary nature of *chüan* five. Stylistically, it is a hotchpotch of reportage: at one moment recording, in true annalistic style, the death of a marquis or the construction of a palace, at another, narrating the content of King Mu's dreams or his poetic expressions.[118] Furthermore, these stylistic inconsistencies diminish any sense of structural integrity that might have given form to the information presented. Given the circumstances of the text's compilation and transcription, coupled with the amorphous style of *chüan* five, I am inclined to believe that it is a repository of events written on strips originally belonging to the text that somehow were displaced and never fully integrated into the *Mu T'ien-tzu chuan*, or strips that may have originally belonged to other texts of the corpus, such as the *Bamboo Annals*, which never really belonged to the *Mu T'ien-tzu chuan.*

There are several sections of *chüan* five that point to strong ties to other portions of the *Mu T'ien-tzu chuan*. For example, the two poems that are found in the fifth *chüan* are thematically and stylistically of the same kind as the poems found earlier in the text. Similarly, the narrative concerning King Mu's visit to the grave of the son of the great Yü 禹, Ch'i 啟, his dream of the mythical Archer I 羿, and his interest in the "Numinous Drum" (*ling-ku* 靈鼓) all contain details that are intimately connected to events narrated in the first four *chüan*.[119] One could also cite the anecdote about capturing the tiger and King Mu's naming of the place where it was caged as an example that resonates with King Mu's patterns of behavior throughout the text. While I attempt to draw some connections between various events narrated in the fifth *chüan* and those in the first four *chüan* (see appendix), it is nevertheless virtually impossible to reconstruct the text with the kind of precision that Edward Shaughnessy brought to his study of the *Bamboo Annals*.[120] There are too many lacunae, and unlike the practice of contemporary transcribers, who use one lacuna symbol to represent one unreadable character, the transcribers of the *Mu T'ien-tzu chuan* used the symbol to represent one or many unreadable characters. It is thus at times difficult to know how much is missing: whether a single character or an entire sentence.

Our inability to reconstruct the text in its exact original form, however, does not preclude our recovering and reestablishing many of the literary features of the *Mu T'ien-tzu chuan*, and it is toward this goal that the present study is directed. As such it differs significantly from the objectives of most earlier commentators, whose interests were largely informed by historical perspectives.

The point of departure for my literary analysis is the recognition that, contrary to the beliefs of most commentators (and even those scholars who view the *Mu T'ien-tzu chuan* from a literary rather than historical perspective), very few (if any) of the places visited by King Mu in the text have actual geographical referents. My observation that many of the place-names in the *Mu T'ien-tzu chuan* also appear in other texts relating early Chinese myths has led me to consider the possible implications of such shared references. Indeed, the concurrence of place-names such as Yang-yü, K'un-lun, and Yen Mountain in the *Mu T'ien-tzu chuan* and in early myths, especially those related to the Chinese flood myths, has led me to question the validity of assigning geographical referents to these place-names.

My literary analysis, then, rests in part on my ability to reconstruct the implicit mythic context alluded to in the *Mu T'ien-tzu chuan*. Because it will rely for its legitimacy and authority on a rigorous attention to textual detail and on the substantial accumulation of shared coherent elements of the mythic traditions and the *Mu T'ien-tzu chuan*, the following chapter is devoted to an exhaustive examination of the tradition of flood myths and of the cosmogonic intentions underlying those myths. Through my analysis I will attempt to recover the cosmogonic intentions which will form the basis for analyzing the literary significance of the references to the mythic traditions in the *Mu T'ien-tzu chuan*. It is hoped that such an analysis, by bringing to light the richness of the narrative features that comprise the text, will also convince readers of the profound revelations the text has to offer when read as the product of a literary, and not a historical composition.

TWO

See Yü Later: A New Interpretation of Chinese Flood Myths

One cannot overstate the importance of the Yü flood myths for a literary appreciation of the *Mu T'ien-tzu chuan*. Even scholars who are not interested in a literary analysis of the text have noted its striking resonance with the "Yü kung" chapter of the *Shang shu* in particular and with the broader political themes of the Yü myths. In general, most discussions of the relationship between the two texts have centered on their shared geographical references. I count at least eleven place-names that appear in both texts and at least two others that though epigraphically distinct in each text may nonetheless be related phonetically (that is, one is a loan character for another). In addition, there are overlaps between places visited by King Mu and those visited by Yü as recorded in other texts.

Although scholars working on the "Yü kung" and the *Mu T'ien-tzu chuan* have emphasized these geographical locations—indeed that has been the major evidence supporting a historical appreciation of the latter text—I believe that the shared references point to another level of signification. The very fact that the two texts, purporting to record journeys occurring at least a millennium apart, refer to similar locations is suggestive of a connection beyond the realm of geography. Rather, I submit they belong to the realm of myth. And only by uncovering the nature of the myth informing both texts can we finally get at the literary signficance of the *Mu T'ien-tzu chuan*—obscured to date by misreading the text in terms of geographically grounded historicity. The present chapter, then, seeks to establish the relevance of the Yü myths to the *Mu T'ien-tzu chuan.*

1

More and more of the recent scholarship on ancient China has sought to reevaluate the nature and significance of Chinese mythology and thereby deepen our understanding of ancient Chinese cultural patterns. In analyzing the early myths, scholars have offered stimulating new interpretations of topics as diverse as the origins of scientific thought, the religious elements of early Chinese philosophy, and the paradigmatic models that inform early Chinese concepts of political legitimacy and social order.[1] The following analysis offers a new interpretation of the origin and significance of Chinese flood myths, especially those concerning the Great Yü's control of the floodwaters. Specifically, it examines the cosmogonic purpose of these myths, which, I believe, should be read as references to celestial phenomena.[2]

The task of interpreting the texts recording Yü's control of the floodwaters was often relegated to the sidelines, in deference to the work of the philologists and historians. The former concentrated on the linguistic connections between mythic elements that could lead to the identification of one mythic figure in terms of another, and the latter sought to connect records of Yü's hydraulic feat with the history of the Hsia dynasty. So dominant was this work that notwithstanding the groundbreaking work of Ku Chieh-kang, Yang K'uan 楊寬, Wen I-to 聞一多, Wei Chü-hsien, Marcel Granet, Henri Maspero, Wolfram Eberhard, and Derk Bodde on the mythological aspect of these traditions, the (cosmogonic) significance, not to mention the literary implications, of this particular tradition has yet to be plumbed. Indeed, even the most historicized account of Yü, the "Yü kung," with its emphasis on Yü's organization of space, points to cosmogonic themes, with Yü's activity constituting the "paradigmatic work of cosmicization."[3]

Surely, as many have noted, a major difficulty in analyzing Chinese mythological traditions lies in the way in which myths were preserved in written accounts. Unlike Western myths, which often take lengthy narrative form, Chinese myths are little nuggets—terse references to what must have been well-preserved oral traditions. Moreover, these references appear in numerous texts, written by members of different schools of thought. And finally, the earliest forms of many of these texts date to the late Chou dynasty, leading some to argue that they are not reliable sources for the study of archaic Chinese myths, but can only be used to understand a late Chou conception of these Myths.[4]

Fortunately, the once-dominant rigid historical and philological principles have been amply qualified, and a new, broader perspective now informs the way scholars use texts to learn about early Chinese mythology. I should state at this juncture my own position on the perceived antiquity—or lack thereof—of mythological traditions. Rather than assuming the existence of a whole or "pure" ur-myth that can be reconstructed, I follow Claude Lévi-Strauss' argument that the intelligibility of a particular Chinese myth is related to its cross-connections to other sets of myths (though I reject his application of a binary model as the only way to map these connections).[5] Moreover, I believe that the significance of the cross-connections existing among many myths validates the notion that myths were repositories of information that were handed down—regardless of the "degree of insight of the people who do the actual telling."[6] Thus, whether one believes that this "knowledge" concerned historical events, ritual, or astronomical events, as I will argue—and even if the actual referents of the myth's language were not clearly preserved or understood—"the stories" persisted, nevertheless, often retaining verbal echoes of their original significance. Myths, that is, remained the preserve of the collective memory for centuries, even millennia. The gradual encroachment of writing on the oral tradition should therefore not be viewed as an obstacle to analyzing or even receiving truly ancient material.[7]

My interpretive framework is informed in large part by the work of Giorgio de Santillana and Hertha von Dechend. John Major summarizes their thesis:

> Myths can be used and were from the beginning intended to be understood by initiates as compendia of cosmological teachings. They showed with a high degree of probability that a single Grand Origin Myth was shared (in terms of structure, though not of course in literary details) by nearly all of the great ancient civilizations of Eurasia, and that it served as technical language for recording all of the essential features of the first of the ancient exact sciences, astronomy.[8]

My examination of the possible cosmogonic intentions of the Yü myth might thus also be seen as a study of a worldview that gave rise to it, namely, a worldview based on astronomical observation of the celestial changes that resulted from the phenomenon called "the precession of the equinoxes."[9] That worldview is represented by "the mythological motif of successive 'world ages' denoting the sequence of equinoctial constellations which precession has gradually rendered obsolete."[10]

Although historical knowledge of precession is traditionally dated to the first explicit description of the phenomenon in writing, the ecliptic and its significance vis-à-vis the location of astronomical seasonal markers is not all that obscure a concept. An awareness of precessionial movement could easily have developed with an understanding of the altered arrival time (that is, the rising, transit, and setting times) of key star groups. These were observable over the span of only three generations, especially for those star groups identified as markers of the beginning of seasons or of the equinoxes and solstices.[11] Such knowledge would have been essential for maintaining the high level of agricultural sophistication suggested by the archaeological evidence of several Neolithic tombs. A number of historians of astronomy have postulated that the Neolithic Chinese knew from a very early time on that certain stars indicated by their acronychal and heliacal rising the times at which the sun passes through the equator from the South to the North (vernal equinox) and the sun's highest position in the northern tropic (summer solstice). Dependent as they were on seasonal regularity, the ancient Chinese must have observed the shift of the position of the solstices and equinoxes.[12]

I will argue even further that the information pertaining to these observations was important enough to have been preserved in an oral tradition.[13] The slow movement of the equinoctial points backward through the zodiac (moving through the entire celestial sphere in 25,920 years) may have allowed calendrical and hence agricultural adjustments to be made without urgency, so long as the equinoctial location continued to occur within or near a specific constellation. The movement of the equinoctial point farther and farther from this constellation must have been regarded with fear, however, especially if there were no nearby bright stars that could be obvious as the seasonal markers. Ancient observers of the sky must surely have experienced a strong sense of displacement and anxiety in reponse to such a "violation of spatiotemporal parsimony and symmetry."[14] A certain few—most likely those charged with the responsibility of observing the heavens—must have been moved to explain what was happening and to preserve this reasoning.

The premise that certain early Chinese cosmogonic myths represent a metaphoric rendition of astronomical and cosmological knowledge is accepted by several modern scholars of Chinese myth. Consider the interpretation by John Major and David Pankenier of the famous myth of Kung-kung 共工 butting Pu-chou 不周 Mountain, which severs the connection between earth and heaven and thus "explains" the northwestern tilt of the heavens; these modern scholars see in this account "a description of the tilting of the ecliptic relative to the celestial equator, the non-coincidence of the paths of the sun and planets with the rotation of the fixed stars around the plane of the celestial equator." Similarly, the myths concerning the great inundation of floodwaters and Yü's control of them represent a tradition based on the obvious changes in the time of arrival of certain constellations on the eastern horizon.[15]

The following discussion first explores the astronomical implications of the flood and illustrates how certain celestial phenomona, astral configurations, and their spatiotemporal relationships are metaphorically represented as the source and cause of the flood in the myths. It then analyzes the myths of Yü in this context. Finally, having established the stellar origin of the Yü flood myths, the discussion elaborates the cosmogonic intentions underlying the myths.

2

Yü takes action in response to a cataclysmic flood. To understand his behavior we must first understand the cause and significance of the flooding. We saw above that the consequences of Kung-kung's act of butting Pu-chou Mountain can be understood as a figurative rendition of the "displacement" of the sun's path along the zodiac (that is, the westward precession of the solstitial and equinoctial points through the zodiac). That Kung-kung's act broke one of the four pillars (literally "the four cardinal points" [*chi* 極]) of Heaven, seen in Wang Ch'ung's 王充 (A.D. 27–97) *Lun heng* 論衡, may be a tacit reference to the shifting of the four equinoctial and solstitial points that occurs with precession.[16]

The earth's southeast tilt that resulted from Kung-kung's butting Pu-chou Mountain implies that there is a gap in the (celestial) northwest. In fact, the name Pu-chou literally means "not complete" and refers to an incomplete circumference or revolution. The image of a celestial rupture that must be mended or bridged is also suggested by a term used to identify the celestial northwest, that portion of the sky which lies between Scorpius and Sagittarius. The *Erh-ya* identifies this area as the "heavenly ford" (*t'ien-chin* 天津).[17] That this celestial space could indeed have been conceptualized as the place that bridges the gap caused by the westward shift of the equinoxes is supported by the fact that the Chinese ecliptic—the major constellations of the Chinese zodiac—runs right through this portion of the sky. Leopold de Saussure argues that the ancient Chinese knew well that the return of the planet Jupiter to "heavenly ford" signaled the end of one Jovian revolution—in other words, the end of one year, and the beginning of the new one.[18] That this area of the sky is associated with some kind of passage or transformation is further underscored by the appellation "heaven's watchtower" (*t'ien-ch'üeh* 天闕) given to the westernmost asterism belonging to Sagittarius, the Southern Dipper (*nan-tou* 南斗).[19] Finally, that the "heavenly ford" may represent a corrective to the effects of the precession of the equinoxes is also intimated by its seasonal associations: it serves to bridge the two quadrants, the eastern Cerulean Dragon (*ts'ang-lung* 蒼龍) and the northern Heavenly Turtle (*t'ien-yüan* 天黿) or Black Turtle (*hsüan-yüan* 玄黿), in which Scorpius and Sagittarius were the seasonal markers for spring and winter, respectively. It thus provided a means for the sun to cross over from the dark, cold, northern winter quadrant to the resplendent and vibrant vernal quadrant.[20]

Since the asterisms belonging to the Heavenly Turtle quadrant directly precede those of the Cerulean Dragon in the zodiac, it is understandable why the cause of the shifting of the equinoctial (and, of course, the solstitial) points was believed to emanate from this part of the sky. Perhaps the ominous associations of the Heavenly Turtle quadrant can be explained by its spatiotemporal relation to the Cerulean Dragon, which served as the harbinger of spring; the shifting of the spring seasonal marker may have been perceived as the work of a malevolent force hidden in the Heavenly Turtle quadrant. Certainly the connection between this quadrant and the season of death—winter—reinforces the image of the Heavenly Turtle as a menacing figure.

Also significant for our present inquiry are the associations of the celestial northern quadrant with water. These are quite compatible with many myths worldwide, in which the source of all waters is thought to be the Milky Way (the "Heavenly River" [*t'ien-han* 天

漢] in Chinese), which is located in the *northwestern* direction of the heavens. In the Chinese system, the Heavenly River, along with the ecliptic, runs *right through* Scorpius and Sagittarius, providing another level of signification for the appellation "heavenly ford" given to that space: it symbolizes the bridging of the Heavenly River, which flows between the (watery) northern and eastern quadrants of the sky.[21]

The common mythical associations between water, floods, and chaos can also be explained in terms of the astronomical significance of the northwestern quadrant of the sky. According to the *Huai-nan-tzu,* the rupture in the northwest caused by Kung-kung resulted in the uncontrollable flowing of waters. Given the proximity of the Milky Way to the celestial northwest (where Pu-chou Mountain is located), it is probable that Kung-kung's act was viewed as the source of the floodwaters. This association is strengthened by an added detail in the *Huai-nan-tzu* passage that describes how the goddess Nü Wa 女媧 "cut off the foot of a turtle with which she reestablished the four cardinal points."[22] The turtle imagery of course recalls the celestial north, the Heavenly Turtle, while the remaining three legs represent the number of cardinal points presumed to be (still) stable. Floodwaters, or more precisely the Milky Way, are thus associated with the displacement caused by the precession of the equinoxes.

The association of the Milky Way with the effects of precession is suggested, I believe, by the ancient location of the seasonal indicators for the vernal equinox: in 6000 B.C. the acronychal rising of Gamma Sagitarrius (right ascension/declination: $10^{h}27.9^{m}$/Ø°55'), which is part of the constellation known as Basket (*ch'i* 萁) and is located right in the Milky Way, was the indicator of the arrival of the equinox.[23] (See figure 2.1.) The Milky Way occupied this postion for almost fifteen hundred years. (Its heliacal setting also marked the autumnal equinox for the same amount of time.) One can perhaps see in this spatiotemporal context a connection between water and the equinox. But why are the waters considered floodwaters, with their suggestion of catastrophe? The answer lies in the celestial movements in the area surrounding the Milky Way.

Phi Sagittarius (right ascension/declination: $11^{h}ø5.4^{m}$/Ø°22'), which is the determinative star for the Southern Dipper, was about eight degrees away and rose just half an hour later than Gamma Sagittarius. In other words, Phi Sagittarius would have been the marker of the vernal equinox about five hundred years earlier. This is significant because a parenatellon (an asterism that rises at the

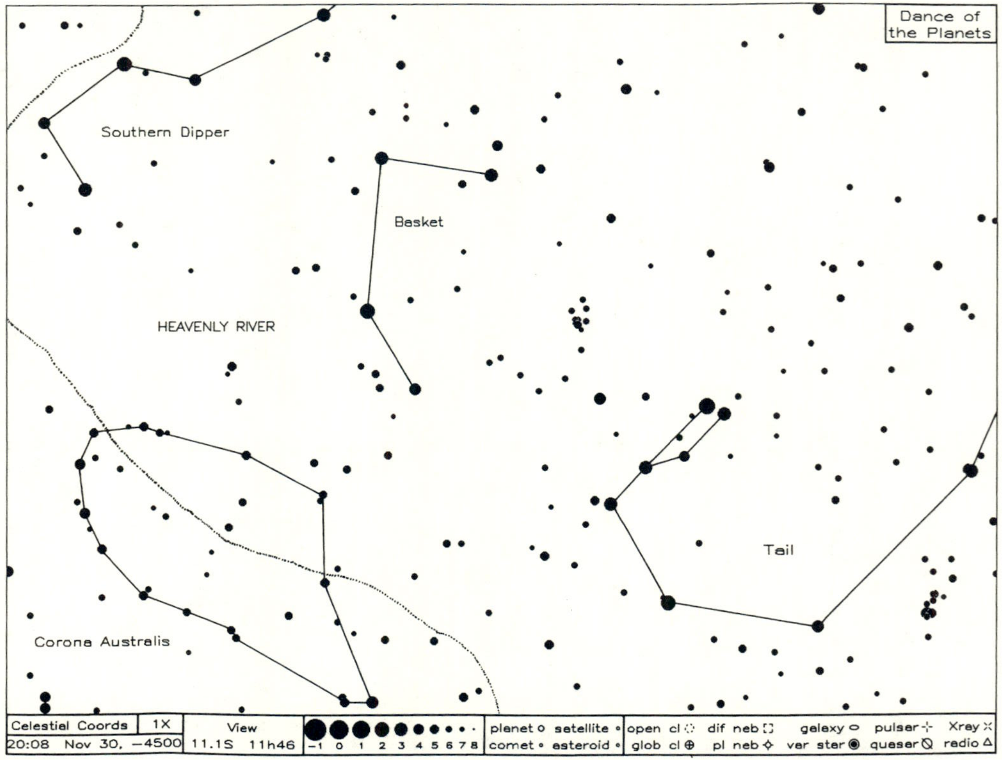

FIGURE 2.1. Chart depicting the relative positions of Basket, Southern Dipper and Corona Australis, ca. 4500 B.C. "Dance of the Planets © ARC Software."

same time as a constellation) of the Southern Dipper, one that was considerably more important in the Chinese conception of the sky than in that of the Western, is a constellation also known by the Chinese as the Heavenly Turtle (*t'ien-pieh* 天鼈), and known in the West as Corona Australis. Given the turtle's aqueous nature, the proximity of the "Heavenly Turtle" asterism to the Milky Way bespeaks the etiology of the name of the constellation as much as its round shape, which is formed by fifteen stars.

During the Western Chou, Corona Australis was a seasonal indicator marking the beginning of winter. This role must have had much to do with the appellation of the quadrant of the sky that it occupies;[24] while the asterisms contained in the other three quadrants are all considered a part of the animal for which the quadrant is named, Corona Australis gives its name (Heavenly Turtle) to the quadrant without even serving as an "official" part of the zodiac.

The calendrical use of such a constellation—one that was not among the twenty-eight lunar stations that marked the places where the sun and moon "rested" on their journey around the heavens—suggests an ancient tradition of the seasonal significance of Corona Australis. There was, in fact, a tradition that during the time of T'ao T'ang 陶唐, Yüeh Shang Kuo 越裳國 presented a numinous thousand-year-old turtle (*shen kuei* 神龜) that occupied an area of three square *ch'ih* 尺. Written on the back of the turtle in "tadpole" script, were all the events concerning the split (between heaven and earth). Yao 堯 ordered that this be recorded, and this was called the Turtle Calendar (*kuei-li* 龜曆).[25]

The connection between a turtle (and the Turtle Calendar) and the events surrounding the sundering of heaven and earth is not gratuitous. Rather, it points to the obsolescence of Corona Australis, to the catastrophic inability of Corona Australis to continue to serve as a seasonal indicator for the arrival of spring. This event, which occurred sometime in the sixth millennium B.C., was a result of precession.[26] The Turtle Calendar may thus refer to a tradition whereby Corona Australis was the basis for an astronomical calender, or more concretely—to the time when Corona Australis was still a marker for the vernal equinox and before it was replaced by the Milky Way. It is thus similar to the appellation Fire Calendar, referring to the use of Antares—the Fire Star—as a basis for an astronomical calendar. The severance of heaven's ties—this great astronomical displacement—must have caused a sense of profound chaos. Heaven could no longer serve as a guiding force for actions (especially agricultural) on earth.

This sense of chaos is also reflected in the metaphor of the flood. The source of that metaphor is vividly depicted in the fact of the proximity of the Heavenly River to Corona Australis and the fact that precession would have shifted the equinoctial points such that the Heavenly River assumed the temporal and spatial dimensions once belonging to Corona Australis.[27] Additional evidence is provided by the multivalent connotations of the word *yin* 淫. Often understood to connote both a sense of excess caused by flooding waters and a sense of debauchery (often sexual), the term is used frequently in the *Tso chuan* to mean "encroach" in the sense of one celestial body encroaching upon another. The combination of these meanings evokes a sense of cosmic disorder, as one celestial body (the Milky Way) "encroached" upon another (Corona Australis).[28]

The term Turtle Calendar also calls to mind the River Chart (*h'o-t'u* 河圖), which is believed by some to depict "the heavenly stars that control nature" and to be a "record of Heaven's Mandate, measuring the period ending and beginning, of preservation and extinction, of Heaven and Earth and of Kings, and the rule of succession of the Register (of heavenly legitimation)."[29] Moreover, there is a likely astronomical interpretation of the imagery associated with the discovery or emergence of the River Chart and its equally numinous counterpart the Lo [river] Chart (*lo-t'u* 洛圖): the former was said to have been carried on the back of a *dragon* and the latter, on the back of a *turtle* (the two asterisms sandwiching the Heavenly River), both of which emerged from a *river* (that is, the Milky Way) and ascended onto *land* (that is, the Heavenly Ford mentioned above). The split in the Milky Way at the juncture between Scorpius and Sagittarius may be the source of this imagery as well as the source of the association between the number nine and the charts, which we will address below. Hsing Ping's annotations to the "Tzu-han p'ien" 子罕篇 chapter of the *Lun-yü*, cites Cheng Hsüan 鄭玄 who states that the writing on the back of a turtle was "a list of the precise degree coordinates for Ursa Major and the lunar stations, the calculations requisite for recording the ascent and decline of kingdoms."[30] Hence, the Lo Chart, like the Turtle Calendar, may be viewed as a mythic repository of information about the calendrical role of Corona Australis. In sum, this rather long excursion into the seasonal function of Corona Australis is a key to unlocking the referents of early Chinese flood myths.

The Heavenly Turtle (Corona Australis) has other mythic associations, as well; for example, a very strong one with Kun 鯀—Yü's father—who figures significantly in the myths. This association of the myths of Kun with Corona Australis is warranted, I believe, by several factors.[31]

We can identify three common motifs that structure the myths concerning Kun, although some of the details about him differ in the various traditional sources: (1) he is the first to try to control the floodwaters; (2) he fails to control the floods; (3) a consequence of this failure is his death at a location called Feather Mountain (*Yü shan* 羽山) or Feather Abyss (*Yü yüan* 羽淵). The term "abyss," it should be noted, is used in at least one early source, the *Book of Changes*, to describe the astronomical space occasionally inhabited by the Cerulean Dragon. It is also said to be the place the dragon enters (and subsequently disappears into) at autumn.[32]

These obvious watery connotations suggest a connection with the watery winter quadrant of the Heavenly Turtle. That Kun is often said to have failed to control the floods because he listened to the advice of an "old turtle" strengthens this hypothesis. Moreover, Kun is identified as the son of Chuan Hsü 顓頊, who is related astrologically to the winter Heavenly Turtle quadrant of the Heavens. And of course Kung-kung's butting of Pu-chou Mountain, which caused the flood, was the result of a cosmic battle with Chuan Hsü—again, connecting Kun's work to control the flood to the astronomical context. (Moreover, Chuan Hsü was supposedly buried in a place called by another appellation for the lunar lodge *hsü* 虛 [Beta Aquarri], which is located in the Heavenly Turtle quadrant.)[33] Finally, the tradition credits Chuan Hsü with the invention of calendrical astronomy (that is, seasonal asterisms), yet another close tie between his place of death, Kun's work to control the floods, and the effects of the precession of the equinoxes. Indeed, this is suggested by Gustav Schlegel's interpretation of the etiology of the name of the lunar lodge *hsü* as referring to a celestial "graveyard": the myth of Kung-kung and Chuan Hsü, and the name of the latter's grave site both may allude to the "obsolescence of the lunar lodge Xu [*hsü*] . . . as the location of the sun at winter solstice (and by implication the equinoctial asterisms as well)."[34]

Kun's failure to control the flood also contributes to my identification of Kun as Corona Australis. The reasons given for his failure are often linked to his strategy for controlling the water. Some sources are very general, stating only that Kun was either belligerent or ineffectual. Others specify that he stole from God on High a special type of "swelling soil," *hsi-jang* 息壤, that had the quality of expanding itself in water.[35] But damming that may work under more ordinary conditions cannot possibly succeed in a situation of ultimate chaos, where the "waters surged up to heaven."[36] In view of the association between floodwaters and the precession of the equinoxes, Kun's failure to stop the rising waters can be seen as a tacit acknowledgment of the impossibility of blocking or obstructing the precession of the equinoxes: the turning of the precessional clock necessitates the continual westward flow (shift) of the equinoctial points. In a view that supports this interpretation, Ku Chieh-kang, Yang K'uan, and others have made the convincing case that the stories of Kun and Kung-kung in fact stem from one original source and need to be read as two versions of the same myth. Kung-kung's butting of Pu-chou Mountain, as we have seen, is also an imagistic representation of the effect caused by precession.[37]

Finally, the association of Kun with Corona Australis is supported by various other details and other appellations. First, after Kun is killed at Feather Mountain, he is said to have "dived into the Feather Abyss," which we have seen may be connected to the celestial north.[38] This verb, "to dive" or "to submerge" (*ch'en* 沈), is also frequently used in Chinese to describe the descent of constellations or asterisms. Second, Kun is sometimes called by the name Black Fish (*hsüan-yü* 玄魚), in which the term "black" (*hsüan* 玄) is the same as that used in the appellation Black Turtle, a reference to the Heavenly Turtle quadrant. Indeed, Kun is said to have been transformed into a three-legged turtle (*nai* 能) after descending into the Feather Abyss. This odd image recalls the myth of Nü-wa cutting off one foot of a turtle to reestablish the four cardinal points.[39]

The death motif, too, links Corona Australis and Kun. Both Moriyasu Tarō and Whalen Lai have pointed to Kun's symbolic function in autumnal sacrificial rites. The term used for the sacrifice to Kun, *chiao* 郊 is often translated as "suburb" or "periphery." In the *Shan-hai-ching* as well as in the *Tso chuan,* Kun is said to have been killed at Feather Suburb (*yü-chiao* 羽郊).[40] The term *chiao* may be a reference to the actual location of Kun's death and subsequent transformation: Kun's (Corona Australis) proximity to the Heavenly River, I have noted, placed it at the periphery of Sagittarius—near the border between the northern and eastern celestial quadrants. This association may also explain the often cited detail of Kun's three-month (or year-long) hibernation, after which his son, the Great Yü, was born; that is, the winter solstice and the spring equinox are separated by three months. In addition, with the obsolescence of Corona Australis as a marker for the spring equinox, it became an indicator of the arrival of winter, also a period of three months.[41]

3

If Kun is correctly identified as a heavenly personage, then to what stellar configuration do the myths of Yü refer? Another ancient calendrical system, the Fire Calendar (*huo-li* 火曆),[42] suggests an answer. This system, which derives from seasonal observations of the fire star (*huo-hsing* 火星) Antares, probably replaced the ancient calendrical system associated with the Heavenly Turtle. Antares, along with two other stars, is situated at the very top of the lunar station Tail (*wei* 尾) which is part of the dragon constellation, or Scorpius. The asterism of which Antares is a part is known as the Heart (*hsin* 心) of the Cerulean Dragon. Remarkably, there exist textual traces of the role played by Antares in ancient Chinese calendariography; its function of marking the spring equinox with its acronychal rising dates to 4500 B.C. (and ends about 3500–3000 B.C., when, due to precession, the asterism known as Room [*fang* 房] assumed this function).[43]

The appellation fire star undoubtedly derives from the red color of this supergiant first-magnitude star. So bright is it that Sui jen 燧人 is said to have discovered fire after having observed Antares, which then led to the practice of using fire to mark the change of seasons (*huo chi shih yen* 火紀時焉). Thus the spring appearance (rising) and the autumnal disappearance (the heliacal setting) of Antares signaled for the agricultural community the time when "the fires should be brought out and brought in." The term "bringing out" (*ch'u huo* 出火) fire presumably refers to the burning of fields to prepare the soil for sowing, a practice documented in oracle bone inscriptions dating from the Shang dynasty. The term "bringing in the fire" refers to the need to ready the hearth for winter. Human activity was thus coordinated with celestial movements. Indeed, Antares played such a significant role in the lives of farmers that the neighboring asterism House (which itself became the seasonal marker) was named Auspicious Farmer (*nung-hsiang* 農祥).[44] Early evidence of this nexus between the dragon constellation and agriculture may be seen in the decoration of a bowl that depicts a reptile/dragon-like figure with a stalk of grain coming out of the mouth. The bowl is considered a remnant of Lung-shang culture (龍山), which dates to about 2500 B.C. (See figure 2.2.)[45]

Epigraphic evidence also points to the calendrical role of Antares: namely, the very form of the graph used to designate the concept of seasonal indicator or celestial mark point, *ch'en* 辰. It appears to be a representation of the tail of a dragon—that is, the tail

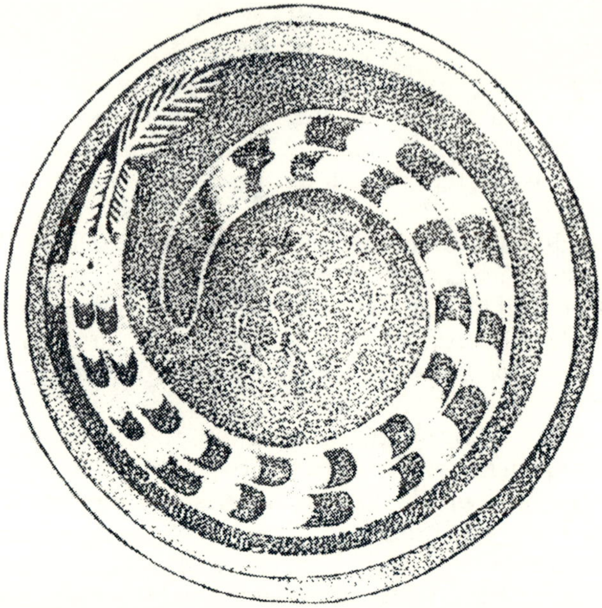

FIGURE 2.2. Dragon with wheat stalk on Neolithic Pottery discovered in Shan-hsi, Hsien-fen district, T'ao-ssu. (Wen-wu ch'u-pan she, *Wang-lai ku-chin shuo*, 1990.)

of the constellation Scorpius ([illegible]). The intimate connection between Antares and agriculture is likewise represented in the form of the graph for agriculture (*nung* 農), a major component of which is the graph *ch'en*, "celestial mark point."[46]

The significance of Antares in shaping the agricultural calendar cannot be overstated. So ingrained was it in the consciousness of those charged with observing the skies that a historian of the Lu court during the seventeenth year of Duke Chao's (525 B.C.) reign claimed that the appearance of Antares in the sixth month of the Chou calendar year (*Chou-li* 周曆) actually demarcated the first month (*cheng-yüeh* 正月) of the year. As P'ang P'u explains, the historian's insistence bespeaks a knowledge of the traditional Fire Calendar.[47] Why the authority invested in Antares as a marker of the vernal equinox continued to have resonance even thousands of years after it ceased to function in this manner, is related to the rationale informing the cause of the flood (and hence the generation of the flood myths) discussed above. Just as the flood should be understood as a reference to the effects of the shifting of the (vernal) equinoctial point from Corona Australis to the imperspicuous Milky Way, so too should the controlling of the flood be understood as the discovery of and settling on a new star to serve as a marker of the vernal equinox. Antares was this star. Its radiance must have been welcomed by the early Chinese who for so long had had no bright star to use as a seasonal marker. Meanwhile the fact that it is situated just outside a branch of the Milky Way must have inspired observers to see in Antares an additional role as savior, as the controller of the flood waters: this is the role that defines the persona of the Great Yü. The myths of Yü's control of the floods are in fact imagistic renditions of the ancient use of Antares as a marker for the vernal equinox.

4

The foregoing analysis of the myths of Kun intimates that Yü's persona, like Kun's, is informed by stellar movements: if Kun is Corona Australis, his son, too, would have his origins in the stars. Indeed, the spatiotemporal relationship of Corona Australis and Scorpius offers a clue to the source of the mythic familial relationship of Kun and Yü. Any star map vividly depicts just how Yü "issues" forth from Kun: Scorpius's tail almost literally touches the head of Corona Australis.[48] (See figure 2.3.) This same spatio-temporal connection may inform the iconography of a late Shang bronze dragon-shaped *kuang* vessel. Depicted on the side of the vessel is a turtle figure trailing the tail of a dragon. My astronomical reading of this iconography would be supported by the archaeoastronomer Feng Shih, who has identified the starlike knob on the top of the vessel as a representation of Antares. (See figure 2.4.)[49]

The physical proximity of the two constellations may, however, be only one of the reasons for describing the relationship in familial terms. The word used to describe how Yü was born of Kun, *fu* 腹, may refer to Yü's inheritance of Kun's (calendrical) position and hence function, much as ancient administrative titles and duties were hereditary. *Fu* is usually translated as "stomach" or "belly," and in the context of Yü's birth it is often understood to mean that Yü was born from Kun's stomach. There is certainly mythic drama in the image of a belly splitting open to allow for Yü's emergence, but another avenue of interpretation suggests itself as well. In sources dating back to Shang oracle bones, the phonetic *fu* 复 itself is a word meaning "return to," "restore," and "recom-

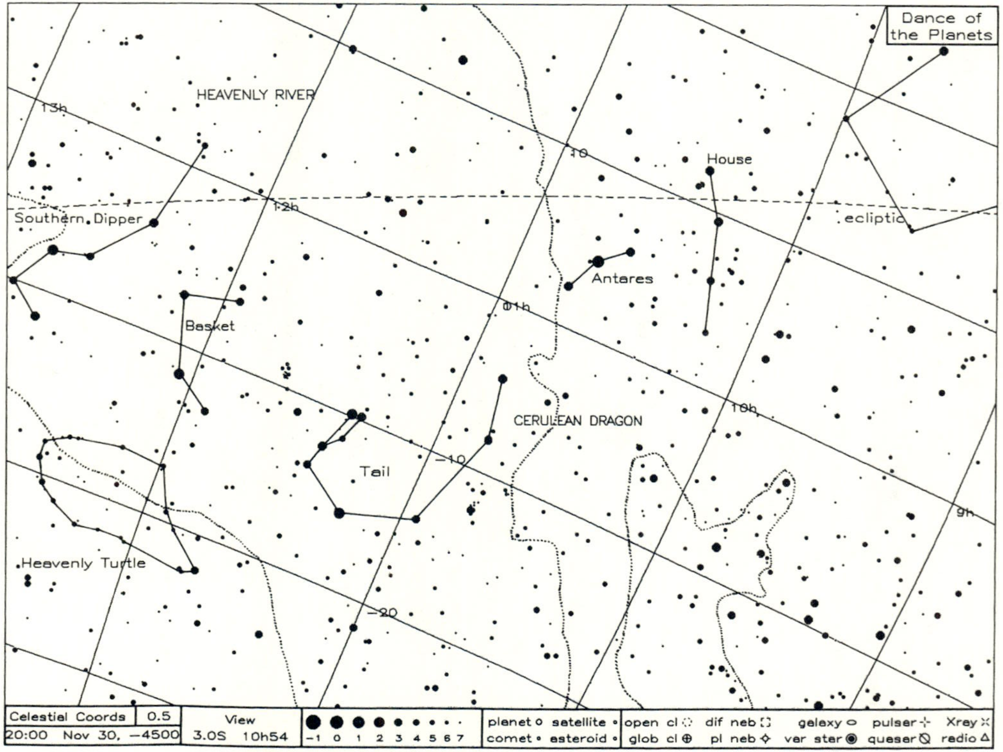

FIGURE 2.3. Chart depicting the relative positions of the Heavenly Turtle (Corona Australis), the Heavenly River and the Cerulean Dragon, ca. 4500 B.C. "Dance of the Planets © ARC Software."

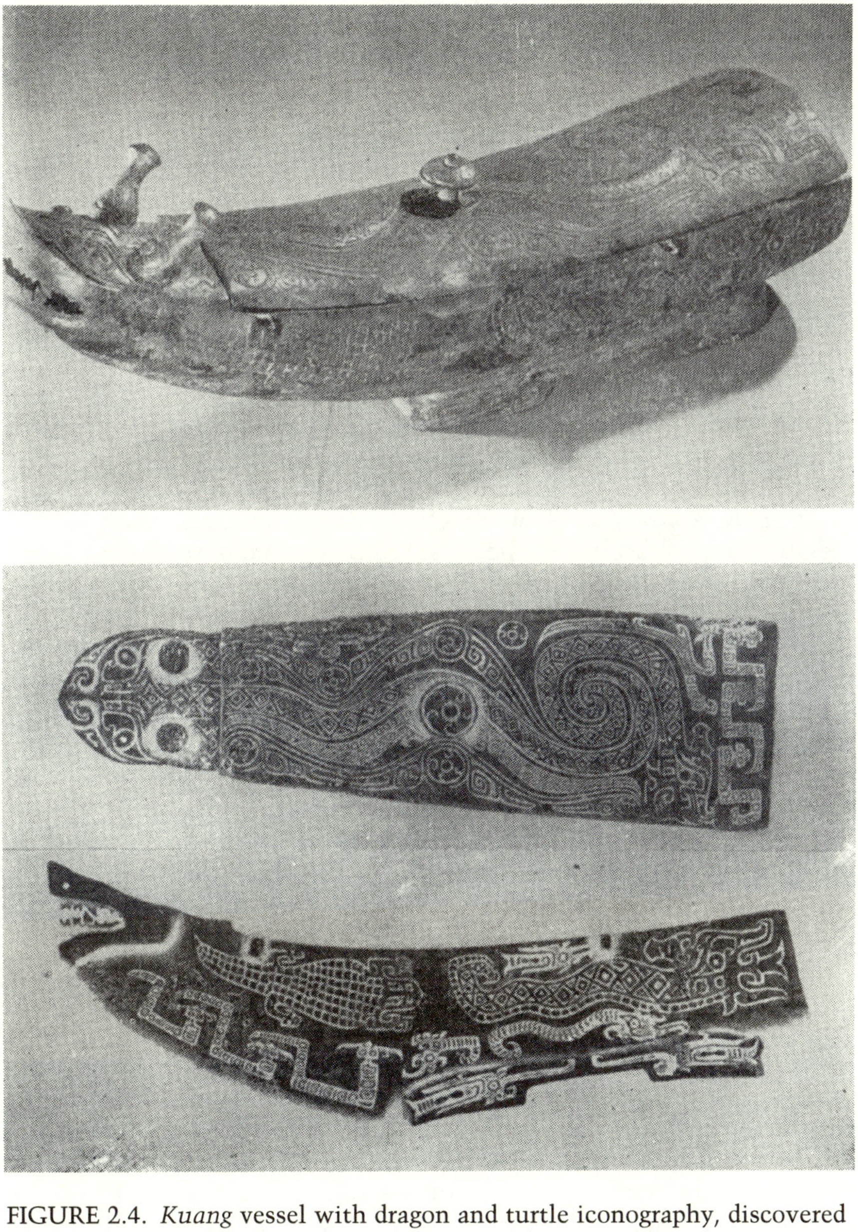

FIGURE 2.4. *Kuang* vessel with dragon and turtle iconography, discovered in Shan-hsi, Shih-lou T'ao-hua chuang. Knob on middle of top part is thought to represent Antares. (Tsou Heng, *Hsia Shang Chou k'ao-ku-hsüeh wen-chi*, plate 42.)

mence"—all rich in temporal nuance. Perhaps, then, Kun's "belly birthing" of Yü is a tacit reference to the restoration of a stable calendrical system, to the recommencing of time—which had been (at least symbolically) disrupted and broken with the obsolescence of Corona Australis.[50] Thus Yü is described in the "T'ien-wen" as "inheriting the same tradition and carrying on the same work of his father" (*tsuan-chiu ch'ien hsü* 纂就前緒). Ch'ü Yüan goes on to ask, "If he continued the work already begun, in what way was his [Yü's] plan a different one?"[51] Whereas many commentators have understood these lines as referring solely to the work of flood control, I believe that Ch'ü Yüan is referring to the broader calendrical function of both Kun and Yü.

This interpretation is supported by a passage in the *Chou-yü* that depicts Yü's accomplishments not so much in terms of water drainage as in terms of altering and correcting the *inappropriate measurements* (*fei-tu* 非度) used by his predecessor, Kun. The context of the passage is clear that these measurements are related to establishing an accurate calender: to ensure that activities on earth accord with events in heaven (*tsai t'ien ch'eng hsiang, tsai ti ch'eng hsing* 在天成象, 在地成形). A myth preserved in the *Mo tzu* seems to contain a veiled reference to Yü's relationship to Kun, although the latter is not mentioned explicitly.[52] In that myth Yü receives an order in the Dark Palace (*hsüan-kung* 玄宮) from Kao Yang 高陽, another name for Chuan Hsü, Kun's father. The term Dark Palace, of course, resonates with the terms used to refer to Kun (*hsüan yü* 玄魚) and the Heavenly Turtle quadrant, which is also often referred to as a palace. We thus have an implicit reference to Yü's succession: he "receives" his orders in the location that has lost its calendrical significance, which accords with Ch'ü Yüan's description of Yü "picking up" or carrying on with a job that Kun could not complete. That Yü was ordered to eliminate a figure who had caused catastrophes of a calendrical nature lends further support to this interpretation.[53]

In the passages describing the flood and its control Ch'ü Yüan employs imagery that recalls the physical relationship of Corona Australis and Scorpius. Most striking is the reference to a Responsive Dragon (*ying-lung* 應龍) that uses its tail to sketch on the land a map of channel-like formations whereby the floodwaters were allowed to drain. Yü then used this sketch to help control the flood. The Responsive Dragon's tail brings to mind the tail of the celestial dragon (Scorpius), which, remarkably, is situated precisely at the place where the Milky Way *splits into two branches*.[54] That

Scorpius's tail should be identified as the Responsive Dragon is also intimated by an account in the *Shih i chi* 拾遺記: "Yü exhausted his energy creating channels, diverting the waters and establishing mountains as the yellow dragon dragged its tail in front and the black turtle carried green-black mud (used to build the channels) in back." The black turtle (*hsüan-kuei* 玄龜), as noted previously, is another appellation for Kun, Corona Australis, while the detail of the dragon "dragging its tail" can surely be seen as a variant of the aforementioned myth of the Responsive Dragon using its tail to draw a map.[55] This is the very spatiotemporal relationship that I have proposed!

Not only did Yü use the drawing of the Responsive Dragon to drain floodwaters, but he also used it to divide the land into "nine regions" (*chiu-chou* 九州).[56] While many traditional scholars, including the one who wrote the "Yü kung" (which narrates the route taken by Yü as he cleared the floodwaters), have enumerated nine terrestrial referents corresponding to Yü's nine regions, there are other interpretive possibilities.[57] Foremost among them is that nine regions refers not to terrestrial locations but to a celestial one: the tail of Scorpius that is formed by *nine* stars. According to the *Canon of Luminaries*, the constellation Tail has a second appellation, "mouth of the nine rivers" (*chiu chiang k'ou* 九江口), perhaps an allusion to the rivers "drawn" out by the dragon's tail.[58] Moreover, if we remember just where Scorpius's tail is situated—right at the little "islet" of celestial space formed by the forking of the Milky Way—then it should come as no surprise that the original meaning of the word "region" (*chou* 州), as its ancient graph vividly depicts , was "islet" or even "sandbar."[59] It may be that the ancient epithet used to refer to China, nine regions, in fact refers to the Cerulean Dragon's (that is, Antares') role—through metonymic association—in establishing a new calendar, a function that is commensurate with the establishment of a reign or a political entity. The fact that the asterism Tail was also called the Controller of Works (*ssu-k'ung* 司空) further underscores these political associations.[60]

The same political associations give nuance to many of the myths concerning the Great Yü, who, according to tradition, was also given the title "controller of works" by Emperor Yao, when the latter appointed him to deal with the floodwaters.[61] The shared title, I believe, is not a coincidence: Yü is none other than the Cerulean Dragon (the asterism Heart, which contains Antares and the tail of Scorpius), whose tail symbolized the new spatiotemporal dimensions upon which the Antares calendrical system was based.

If the foregoing analysis is correct, it provides a clue to understanding the profound significance of the number nine in Chinese culture; more specifically it explains why that number is so intimately connected with the manifestation of political power. The nine dragons that emblematized the king's prerogative may be associated with the function of the Cerulean Dragon's tail in demarcating the boundaries for a new calendar;[62] and the nine squares that make up the grids of the Lo-shu and the Ho-T'u may emblematize the power attendant upon comprehending the significance of Scorpius' function. Indeed, Scorpius' tail can also be seen as the source of the cosmological significance of the notion of *yang* (of yin-yang theory). The constellation is the essence of virility because its tail can be seen clearly in the evening sky during the regenerative and productive seasons, spring and summer. The fact that the line statements of the pure *yang* hexagram detail the seasonal movements of the Cerulean Dragon, coupled with the fact that *yang* (unbroken) lines in the succeeding hexagrams are referred to by the number nine underscore this connection.[63]

The identification of Yü as an anthropomorphized rendition of this constellation accords with scholarship that has seen in the portrayal of Yü—indeed, in his very name—vestiges of a totemic tradition of worshipping the dragon or reptilian creatures. Wei Chü-hsien, Moriyasu Tarō, and others have all paid close attention to the prominent associations between Yü and the dragon that suffuse many myths. Yü is said, for example, to carve out Dragon Gate as a first step of flood control; a green-black dragon was said to have been born in the peripheral suburb as Yü started his work—imagery that may refer to the spatiotemporal dimensions of the dragon constellation; Yü's boat was said to be carried by a yellow dragon; and a "numinous dragon" (*shen-lung* 神龍) was said to have led the way on Yü's travels, in some cases to a place where a great turtle and an alligator made a bridge for him to cross. The number nine also figures importantly in many of the Yü myths: Yü established the nine regions, the nine mountains, the nine rivers; and he created the nine cauldrons, considered to be the emblem par excellence of political legitimacy.[64]

These two elements, the number nine and the dragon, are simultaneously present in one of the names given to Kun's (and Kung-kung's) son: Kou-lung 句龍. Ku Chieh-kang and Yang Kuan have argued that the *kou* of *kou-lung,* meaning "hooked" or "curved," is in fact another way of writing the word *ch'iu* 虯, which, according to several philologists, is related to the word "nine" both phonetically and epigraphically. The binome *ch'iu-long* 虯龍, "hooked dragon," is certainly an apt description of the tail of the Cerulean Dragon and thus an appropriate appellation for Kun's son, Yü.[65]

Indeed, the graph signifying Yü's name itself points in this direction. The earliest epigraphic evidence for the graph Yü is on a bronze vessel, the *Yü yen* 禹甗 dating from the ninth century B.C.: Yang K'uan correctly analyzes the structure of the graph: it represents the number nine superimposed on the graph usually read as signifying "snake" or "reptile"[66] 虫. According to Ch'iu Hsi-kuei, the nine component represents a later epigraphic development, similar to the evolution of the lower part of the graph for ten thousand (*wan* 萬, written as on oracle bone inscriptions).[67] In his analysis of the oracle bone graph *hai* 害 (to harm), which comprises a foot above a reptile element, Ch'iu argues that the reptile component of the graph , was a phonetic signifier that in later paleographic sources was written as Yü 禹. Thus, we can assume the original graph for Yü was comprised of only the reptile element.

Just what reptile Yü's name was supposed to signify becomes clear once one compares the graph used to represent Yü's name and the most ancient form of the Cerulean Dragon constellation (that is, the Tail, Antares and the two stars next to it, and the four stars constituting House directly above Antares).[68] The uncanny resemblance between the curve of the tail, the arrowhead-like formation of the combined asterisms Heart and House, and the reptile graph (see figure 2.3), together with Ch'iu Hsi-kuei's philological reconstruction of the ancient phonetic significance of the reptile graph, suggest that Yü's name is a pictographic representation of the lower half of the celestial dragon.[69]

5

Many other elements of the Yü flood myths can be explained in light of Yü's true identity. For example, crediting Yü with teaching the Chinese the rudiments of agriculture can be understood as a reference to the time when the rules for farming were connected to the annual rising and setting of Antares. That he was called Hou T'u 后土, "Master of the Earth," and was worshiped as the God of the Soil (*she* 社) after his death surely points to this agricultural connection.[70] Likewise, the phrase "to govern" (*tien* 甸), which is used to describe Yü's activities at least three times in the *Shih ching* and which connotes the sense of governing the agricultural production of the land outside the capital, can be understood as an allusion to Yü's/Antares' calendrical and hence agricultural function.

Details concerning Yü's death and marriage are also clarified when read in an astronomical context. In the course of controlling the flood, Yü is said to have disembodied himself at a place called Yang-yü 陽紆.[71] In several sources Yang-yü is described as the source of "the river." While many philologists believe this refers to the Yellow River, I suggest that Yang-yü is instead more probably associated with the Heavenly River. In the *Shan-hai-ching*, Yang-yü is identified as the site of Dragon Gate, which Yü had to open in order to control the floodwaters.[72] A clue to the exact location of Dragon Gate may be provided in the name Yang-yü itself.

A salient connotation of this proper name concerns the sense of boundary. The term *yang* 陽 is often used in ancient texts to connote a bank of a river or a slope—often the south side—of a mountain. Furthermore, all of the various forms of the graphs *yü* 于 used in ancient texts connote a sense of boundary, usually one imposed by the bend in the course of a path, either of water or mountains. The graph used on oracle bone inscriptions indeed resembles a waterway that at one point diverges from its course.[73] The name Yang-yü thus signifies an area "that bends, diverts from the main course." As we have seen, the area of the Milky Way in between the tail of Scorpius and Corona Australis fits this description perfectly.

Yü's act of disembodiment is not, as Granet argues (following the *Huai-nan-tzu*), a reference to a form of self-sacrifice. Rather, it depicts in imagistic terms the fate of the Cerulean Dragon constellation once winter begins. In ancient China, the heliacal setting of Antares marked the end of autumn, and in turn the approach of winter. The Cerulean Dragon was believed to descend at this time into the abyss, the watery environs of the celestial north, the quadrant of winter. The nature of the descent was such that each night toward the end of autumn a part of the Cerulean Dragon's body would already have "sunk" below the horizon by the time the sky was visible after sunset. This celestial phenomenon is the source of the image of a disembodied Yü.[74]

That the process of disembodiment began toward the end of autumn, after the autumnal equinox, provides a clue to the significance of the name of the location where Yü is said to have died. At least six different sources place Yü's death at a place called K'uai-chi 檜稽, usually identified as K'uai-chi Mountain in Shao-hsing 紹興

prefecture, Chekiang 浙江.[75] Given the aforementioned astronomical significance of Yü's disembodiment, however, one would expect that the location of his death would also contain similar nuances. And indeed it does. According to the "Treatise of Astronomy" ("T'ien-kuan shu" 天官書) in the *Shih chi*, there is a constellation of multiple stars called K'uai-chi that is situated just south of the asterisms Stomach (*wei* 胃) and Bondslave (*lou* 婁). These two asterisms, located in the western quadrant, are associated with autumn and, more specifically, with the harvest. The asterism Stomach, in fact, is very close to the Pleiades (*mao* 昴), which about 2400 B.C. was the seasonal marker for autumn.[76] At this time Antares would have been setting just about one hour after sunset. Yü's death at K'uai-chi thus may very likely refer to the disappearance of Antares.

Yü's death by submersion into the abyss—the celestial space associated with winter—is only temporary, of course, because he reappears right after sunset at the vernal equinox. This segment of time during which Antares did not perform a calendrical function is also reflected in the Yü myths. Interestingly, Yü's (Antares') activities during this time are described in domestic and sexual terms.

In most accounts Yü is said to have married a "lady of the T'u 涂 clan."[77] Many scholars have identified the T'u as a tribe Yü must have met on his journey through western China. We should now be sensitized, however, to the possibility of other interpretations. One derives from the two graphs conventionally used to write the graph *t'u*: both contain the water signific and both connote a sense of creating a boundary—but with a difference. One, 塗, means "to mire, to stop up," to create a boundary by piling something up, and the other, 涂, means "path on the bank of a canal" and thus refers to the natural tendency of water to seek its own level, in contrast to artificial damming. The association of these two meanings of the graph *t'u* with the methods used by Kun and the Great Yü, respectively, to control the chaotic floodwaters, strongly suggests that the location known as T'u may, like Yang-yü, be found in the heavens. Certainly the images concerning a division of water bring to mind the forklike division of the Milky Way in the area between Scorpius and Corona Australis, the very area associated with the winter, at just the time time when Yü is not "performing" his duties. Furthermore, at least one source identifies the lady of T'u as Nü Wa, the one who mended the break in the sky by propping up the three-legged turtle. In other sources the lady of T'u watches Yü as he passes (*t'ung* 通) Hsüan-yüan 軒轅 Mountain and is transformed into a three-legged turtle (some scholars read this as a bear).[78] With Hsüan-yüan a perfect homophone of Heavenly Turtle, this myth probably refers to the disappearance of the Cerulean Dragon constellation and its "passage" through the Heavenly Turtle quadrant, that is, winter, before it rises again in the spring. Thus, the lady of T'u is also associated with the winter quadrant.[79]

Other references to Yü's marriage and domestic life strengthen this contention. He is frequently described, for example, as either marrying his wife or only resting with her on *hsin* 辛, *jen* 壬, *kuei* 癸, and *chia* 甲 days, which refer to the last three and the first terms of the denary calendrical system ("stems" *kan* 干) used in ancient China. The significance of this sequence of days, as Leopold de Saussure brilliantly points out, is that in calendrical terms they represent four periods of time: *hsin* is the time beginning with the autumnal equinox and ending with the first month of winter; *jen* is the time beginning with the first month of winter and ending with the solstice; *kuei* starts with the solstice and ends with the first month of spring; *chia* begins with the first month of spring and ends with the vernal equinox, the time when Antares makes its appearance.[80] That these four segments of time are neatly halved by the winter solstice, a time associated with marriage, conception, and regeneration, points to the true significance of the terms: as the time when Yü is not "working" in the sky, it is a period when he can devote himself to domestic affairs.[81]

There remains one last detail, frequently seen in the Yü myths, that lends itself to the astronomical interpretation advanced here: Yü's "hemiplegic gait," usually attributed to his great efforts to control the flood. Jane Sellers has suggested that myths all over the world feature lame gods, often celestial gods who are shot down by precessional lag.[82] Yü's dragging foot is so clearly of a "lagging" nature that it invites a similar interpretation. As noted above, by about 3000 B.C. Antares was no longer the first bright star seen after sunset on the day of the vernal equinox; that function had been assumed by stars belonging to the asterism called "House." This shift was not yet disastrous, since Antares still followed closely behind; but over the next two thousand years, Antares slowly but surely lagged more and more. It appeared later and later in the evening of the vernal equinox—until the asterism Horn (*chiao* 角), almost 45 degrees away, eventually took over its old function. This, then, is the celestial phenomenon signified by Yü's lameness.

A word should be said about the Taoist tradition of a Dance of Yü (*Yü bu* 禹步) that both derives from and emulates Yü's lame gait.

Descriptions of the dance, at least as they are preserved in Taoist texts, speak of the dance as constituting *nine* steps, even though the dance supposedly traced the configuration of Ursa Major, the Big Dipper, which today has only seven stars visible. Joseph Needham has suggested that precession may have shifted the apparent circumpolar position of two stars belonging to Bootes, which may have been considered to belong to the Big Dipper. Taoist texts have always explained the additional two steps in terms of "lost stars" or "black holes." Given the dance's associations with Yü's lameness, and given its supposed magical function of imbuing the dancer with an ability to "pace the void"—to borrow Edward Schafer's eloquent translation—and hence control astral movements, the dance may reflect the adoption of a different (perhaps at that time more stable) stellar configuration—the Big Dipper—to take the role of the now incapacitated Yü. The passage in the *Tso chuan* shows us that by the sixth century B.C. Antares could not even be used as an indicator for spring anymore; it had precessed to the point of appearing in the summer months. The connection between Yü and the Big Dipper may be a tacit reference to functional similarities of the two stellar configurations.[83]

Another possibility is that the nine steps of the dance correspond to the nine stars of Scorpius' tail. One scholar has linked the motif of Yü's lameness to his error in stepping on a drum instead of a stone, an act that so embarrassed his wife (Lady T'u) that she turned to stone.[84] This event occurred while Lady T'u was watching Yü pass through Hsüan-yüan, a tacit indication that Lady T'u and the Heavenly Turtle quadrant are closely related. That Lady T'u consequently gave birth to a son who presumably took over his father's role as Yü did for Kun (we shall address this in further detail below in chapter 5), further links Yü's lameness to the waning abilities of Antares. The Taoist Pace of Yü may thus be seen as a representation of this drama, the knowledge of which empowered those who control (or understand) the workings of the cosmos.

We also find a similar astronomical referent to the name of a mythic figure who may be seen as a later evolution of Yü. In a well-known passage in the *Tso chuan,* the sequential rising and setting times of Antares and Orion, respectively, are represented mythologically as the result of the inability of two brothers, O Po 閼伯 and Shih Ch'en 實沈, to get along with each other. Their father, Kao Hsin 高辛, ordered the older, O Po, to reside on Shang hillock 商丘 to control the "celestial mark point" (Antares), while Shih Ch'en was ordered to reside at the Great Hsia 大夏 to control Shen 參

(Orion).[85] The text continues that the Shang rulers followed the movements of O Po and thus recognized *ch'en* (Scorpius) as the Shang star (*Shang hsing* 商星). Thus, although Antares could not have been a marker for the vernal equinox by the time of the Shang (1576–1046 B.C.), it nonetheless remained a star of great significance. Indeed, the name O Po bespeaks the nature of the seasonal movements of Antares at that time—movements that had altered over the span of two millennia. The word *o* means "restraint" or "hindrance" and thus recalls the illusion of stars being hindered from rising at their "proper" (traditional, equinoctial) time.[86] The duties of O Po also reflect this nuance: as the "controller" (*chu* 主) of Antares, he presumably had to observe its movement and make appropriate ritual and calendrical adjustments to accommodate its ever-changing times of rising.[87]

Lastly, the apparent connection between the enactment of the Pace of Yü and the magical recipes for the expulsion of or domination of demons, especially those associated with water, also deserves notice.[88] The magical efficacy of the practice may be linked to Yü's control of flood waters, which is an imagistic representation of Scorpius' "successful crossing" of the Milky Way. As we shall see in the following two chapters, the crossing of a body of water was a frequent metaphor for the actualization of a desired transformation. The dance's signficance in the recipes may thus be understood as a means to effect the desired transformative cure.

6

In the foregoing discussion I have proposed that the observable workings of precession lie at the root of the myths of Yü and that the specific myths concerning Yü's control of floodwaters were created to deal with a distressing alteration in the sky, not on land. However, the metaphor of a flood and even that of a dragon derive from life on land. We will thus shift our attention from the skies toward earth, if only briefly, to probe the possible sources of these metaphors.

According to Chang Kuang-chih, the climate and the terrain of the central plains of Neolithic China were vastly different from today's arid conditions. China had been much wetter and warmer in those days, as the melting of ice sheets and glaciers, which began at the onset of the Holocene period, raised the sea level to "at least 6–7 meters above the present level at the height of post-Pleistocene transgression perhaps during 6000–5000 B.C."[89] Several paleoclimatologists have shown that there occurred, as a result, great floods. Indeed, these paleoclimatologists posit that these floods must have been actual referents for the "deluge stories common to many traditions." And John Major suggests that the floods were a source of a flood metaphor that "more probably refers to cosmology (that is, the consequences of the splitting apart of heaven and earth) than to a single event preserved in the collective human memory"—an apt linking of the floods and the flood myths of ancient China.[90]

The humid conditions supported life—elephant, water buffalo, and rhinoceros—that could not have existed in the northern Chinese climate of later times. Of import to us is the apparent proliferation of reptiles known today as *Alligator sinensis* (*yang-tzu o* 揚子鱷)—that require both land (to lay their eggs) and water to survive.[91] The ancient word for alligator in Chinese was *t'o* 鼉 (the modern term *O* was not used in any pre-Ch'in texts). According to Li Shih-chen 李時珍, author of the *Great Materia Medica* (*Pen-ts'ao kang-mu* 本草剛目), the oldest form of the *t'o* graph was a "pictographic representation of the head, body, feet and tail of the animal." The *Shuo-wen* dictionary describes the *t'o* as an "aquatic reptilian (*shui-ch'ung* 水蟲) that resembles the lizard and measures over ten feet in length." Some archaeologists have suggested that the *Alligator sinensis*, along with the turtle, was considered a numinous animal, on the basis of the polished and refined scales of both species found in Neolithic graves of the Ta Wen-k'ou 大文口 culture.[92] Several ancient textual references to characteristics of the *Alligator sinensis* also highlight its symbolic significance: the alligator appears to have been the physical referent for the numinous reptile known as the dragon.

Among the most important of the alligator's characteristics is its thunderous bellow. A. A. Fauvel, one of the earliest scholars to investigate the alligators of China, believed that the "very name *T'o* is an imitation of the explosive noise made by the Alligator." While the quality of the *t'o*'s skin was very thick and well-suited to making drums, the resounding bellow of the alligator itself may have been the true inspiration for the early Chinese use of alligator skin for this instrument. The *Shih ching* makes reference to the sound of a drum made from *t'o* skin and meant to sound like the cry of the alligator, pointing therefore to a similar conclusion. The connection also surfaces in myths where the *t'o* is represented as an official of music.[93]

The resemblance of the alligator's bellow to thunder may have inspired ancient Chinese conceptions of the thunder god: thunder was believed to be the "drum of Heaven and Earth," and in some accounts the god of thunder is described as a dragon. The alligator's thunderous bellow may also explain the connection between rain and the dragon: Ch'iu Hsi-kuei has shown that the fabrication of an Earth Dragon (*t'u-lung* 土龍) often accompanied prayers for rain.[94] It should therefore come as no surprise that the term Earth Dragon was another appellation for the *t'o* alligator. We may even have extant remnants of the so-called Earth Dragon in several bone figures collected by L. C. Hopkins in 1911.[95]

Closely connected to the phenomenon of thunder and rain is the concept of seasons. Just as the drum establishes the temporal beat of a musical piece and was used to demarcate the nightly divisions of time in ancient China, so too did thunder and the rain that followed function as seasonal markers. The ancient almanac, the *Hsia hsiao cheng* 夏小正, states that "in the first month [i.e., the month of the spring equinox] it must thunder." A later almanac, the "Yüeh-ling" 月令, associates the initial roar of thunder and its final resounding effects with the vernal and autumnal equinoxes, respectively.[96] In light of these connections, can it be a coincidence that the "inactive season of the wild alligator extends roughly from mid-November to mid-March"—roughly the same period of time that divides the two equinoxes?[97] Surely the concept that it is the Earth (rather than the Heavens) that emits (*ch'u* 出) and retrieves (*shou* 收) thunder—activities spanned by 180 days—seems to tie the seasonal phenomenon of thunder to the hibernation of the alligator, especially when we remember that the alligator is also called Earth Dragon.[98] The seasons that are correlated with the time one hears or ceases to hear thunder are exactly those that accord with the appearance and disappearance of Scorpius. The watery milieu of the flood myths is appropriate to the culture because the Chinese assigned to the emergence of the alligator (after hibernation) and the Dragon constellation the beginning of the rainy season. Observations of the alligator's living habits may thus have informed the selection of the metaphor of the Cerulean Dragon for Scorpius.[99]

Linguistic evidence suggests that the *t'o* and the *ch'iu-lung* (the Cerulean Dragon) shared the same referent. From an etymological standpoint the *t'o* graph is problematic because the component usually identified as the phonetic, itself a unique graph meaning "alone" (*tan* 單), appears to be very dissimilar in pronounciation. Thus Axel Schuessler reconstructs the archaic pronunciation of this latter word as *tar, and suggests *dal for *t'o*. Yet his reconstruction of the word for "to hunt" (*shou* 狩), which clearly, in its most ancient form, , also consists of the same phonetic, is given as *?-jew? He provides a similar reconstruction for the phonetic final of the word "autumn" (*ch'iu* 秋): *tshjew, a graph that in oracle bones depicts a turtle-like reptile.[100] The phonetic similarity of "autumn" and "to hunt," combined with the fact that the *t'o* alligator was recognized as a close relative of the *yüan* 黿 turtle,[101] an identity that may have informed the special connection between the turtle and the dragon in early Chinese cosmological (and astronomical) thought, leads me to believe that the words *t'o* and *ch'iu* not only were pronounced similarly but also may have in fact both shared the alligator as their referent.

While most scholars accept T'ang Lan's identification of the oracle bone turtlelike graph as the word for "autumn," no one, to my knowledge, has explained why such an animal would be used to represent this season. The significance of this association, I believe, is astronomical. The *ch'iu-lung*, that is, the Cerulean Dragon, while having lost its function as marker of the vernal equinox, nonetheless still marked the arrival of the autumnal equinox in 1500 B.C. In fact, the position of the autumnal equinoctial sun was right in the Cerulean Dragon constellation. The word "autumn" very possibly signifies the time of the conjunction of the sun and the constellation. The apparent early usage of the term *ch'iu* to refer not to the season but to the asterism itself lends force to this interpretation.[102] Certainly the fire element that often adorns the turtlelike graph calls to mind the appellation Fire Star which was given to Antares, the major star of the *ch'iu-lung* constellation.[103]

7

The alligator as the source of the metaphor of the dragon bears on a cosmogonic interpretation of the Yü flood myths. This amphibious animal represents the mediating qualities of one who negotiates both land and water. It offers a model for cosmogonic conceptualization: the cosmos of the Yü flood myths originates in the balance of aquatic and tellurian forces: the telluric stage represents the stability that marks the creation of the cosmos, but such a cosmos would not be possible without the aqueous stage. If Yü's actions can be viewed as a metaphor for the ontolog of a new world (the identification of Antares as a viable fixed point established for the Neolithic Chinese a reliable new astronomical/seasonal orientation),[104] this new world could not have come into being without the confusion wrought by the Milky Way's displacement of the former world.

This investigation has assembled the data pertaining to the flood myths in order to examine the cosmogonic "intentions" underlying the myths of the Great Yü. The Yü myths reveal how the specific celestial territory between Scorpius and Corona Australis—where the activities of Yü "occurred"—marked for the ancient Chinese the point of transition between the primal forces of life and death. The cosmogonic significance ascribed to this celestial territory derives from its association with the effects of the gradual shift of the position of the equinoxes. The Chinese, I believe, associated this shift with a change in the "world order," with the "death" of one age—Kun's/water—and the "birth" of another—Yü's. It essentially galvanized the Neolithic world: this was the time when cosmogony was born. It is within this context that we can appreciate the great rhetorical power of the metaphor of Yü as a sage king: it tames the fear caused by the movements of precession by invoking a cosmos that operated in an orderly, systematic, and predictable fashion. The world, in other words, was not a place where chaos reigned. Rather, Yü emblematized the ideal of the sage ruler, the embodiment of the earliest human capacity to observe, measure, and predict celestial changes resulting from the precession of the equinoxes.[105]

The stars were the true sages of the early Chinese. Their patterns taught the people to measure, to count, and to cultivate. The stars gave the early Chinese their tools of thought and stimulated imagistic expression; they prescribed behavior and legitimized their rulers. They allowed the people to establish order and maintain it in their world. The preservation of astronomical knowledge pertaining to the stars over many millennia attests to the inherent cultural significance of this information. Its transmission through an oral mythic tradition became a symbolic mode of recounting and overcoming challenges to world order. This metaphorical form, in the end, permits us to perceive a cosmogonic hermeneutic of the Yü flood myths. It remains to be seen how this hermeneutic functions in the *Mu T'ien-tzu chuan.*

THREE

Toward an Aesthetic of Symbol in Early Chinese Thought

The complexity of the cosmogonic hermeneutic of the Yü myths suggests that their appearance in the *Mu T'ien-tzu chuan* signifies more than mere textual borrowing. The references to the Yü and other myths in the *Mu T'ien-tzu chuan*, can be read as a reference to the symbolic significance of the celestial territory—lying between Scorpius and Sagittarius—which marked for the ancient Chinese the point of transition between the forces of life and death. The concepts of "symbol," and the literary process by which symbols signify, "symbolic operation," are critical to an appreciation of the potential for a literary interpretation of the *Mu T'ien-tzu chuan.* This brief chapter thus presents my understanding of these terms and thereby establishes the interpretive framework for my analysis of the *Mu T'ien-tzu chuan.*

1

My usage of the term symbol and its variants (symbolic, symbolism) is informed by the brilliant work of Nicolas Abraham.[1] Initially developed as a heuristic tool to facilitate the discussion and clinical practice of psychoanalysis, his theories of the symbol and symbolic operation have remarkable resonance not only with the dominant mode of literary signification within the *Mu T'ien-tzu chuan* but also with the concept of symbol in traditional Chinese aesthetics and philosophy.

The premise informing Abraham's work is that the interpretation of a symbol is never a simplistic act of substitution:

> We are used to treating symbols like archaeologists who attempt to decipher the written documents of an unknown language. What is given is "something" with a meaning. Many of us live with the convenient misconception that in order to decipher [the document] it is sufficient to add meaning to the "thing" or the hieroglyphs. . . . Yet in so doing [we] merely convert one system of symbols into another and this latter system still stops short of laying open its secret. Actually, the reading of a symbolic text cannot be content with registering one-to-one equivalence between two terms. The work of deciphering will be completed only if we restore the entire circuit of functions involving a multiplicity of subjects and in which the symbol-thing is simply a relay.
>
> Here a first distinction must be made between, on the one hand, the symbol-thing considered as a hieroglyph or symbolic text—the *lifeless symbol*—and, on the other hand, the symbol included in a process, the *symbol in operation,* endowed with meaning and implying concrete subjects, together considered a functioning unit. *To interpret a symbol consists in converting the symbol-thing into an operating symbol.* A *thing* must never be taken as the symbol of another thing.[2]

Citing the ancient Greek usage of the term *symbolon* as referring to a piece of pottery that was broken in two prior to someone's voyage, so the two pieces could be rejoined upon the traveler's return (and thus used as a sign of identification), Esther Rashkin explains that "Abraham's theory of the symbol can be extrapolated from these two meanings (i.e., the two pieces individually as well as to the act of putting the two pieces together)."[3] She further elaborates: "When we read a text we read its symbols. We read fragments of semantic or phonetic elements that, if joined to their missing parts, would signify something (a drama, scene, or simply a lexical or phonetic element) that must for some reason be kept hidden or out of circulation."[4] As Abraham himself states in another text, "Symbols are data that are missing an as yet undetermined part, but that can, in principle, be determined."[5]

The reason why symbols are by essence fragmentary is related to the psychoanalytic circumstances that lead to their production: symbols are produced in the wake of devastating emotional consequences of a trauma, which, because of their painful associations, must be entombed or "consigned to internal silence."[6] The process of "entombment" is activated when the consequences of a trauma cannot be assimilated (Abraham's "introjected") into the psyche of a subject. Symbols evolve as traces of the trauma that is kept out of conscious psychic circulation. As Nicholas Rand states succinctly, Abraham's "treatise on symbol is also a theory of disasters."[7]

Interpreting symbols, one reconnects them with their absent complements. The very nature of the symbol itself determines the mode of the rejoining, or "symbolization": just as "the shape and pattern of the jagged edge of the piece of pottery reveal the direction or "sense' in which it must be held to fit its complement,"[8] so, too, is a textual symbolic fragment composed of elements that allow us to reconstruct what its complement might look like. At the basis of the theory of the symbol, then, is also a "theory of readability" which "demonstrate[s] the feasibility of interpretation in the face of seemingly insurmountable obstructions" and "shows how signification can be reinstated after its collapse." Reading symbols consists in rescuing "choked or subverted signification."[9]

To recapitulate, symbols are symbols by virtue of the absence of a posited counterpart, and they are readable as symbols only in that the absent counterpart can be reconstructed. Thus do symbols simultaneously conceal and reveal their source of meaning, a dual function that derives from processes involving their creation. Abraham posits that the essence of "being" "is only possible in a symbolic mode." "[R]eturn[ing] to the basics of physics and to the dyadic structure of the atom to describe the origin of being . . . as a symbolic operation involving the constant oscillation between a negative and a positive pole,"[10] Abraham argues that

> in formal terms one can say: A is A only if one can somehow say that A *implies* B in the form of *not*, that is, if A symbolizes *with* B. . . . It is clear that the single symbol alone is not sufficient for being. . . . [T]o say that A corresponds to B signifies that it is not closed in upon itself but is in some sense *in communication with* B. *For A to be A and not B it must itself accomplish this act of discrimination.* Such is its symbolizing operation.[11]

As Rashkin explains: "The origin of being is a communication or co-symbolizing between two entities constituted by mutual negation, that is, by repeatedly articulating their difference from one another. A symbolizes with B in its absence."[12]

The conception that being or the apprehension of experience is realized in terms of the relative presence or absence of opposites is not unfamiliar to Chinese thought. Indeed, there is a striking resemblance between Abraham's theories and a Chinese archetypal pattern of conceptualization dubbed by one scholar as "complementary bipolarity."[13] Most important for the present discussion is the pattern of "mutual implication . . . whereby qualities of experience are often perceived to be most essentially present at the time of their nominal absence."[14] There is nevertheless an intrinsic difference between the two theories, a difference that lies in their orientations: whereas the concept of "mutual implication" is epistemologically oriented—in that absence and presence are always conceived in terms of an already assumed quality of being—the concept of the symbol is ontologically oriented, in that absence and presence are conceived in terms of being and nonbeing. Symbols function as signifiers of an ontological conflict between being and nonbeing, their generation then resolves this conflict.

Abraham "postulates that if the origin of being is grounded in the otherness or difference of a perpetual symbolic operation, at the origin of the symbolic operation itself is 'the impossibility of being or . . . active nonbeing tending toward being.' The symbolic operation is thus understood by Abraham as a response to the blockage of being; as the means by which nonbeing is transcended, that is, an obstacle surmounted."[15]

The process of transcendence implied in the symbolic operation has far-reaching ramifications for the interpretation of the literary function of the symbol, especially the positing of an "absent text" that must be reconstructed if the symbolic elements of a text are to be understood. More than just an "element of [a] text with external reference"[16] or just a means of "calling attention to its otherness of reference,"[17] symbols are "traces that give voice to their *founding* silence."[18] That silence must be made audible if the symbolic meaning of a text is to be revealed.

The notion that silence, generated by an act of concealment, can generate a specific form of discourse is also not foreign to Chinese tradition. Consider the traditional interpretation of the form of discourse employed in one of the five Chinese classics, the *Spring and Autumn Annals.* The Kung-yang tradition states unequivocally that "the Spring and Autumn Annals [are written to] hide [the flaws of] the exalted; to hide [the flaws of] kinsmen; to hide [the flaws of] the virtuous"[19] (春秋為尊者諱, 為親者諱, 為賢者諱). Whether this discursive form represents a means of overcoming an obstacle to being cannot be verified; that Confucius associated it with the maintenance of order, however, suggests that it served a mediating function in a time of chaos.[20] The significance of the concealing mode of discursive representation eventually evolved into what can be called a virtual "aesthetics of concealment."[21] While it is surely linked to the historical tradition of silencing, this latter manifestation is described more in terms of the profundity of aesthetic inspiration than in terms of psychoanalytic trauma, though the two are by no means mutually exclusive. Indeed, the earliest and most extensive treatment of the "aesthetics of concealment," found in Liu Hsieh's 劉勰 (465–522) *Wen-hsin tiao-lung* 文新雕龍, often cites the *Book of Changes* to illustrate its points. We shall see that the production of the *Book of Changes* is inextricably bound up with an obstacle to being.

Abraham's theory enables us to recast the mythic formulation of the flood and Yü's control of it. We can interpret it as a symbolic response to the obstacle to being caused by the astronomical reality of precession, which rendered obsolete the seasonal function of a constellation and hence hindered the ability of the ancients to read and control time. Since the prestige and influence of the observers of the sky—most likely shamans and diviners[22]—derived from their control of the inextricable connection between establishment of a calendar (and the astronomical work on which it was based) and political power and social status, the realization that their knowledge was becoming obsolete, and that this would have been apparent to everyone, must have presented a frightening threat to their sense of security. Furthermore, the fact that they did not comprehend the true reason as to why the framework of time and space had gone awry, must have made the enigma all the more traumatic. Certainly, the inability to provide a reason for the astronomical displacement could have jeopardized their position. The symbolic Yü myths at once reveal and conceal the true object of discourse: astronomy. They constituted a linguistic, symbolic response to the obstacle to being on the part of the early knowers of astronomy, who confronted the need to provide an explanation for something they did not truly understand. Even as these astronomical sources of signification lie beyond perception, they can nonetheless be reconstructed from traces within the mythic texts.[23]

The myths as symbol function as linguistic resolutions to an obstacle to being by facilitating and signifying the means to transcend it. The Yü myths are symbols on two levels of discourse—the encrypted astronomical and the anthropomorphized. The astronomical discourse is the information that must be explained if those who possess it are "to be," while the anthropomorphized discourse is the symbolic form that the explanation took. The anthropomorphized discourse is symbolic because in concealing and revealing traces of the astronomical discourse, it symbolizes the conflict generating its own production. The latter, in other words, is the means by which its creators transcended their own obstacle to being. We will examine below the profound aesthetic developments in Chinese literature that I believe were informed by this specific mode of expression. We might note here, however, that as a discursive mode that reflects on its own production, the Yü myths are an ideal mode for speculation about cosmogony, or origins.

My symbolic analysis of the Yü myths "deciphers" the "traces left by the silencing or displacement" of the astronomical discourse, and "retraces the steps and operations constituting that displacement."[24] Symbolic reading does more than merely attach an "outside" meaning to signifying elements: it carries the symbol "back to the place of its co-symbol,"[25] which in the case of the Yü myths is situated in the astronomical reality of Neolithic China. This mode of reading allows one to uncover the astronomical and hence cosmogonic intentions underlying the generation of the myth.

One may perhaps object to my willingness to use Western theories—Abraham's in particular—that embody "cultural presuppositions" which have not been shown to accord with similar attitudes toward the significance of symbols in classical China. In fact, however, it is my contention that a comparable understanding of symbol is rooted in a similar set of assumptions in ancient China. Specifically, the dynamic function of a symbol as signifier of its own process of generation is implicit in the most ancient connotations of the Chinese term that best accords with this concept, *hsiang* 象.

In assigning the translation "symbol" to the term *hsiang*, I do not mean to devalue other English terms that have been used, such as "image" and "figure."[26] Rather, I mean to offer a different conceptual possibility for the underlying meaning of the word; this new perspective is derived from the usage of *hsiang* in two early Chinese texts, the *Tao teh ching* 道德經 and the *Appended Words Commentary to the Book of Changes* (*Hsi-tz'u chuan* 繫辭傳).

I should distinguish my approach from that of Toshihiko Izutsu, who also examines the philosophical essence of *hsiang*—

which he terms "image"—in these same two works and employs what could be called a psychoanalytic perspective.[27] Izutsu's examination of the problem "relating to the fundamental structure of image-making or image-producing mechanism of human consciousness" appears on the surface to be congruent with Abraham's theories. Izutsu, too, is interested in the "problem of how images emerge out of their ultimate source, which is the No-Image," and he presents a psychoanalytically informed "model of consciousness" consisting of two strata to elaborate his theory.[28] Izutsu identifies the symbolic images of Taoism and the *Book of Changes* as those that "unlike the sensory images . . . emerg[e] from the darkness of the B-stratum of consciousness, [and] do not go up straight to the A-stratum, but remain as a rule lingering between the two strata," a place he calls the "M-region" or "*mundus imaginalis*."[29] Therein lies the distinction between Abraham's theory of symbolic operation and Izutsu's theory of image production: Abraham's symbols do not preexist the trauma or crisis that generates their production, whereas Izutsu's images are latent potentials that are expressed "when the B-stratum of consciousness becomes activated in a peculiar manner, as when, for instance, one is in a state of shamanic ecstasy, contemplative concentration, or magico-religious excitation."[30] Thus, both theories view the expression of images and symbols as deriving from a form of stimulation. But Abraham posits a specific function for this expression—transcendence of an obstacle to being—whereas Izutsu sees it merely as a more nuanced and more profound means of reflecting reality, the images or symbols of Taoism and the *Book of Changes* being reflective of "different attitudes taken toward the problem of how images emerge out of their ultimate source (No-Image)."[31]

I follow Abraham and view the concept of symbol in these two philosophical systems as reflective of the same attitude. My analysis suggests that this shared attitude derives from the fact that both Taoism and the *Book of Changes* have as the source of their symbolic stature the same obstacle to being.

2

I argue that the Yü myths constitute the linguistic manifestation of a transcendence of a hidden obstacle to being effected by the precession of the equinoxes and that cosmogonic intentions underlie the symbolic operation governing the creation of the myths. It is therefore noteworthy that one of the earliest texts in which the term *hsiang* was used, the *Tao teh ching,* is also concerned with cosmogony; that is, that there is a connection between the Yü myths and early Taoist philosophy, and it is not coincidental.

I believe that there is ample evidence to argue that the tenets of early Taoist thought have as their antecedents the same specific celestial phenomena as the myths. Their difference lies in the presentation: whereas the myths merely describe them, Taoist thought represents the implications of precessional effect in coherent philosophical terms.[32] I would go so far as to suggest that the effects of precession may account for the "consistent inner logic, a 'central idea,' or a mythically grounded pattern of religious convictions and procedures" that Norman Girardot has so brilliantly illuminated in his work.[33] While the scope of the present study precludes delving into this cultural nexus for the evidence needed to validate my hypothesis fully, a brief discussion of certain structural features of early Taoist philosophy that are related to the use of the term *hsiang* in the text should establish the validity of its underlying premise and, one hopes, invite more detailed examination on the part of future scholars.[34]

Chapters 41 and 42 of the *Tao teh ching,* also known as the *Lao tzu* 老子, have long been recognized as containing the core of the text's cosmogony. In these chapters the cosmogonic process leading to the birth of phenomena is described:

> The Tao gave birth to the one.
> The one gave birth to the two.
> The two gave birth to the three,
> And the three gave birth to the Ten Thousand Things.[35]
> (道生一，一生二，二生三，三生萬物)

According to Norman Girardot, this delineation of the transformation from three to the ten Thousand Things represents "a moment of rupture with, or fall from, the creation time."[36] While Girardot holds that the "causality of why and how there was a fall from paradise is never made completely clear,"[37] I contend that there is a symbolic "trace" that points to the source of the causality, and Girardot himself calls attention to it: it is the important principle of "Tao's *creatio continua* . . . the cyclic interplay between creation and destruction."[38]

Precession, I believe, accounts for the idea of a "cyclic interplay between creation and destruction," because its movements "consist of regularly recurring replacement coinciding with a universe out of order."[39] When precessional movement caused the vernal equinox to recede from the vicinity of a familiar constellation, the universe could be said to be in a state of chaos, the equinox lacked any home; the pole was displaced from its center.[40] The sighting of or settling on a new determinative constellation to replace the old, nonfunctional one could, however, be perceived as a reconstitution of lost order. Therein lies the source of the cyclic interaction between creation and destruction. Precessional movement accounts for the overweening sense of upheaval, ruin, and a lost world order that we find on the plane of myth and Taoist thought—it is a sense too drastic to have derived from an occasional disturbance of the regular succession of the seasons.[41] As a continuous, nondiurnal, nonseasonal motion that alters the position of the stars, precession accounts for the "paradoxical idea of an ordered chaos" implied by the condition of the "period of the three," which, as described by Girardot, is a "chaos condition with its own internal principles of organization."[42]

Taoism constitutes a philosophical response to the obstacle to being posed by precessionally caused astronomical events.[43] It is the formalization of the observation that "landmarks" of cosmic recurrence, such as stellar equinox markers, ceased to function after a time and that new ones needed to be chosen, an act that was likened to a return to chaos and the subsequent ushering in of a new age. The agent of this transformation, according to the *Tao teh ching*, is the Tao, which is responsible for the motion of the cosmic structure; indeed, it is more powerful than the cosmos itself. Given that the precession was observed through its effect on the equinoxes, the Tao's power would be most evident in its ability to change the positions of the constellations. Therein lies the symbolism of turbid water in Taoist thought: the imagery refers to the Milky Way whose displacement/replacement of the Heavenly Turtle constellation best captures the power of the Tao—its power of precession. Taoism envisions the watery environs as representing an earlier state of the cosmos, transformed by the Tao into the current world age—the age symbolized by Yü, when Antares served as the standard. Although the shared symbolic significance of the Taoist water motif and the flood myths lends further support to the possibility that both are a response to the same cultural phenomena, each response is nevertheless unique.

The displacement of Corona Australis by the Milky Way was the crisis that generated the Yü flood myths; the establishment of a new (calendrical) order by using Antares as a seasonal indicator—

Yü's hydraulic feats—was the means by which the crisis was symbolically transcended. In Taoism, however, the establishment of order was viewed negatively, for it effected the establishment of phenomenal boundaries (the Ten Thousand things), which in turn established a means for phenomenological differentiation, an act that ultimately effaced the power of the Tao (which was signified by the chaotic unintelligibility of the Milky Way).[44] The establishment of "order," then, is the crisis to which the symbolic system of Taoist philosophy responds. It seeks to transcend the crisis through what Girardot has identified as its "religious" function: a salvation, a "deliverance possessing cosmic implications." Taoism, in other words, constitutes a symbolic response to the "obstacle to being" posed by the disintegration of the "original wholeness"; it "provides a means of periodically recovering in this lifetime a condition of original wholeness, health or holiness."[45] Whereas Girardot looks at this aspect of Taoism from the "receiving end," that is, from the stance of the salvational aspect of an already established system of symbols, I am interested in looking at Taoism from the other side, from the perspective of revealing the source of its symbolic mode of representation.

This rather long digression into the possible astronomical origins of the tenets underlying Taoism demonstrates how the specific conceptual model for symbol that I have employed is implied in the use of the term *hsiang* in the *Tao teh ching*. The term *hsiang* appears four times in the text:

> Chapter 14: "the *hsiang* that derive from non-*hsiang*,[46] this is called undifferentiated chaos" (無象之象，是謂忽恍).
>
> Chapter 21: "As for the Tao's making of phenomenon, it [arises from] chaos, it [arises from] undifferentiation; within chaos and undifferentiation there is *hsiang*" (道之為物，唯恍唯忽，忽恍中有象).
>
> Chapter 35: "Upholding/maintaining the great *hsiang*, all under heaven has direction [i.e., a direction toward which existence can evolve]" (執大象，天下往).
>
> Chapter 41: "The great *hsiang* has no shape. Tao is hidden and nameless"[47] (大象無形，道隱無名).

The condition of *hsiang* as represented in these passages resembles that of symbolic operation: it is the undifferentiated, whole state of being that is obstructed and obscured with the production of phenomena attendant upon the establishment of order; and it also signifies the means to transcend this state of obstructed undifferentiation—the means to "become" (whole) again through symbolization (*hsiang*). *Hsiang* are *hsiang* only by virtue of the absence of a posited counterpart (non-*hsiang*), which is identified in chapter 14 as chaos. *Hsiang* symbolizes with chaos in its absence, and as such it demarcates the crisis that led to its very production. The production of *hsiang* presupposes this absence, since, according to chapter 21, it is the phenomenological state (absence) of chaos or being (*tao chih wei wu*) that stimulates the generation of *hsiang*. In other words, as is intimated in chapters 21 and 35, in demarcating the obstacle to being, *hsiang* embodies the possibility for representation, which in ontological terms suggests phenomenological existence. The fact that *hsiang* signify the state of affairs leading to their own elision is paradoxically reflected in the text's insistence on the amorphous nature of *hsiang*, coupled with the repeated characterization of the Tao as "hidden." Both ultimately suggest that existence can only be perceived symbolically; that is, being is perceived as a response to its own disjunction.[48] *Hsiang*, like Tao, is thus perhaps best understood as referring to a process similar to that of symbolic operation, a process whereby that which is hidden and nameless is manifested in the phenomenological world.[49] *Hsiang* thus provides the means to unveil its own hidden mysteries.

This interpretation suggests a response to those skeptical of a philosophical tradition that at first claims "the Tao that can be spoken is not the eternal Tao," only then to provide a text of considerable length dedicated to what appears to be "speaking the Tao."[50] The implicit paradox is mitigated when we interpret the *Tao teh ching* not as a text that "speaks the Tao" but as one that *symbolizes with* the Tao. This manner of articulation is congruent, I believe, with the intuitive awareness of what constituted the Tao: its force (precession) operated symbolically, for how is precessional movement perceived but as the principle of demarcating displacement so essential to the operation and function of a symbol? The *Tao teh ching* represents displacement as the inaccessibility of the Tao to human language.

Given the shared object of discourse of flood myths and Taoism, the emphasis on the unspeakable aspects of the Tao may be construed as a tacit reference to the desire to keep the knowledge central to the philosophy hidden, as much as it may be an admission of the ineffable nature of the Tao itself. Viewed in this light, Girardot's suggestion that a process of indoctrination may be implied in the *Tao teh ching*, one that concluded with a "return to turbid waters" (knowledge of the significance of the Milky Way) deserves close attention.[51]

In light of the foregoing discussion, the close epigraphic and etymonic connection between the word *hsiang* and that of *wei* 為, "to do," "to act as," "to become," of which the character *hsiang*, originally a pictograph of an elephant, forms the major component,[53] can be considered supplementary evidence supporting my interpretation of the meaning of the term *hsiang* in early Chinese texts. Peter Boodberg argues that the two words are linked through the etymon *TSNG, which is retained even in the modern pronunciation of the word *ts'o* 作 "to make," and often forms a binomial compound with the term *wei*.[53] Takada Chūshu 高田忠周 has also provided evidence of similar contextual usages of the terms *hsiang* and *wei* in early texts.[54] The linguistic connection between the two words reveals in the concept of *hsiang* a connotation similar to the dynamic notion of symbol as process. Indeed, the close relationship between the concept of "inaction" (*wu-wei* 無為) and chaos, itself defined in the *Tao teh ching* in terms of *hsiang*, suggests some overlap of the meanings of the terms. In one edition the graph for *hsiang* was written in a form that greatly resembles that of *wei*.[55] The linguistic connection signifies that the process of symbolization, and its attendant connotations of transcendence, is intimately connected to one of becoming.

3

Connotations of transcendence and becoming also determine the contextual use of the term *hsiang* in the *Appended Words Commentary*, a text that was probably composed in the third century B.C.[56] As is well known, the *hsiang* referred to in the *Appended Words Commentary* consists of the sixty-four hexagrams. These are formally the sixty-four mathematically possible combinations of two primary graphs, a broken line and an unbroken line, and they represent the concepts of yin and yang respectively.[57]

The first mention of the term *hsiang* occurs in the fifth sentence of the text: "[Just as] in the heavens [flux and transformation] bring *hsiang* to completion and on the earth [flux and transformation] bring forms to completion, flux and transformation are made manifest [in the *hsiang* of the hexagrams]"[58] (在天成象，在地成形，變化見矣). Part of a sequence of sentences in which "the first part of each . . . has been taken to refer to phenomena in the realm of heaven-and-earth, and the second parts are understood as referring to the hexagrams and lines in the *Change*,"[59] this sentence reveals *hsiang* as an element that, through its mutual function in heaven and the text, is emblematic of the nature of the relationship between the two. Indeed, in an incisive analysis of the "claims" and underlying themes of the *Appended Words Commentary*, Willard Peterson argues that "the technique [for divination], for which the text of the *Change* is the written repository, duplicates relationships and processes at work in the realm of heaven-and-earth."[60] While Peterson never explicitly draws attention to the role of the term *hsiang* in manifesting this association, his reasons for translating *hsiang* as "figure" (which I modified in the translation above) intimate an awareness of this function. His arguments revolve around the semantic multivalence of the word "figure," which "is an image or likeness, but it is also a form or shape, a design or configuration or pattern, and a written symbol; 'to figure' is to represent as a symbol or image, but also to give or bring into shape."[61] The dynamic connotations of Peterson's definition for the term "figure" are also captured by my use of the term "symbol" although the former does not encompass all of the particular nuances attendant upon my understanding of the latter term. For this reason, I prefer to translate *hsiang* as "symbol." Moreover, in the last chapter of this study I will use the term "figure" to designate specific literary operations involving symbols, rhetorical figures.

Peterson's observation that the divination technique both manifests and mirrors the processes embodied in the cosmic principle of change is premised on his interpretation of a passage in the first portion of the text (*Chou-i cheng-i*, vol. 1, 79) in which the word *p'ei* 配, translated by him as "matches," signifies the complementary nature of the work conducted both in the realm of heaven-and-earth and in the text of the *Book of Changes* itself.[62] By "matching" Peterson means "to duplicate," a process that he claims vitiates the "epistemological problem" of determining just "how . . . a divination text connect[s]' with the cosmos."[63] I share Peterson's concern not to portray the relationship between the *Book of Changes* and the cosmos as one of mere imitation, or substitution, but I do not agree that the term "duplicated" achieves his objective. I would suggest that the *Book of Changes* and the cosmos can be viewed as co-symbols; the text symbolizes with the cosmos (in the latter's absence). *Hsiang* both signify and facilitate this process. The aptness of this conceptual framework for viewing the relationship between the text and the cosmos reflected in the *Appended Words Commen-*

tary becomes even more apparent once the ontological implications of the symbolization process are recognized as having everything to do with the nature of the relationship.

Recalling that in Abraham's theory the symbol is manifested through the process of transcending an obstacle to being, it is striking that the composition of the *Book of Changes* is posited in terms of a response to times of trouble: "Did not the makers of the *Change* have anxiety and tribulation" (作易者，其有憂患乎)?[64] As an amalgamation of the results of many separate divinations over a long period of time, which served as a manual of ready reference of the consequences of relevant past divinatory determinations,[65] the *Book of Changes* was a "filing system for a natural novelty." To continue Joseph Needham's eloquent description, it met that need which

> was one of the greatest stimulating factors of primitive science, namely the need for at least classing phenomena, and placing them in some sort of relation with one another, in order to conquer the ever-recurring fear and dread which must have weighed so terribly on early men. Any hypothesis would be better than none, but hypotheses which would take some of the terror out of disease and calamity there must at all costs be.[66]

The prognostications derived from the hexagrams and the technique for divination that led to the prognostications thus function as means for transcending obstacles to being.

While the context of divination makes clear the symbolic function of the *Book of Changes* in practice, yet to be elucidated is why the *hsiang* were viewed as the concrete manifestation of the text's prognosticating abilities. Put otherwise, what obstacle to being gave rise to the symbolism of the hexagrams themselves? If we remember that symbols co-symbolize by "filling in" information that is absent yet implicit, one would expect the hexagrams to be readable as symbolic traces of a hidden, unspoken reality about the workings of the principle of change within the cosmos. Since it was the *Appended Words Commentary* that posited the co-symbolic nature of the relationship between the cosmos and the text, it should come as no surprise that the same text provides clues about how to interpret these traces.

A key statement in the *Appended Words Commentary* holds that "sages established symbols [rather than relying on words] in order to exhaust their meaning" (聖人立象以盡意).[67] Frequently noted by critics, the metalinguistic implications of the statement are nonetheless rarely probed; rather, the statement is understood in purely negative terms, as an example of the Chinese awareness of the inadequacy of language. I believe, however, that this statement tacitly affirms the symbol's function as a sign of hidden realities, realities that somehow were obstacles to being. Another statement found earlier in the text seems to confirm this:

> Sages, having the means to manifest the mysteries in all-under-heaven and imitate them in their form and characteristics, symbolized particular phenomena [of the manifest mysteries] as [an] appropriate [means for revealing the aspect of the mysteries relevant to the proper management of human affairs]. For this reason, they are called symbols.[68]
> 聖人有以見天下之　而擬諸其形容，象其物宜，是故謂之象

Here symbols are portrayed not only as related to the hidden mysteries of the cosmos but also as signifiers of them. Peterson's description of the function of the text can in fact be applied to that of the symbols: "The *Change* is the medium . . . in the sense of being the means of passing from the realm of what is intelligible to us to the realm of what is not directly or only imperfectly knowable . . . the technique and the text of the *Change* include, and mediate between, the unknown and the known."[69] Peterson's "mediation" resembles Abraham's symbolic operation; both imply an ability to know and make knowable that which is hidden.

But what is it that is unknowable and how does it relate to the specific symbols comprising the *Book of Changes*? In the *Appended Words Commentary* the unknowable is identified as the principle underlying cosmic change, which "is without conscious thought and is without purposive action."[70] The phrase "without purposive action" (*wu-wei*) recalls the description of the ineffable Tao in the *Tao teh ching* and alerts us to the possibility that the unknown referred to in the context of the *Book of Changes* and the *Tao teh ching* both have their locus within a similar vision of an obstacle to being, the transcendence of which generated the *hsiang* of the text. Indeed, the pointed use of the term *hsiang* to refer to astral entities displayed by heaven, as well as the process of their symbolization (that is, "the sages symbolized them [the astral entitites] in the *Book of Changes*") suggests that the process of symbolization itself is closely connected to heavenly bodies. *Hsiang* is the only word used in the *Appended Words Commentary* to refer both to an object with prognosticating capabilities and to the means by which these capabilities are made knowable.

The text intimates that the symbols, the mediator between unknown and known, derive their potency from their connection to Heaven, or more specifically, from astronomical phenomena. Consider, for example, the implications of the following passage interpreted by Peterson as a description of the types of symbols (Peterson's "figures") included within the *Book of Changes*:[71]

> In consequence of this [that is, that there is nothing more efficacious for the penetration of the mysteries of the cosmos and establishment of ill and good fortune than divining by yarrow and turtle] Heaven engenders numinous phenomena, the sages modeled [the *Book of Changes*] on them.
> 是故天生神物，聖人則之
>
> Heaven and earth have flux and transformation and the sages imitated them [in the *Book of Changes*].
> 天地變化，聖人效之
>
> Heaven dangles symbols [in the form of astral bodies] making manifest ill and good fortune. The sages symbolized this [in the *Book of Changes*].
> 天垂象見吉凶，聖人象之
>
> The [Yellow] River gave forth the Chart and the Lo [River] gave forth the Writing. The sages modeled [the *Book of Changes*] on them.
> 河出圖，洛出書，聖人則之
>
> The *Book of Changes* having these four symbols, is the means by which it shows.
> 易有四象，所以示也

Peterson's contention that each section of this passage refers to the "prognosticating capabilities of the figures [*hsiang*] in numinous things (that is, the carapace, the scapula, and the milfoils), omens, astrological signs and numerological devices"[72] respectively—ingenious though it is—is not without its problems. It necessitates, that is, three different readings of the term *t'ien* 天, a practice that is not found anywhere else in the text. Peterson's insights can be reconciled with a more consistent reading of the term "Heaven," however, by viewing each section as consisting of descriptions of symbolic responses to a common obstacle to being, namely some heavenly phenomenon.

The focus on the movements of the Cerulean Dragon constellation in the line statements of the first hexagram, *ch'ien* 乾, a pure Yang construction with its six unbroken lines, offers a context for interpreting the meaning of the astral symbols referred to in the passage above. To follow my analysis of the Yü myths, moreover, especially with regard to their underlying cosmogonic intent, the first hexagram's hexagram lines, with their references to dragons, may have as their hidden referent the role played by the Cerulean Dragon in transcending the obstacle to being caused by the displacement of the Heavenly Turtle asterism.[73] Moreover, the watery associations of the name of the second hexagram, *k'un* 坤, a pure Yin configuration composed of six unbroken lines (and written as "river" *ch'uan* 川 in the Ma-wang-tui manuscript of the *Book of Changes*) may reflect the spatiotemporal context informing the cosmogonic signficance of the Cerulean Dragon.[74] One might go so far as even to suggest that the broken-line configuration of *k'un* represents the cosmic gap that is symbolically represented by a cataclysmic flood. It is perhaps not so coincidental that the phonetic reconstruction of the name of the second hexagram *k'un* (k'wən) is virtually identical to that of Kun. The solid lines of the *ch'ien* hexagram may thus represent the bridging of the cosmic gap, symbolized by Yü's controlling the floods.[75] Indeed, if the first hexagram of the *Book of Changes* is an account of the seasonal behavior of the Dragon constellation, does it not follow that Kun/k'un is the abyssal, watery parent? That *ch'ien* in its other reading means "dry" and thus represents the cosmogonic significance of Yü's draining of the floodwaters suggests that astronomical/cosmogonic connotations are also embedded in the wet/chaos associations of Kun/*k'un*.[76] While this is at best an informed speculation, it provides a possible explanation for why *ch'ien* and *k'un* are perceived "as the two fundamental aspects of cosmic processes and of the *Change*."[77] Change refers to the dynamic (perceived to be cosmic) motions that effected the transformation from wetness to dryness, a transformation that represented a transcendence of the astronomical obstacle to being. That the ancient meaning of the term "change" itself connoted a transformation from a state of wetness to dryness—in oracle bone inscriptions the word denoted the dissipation of rain and the emergence of the sun—lends further support to this interpretation.[78]

The sense of transcendence that I am arguing for seems to be implied in the following passage in the *Appended Words Commentary*:

> A shut door is called *K'un*; an open door is called *Ch'ien*. One closing and another opening is called flux. Reciprocally alternating, [the flux] is never exhausted, [this is] called transcendence. Once manifested, [this transcendence] is called symbol.[79]
> 闔戶謂之坤，闢戶謂之乾;一闔一閉謂之變，往來不窮，謂之通，見乃謂之象

The closed door refers to the blockage to reading posed by the Heavenly Turtle, *Kun/k'un* (who of course is represented symbolically as failing to control the floodwaters because he uses "blocking" or damming techniques), while *Ch'ien* is described as an open door because it symbolizes a new beginning, the replacement of the displaced Heavenly Turtle marker with Antares and the beginning of a new calendrical system, a new world age. *Hsiang* are thus presented as the symbolic responses to, or "manifestations" of, the ineffable force of transformation reflected in the process of replacement.

The relationship between Heaven and the *Book of Changes* is co-symbolic and is manifested as a chain-like phenomenon.

1. Heaven produced symbols—the changing position of stars (that is, seasonal indicators and the pole stars)—as a response to an ineffable force stimulating the otherwise "still and unmoving"[80] cosmic process.
2. Heaven's symbols can be "read" only by those, the sages, who comprehend the hidden source of their generation.
3. In "reading" Heaven's symbols the sages transcend the mysteries of the cosmos, which are so deep as to preclude comprehension by common people.
4. The sages' transcendence is manifested symbolically first in their production of the hexagrams, and then in the text of the *Book of Changes.*

As symbols whose existence derives from and whose content reflects its own unstated relationship with Heaven, the hexagrams of the *Book of Changes* can be said to co-symbolize with Heaven, or more appropriately, they co-symbolize with the principle of change. We readers can know about things that are hidden and mysterious by means of *change*, that is, through symbolic operation. Witness the *Appended Words Commentary*'s assertion that "being the *change* is a matter of providing symbols" (易者象也).[81] It provides a remarkable ancient Chinese corollary to Abraham's conviction that "being . . . is only possible in a symbolic mode."[82]

This discussion has sought to show how the concept of symbolic operation delineated by Nicolas Abraham accords with conceptions of the symbol in ancient Chinese thought and, more importantly, how the concept can be used as a heuristic device to elucidate the meaning and literary significance of certain texts. Although the symbolic operations examined herein are related to cosmogonic conceptions of origins, it is not meant to imply that symbolic operations are possible only within these parameters. The value of the concept of a symbol does not hinge on any preconceived constellations of signification.

The concept of the symbol, as it relates to the organization of the elements of the Yü flood myths and the representation of specific modes of philosophical theorizing, allows us to consider elements of other texts that pertain to these systems of thought and expression as possible signs of a co-symbolic connection. Thus, the figures of K'un-lun, Ho-tsung, and Hsi-wang-mu all constitute symbols that are part of the same system of traces, the same symbolic operation that gave form to the Yü myths. I will argue, therefore, that the elements contributing to the image of K'un-lun, Ho-tsung, and Hsi-wang-mu may be interpreted as fragments of a more complete scene that reveals their role as components of the cosmological function of transformation.

FOUR

Symbolic Foundations of the *Mu T'ien-tzu chuan*: K'un-lun, Ho-tsung, and Hsi-wang-mu

The cosmogonic significance ascribed to the celestial territory between Scorpius and Sagittarius, discussed above, also informs the development of the mythic traditions of K'un-lun Mountain, the River God, Ho-tsung, and Hsi-wang-mu: all are associated with the shift. The specific organizational and conceptual structures that express the shared cosmogonic intent of the myths of K'un-lun, Ho-tsung, and Hsi-wang-mu, are at once manifested and obscured by the linguistic elements of each tradition. The extensive intertextuality of these mythic traditions reflects the complexity of the structures underlying the myths. Aided by the hermeneutic concept of the symbol delineated in the previous chapter, our examination aims to reveal the cosmogonic nature of these structures.

1

Not surprisingly, most discussions of K'un-lun in the *Mu T'ien-tzu chuan* have focused on the mountain's geographical location rather than on mythic significance. I propose, instead, that K'un-lun Mountain, identified by scholars as being anywhere from

Sinkiang to Persia, functions as a symbol that transcends conventional categories of history and geography.

In addition to appearing in the *Mu T'ien-tzu chuan*, K'un-lun is described in five or six other sources.[1] The details vary, but three features recur frequently enough to suggest a generalized notion of its function: K'un-lun is a mountain; it is located in the northwest; and it is the source of all rivers. The mountain motif is rich. K'un-lun is a peak of remarkable height; so high, is it, according to one text, that "besides Archer I 羿"—and in another text "without the aid of a dragon"—no one can surmount the staggering cliffs.[2] Several scholars read this to mean that K'un-lun is an *axis mundi* connecting heaven and earth.[3] This is a viable interpretation that does not conflict with the scholarship that is principally interested in identifying K'un-lun's exact location on earth. Another source suggests that K'un-lun lies not within the Chinese landscape but within the celestial realm; this is based on descriptions of Archer I, who alone can climb K'un-lun and who is said in other texts—such as Ch'ü Yüan's "T'ien wen" and the *Huai-nan-tzu*—to be the one who shot the nine suns from the sky.[4]

I emphasize this element of sun shooting because many myths describing the demise of either the sun or figures related to the sun have been interpreted as an imagistic account of the gradual westward shift of the solstitial and equinoctial points through the ecliptic or zodiac—the same phenomenon that gave rise to the Yü flood myths. If, as Chang Kwang-chih has suggested, the appearance of ten suns in the sky in the Archer I myth represents the reappearance of primordial chaos, then this chaos may be an imagistic representation of the astronomical displacement that occurs when the sun cannot be placed within the realm of a constellation.[5]

The location (and significance) of K'un-lun is, I believe, related to the role of Archer I. If K'un-lun can be scaled only by someone who can remedy the chaos, its location may be connected to the location of the displacement of the sun's path. The myth of Kung-kung's butting of Pu-chou Mountain as a result of a battle with Chuan Hsü provides a context for this connection—as we have seen, it is a mythic rendition of the results of precession. Recall, too, Pu-chou Mountain's close proximity to K'un-lun Mountain and its location in the (celestial) northwest.

Support for this line of reasoning is provided by the "T'ien-wen." In an extended passage the poem consistently alludes to celestial mythic elements, a category to which Archer I belongs. The topic of the passage is a place where "people don't die," where

Black River (*Hei-shui* 黑水) and Three Dangers [Mountain] (*San-wei* 三危) are located in places that figure significantly in the topography of K'un-lun. Let us examine the celestial dimension of Ch'ü Yüan's references:

> The Black River, the Black Pool, Three Dangers [Mountain], where are they located? Extended years with no death, how does long life end? Where does the Ling Fish reside? What environs are occupied by the Ch'i Bird? Where did [Archer] I shoot the suns? Where did the birds let go of their feathers? Yü's ability enabled him to contribute benefits, he descended to survey the land below. Where did he obtain that girl from T'u Mountain, with whom was he man and wife at T'ai-sang?[6]
> 黑水玄趾三危安在 延年不死壽何所止
> 鯪魚何所鬿堆焉 羿焉畢日鳥焉解羽 禹之力獻功
> 降省下土方 焉得彼塗山女 而通之於台桑

All of the locations that figure in each of these questions are symbolically connected to the celestial gap between Scorpius and Sagittarius; to bridge that gap is to arrive at rejuvenation—rebirth. The appellation Black Pool shares its modifier "black" with the Black Turtle of the Heavenly Turtle quadrant. Moreover, the term pool (*chih* 趾) connotes a body of water that is blocked (dammed) by an islet, an image that resembles the topography of the celestial gap. It also resonates with details of the Kun myth: both Black Water and Three Dangers (Mountain) contain similar referential connotations.[7]

The Ling Fish, too, is associated with the heavens. The *Shan-hai-ching* describes it as living in the depths of the oceans, and the commentators compare it to a four-legged amphibian like a turtle. Another passage of the *Shan-hai-ching* describes a dragon fish (*lung-yü* 龍魚) that lives on a mountain and is used by gods and sages (in one text shamans) to "travel the nine wilds." Su Hsüeh-lin equates the Ling-yü with the Lung-yü because, according to the commentary to the "T'ien-wen" and the text of the *Shan-hai-ching,* they resemble the turtle. Amphibians, of course, frequently represent transformation in myths. The additional detail that likens the Ling Fish (and the Lung Fish) to a *pieh* 鱉 (turtle), however, suggests the unique function of a certain celestial turtle who is also involved in transformations, specifically seasonal ones.[8]

That the reference following the Ling Fish is to a Ch'i bird highlights this celestial/seasonal nature of transformation: whereas the turtle/fish symbolizes the watery depths of winter, the bird, which soars to great heights, symbolizes the ascent of spring (which itself is marked by the ascent of Scorpius, the dragon constellation). The same imagery figures in the famous passage in the *Chuang tzu* that describes the transformation of the huge K'un (鯤) fish—associated with the north—into a P'eng (鵬) bird. Su Hsüeh-lin associates Chuang tzu's *k'un* with Yü's father, Kun, on phonetic grounds; others have read Chuang tzu's *p'eng* as a reference to the phoenix (*feng* 鳳). Indeed, one finds an epigraphic (and perhaps phonetic) relationship between the graphs for phoenix and dragon (*lung* 龍) in oracle bone inscriptions. That the dragon could fly and so noticeably ascended the sky in the spring, invested the animal with birdlike qualities. This seasonal symbolism is reflected in both ancient texts and artwork. Su Hsüeh-lin has noted that many ancient descriptions of turtles refer to "eagle-like beaks" (*ying-wen* 鷹紋); and several Han stone carvings of Hsüan Wu 玄武, another appellation for the Black (Heavenly) Turtle, depict him with the claws of a bird.[9]

If the sequential association between the Ling Fish and the Ch'i Bird does in fact symbolize the transformation underlying the change of seasons, then Ch'ü Yüan's repeated questions about where these creatures live can be understood as referring to the celestial location that effects this transformation. Viewed in this context the next two lines of Ch'ü Yüan's lyric take on significance: both clearly refer to Archer I's shooting of the suns and both seek to identify the location at which Archer I shot and the location where the sun's (bird's) feathers subsequently dropped. Archer I, it appears, should be situated in the space between Sagittarius and Scorpius.

The questions following the two about Archer I concern the origins of Yü's wife, Lady T'u. I stress the locative qualities of the particle *yen* 焉 in this setting: while the *yen* that begins the strophe containing the question is usually translated as "how," the questions preceding this line have a spatial orientation and most repeat the use of *yan* as a question word for "where." This does not obviate the preferred reading but rather highlights the implied spatial nuances of where the action occurred. One could thus diagram the semantic implications of this reading as: where→in what environment→under what circumstances→how→did Yü obtain Lady T'u?

Lady T'u (or more specifically, the space T'u, as we saw in chapter 2) yet again returns us to the celestial area between Scorpius and Sagittarius. Its generative capacity in giving birth to spring and the new year makes it an appropriate symbol of marriage and sexual union. Moreover, the mulberry forest in the last line of this section is an allusion to spring itself: Yü passed through (*t'ung* 通) Lady T'u, that is, he completed the process at Sang-lin, the place associated with the birth, and the rise of the daily and, even more significantly, vernal sun.[10]

Surrounded as it is by mythic elements connected to the cosmogony of the area between the Heavenly Turtle and the Cerulean Dragon quadrants, the reference to Archer I—the place where he shot the suns, the place where the feathers dropped—must be related to the same celestial phenomena. We now turn to the text of the *Mu T'ien-tzu chuan.*

The first reference to the mythic configuration of K'un-lun Mountain, Ho-tsung, and Hsi-wang-mu that I will examine also involves Archer I since the cross-connection between him and K'un-lun Mountain led to the discovery of their astronomical significance. In *chüan* 5 of the text (SPTK ed., 5.3a), King Mu dreams that Archer I shoots T'u 塗 Mountain. This terse narration can be interpreted as a projection of the king's desire both to tear down and to re-create. Archer I's act is at once destructive and constructive: in destroying the suns, he is also an agent of rectification; he has eliminated the sources of primordial chaos. This double function links Archer I to the regenerative quality of T'u Mountain, itself a symbol of the area between Scorpius and Sagittarius. Indeed, these associations of destruction and rebuilding are also implicit in the two most common graphs for the name *t'u*, which we have seen reflect the methods used by Kun and the Great Yü, respectively, to control the chaotic floodwaters. Whereas Kun piled up earth to stop the floodwaters, the Great Yü dug canals so that the waters could flow naturally. The one failed and died as a result at Feather Mountain; the other succeeded and, earned for himself accolades as a cultural hero. That Kun needed to be killed or destroyed, in some sources by his son the Great Yü himself, before the latter could succeed, further ties the notion of destruction and regeneration to King Mu's dream. In ancient China, moreover, the very act of shooting arrows was invested with regenerative significance; it was often associated with activities occurring during the winter solstice, the transitional point between seasons.[11] King Mu's dream thus connects him to this regenerative process.

This line of interpretation is supported by other references to the Archer I myth in the *Mu T'ien-tzu chuan*. We have seen how the suns shot down by Archer I are described as birds, the shooting of which results in the "shedding of many feathers" (*chieh-yü* 解羽). Similar imagery appears in the *Mu T'ien-tzu chuan*: King Mu spends a considerable amount of time at a location near K'un-lun Mountain that is known as the "place where many feathers were shed," Feather Mountain (*yü-ling* 羽陵).[12]

The astronomical associations of Feather Mountain through its connection to Yü's father, Kun, and by extension to the watery Heavenly Turtle quadrant have been delineated in chapter 2. This was corroborated by the analysis of the "T'ien-wen" passage above. The myths of K'un-lun Mountain are celestially referenced in other ways, as well, as is illuminated by the remarkable similarities in the myths concerning Kun and K'un-lun Mountain.

To begin, the Feather Mountain visited by King Mu recalls the name of another Feather Mountain (*yü-shan* 羽山)—the place where Kun was killed for failing to control the floodwaters. This mountain was linked by its associations with an abyss (the celestial area below the equator) to the watery winter quadrant of the Heavenly Turtle. And water, as noted above, is intrinsic to K'un-lun, described in several texts as the source of all waters. Since the Milky Way, too, has been designated as the source of all terrestial waters,[13] it must be that K'un-lun is situated in proximity to it.

This observation is strengthened by the fact that several bodies of water closely connected with K'un-lun Mountain have names that resonate with terminology used to describe the Heavenly Turtle quadrant, itself situated right next to the Milky Way. For example, a body of water called Jo Waters (弱水) is described in several texts as circling—sometimes three times—the foot of K'un-lun Mountain.[14] Most commentators identify Jo Waters as the place where the sun sets and thus infer a geographical referent. The use of the term abyss (*yüan*) to describe Jo Waters in at least one text is suggestive of another possibility, however—that like the place where Kun was killed (Yü Mountain/Yü Abyss), Jo Waters is associated with the Heavenly Turtle quadrant.[15]

An even closer association between Kun-lun Mountain and the Heavenly Turtle quadrant is intimated by King Mu's visit to Black Pool (*hsüan-ch'ih* 玄池) while at K'un-lun. The appellation Black Pool is almost identical to the one referred to by Ch'ü Yüan in his "T'ien-wen." The modifier "black," as we indicated above, is used in an alternative appellation for the Heavenly Turtle quadrant, Black Turtle. One commentator of the *Mu T'ien-tzu chuan* identifies the Black Pool with a place called Submerged Abyss (*ch'en-yüan* 沈淵), which he locates, according to the *Shan-hai-ching*, west of Chuan Hsü's grave.[16] The submerged abyss is rich in cosmogonic associations. First, it concentrates allusions to both the place (*yüan*) and the manner (*ch'en*) in which Kun died. Second, the abyss is in the vicinity of Chuan Hsü's grave, which we know is located within the Heavenly Turtle quadrant. If T'an Ts'ui's identification is valid, then Black Pool and K'un-lun Mountain must be seen as elements of a topos connected to the Heavenly Turtle quadrant.

Other details of K'un-lun's environs point in the same direction. The modifier "suspended" (*hsüan* 縣), which is often used to describe K'un-lun's ethereal status, evokes that sense of gap which defines the essence of chaos—itself represented by the figure of Kun. The gap marked by K'un-lun's suspension is the same gap that separates the winter and spring quadrants—the Milky Way, that watery void that "links the uncreated one and the created two into a meaningful whole."[17] That the character "black" (*hsüan*), which figures so significantly in the Kun myths, often substitutes for the homophonous character "suspended" reinforces the connection between them and the K'un-lun myths.

The flora of K'un-lun are also suggestive of a relationship with the Kun myths. For example, the specific reference in the *Mu T'ien-tzu chuan* to *huan* 雚 (*Scirpus lacustris*), *wei* 葦 (*Phragmites communis*), *wan* 莞, and *fu* 蒲 reeds as part of the topography of K'un-lun links the mountain to Nü Wa's Heaven-mending effort (which also included cutting a *turtle's* leg), Kun's flood control endeavors, and the location of Kun's death. Thus, Nü Wa piles up the ash of burnt reeds (*lu* 蘆, *Phragmites roxburghi*) to stop the wild waters in the *Huai-nan-tzu*. The *Shan-hai-ching* speaks of reeds piled up (*fu-lu* 蒲蘆) near a sandbar in a river as the distinguishing feature of the place where Yü's father (Kun) died and was transformed (*Yü fu chih so hua* 禹父之所化). And, in the "T'ien-wen," Ch'ü Yüan questions why Kun was branded a criminal when he "planted black millet and managed his affairs [of flood control] with the use of *fu-wan* reeds."[18] These two lines perplexed the commentators, who offered a plethora of interpretations, but all concur that they refer to Kun's work and that the *fu-wan* are a type of water plant, probably reeds.

These reeds take on cosmogonic significance because of their relation to Kun's method of flood control. Su Hsüeh-lin is insightful in connecting the reed motif to the "swelling soil" that both Kun and Yü use in their efforts to control the floods, but because she insists on identifying the term *hsi-jang* as the shortened transliteration of the Sumerian god Gilimma, she fails to illuminate the significance of the soil/reed connection. Ch'ü Yüan's question provides a hint: it is related to Kun's method of management—reflected in Ch'ü Yüan's use of the term *ying* 營 twice to refer to Kun's [failed] work. Though his failure is sometimes explained by his theft of soil from God on High, John Major's comment seems more pertinent—that the different results achieved by Kun's and Yü's use of the swelling soil is a function of the differences between using soil to dam waters and using soil to create channels through which excess water can flow.[19] The references to blockage in connection with reeds both in the Nü Wa passage and in the passage describing Kun's place of death (sandbar) suggest that his method of managing the floods with reeds in the "T'ien-wen" also employed blocking techniques. K'un-lun, with its abundance of the "blocking" reeds, is thus contextually related to Kun, or more specifically, to the cosmogonic function of the Heavenly Turtle quadrant.

There is also a remarkable resonance between the name of K'un-lun's highest mountain, Ch'ung 舂 (also written as 鍾) and Kun's supposed native land, Ch'ung 崇. Both the Chi-chung *Bamboo Annals* and the *Kuo-yü* refer to Kun as Count of Ch'ung, Kun (崇伯鯀). Scholars such as Ku Chieh-kang have identified this Ch'ung as a specific geographical location, perhaps Sung Mountain. This identification is based largely on Wang Nien-sun's persuasive argument for the close phonetic resemblance of the words *ch'ung* 崇 and *sung* 崧. The same phonetic argument can be made for *ch'ung* 舂 and *song* according to an entry in the *Fang-yen* on the *ch'ung-shu* 舂黍 locust (*Gompsocleis mikado*), which is also written as *sung-hsü* 蜙蝑. The strong semantic overlap between another meaning of Kun's native Ch'ung, "to pile on high," and the method Kun uses to stop the floodwaters also indicates more than a superficial connection between the mountain and Kun.[20]

Another relevant detail is the absence of sunlight in the environs of Ch'ung Mountain, which is likely related to the fact that it is the place where the birds (that is, the sun) rest (after setting).[21] Ch'ung Mountain, in other words, is equated with the watery underworld through which the sun must pass before it rises again. This concept is graphically represented in the ancient character meaning "yesterday" or "previously" (*hsi* 昔, 㫺). The symbolism is equally relevant to the yearly passage of the sun, whereby the night is represented by the winter months, that period of time associated with the Heavenly Turtle quadrant.

That Ch'ung Mountain can be understood as a topographical representation of the Heavenly Turtle is indicated by its most famous inhabitant, the Torch Dragon (*chu-lung* 燭龍). In chapter 2 I alluded to the possibility that this Torch Dragon may in fact be the ancient Regulator of Fire Chu-jung 祝融, whose story itself is a mythic rendition of the function of Antares (the Fire Star) in early Chinese agriculture. In fact, the *Tso chuan*'s record that the Hsia dynasty began with the "descent of [Chu] Jung to Ch'ung 崇 Mountain,"[22] reiterates this implicit connection while it also shores up the identification of Kun's home Ch'ung as K'un-lun's Ch'ung Mountain. The affinity of Chu Jung and the Torch Dragon for Ch'ung derives from the actions of the Cerulean Dragon (Scorpius): it appears in the spring after having resided for almost six months in the watery abyss and is in fact thought to have been born out of it (from Kun, the anthropomorphic manifestation of the Heavenly Turtle quadrant). As a place that effects regeneration, moreover, Ch'ung is the ideal residence of the symbol of regenerated life, the Cerulean Dragon, and its other incarnations Chu Jung and the Torch Dragon.

Percussion instruments also figure in the imagery connecting Kun and K'un-lun. Drums, especially those made of alligator skin, symbolize both a spatiotemporal context (the Heavenly Turtle quadrant, parent of the *ch'iu* dragon—Scorpius) and the function of that context, namely, to regulate the rhythm of the seasons.[23] The creation of order through rhythm is also implicit in both of the characters used to write Ch'ung Mountain: the graph used in the *Mu T'ien-tzu chuan* represents the act of pounding grain with a pestle and mortar, one of the oldest means of producing rhythm, while the other graph was commonly used to designate bells. Both probably figured in seasonal rituals and dances; and the bell in particular was traditionally associated with the autumnal equinox.[24] An entry in the *Shan-hai-ching* gives a familial connection to percussion instruments and the mountain: the "son" of Ch'ung Mountain, it states, was called "drum" (*ku* 鼓).[25]

Music produced by bronze bells was believed to capture the essence of endurance, with its "unending" (*pu chong* 不終) resonance of sound."[26] This sonorous quality invested the instrument with cosmological significance. In fact, in Western Chou inscriptions the word for "unending" was written with the graph for "winter" (*tung* 冬, **tong*); winter was perceived as the end, the marker of the completion of a solar year. The bell's ability to play "undendingly" implies a regenerative force, a sense of progression and growth. The association with the last seasons of the year may derive from the homophony between the words for "winter" and "bell." The semantic nuance of termination implicit in the term "to end" (*chung*), coupled with the phonetic similarity between this term and that for "bell," may also have informed the shared cosmological associations of both words. Once again, therefore, we encounter a relationship in the underlying structure and purpose of the Kun and the K'un-lun myths. We will examine the relevant symbolism of percussion music in the next chapter.

Yet one more piece of evidence indicates similar cosmogonic intentions. This is the striking linguistic resonance between the archaic pronounciation of the two names under consideration: Kun is pronounced *kwən; *k'un* is pronounced the same way; and *lun* is pronounced *lwən.[27] This, in addition to the many images shared by both myths, raises the possibility that the proper names K'un-lun and Kun refer to the same place, via two different linguistic forms.

The research of Peter Boodberg supports this hypothesis, arguing for an etymonic rather than an ideographic analysis of Chinese graphs. Premising his thesis on the evidence gathered by Karlgren and Maspero on the existence of complex initial consonantal groups, he proposes that archaic Chinese possessed a variety of consonantal Anlaut complexes, which he signifies with the symbols *G^wL, *G^wS, and *G^wN. As the language developed, these glottological principles ceased to operate. Consequently, "words were 'reconstructed' into the primitive reading by affixing to one graph a graph read with the needed phonetic determinative." Boodberg cites the example of the term *chü-lou* 句婁, "mountaintop," which he reads as a "binome consisting of two independent graphs, the purpose of which would be not so much to represent two words as to render an obsolescent *gləu." By this reasoning, K'un-lun can be read as a "reconstruction" of the word Kun. Boodberg then posits that the etymons *GLUNG and *GLUN, the latter of which is the archaic glottological rendition of Kun, are related to the concept of chaos and are reflected in various terms such as *hung* 洪 (*GLUNG), "flood," having to do with the notion of chaos. According to Boodberg, "most names of the mythological characters in the Flood Story are but variations of only two or three original etymons which composed the primeval myth of the creation legend."[28]

K'un-lun Mountain represents a variant concretization of the cosmogonic concept of Kun. It is the "source of all waters," which functions on one level as the quintessential symbol of the gap that constitutes chaos. It consists of several (nine in most sources) levels (that is, it is a "pile" of a mountain) that reflect the method used by Kun to control the flood, while the number may tacitly refer to the means by which Yü succeeded. And it is located in the northwest, precisely the position of the Heavenly Turtle (Kun) in the celestial realm.[29]

The significance of these associations for my interpretation of the *Mu T'ien-tzu chuan* lies in the intimate connection between astronomical phenomena and Chinese cosmological beliefs: the effect of the precession of the equinoxes was associated cosmologically with a change in the world order, with the death of one age and the birth of another. In other words, the specific northwestern celestial territory symbolically marked the point of transition from the primal forces of chaos to order. K'un-lun functions as a border, both dividing and connecting, and thereby effecting this *transition.* It symbolizes the chaos associated with Kun, while also demarcating the place where Kun died and was transformed, and hence the place where the cosmos, in the form of the Great Yü, was born. It thus embodies and distinguishes between the old and the new.

2

Ho-tsung Po-yao is the first mythical figure encountered in the *Mu T'ien-tzu chuan.* I call him such because I will argue that he is an incarnation of the River God, who himself is (textually) associated with the flood myths. It must be noted, however, that many readers of the *Mu T'ien-tzu chuan* take Ho-tsung Po-yao to be a bona fide human descendant of the first person enfeoffed with an area of land in Western China and assigned the task of governing the river.[30]

King Mu's interaction with Ho-tsung Po-yao occurs in the first *chüan* of the text, and the narration continues for almost four pages. Despite the thematic and structural significance of the passage, very few scholars have treated it in more than cursory fashion. Perhaps those who wished to see the text as purely historical preferred to disregard the supernatural overtones. For the most part, scholars who do discuss the passage are earnest philologists, more interested in the geographical location of the event or the political lineage of the alleged enfeoffment of Ho-tsung Po-yao than in the literary significance of the events. I will diverge from this well-established line of scholarship and suggest that Ho-tsung Po-yao, at least as he is portrayed in the *Mu T'ien-tzu chuan,* is a mythic construct and thus transcends conventional categories of history. The significance of his role with regard to King Mu lies in our understanding of the hermeneutic "function" of his actions.

Several details of the narration seem to support this position. First, and arguably most importantly, King Mu meets Ho-tsung Po-yao in the location of the residence of Po-yao's "ancestor," Ho-tsung Wu-i 無夷, which I, following almost all other commentators, read as Feng-i 馮夷.[31] This residence is consistently described in other texts as being situated "three *jen* 仞 measures into the great abyss beyond the extreme [i.e., cardinal point]."[32] The diction of this description, especially the use of the term abyss, locates Feng-i's home outside the Chinese landscape and instead in the celestial realm.[33] One text identifies Feng-i's home as the source of all rivers, precisely the imagery used to describe K'un-lun.[34] The *Cheng-i* commentary to the "Hereditary House of Chao" (趙世家) of the *Shih chi*, which states that Ho-tsung is a location on the top of Dragon Gate river (*lung-men*), further corroborates this interpretation. Dragon Gate designates the first area opened by Yü (that is, the tail of the Cerulean Dragon constellation), an act that resulted in his successful draining of the floodwaters.[35]

That Feng-i's residence is indeed associated with the area dividing the spring Cerulean Dragon and the winter Heavenly Turtle quadrants is also indicated in its proper name, Yang-yü, which, as shown in chapter 2 refers to the area of the Milky Way between the tail of Scorpius and Corona Australis. The character *yü* is also etymologically related to the graph meaning universe or world (宇), further heightening the cosmogonic undertones of the place-name. The name Yang-yü may thus signify an area that demarcates the beginning and end of "world ages," an appellation that accords nicely with the effects of precession.[36] Last, we should recall that the Great Yü himself "disembodied himself at Yang-yü," and in some other versions of the myth, changes into a *nai* ("three-legged turtle"), after he crosses over a mountain named *hsüan-yüan* 軒轅, a homophone of the name Heavenly Turtle. The cosmogonic significance is unmistakable.

But just who—or what—is this Feng-i? Girardot has suggested that Feng-i is a "mythological chaos figure like Emperor Hun-tun." In Ch'ü Yüan's "T'ien-wen" the term *feng-i* 馮翼 is the formless gap that preceded yet also facilitated the creation of the cosmos.[37] If the referent for the cosmogonic notion of a watery gap–like chaos is the Milky Way, as I have postulated, then Feng-i's connection to water, especially rivers, is very telling for our analysis. In this regard, Feng-i's association with the River God is especially significant.

The earliest texts to make this association explicitly were those discovered at Chi-chung—the *Bamboo Annals* and the *Mu*

T'ien-tzu chuan. Wen Ch'ung-i believes that this association is unsubstantiated by most other textual traditions and cites the "spurious" ("forged") nature of the Chi-chung books as negative evidence for his contention that those two texts are a conflation of two discrete mythic traditions. Wen's argument is understandable in light of the apparent inconsistency with which the term Feng-i is used, alternately as a proper name, a precosmos state, and the name of a dance, but he ignores how these variant elements in fact represent images that "summarize a central mythological idea and condense in an ideal-typical way the basic structure or logic of a set of myths."[38] In other words, when analyzed within the context of the flood myths, seemingly disparate threads of the Feng-i myths come together as a tightly woven fabric. Once this fabric is closely examined, the (mythic) rationale underlying Feng-i's identification as the River God will be clear.

Consider, for example, the detail recorded in both the *Chuang tzu* and the *Huai-nan-tzu* that Feng-i "obtained the Tao" and either "roamed the great river" or "submerged himself in the great river."[39] The word *ch'uan* 川 for "river" is relatively rare; its use therefore demands attention. Could it reflect a deliberate attempt to distinguish this body of water from the Yellow River, the "great river" believed to be the referent for the term *ho* in most early texts?[40] The mention of "submerging" recalls yet another body of water—the abyss by the Milky Way in which Kun submerged himself. While some late accounts offer euhemerized explanations for Feng-i's drowning, the fact that Feng-i is also described as "ascending K'un-lun Mountain" and "opening Heaven's door,"[41] as well as "frolicing amongst the *nine* rivers" and "riding on a white *yüan* turtle to follow the patterned fish,"[42] places Feng-i more appropriately within a cosmogonic context. Certainly the images of K'un-lun in combination with those of the *yüan* turtle suggest a connection between Feng-i and Kun.

I am by no means the first to note this connection. Su Hsüeh-lin and Yang K'uan have both written persuasive studies that identify Kun, Kung-kung, and Feng-i (whom they see as the River God) as one and the same mythic figure. Both Su and Yang highlight the consistent overlap of imagery pointing to the place and act of submergence of the three figures, as well as their apparently malevolent intentions toward man—all three are described as "wreaking havoc" (*tso-sui* 作祟), an expression that can be traced back to oracle bone inscriptions. Su Hsüeh-lin also underscores the prevalence of turtle imagery in many accounts of the three figures.[43] Su's thesis that the source of this imagery lies in the Assyrian myths of Kudarru, another form of Tiamat the god of chaos, is fascinating and deserving of serious attention as material and textual sources increase and our comparative skills become more sophisticated. Nonetheless, there is also evidence of an indigenous context for the turtle imagery in early Chinese cosmogony. It must not be ignored.

Notwithstanding the obvious overlaps in the myths of Kun, K'un-lun, and Feng-i, they are not simply linguistic variants of the same myth. Rather, each mythic tradition represents a specific "symbolic angle" with its own unique perspective. Thus, Kun embodies the cosmic flaw that precipitated the catastrophe that was later identified as chaos; K'un-lun, functions as a concrete manifestation of the spatiotemporal coordinates that mark the process of transformation from chaos to cosmos; and Feng-i's role concerns the actual transformation from chaos to cosmos.

Feng-i's function can be likened to the classic mythic ferryman who guides passengers to and from the realm of the dead. The term *tsung* in his official "title," "Ancestral [Source of the] River" (*ho-tsung*), is explained as a representation of the place where ritual sacrifices to the ancestors of the royal lineage were performed;[44] Feng-i's function, it would seem, is somehow linked to the spirits of the dead.

Indeed, water and death have a strong association in Chinese mythology, not only in the textual tradition but also in art. It may be, thus, that the Milky Way was perceived in China as in many cultures as a bridge crossed by the souls of the dead as they enter the realm of the underworld.[45] These associations of the environs of K'un-lun—and by extension the Heavenly River—seem to be implied in texts that situate the palace of the Yellow Emperor there. Sarah Allan has argued that the Yellow Emperor represented the inverse of the mythic origins of the Shang, the Black Crow, and thus "may have originally been the Lord of the Underworld, the counterpart of Shang Di, the Lord on High."[46] Another name for "Yellow Springs," "Nine Springs" (*chiu-ch'üan* 九泉), brings to mind the spatiotemporal significance of the nine stars of the tail of Scorpius—located right in the branch of the Milky Way, thus suggesting a connection between the underworld and that space.[47] Indeed, that a cognomen for the Yellow Emperor, *Hsüan-yüan shih* 軒轅氏, is homophonous with the Chinese appellation of the Heavenly Turtle quadrant is more than a coincidence. Ch'en Meng-chia has suggested that the Yellow Emperor's other name resonates with the story of Yü passing through a mountain of the same name, which we alluded to above.[48]

Feng-i's proper name is even more explicit about his cosmogonic function. The term *feng* has been glossed in the *Shih ching* as "treading on water," or "crossing water without a boat," and it seems to be the name of a dance across water in the piece called "Wandering Afar" (*yüan-yu* 遠游) of the *Ch'u-tz'u*.[49] The body of "water" that can be crossed without the aid of a boat is none other than the Heavenly River; crossing it is tantamount to effecting the transformation from chaos to cosmos, from death to (re)birth. Marcel Granet has shown that rituals involving the crossing of water were especially significant at the times of the equinoxes and solstices. The later evolution of the connotation "to lean on" or "to depend on" for the word *feng* seems especially fitting—those who want to regenerate themselves must rely on Feng-i, for only he can assist them across the (Heavenly) River.[50]

Ho-tsung's function as a vehicle for transportation across the watery divide is implicit in the turtle imagery that often figures in descriptions of him. For example, in the passage of the *Shih i chi* that we cited above in chapter 2, the Water Spirit (*ho-ching*) is described as a black turtle. Similarly, in a passage in the *Chuang tzu*, one Sung Yüan-chün 宋元君 dreams of an emissary of Ho-po who is described upon Sung's waking as a "numinous turtle." One also finds the turtle's role as facilitator in passages that describe it transporting Yü, and even King Mu, across a confluence of waters called "nine rivers" (*chiu-chiang*). Indeed, the turtle as a vehicle enabling passage through a difficult part of a journey is a fairly regular trope in Chinese literature.[51] The role of facilitator is also implied when the River Spirit presents Yü with the River Chart, which the latter used to control the floods.[52]

Ho-tsung's role as mediator and transmitter is foregrounded in the *Mu T'ien-tzu chuan*: he is the medium for God on High's order initiating King Mu's western sojourn and the king's guide on the journey. That King Mu must rely on Ho-tsung to cross the depths of chaos is intimated by the term "quickly" (*mu* 鶩), which appears in the narrative of the journey to Feng-i's residence. This anomalous use of an adverb in a text otherwise devoid of modifiers other than colors is all the more striking in its resonance with a phrase in the *Huai-nan-tzu* that describes Feng-i as one able to "quickly pass through chaos" (*mu huang-hu* 鶩恍忽).[53] The use of the term in the *Mu T'ien-tzu chuan* shores up the suitability of Ho-tsung's cosmogonic function as "tour guide," for the entire *Huai-nan-tzu* passage is devoted to describing his unique abilities to move through the cosmos.

3

K'un-lun's role as a concrete manifestation of the process of transformation from chaos to order is complemented by the function of its most famous inhabitant, Hsi-wang-mu, a complex and important member of the Chinese pantheon. Her cosmogonic function and the development of various traditions surrounding her in early literature have greatly interested scholars of early Chinese thought.[54] Although my primary interest is in analyzing her literary significance in the *Mu T'ien-tzu chuan,* this analysis also seeks to shed light on some of the larger questions and issues concerning her mythic significance.

Hsi-wang-mu's function in the *Mu T'ien-tzu chuan* accords with that of the other mythic elements considered thus far: she, like K'un-lun Mountain and Ho-tsung, represents the rejuvenating power inherent in the process of transformation from chaos to cosmos. This power was identified as immortality in some of the traditions surrounding her. But I will try to show that Hsi-wang-mu's significance lies not in her ability to extend life per se but in her ability to renew and reinvigorate life through transformation.

Several scholars have noted the antiquity of Hsi-wang-mu myths, with some even arguing that the most ancient record of worship devoted to her dates to Shang oracle bone divinations. Ch'en Meng-chia was the first scholar to venture a connection between the "Western Mother" (*hsi-mu*) and "Eastern Mother" (*tung-mu*) of oracle bone inscriptions and the Hsi-wang-mu referred to in later texts. In a thorough and illuminating discussion of the different traditions of Hsi-wang-mu, Riccardo Fracasso has argued that the evidence for this link is too scarce to be convincing: there is only one extant reference to Hsi-mu in oracle bone inscriptions. Even though the *Ho-chi* concordance of oracle bone inscriptions now lists three inscriptions containing references to a Hsi-mu, Fracasso is nonetheless justifiably cautious.[55] Nevertheless, his categorical dismissal of the possibility of any connection between Hsi-mu and Hsi-wang-mu is perhaps too extreme a position, for the question is still open. It may be that an exploration of Hsi-mu will lead to a deeper understanding of other mythic traditions that have a bearing on those of Hsi-wang-mu.

Especially relevant are the theories positing a relationship between Tung-mu (Eastern Mother) and Hsi-ho 羲和, the mythic mother of the suns.[56] If Tung-mu is identified with the birth of the sun, or at least the location where the sun begins its daily journey, then Hsi-mu logically should refer to the deity who deals with the termination of the sun's journey. Termination, of course, implies closure, death, or absence. But because the sun appears every day (the Shang believed there were ten suns that rotated), the termination was viewed not as eternal but rather as a transformation. Hsi-mu, then, may have facilitated this process.

The myths of Hsi-wang-mu also contain elements that link them to the sun's path and a process of transformation that occurs in the west. She inhabits K'un-lun Mountain, a mythic location related to the annual path taken by the sun. It is thus noteworthy that the verb used to narrate King Mu's visit to Hsi-wang-mu "to play host to" (*pin* 賓)—a verb that is not used anywhere else in the text—also appears in oracle bone inscriptions as a ritual performed for the sun or an ancestor.[57] Several of the commentators point to the uniqueness of the term at this juncture, and one speculates that its use here signifies the superior status of Hsi-wang-mu.

Another indication of a connection between Hsi-wang-mu and solar processes appears in King Mu's ascent of Yen Mountain 弇.[58] The name Yen, which means literally "to cover or conceal," calls to mind the graph *mo* 莫, the ancient graph of which depicts the sun being covered or enveloped by grass; it was a technical term in Shang oracle bone inscriptions for evening.[59] Thus, Yen Mountain is often glossed as the "place where the sun enters [the depths]" (*ju jih chih ch'u* 入日之處).[60] King Mu makes explicit the connection between Hsi-wang-mu and Yen Mountain: he identifies Yan mountain as "Hsi-wang-mu's Mountain" in an inscription on stone.[61]

The tiger iconography so often found in Han dynasty depictions of Hsi-wang-mu, as well as the early verbal descriptions of her, also adumbrates the association between the goddess and the sun. The antiquity of the association of the tiger with the celestial west is suggested by the discovery of the clamshell figures of a dragon and tiger, separated by the figure of the Big Dipper, in a Neolithic grave in P'u-yang. The tiger, a ferocious animal whose huge, gaping mouth formed the primary element in the earliest examples of the written form of the word signifying it,[62] was emblematic of the ravenous forces that engulfed the sun as it descended from the sky.

Yet the tiger represented more than the obliteration of brightness. Rather, its open mouth, frequently depicted on Shang bronzes, may also have signified a passageway between light and dark, this world and the other world, life and death. Or it may have symbolized a way of crossing the threshold. Mircea Eliade has shown in this regard that thresholds are "symbols and at the same time vehicles of passage from the one space to the other." Chang Kwang-chih has suggested that the clamshell figure of the tiger discovered at P'u-yang was conceived as a numinous animal that could effect transformation by carrying shamans to other worlds.[63] Perhaps the depiction of Hsi-wang-mu's traditional habitat as a cave or crevice, which was assimilated to the mouth, reflects an ability to achieve new modes of existence.

Suzanne Cahill suggests along similar lines that the representation of Hsi-wang-mu in connection with bestial iconography indicates a close connection between the role of the goddess and that of shamans in early Chinese society.[64] As ones who communicate with spirits, shamans transcend the mortal barriers that preclude interaction with other modes of being. Since Neolithic times the dragon and the tiger were viewed as facilitators of this ontological passage from one mode of being to another. And it is their function as symbols of the temporal and spatial points of transition of the sun, both diurnal and annual (that is, as constellations), that invests these animals with their transcendental powers to begin with.

That Hsi-wang-mu in some way represents the process of transition associated with the sun's passage accords with the symbolic significance of her primary domus, K'un-lun, which concretized the concept of Kun and was linked to the process of regeneration. In fact, the location of Hsi-wang-mu at a Turtle Mountain (within the environs of K'un-lun) in the *Shan-hai-ching* connects Hsi-wang-mu to K'un-lun with precisely the same imagery that led to the discovery of Kun's cosmogonic role. Turtles and mountains then, are long-standing complements to the icon of Hsi-wang-mu; we see this as well in Han dynasty tomb paintings.[65]

Hsi-wang-mu's consistent depiction alongside turtles and tigers is related to the seasonal associations of both animals with autumn and winter. What in late Warring States terminology was expressed as a metaphysical force, *yin* 陰, was in earlier texts and later in iconography represented as images of the half of the year when the tiger and turtle celestial quadrants were home to the sun. This combining of what we consider two seasons as one long period in fact supports the general scholarly belief that the division of the year into four seasons was a relatively late invention. Shang oracle bone inscriptions, for example, show no indication that summer and winter were conceived as distinct temporal periods.[66] Rather, the temporal perspective of the inscriptions is of a bipartite division into spring and autumn. Kominami Ichiro concurs, commenting that "extreme West" in early texts referred to the season of winter as well as autumn.[67]

Hsi-wang-mu's association with the tiger and the turtle thus connects her to chaos, best understood "as [a] grinning gulf, the yawning dawn of creation . . . the basis of a cosmogonic process."[68] As we have argued, chaos was also conceived more concretely as the gap in the northwestern quadrant of the sky. Since it is from this gap that Yü (Scorpius) emerges to establish (calendrical) order, the gap was invested with regenerative powers frequently portrayed in sexual terms. It is thus not insignificant that a common motif in descriptions and depictions of Hsi-wang-mu—the nine-tailed fox—also figured prominently in the sexually nuanced myth of Yü's meeting Lady T'u and the subsequent marriage. We noted in chapter 2 that the latter's name, T'u, is related to the area dividing Scorpius and Sagittarius. This association is also reflected in the number of the fox's tails: it symbolizes the regeneration produced by Scorpius's tail, comprising nine stars.[69] The attendant iconographic detail of the nine-tailed fox, then, associates Hsi-wang-mu with the creative and positive aspects of chaos.

The rather obscure imagery in a few of the line statements in the last hexagram of the *Book of Changes*, "Have not yet Crossed" (*wei-chi* 未濟), together with the hexagram's name itself, seem to bespeak a similar symbolic nexus. There we encounter mention of a fox wetting its tail as it "is on the point of crossing over a stream."[70] The repeated allusions to distress and inauspiciousness hark back to the ominous associations of the Milky Way. Yet reference is also made to auspicious success occurring after three years, the symbolic equivalent of fording the waters or establishing order after chaos (as in the case of the birth of Yü). While this hexagram makes no mention of Hsi-wang-mu, nor of any other female figure, there is in the preceding hexagram a reference to a "matron" (*fu* 婦) who loses her "hairpiece" (*fu* 茀). Given the name "Already Crossed" (*ji-chi* 既濟), the two hexagrams are obviously inextricably connected. In addition to the shared images of "wetting a tail" and success following a three-year span of time, the image of a thread being either spun or tangled also occurs in both hexagrams. We shall see that the motif of weaving, too, is an important, albeit often implicit, feature of the Hsi-wang-mu mythic tradition.

Once Hsi-wang-mu's significance, like that of K'un-lun, is seen as deriving from the transformation from chaos to order, the celestial associations attendant upon other details concerning her cosmic powers and function also emerge. Two details in particular, the special function of Hsi-wang-mu's unique *sheng* 勝 headdress and her relationship to the myth of the Weaving Maiden, bring the elements of Hsi-wang-mu's symbolic identity into even sharper focus.

Michael Loewe offers a penetrating examination of the cosmic role played by Hsi-wang-mu in early Chinese thought, drawing attention to the relationship between Hsi-wang-mu's headdress and the state of the cosmos. Citing the *Huai-nan-tzu,* he illustrates how, by breaking the headdress, Hsi-wang-mu in effect disturbed the cosmic cycle.[71] This reference to a break links Hsi-wang-mu to the astronomical context of the gap caused by the displacement of the Heavenly Turtle. Given the frequent connection between Hsi-wang-mu and the nine-tailed fox, a motif that signifies Antares' winter, "domestic" sojourn in the north celestial quadrant, the headdress motif as well probably has stellar origins. Like Kun, who is responsible for both the catastrophe and its remedy through engendering Yü, so Hsi-wang-mu, as the symbolism of her headdress indicates, was associated with both, the cause and remedy of the cosmic break.

Several scholars have noted the metaphorical implications of the ties between the term *sheng* and other words associated with weaving. These ties, they believe, inform the metaphorical conception of Hsi-wang-mu as "posssessing the power to renew the cosmic cycle . . . by weaving a web of continuity and rebirth."[72] First, the term *sheng* refers to the weaving spool, or the part of a loom that holds the warp threads;[73] and second, a binome containing the term, *tai-sheng* 戴勝, which also appears in texts depicting Hsi-wang-mu, is identified in the "Yüeh-ling" 月令 chapter of the *Li chi* as a "weaving bird" that "descends onto the mulberry trees" in the third month of the year.[74] The "Yüeh-ling" passage refers to the month after the vernal equinox, the time when the silkworm begins spinning its chrysalis. In linking the human activity of weaving to the seasonally determined activities of the silkworm, the use of the term *tai-sheng* in the "Yüeh ling" passage also suggests a connection between stellar movements and the invention of the cosmic weaving metaphor—an interpretation supported by the common appearance of star configurations on paintings and stelae depicting weaving and Hsi-wang-mu.[75]

Additionally, there are myths of the Weaving Maiden, which, not incidentally, derive from stellar movements. Michael Loewe, following Izushi Yoshihiko and Kominami Ichirō, has made a convincing case for a connection between the myths of Hsi-wang-mu's visit to Emperor Wu Ti and the meeting between the Weaving Maiden and the Oxherd. One must see these shared motifs as a late (post-Han) literary development, however, for as both Wang Hsiao-lian 王孝廉 and Hsü Ch'uan-wu 徐傳武 have pointed out, the earliest strata of myths concerning the Weaving Maiden did not include her attachment to the Oxherd. In the *Huai-nan-tzu,* the Weaving Maid marries a Taoist adept (*chen-jen* 真人) who "wanders in the wastes" and in a lyric written by the commentator of the *Ch'u tz'u,* Wang I 王逸 (89–158), the Weaving Maid marries Fu-yüeh 傅說, a figure usually identified with the Cerulean Dragon constellation. Moreover, the reference to the Weaving Maid in the *Shih ching* does not portray her as one of a couple, even though it is adjacent to a reference to the Oxherd.[76]

The apparent single status of the Weaving Maid in the earliest strata of the myth suggests that her significance derived originally from activities other than her relationship with the Oxherd. Since several texts allude to the Weaving Maid's inability to do her job, it may be likened to Hsi-wang-mu's breaking of the (weaving) *sheng,* with its catastrophic consequences. There is a strong possibility that the myths of the Weaving Maid and Hsi-wang-mu stem from a single tradition that viewed the cosmic gap as a tear in a cosmic fabric that was maintained if not produced by a female, whose traditional societal role was to weave.[77]

The venerable history of weaving in China may explain its metaphorical application to Chinese cosmogony. The hand-spindle is the oldest textile-technological implement, having been in continuous use over the last seven thousand years.[78] Its importance to society can be gauged by the abundance of whorls discovered at numerous Neolithic sites. Its significance is even reflected in the earliest form of the language, oracle bone inscriptions, where specific graphs depicting the hand-spindle, with or without whorl, apparently signify the verb "to turn" or "to transfer." "The ancient graph for *chuan* 專" as Dieter Kuhn explains, "depicts a hand-driven instrument which is round . . . the small circle of the graph could be the whorl and the big, round or oval-shaped body may depict the spindle-shaft with the yarn wound around it."[79] That the pictograph signified not only an object but also the movement necessary to use the object and the result of that motion, such as the completion of some form of transference, contributed to its applicability as a cosmogonic trope, wherein because of precession the determinative constellations are displaced and then replaced by others newly suited to do the same job. It may thus be that the whirlpool patterns and diagrams "traditionally understood as representations of the *yin-yang* elements" that decorate excavated whorl reflect an early association between weaving and cosmogony.[80]

Hence, the Weaving Maiden constellation is located in the northern quadrant of the sky, within the spatiotemporal coordinates of cosmic disaster. One scholar has even suggested that the lunar lodge Girl (*nü* 女), located right next to the lunar lodge Waste was the original referent for the Weaving Maid appellation.[81] We have already noted that the appellation Waste may reflect the obsolescence of the lunar lodge as a marker for the winter solstice, the beginning of the solar year. Since the Girl lunar lodge lies directly west of Waste, the former's assumption of the latter's role may have been conceived as a metaphor for the reparation of the tear in the cosmic fabric.

There is some paleographic evidence pointing to an association between the lunar lodge Girl and myths depicting reparation of the cosmos, but the context of the chaos is presented in terms of the flood and not weaving. Written on a recently discovered lacquered clothes chest dating from the fifth century B.C. is the earliest example of the names of the twenty-eight lunar lodges.[82] There are two graphs used to signify the Girl lunar station 沷女. Ch'iu Hsi-kuei has transcribed the first of these graphs as 沷, and has suggested that it is an alternate form for the graph 魃 which is the name of a female ghost/spirit who is called upon to aid the Yellow Emperor in his fight with Ch'ih-yu 蚩尤 which resulted in floods.[83] Often described as a spirit of drought because she dried up the excessive waters, Pa-nü, who served the Yellow Emperor, is frequently linked to the Responsive Dragon—alias Yü—who was also called upon to aid the Yellow Emperor. This association suggests that Pa-nü's role has as much cosmogonic significance as Yü's: like Yü, she neutralizes the catastrophic events demarcating the end of a world age and has a role in establishing a new one.

Although the links between Pa-nü, the Girl lunar lodge, the Weaving Maid myths, and those of Hsi-wang-mu are at best speculative, the structural and thematic similarities of the three traditions is striking. Each of these traditions was closely related to astronomical realities pertaining to the north or northwestern celestial realms—for the ancient Chinese the point of transition between the primal forces of life and death. These divine women are agents of this transition, symbols of regenerative power; they inhabit the location where the transformation from birth to death and from death to birth is effected.

Recapitulating the central argument of this chapter, I have tried to show that Hsi-wang-mu, K'un-lun, and Ho-tsung are interrelated mythic sites. Their symbolic significance is also reflected in the cosmogonic function of the celestial Heavenly Turtle quadrant. And there is overall an intimate connection between astronomical phenomena and Chinese cosmological beliefs. Specifically, the northwestern celestial territory symbolically marked the point of transition between the primal forces of chaos and order. K'un-lun's function as a connective or border, represents its role in effecting this *transition;* Ho-tsung, who as the ruler of water, or more specifically the Heavenly River, assists those who want to regenerate themselves by enabling them to cross the (Heavenly) River, just as Yü (Scorpius) does to control the floodwaters; Hsi-wang-mu, possibly once responsible for the sun after its descent, eventually assumed the role of caretaker if not producer of the cosmic fabric rewoven every year in the pattern of the sun's annual journey. Connected to the chaos associated with Kun and the place where Kun died and was transformed, the three symbols hence are also associated with the place where order, in the form of the Great Yü, was born. The ancients clearly needed to displace the disaster of displacement with a discourse of regeneration.

The remainder of this chapter returns to the narration of King Mu's trip to K'un-lun in the *Mu T'ien-tzu chuan*. It can now be shown that what we have is not a historical narrative but a literary articulation of a symbolic journey involving rebirth, that is, the emergence of the king's new identity. It then follows from the symbolic context of the journey that King Mu himself represents a fictive character and not a historical personage.

4

The fictional status of the *Mu T'ien-tzu chuan* is affirmed by my examination of the cross-connections between aspects of the Ho-tsung, K'un-lun, and Hsi-wang-mu myths. I have uncovered a privileged plane of meaning, an "esprit which elaborates them [the myths] by means of the world of which it itself is a part."[84] It is an esprit related to specific celestial phenomena that the ancient Chinese conceived in a coherent pattern. We can now show that many elements of the text of the *Mu T'ien-tzu chuan* also touch on the astronomical/cosmological significance of the myths.

Indeed, an abundance of details in the *Mu T'ien-tzu chuan* narrative supports this interpretation. For example, the description of the physical environs of K'un-lun, especially K'un-lun's Ch'ung Mountain (the original specific destination mentioned by God on High in his command to King Mu), consistently portrays K'un-lun as the place that demarcates the end of one year's seasonal revolution and the beginning of another—and by extension, as the place that facilitates this transformation. The celestial associations of Ch'ung Mountain are apparent in the descriptions of it in the *Mu T'ien-tzu chuan*, as "the place where flying birds roost."[87] Echoing the motif of the sun as a bird in the myths surrounding the figure of Archer I, Ch'ung Mountain can be seen as demarcating the watery location that the sun must traverse before it begins its daily or seasonal ascent and revolution.

A connection between birds, the sun, and crossing waters is also intimated by the name of a place in the vicinity of K'un-lun and visited by King Mu—Ju Waters 溽水.[88] The *Shan-hai-ching* describes Ju Waters as emanating from Bird Mountain. The bird imagery used to describe Ch'ung Mountain immediately comes to mind, especially because feathers are also collected there by King Mu's retinue.[89] Moreover, several dictionaries define the term *ju* as a synonym and homonym of the word *ju* 濡 "to wade across the river" (*she ch'uan* 涉川), which suggests a link with the role of Ho-tsung, that is, to aid in crossing the river.

This same phrase appears with great frequency in the hexagram statements of the *Book of Changes*, referring mostly to an action that would be beneficial to the diviner. The phrase "crossing water" would seem then to function as a trope for some type of successful action and should not be understood literally.[90] A clue to the significance of this trope emerges from the specific temporal context for the appropriateness of "crossing water"—three days before or three days after a *chia* 甲 day—given in the eighteenth hexagram, Ku 蠱, (written as 箇 in the Ma-wang-tui manuscript, where it is the sixteenth hexagram).[91] *Chia*, the first calendrical term of the sexagenary cycle, was often associated with the first month of spring; in this hexagram it may function as a point of transition (between the before and after) and thus carry seasonal connotations. Because the connotations of the first two hexagrams stem from the astronomical relationship between Scorpius and Corona Australis, which are separated by a *river* (the Milky Way), the phrase "crossing water" may be interpreted as a trope for the seasonal transformation manifested in the movements of the Cerulean Dragon constellation.[92] The importance of this trope for the *Book of Changes* may also be gleaned from the names of the last two hexagrams, "Already Crossed" and "Have not yet Crossed," as well as from the obvious symbolism of the imagery used in the line statements, some of which I examined in the context of Hsi-wang-mu.

We have already seen how the symbolism of crossing water is intimated by Feng-i's name, which can mean to cross water without a boat. It is also reflected in the name of another place visited by King Mu, Hu-lu Mountain 瓜纑, which is close to Ju Waters. *Hu-lu*, of course, refers to a round gourd (the calabash) that in ancient times was tied to the waist to allow people to float across water. In one tradition of flood myths the *hu-lu* gourd serves as a means for Fu Hsi 伏羲 and Nü-wa to evade the dangers of the flood, and in early Taoist texts it is a symbol for chaos.[93] In a passage of the *Book of Changes*, a prognostication of "there will be no great harm" is reached for the proposition of "using an empty *hu* [-*lu*] gourd to cross (*feng* 馮) a river." Chuang tzu also uses this imagery as a metaphor for transcending established conventions.[94]

The *Mu T'ien-tzu chuan* adds the detail that Hu-lu Mountain has three rings, which anchors it to the imagery of the Heavenly Turtle. While the often seen connection between the *hu-lu* gourd and floodwaters and the motif of chaos is enough to warrant such an association, the number three, which figures significantly in the myths of Kun (the number of feet he has after transforming himself into a turtle; the number of months or years it takes to give birth to Yü) ties the *hu-lu* symbolism of the *Mu T'ien-tzu chuan* text to the number of months during which the sun occupies the Heavenly Turtle quadrant. The abundance of references to the numbers three (eleven), and its multiples, thirty (seven), three hundred (fifteen), and three thousand (five) in the text—much more than any other number or its multiples—is suggestive of a context charged by K'un-lun's cosmological significance.[95] K'un-lun itself is described in one text as comprising three corners.[96]

King Mu visits the palace of the Yellow Emperor immediately after ascending K'un-lun, which further solidifies the symbolism inherent in many of the place-names of the *Mu T'ien-tzu chuan.*[97] Also called *Hsüan-yüan chih kung* 軒轅之宮, "the palace of Hsüan-yüan," the name is homophonous with the Heavenly Turtle. In light of the resonance between the Yü flood myths and those involving the Yellow Emperor, Ch'en Meng-chia's suggestion that the Yellow Emperor and the Heavenly Turtle are one and the same mythic figure demands new attention.[98]

Black Pool (*hsüan-chih* 玄池), where King Mu rests and has music played for *three* days, and where he plants a grove of bamboo, is another place-name that evokes the symbolic context of the Heavenly Turtle. In addition to the obvious resonance between the use of the word "black" *hsüan* as modifiers for both names, and the similarities between the appellations of this Black Pool and the one mentioned in the "T'ien-wen," which we have seen is related to the cosmogonic area between Scorpius and Sagittarius, the added detail of the bamboo grove may also place Black Pool in the vicinity of the Heavenly Turtle: in the *Shan-hai-ching* a bamboo grove is situated right at the grave of Chuan Hsü, which we have already identified as linked to the lunar lodge Waste within the northern celestial quadrant. Chuan Hsü, of course, is the father of Kun and the ruler of the Heavenly Turtle quadrant. In the same passage of the *Shan-hai-ching,* moreover, a body of water in which Chuan Hsü was supposed to have bathed is located right next to the bamboo grove. On the basis of the bamboo imagery, T'an Ts'ui identifies this body of water, called "submerged abyss," as the Black Pool visited by King Mu.[99] The overlap of such charged terms as submerge, abyss, and black speaks to a deeper symbolic level than even T'an Ts'ui observed.

The association between K'un-lun and the place where the sun submerges into watery depths may also be implied in the proper names of several of the figures whom King Mu visits at K'un-lun. Most intriguing are Mo-chou 膜晝 and Ch'ien-shih 潛時.[100] The second component of the names, *chou* and *shih,* both contain the sun radical in their graphs: *chou* means "sunlight" or "day," and *shih* means "season."[101] The name Ch'ien-shih, taken literally, means "to bury, to sink, to hide the season" or "the season that is buried." Given that Ch'ien-shih entertains King Mu at Feather Mountain—the place where Archer I "shot" or "killed" the suns and where Kun submerges into the (celestial) abyss—his name seems to be an indirect reference to the spot where the sun completes one revolution and begins another. That King Mu arrived at Ch'ien-shih's land during the first month of autumn, the season traditionally associated with the sun's submerging into the watery depths, only deepens the cosmological nuances of the name.

The first graph of the other name—*mo*—is more problematic, for it does not appear in any other extant ancient text. In the *Mu T'ien-tzu chuan,* furthermore, the graph frequently appears with another graph meaning "to bow" (*pai* 拜), which has led commentators to interpret the compound as a form of ritualistic kneeling.[102] The rationale informing this understanding is for the most part anachronistic, however; a methodologically sounder, more fruitful interpretation can be derived from a philological analysis of other graphs belonging to the same word family.

Mo belongs to a family that derives from the word *mo/mu* (莫), the character for which is the pictograph of a sun surrounded by four grass radicals; the word means "late evening" and connotes the setting sun surrounded, submerged, or hidden. One meaning of this graph is "not" or "not have," implying the displacement, or absence, of something (that is, the sun). Other similar words belonging to this word family—"quiet," "settle," "silent," "cover," and "grave"—also evoke this sense of absence. These linguistic resonances provide a key for interpreting the term *mo* as it appears in the *Mu T'ien-tzu chuan.*

Thus, Mo-chou's name can be read literally as "absence or submersion of sunlight." The land with which King Mu enfeoffs him is located on the slope of the river, perhaps a reference to the Heavenly River and not, as most commentators assume, to the Yellow River. The Heavenly River, of course, runs between the northern winter and eastern vernal celestial quadrants.[103]

The names of three other figures whom King Mu visits, while not as explicitly referential, nonetheless contribute to the underlying symbolism of the *Mu T'ien-tzu chuan.* The second graph of the name Chü-lu 居盧, for example, phonetically and graphically resembles the word for madder-plant, the type of reed that figures significantly in the flood myths pertaining to both Nü-wa and Kun.[104] As we have seen, reeds were employed to control the reckless waters. The symbolic use of reeds seems deliberate: they are noted as part of the terrain of K'un-lun, with its numinous associations and God on High's command that King Mu go there. Indeed, the fact that reeds were an identifying feature of the place where Kun was transformed, links the plant to the process of transformation itself.

The name I-lü 剞閭, with its reference to a gate or threshold, also connotes a transformation that echoes the cosmological function of K'un-lun and its environs.[105] The "Yüan-yu" poem of the *Ch'u tz'u* refers to a location Wei-lü 微閭, the first character of which, suggests Ku Shih, may be a loan character for the character *I* if not variant of it.[106] The term is used in the poem as a location connected to the place where the sun sets in the evening, and it is glossed as being related to the door of Heaven, Ch'ang-ho 閶闔. Both names, then, are associated with the environs of K'un-lun, itself often described as Heaven's door. The frequent references to the asterisms situated between Scorpius and Sagittarius as gates and thresholds concretizes the metaphor: the sun must pass through Heaven's gate as it embarks on a new year's journey, and as such it effects transformation. King Mu's performance of a *chiao* sacrifice (those connected with Kun) within the environs of I-lü further strengthens the symbolism of the name.

The term Fu 鳧, "wild duck," part of another proper name in the *Mu T'ien-tzu chuan* (Wu-fu 無鳧), also bears on our concerns, as we see from its connotations in early Chinese poetic and ritual texts. In the poem "Wild Duck and Gull" (Fu i 鳧鷖) of the "Ta-ya" section of the *Shih ching,* the movement of the wild duck across a river is the major trope of this ritualized communication with ancestral spirits.[107] The rhetorical force of this trope derives in part from the duck's imputed route—from the sand, to the islet, to the confluence of two rivers, and finally to the other bank of the river—a journey that symbolizes both the successful transmission of the message to the ancestors and the attendant good fortune.

Moreover, according to one ancient dictionary, the ability to swim and stay afloat informed the use of the name Fu to designate the official responsible for production of musical instruments, especially percussion instruments such as bells.[108] No reason is offered for this etymology, but the connection between the duck and the instruments may derive from the linguistic resonance between the term for bells, *chung* 鍾 and the name of Ch'ung Mountain. If the mountain symbolizes the regenerative properties of the watery environs of the Heavenly Turtle quadrant, the duck's ability to stay afloat and reach the other side may, like the bell's ability to ring in "succession without ever breaking,"[109] symbolize the successful transformation from one world age to another or more mundanely from winter to spring. Bells in the text, we shall see, have significance beyond pointing to K'un-lun's cosmogonic function; they also shed light on King Mu's motivation to travel.

Thus, we see that King Mu's trip to K'un-lun, his association with Ho-po, and his meeting with Hsi-wang-mu, as represented in the *Mu T'ien-tzu chuan* are not historical narrative but a literary articulation of a symbolic journey. It is a tale of rebirth, of the emergence of a new identity. King Mu does more than go "west" he travels, rather, to the "depths of the abyss"—the locus standi of cosmic disaster—which must be measured again and again as the precessional clock moves on.[110] King Mu's trip to the place where the measures for redrawing the map of the heavens are stored can be read symbolically, as the next chapter illustrates, as a need to redefine the standards of his own world and thus reestablish political legitimacy.

FIVE

The Generation of Symbolism in the *Mu T'ien-tzu chuan*

I have argued in the foregoing discussion for the need to view K'un-lun, Ho-tsung, and Hsi-wang-mu as symbolic constructs, cryptic references to the transition between the primal forces of chaos and order. This conceptualization of K'un-lun, in particular, opens the way to interpreting the journey taken by King Mu not as a historical narrative but as a literary articulation of a symbolic passage to a new identity. The text, moreover, can also be read on another level, as reflecting the emergence of a collective identity: that of the Chou dynasty. That King Mu's journey is initiated by Heaven's command, for example, parallels the Chou view of the heavenly origins of their political legitimacy. King Mu's poetic monologues ponder his posthumous reputation. They reflect a "concept of eternity focused on an open-ended, generalized biological future, not on the past" that David Keightley argues is evident in the use and inscription of ritual bronzes. Coupled with the king's obsession to expand and redefine the dynasty's boundaries by placing markers wherever he goes, these two textual patterns seem to signal that underlying his effort to reconstruct the territory or "identity" of the dynasty is his desire to determine his personal posthumous reputation.

1

Why the Chou would need to redefine itself is connected, I believe, to the preoccupation of the dynasty's early rulers with maintaining legitimacy and preserving political control. Recent scholarship has shown that their political and cultural control over the inhabitants of the Yellow River basin and beyond was neither as broad nor stable as had been traditionally believed.[1] Paleographical and even some literary sources offer evidence of the Chou court in a state of constant military and political upheaval,[2] with the greatest threat coming from the warlike neighboring tribes, perceived by the Chou to be "barbarians." King Mu's own father, King Chao 昭, drowned with his entire army during a military and "metal" (*chin* 金) mining expedition against the southern Ch'u tribe, a catastrophe that had disastrous political ramifications.[3]

Given the Chou struggle for political and cultural supremacy, the paucity of references in the extant records to a recreational western journey undertaken by King Mu is not surprising. Ssu-ma Ch'ien makes no mention of it in the Chou Dynastic Annals,[4] but in the "Chao Family Genealogy" ("Chao shih-chia" 趙世家) speaks of King Mu's meeting with Hsi-wang-mu and his subsequent "pleasure such that he did not return" (*lo erh pu kuei* 樂而不歸).[5] Ku Chieh-kang has suggested that Ssu-ma Ch'ien considered the story of King Mu's trip to be spurious and thus did not deem it worthy of inclusion in the Dynastic Annals, relegating it instead to a less significant section (vis-à-vis the Chou Kings) of his historical work.[6] Extant paleographical evidence corroborates Ssu-ma Ch'ien's historical intuition: numerous inscriptions refer to military excursions and defensive battles during King Mu's reign, but none mention a long journey to the western regions of the empire.

Notwithstanding the lack of documentation in the historiographic materials, there appears to have been an oral version of the journey that served as the source for the relevant (albeit passing and oblique) references in the *Bamboo Annals*, the *Tso chuan*, and the *Chou-yü*.[7] These texts and the *Mu T'ien-tzu chuan* record many similar details, suggesting that all hark back to the same text or oral version.

The apparent discrepancy between the events recorded in the *Mu T'ien-tzu chuan* and those in various historical texts, as well as in the paleographical record, is of course the main source of the debate over the historicity of the former text, as outlined in chapter 1 above. In the following analysis, I propose that the events narrated in the *Mu T'ien-tzu chuan* be considered in terms of the generation of symbols, as discussed in chapter 3 above. The story of King Mu's travels, at least as reflected in the *Mu T'ien-tzu chuan*, actually constitutes a tale of a crisis, of its collective transcendence, of the symbols that emanated from it, and of the memory that preserved it.[8]

The complexity of the processes of recall involving "selection, formation, and re-formation of original experiences" that become "products of later alteration, structuring, selection, and improvement" is pertinent to our understanding of the particular representation of King Mu in the *Mu T'ien-tzu chuan*.[9] King Mu's martial vigor (as recounted in several texts and implictly reflected in the numerous bronze inscriptions recording military victories), coupled with his apparent longevity, surely contributed to the enduring memory of a strong if not successful ruler.[10] But notwithstanding our acknowledgment of the subjectivity of the rhetoric of the bronze inscriptions,[11] these factors do not adequately account for the journey as related in the *Mu T'ien-tzu chuan*.

We have already identified obstacles to being as the force underlying the generation of symbols, which, by their nature conceal the very event that produced them.[12] It is thus an essential element of our symbolic understanding of the *Mu T'ien-tzu chuan* that the details of King Chao's death were kept hidden by the Chou court. Indeed, discussion of the topic was prohibited.[13] The ambiguity surrounding both the details of the event itself and the manner in which the memory of it should be preserved created an environment that set in motion the dynamics of "symbolic-operation."[14]

King Chao's death constituted an obstacle to being for the entire Chou court. The court was surely concerned that it would have difficulty maintaining political legitimacy were news of the untimely and inauspicious event to leak out. Indeed, the situation must have been all the more critical given the efforts of the early Chou court to legitimize its authority following the overthrow of the Shang dynasty.[15] The Chou, it is known, invoked the concept of a Heavenly Mandate (*t'ien-ming* 天命) bestowed by Heaven on moral grounds to justify their actions.[16] David Pankenier has argued that the Heavenly Mandate refers to a remarkable conjunction of five planets that occurred in 1059 B.C. and that was believed to have political portent.[17] The Chou in turn invested this astronomical event with a moral charge and used it to justify their challenge to the previous dynasty's genealogical claim to rule. Surely, the precariousness of the Chou court, as highlighted by King Chao's ignominious death, was seen as a threat to their heavenly sanctioned rule.

That such anxiety plagued the court is vividly illustrated in a bronze inscription dating from the reign of King Mu (discussed above in chapter 1). The *Mao Pan kuei*, comprising 197 characters, is a linguistic portrait of the anxious state of the court when King Mu was still young enough to refer to the object of the vessel's inscription, Mao Kung 毛公 as "Father" (*fu*).[18] Edward Shaughnessy has recently advanced the theory, which I reject, that the *Mao Pan kuei* inscription records the commemoration of a military victory in the eastern part of China between the thirty-fifth and thirty-seventh years of King Mu's reign.[19] Rather, I contend, the different rhetorical styles reflected in the speech of King Mu and the Duke of Mao (Mao kung) sketch a context in which the king is younger than the latter and in which the latter was in a position to serve as mentor to the king.

The inscription opens with four different charges given by King Mu to three different people: Mao the Elder 伯 was charged with taking up the position and duties of a Duke Ch'eng of Kuo 虢成公; and an Elder of Wu 吳 and an Elder of Lü 呂 were each charged with following the just-promoted Duke of Mao on a military expedition against the eastern countries. From the nature of the responsibility invested in him, the Duke of Mao was obviously an experienced warrior. Moreover, as the great-grandson of King Wen, the duke must already have been a respected elder by the time King Mu reigned.[20] Indeed, the king's reference to the duke as "Father" in the charges given to the two lieutenants indicates a generational gap.

A similar linguistic example can be seen in certain phrases and words used in the duke's speech to report to "those above" (Heaven or the ancestors). He states, "The people are reckless . . . in darkening Heaven's Mandate [they] therefore lost it [i.e., transgressed]" (唯民亡 (拙) 昧天令，故亡).[21] He then continues, "It is only with pious thoughts of power that one can avoid transgressing [Heaven's Mandate]" (唯敬德，亡攸違). Not the usual formula for extolling the virtues of the king upon successful completion of a mission for him, the duke's comments contain an unstated message. His bald reference to the "loss" or "transgression" of "Heaven's Mandate" reflects the precariousness of the situation in which he and others found themselves. One may infer that this reflects the general sentiment of the Chou court because the Duke of Mao, the royal family, and the Chou court were so closely connected.

The Chou must have realized soon enough that they would have to demonstrate the legitimacy of their genealogical mandate if they expected to perpetuate their rule. The Chou needed to overcome this obstacle to being by redefining the Heavenly Mandate to support their claim to power. If we accept David Keightley's argument that bronze inscriptions from the late Western Chou evince a shift in early conceptions of eternity from backward memory to foward expectation,[22] the *Mu T'ien-tzu chuan* may be construed as a symbolic representation of the source of this conceptual shift—a conceptual shift needed by the Chou to transcend the obstacle to being posed by the ignominious death of King Chao. It is this desire for transformation that is represented in symbolic fashion by K'un-lun, Ho-tsung, and Hsi-wang-mu.

On a more personal level, the obstacle to being confronting the fifteen-year-old heir apparent, King Mu,[23] upon King Chao's death may have been compounded by ambiguities surrounding his paternity. An intriguing dialogue in the "Chou-yü" relates that King Mu's mother was "a woman of two virtues" and that her son King Mu was the offspring of an alliance other than the one with King Chao.[24] While the text presents the event in supranatural terms, stating that King Mu's mother was impregnated by the ghost of Yao's disgruntled son, Tan-chu 丹朱, the fantastic nature of the story should not vitiate the tradition that regards the paternity of King Mu as ambiguous.[25] Indeed, Tan Chu's status as a son whose hereditary right to rule was negated by his father's abdication in favor of Shun[26] makes him an appropriate "father" of King Mu, the representation of whom, as we shall see, symbolizes with the Chou need to justify their genealogical claim to rule. Whether in fact the symbolic discourse of the *Mu T'ien-tzu chuan* also derives from an obstacle to being posed by a concealed illegitimacy cannot be textually verified; nevertheless, King Mu's preoccupation with his inadequacies as king, and his concern for posterity are suggestive of psychic turmoil.

King Mu's situation could have been further exacerbated by certain astronomical events that were occurring during his reign. By far the most crucial and threatening was the imminent obsolescence of the Vermilion Bird constellation (*ch'ih-niao* 赤鳥) as a marker of the summer solstice. The Vermilion Bird would have begun to outlive its usefulness early in the first millennium B.C. According to the information preserved in the "Yao tien," which, scholars have calculated, accurately describes the astronomical realities of the eleventh century B.C., the Bird star (*Niao hsing* 鳥星) Alphard would appear on the meridian (*chung-hsing* 中星) at the vernal equinox, about 103 degrees.[27] With the sun 15–18 degrees below the horizon (astronomical twilight), the location 105 degrees or so would have been on the meridian at nightfall. Subsequently, however, because of precession, this location would have become less accurate as a marker of the vernal equinox (and hence the sun's location at summer solstice). Thus, by the time of the T'ai Ch'u 太初 calendrical reform of 104 B.C., it was at least 14–15 degrees out of position, forcing the adoption of new celestial mark points.[28] How precise the requirements of Western Chou astronomers were is not known, though they were probably rather flexible. After a shift of five or so degrees, though—as the situation was during King Mu's reign—the court astronomers had surely begun to notice.[29]

The obsolescence of the Vermilion Bird would have been considered particularly threatening because of its significant role in the myths of the conferral of Heaven's Mandate on the Chou. Allusions to a Red Crow in Chou texts have been interpreted by one scholar as an imagistic rendition of the Vermilion Bird quadrant, the site believed by the Chou to have heralded the transfer of Heaven's Mandate from the Shang to themselves.[30] Perceived as having effected the transition of the Chou people from one of many tribes serving the Shang to the tribe designated to rule China, the Red Crow was invested with great significance for the Chou's political (and cultural) identity. If this symbol no longer functioned as it had when the dynasty was founded, it surely would have aroused great fear, especially in light of such other ominous portents as King Chao's death.

My argument, then, is that the *Mu T'ien-tzu chuan* is the linguistic expression of a symbolic operation in which the account of King Mu's journey is a co-symbol of the crisis that posed an obstacle to being for the Chou. In other words, the need on the part of the Chou to suppress events related to King Chao's death propelled the creation of the text.[31] In both concealing and revealing the true object of its own discourse, symbols serve the public function of relieving anxiety over the ambiguity that led to their creation, even as they obscure the very source of the anxiety. The surface meaning of the *Mu T'ien-tzu chuan* reflects this public function.[32] Most pronounced are King Mu's actions to rectify a situation in which the established social machinery had broken down, to obliterate situations where "previously accepted norms [had] become problematic."[33] Endemic to most crisis situations, this breach of normalcy and the inability of precedent to affirm authority necessitates "collective adjustments."[34]

This portrayal of the way a group collectively overcomes crisis, or obstacles to being, accords with events that occurred during what other scholars have labeled a turning point in Western Chou history, namely, King Mu's reign.[35] It also suggests an explanation for several major motifs in the *Mu T'ien-tzu chuan*: the repeated provision of the etiology of place-names in terms of King Mu's actions; King Mu's penchant for leaving records; his establishment of new regulations; and his obvious concern with posterity.[36] "For collective adjustments to be made successfully, men must (re)define the situation [i.e., establish new etiologies for place-names] and develop behavioral patterns better suited to the new life conditions."[37] The representation of King Mu's actions in the *Mu T'ien-tzu chuan* reflects similar concerns.

Myths and legends in ancient China, according to Sarah Allan, served to mediate social contradictions.[38] Thus, the lore surrounding King Mu's frequent military expeditions, which must have figured in the oral account from which the narrative of *Mu T'ien-tzu chuan* derives, was most likely born of a social need. In this case King Chao's disgrace constitutes the founding silence of the *Mu T'ien-tzu chuan*. The text's representation of King Mu's desire to leave "no ground untouched by the tracks of his chariot"[39] reflects therefore a process of symbolization that both signifies and facilitates the Chou transcendence of that ignominious event. King Mu's journey is the symbol of the unstated need of the Chou court to reify its poltitical identity.[40]

In proposing that the *Mu T'ien-tzu chuan* is an articulation of a crisis that befell the historical King Mu and the Chou court, I am not arguing that the text is in any way a historical representation. It is, rather, a symbolic representation. The *literariness* of the text can be grasped in light of certain events that antedate the composition of the written text by more than five hundred years but that nonetheless serve as its unstated referent and inform its articulation. These are events that occurred during the middle of the Western Chou period.

I read the *Mu T'ien-tzu chuan* on two levels: on the level of symbol as signifier for the process of the text's own production; and on the level of the rhetorical devices used to *symbolize with* this process. More specifically, my interpretive framework builds on the premises that (1) the *Mu T'ien-tzu chuan* is a symbol for the obstacle to being that led to its own generation, namely, a crisis of legitimacy experienced by the Chou court after King Chao's startling death; and that (2) this symbolic level of reference is communicated through allusions to cosmogonic myths which themselves tacitly transmit information pertaining to their own generation. I understand these mythic allusions to be co-symbols that speak of the source of their founding silence, in other words, that *symbolize with* the King

Chao crisis. My reading of the text thus entails the detailed elucidation of these allusions.

2

To commence, we focus on an episode that serves as the *locus standi* of the symbolic discourse in the text—the episode in which God on High mandates that King Mu travel to K'un-lun. Herein lies the structural and rhetorical basis for symbolization in the *Mu T'ien-tzu chuan*.

God on High's command implicitly connects him with the processes that produced the *Mu T'ien-tzu chuan*. In transmitting God on High's message to King Mu, Ho-tsung, too, is involved in these same processes.[41] Ho-tsung is the mediator between human and spiritual expression, the latter often hidden and hardly accessible. Ho-tsung's narrative function is to mediate between two contradictory rhetorical objectives—concealing and revealing. Ho-tsung signals another concealed "origin" of the text by himself symbolizing symbolic articulation: he is a site of discursive interaction where the putative origins of the narrative (the stated discourse of travel) symbolize with a concealed discourse of another possible origin (the cosmogony of the early Chinese flood myths).

Ho-tsung's connection to the flood myths, especially those concerned with the actions of Kun or the Heavenly Turtle quadrant, provides the context for reading the "jagged edge" of Ho-tsung, the symbol, as a signpost pointing to the absent discourse of King Chao's drowning. His "residence" situated directly within the symbolic space of the Heavenly Turtle quadrant, Ho-tsung is related to the source of chaos, with its ominous watery associations determined by the Milky Way's apparent displacement of Corona Australis as the marker for the spring equinox. These, in turn, symbolize with the watery death of King Chao and with the sense of chaos that pervaded the Chou court in its wake. In transmitting God on High's command, Ho-tsung is also the "ferryman," the one who transports others across the symbolic space of the Milky Way, Heaven's River. Ho-tsung is the designated leader and intiator of the journey; only he can transport King Mu "safely across the water," an act his father failed to do. By fording the river, King Mu symbolically mitigates King Chao's disgrace by experiencing his own transformation and that of the Chou court. Moreover, Ho-tsung's connection to the three-legged turtle, itself a symbol of cosmogonic transformation from chaos into cosmos, further shores up his symbolic role as facilitator of King Mu's transformation.

Other elements of this episode, too, underline its function as a signifier for the process of symbolization that led to the production of the text. For example, God on High's command that King Mu travel to K'un-lun to view its treasures is preceded by an order that the king "diligently attend to the seasonal sacrifices to his ancestors." The juxtaposition of these orders links sacrifice to ancestors with travel to the watery chaos of K'un-lun—making a symbolic connection between the discourse of King Chao's death and that of flood myths.

The personal name of King Mu's guide, (Ho-tsung Po-)*yao*, suggests a similar thematic union. Early usage of the word *yao* exhibits a cluster of meanings that share connotations of destruction; the term also refers to one who died an untimely or premature death. These overlapping connotations reflect the different levels of symbolic discourse in the *Mu T'ien-tzu chuan*: connotations of destruction represent the manifest discourse of the cataclysmic flood myths, while connotations of untimely departures from earth represent the hidden discourse of King Chao's death.

We have seen how the Heavenly Turtle, because of its role as the site of the displacement of seasonal regularity and as the provider of the means to readjust, again and again, to the never-ending precessional clock, is vested with the cosmogonic function of rejuvenation. It is this role that proves to be the most significant for the symbolic message of the *Mu T'ien-tzu chuan*. King Mu's trip there is motivated by a need and desire to rejuvenate the Chou dynastic claim to legitimacy.

Given this objective, it is not surprising that the symbolic destination of King Mu—the Heavenly Turtle quadrant—figured importantly in the lore surrounding the establishment and legitimacy of Chou rule. An astronomical description in the *Chou-yü* identifies an observation of Halley's Comet in the Heavenly Turtle quadrant in late 1059 or early 1058 B.C. Taken to be another physical manifestation of Heaven's conferral of the mandate to rule China on King Wen of Chou,[42] it is a precedent for the symbolic relationship between the astronomical landscape of the Heavenly Turtle quadrant and the legitimization of Chou rule.[43] Since it is the astronomical discourse that constituted the unstated, hidden referent in the discourse of the flood myths, it is reasonable to read K'un-lun's literary function in the *Mu T'ien-tzu chuan* as also symbolizing with an unspeakable discourse, the one informing K'un-lun's symbolic function.

There is another tie between the Heavenly Turtle quadrant and notions of legitimacy. Not only does the quadrant figure significantly in the conceptualization of the conferral of the Heavenly Mandate on the Chou, but it also serves as the genealogical justification for Chou rule. The same passage of the *Chou-yü* states that Chou ancestry evolved from the Heavenly Turtle: the ancestry is traced back on the maternal side to Chuan Hsü, the ruler of the Heavenly Turtle celestial space.[44] K'un-lun, then, is the place where both heavenly and genealogical legitimacy coexist, conflated and transformed into a new form of legitimacy. Kun's regenerative cosmogonic role suggests more clearly K'un-lun's function within the *Mu T'ien-tzu chuan*: it mediates between discordant views of legitimacy in response to the obstacle to being confronting the Chou.

Indeed, the very first mention of the mountain in the *Mu T'ien-tzu chuan* alludes to this. God on High commands King Mu to go to Kun-lun's Ch'ung Mountain so as to "observe [and collect] the treasures there."[45] Denoting "riches," the term for "treasure," *pao* 寶 is also rich in political overtones: *pao* were the precious objects kept by a ruler as signs of his investiture by the spiritual powers of heaven. The chart—presumably the River Chart (*ho-t'u* 河圖)—presented to King Mu to aid him on his journey is one such example.[46] Several historical texts, such as the *Bamboo Annals* and the "Ku ming" 顧命 chapter of the *Shang shu*, refer to the River Chart as a "precious part of imperial regalia, indeed an artifact which sanctioned the political legitimacy of the one who possessed it."[47] Moreover, the River Chart was believed by some to be a "record of Heaven's Mandate, measuring the period ending and beginning, of preservation and extinction, of Heaven and Earth and of Kings."[48] The River Chart, as noted in chapter 1, is linked with the celestial world, a connection that fits in nicely with the interpretive frame suggested thus far.

According to Pankenier, "The original esoteric Diagrams were in fact depictions of the configuration of the five visible planets during a conjunction,"[49] the very type of astronomical event taken to be the manifestation of the Mandate of Heaven. One such conjunction, which occurred in 1576 B.C. at "the ford on the Celestial River between the regions of the sky occupied by the Dragon and Turtle asterisms,"[50] offers an astronomical interpretation of the "discovery" or "emergence" of the River Chart, namely, that it was carried on the back of a *dragon* or *turtle*, which emerged from a *river* (the Milky Way) and ascended onto *land* (the ford). The causal relation between God on High's command to King Mu to go to K'un-lun and the unveiling of the chart creates a powerful configuration of symbols pertaining to the establishment of a new form of legitimacy.[51]

There seems to have been some connection between the River Chart and the Yellow Steed (*ch'eng-huang* 乘黃) that Ho-tsung mounts "to lead the way for the Son of Heaven and exhaust the Western lands."[52] The *Mo tzu* refers to both and connects their appearance to the bestowal of the Heavenly Mandate on King Wen of the Chou: "[When] Heaven mandated King Wen to attack the Yin . . . the river put forth the Green Chart, the land put forth the Yellow Steed."[53] Ku Shih states that the Yellow Steed was necessary to "execute ancient rites" but does not explain why that was so. Nonetheless, the association of the Yellow Steed with the founding of the Chou dynasty yields an appropriately symbolic vehicle to "lead King Mu to exhaust the Western lands."[54]

King Mu's impulse to collect precious objects along the way is set in relief by K'un-lun's symbolic function as rejuvenator of political legitimacy. King Mu's decision to uproot two types of plants and "bring them back to China," for example, are tangible representations of the "treasures" King Mu seeks at K'un-lun to create a new standard of legitimacy.[55] Similar to the plant that Gilgamesh is given for "rejuvenation" (though not for obtaining immortality), the plants symbolize with the Chou wish to perpetuate their ruling line and reverse the process of erosion. The generative function of the plants is reflected in the modifier of and name of another plant, *chia* 嘉 and *tzu* 孳, which mean "growth" or "increase" and "breed," or "copulate," respectively. Moreover, the word *tzu* is a perfect homonym of *tzu* "son" (*tsiəg).[56] This archaic pronunciation, according to Boodberg, goes back to "*GSIG—*BSIG, an etymon probably meaning 'child,' 'progeny,' which very likely gave rise to the supposed surnames of the first dynasties [Ssu 姒, Tzu 子, Chi 姬]."[57] The dynastic associations of this etymon may explain why King Mu, *immediately upon* (*yü shih* 於是) hearing that the tree "is not afraid of snow or cold" (winter, that is, equals death) decides to bring it back to China.

The *Sonchus oleraceus* (*k'u* 苦) plant, which the king eats and which like the *tzu* tree blossoms in winter,[58] illuminates another symbolic level in the text. The plant's reedlike qualities (highlighted by the common association of the *k'u* with the *t'u* 荼 plant, as in the binome *k'u-t'u* 苦荼) connects influences outside the narrative context of the trip with the specific textual element that preserves the unspoken discourse while cryptically revealing its contents. A common ingredient in soups (*keng* 羹), that "participated . . . in the Chinese calendrical drama of the yearly regeneration of human existence," the *k'u* and similar plants "insured a successful passage from the unseasoned chaos time back to the seasoned order of civilization."[59] This same symbolism is implied in the connection between eating soups (out of *pien* 籩 and *tou* 豆 vessels) and performing the *chiao* sacrifice as recorded in the *Li chi*.[60] Ingesting the *k'u* plant thus mirrors the objectives of King Mu's trip: to visit and thus imbibe the regenerative nutrients of "chaos time" and thereby rejuvenate his authority and that of the Chou. That the *Shih ching* links these plants in the poem "Mien" 綿 to the origins of the Chou dynastic lineage heightens their symbolic significance in the *Mu T'ien-tzu chuan*.[61] The designation of the *k'u* plant, one of only two references to an actual food—among twenty-four general references to feasting in the text—highlights its role in the symbolic operation governing the organization of the text.[62]

Similar functions are carried out by references to the vast number of "jade implements" (*yü-ch'i* 玉器) hoarded by King Mu. Ch'en Feng-heng elaborates on the type of implements that would probably be of interest to the king, with the *kuei* 圭 and *chang* 璋 foremost among them.[63] As implements that were necessary for the ritual assertion of political legitimacy, they would certainly have appealed to King Mu. The hyperbolic enumeration of the number of implements collected by him—ten thousand pieces—underscores the sense of urgency motivating his activities.[64]

Moreover, the place where the jade was collected was allegedly called "the archives of [ancestral] documents" (*ts'e-fu* 冊府) by the "former kings," that is, King Mu's ancestors, yet another link to dynastic legitimacy.[65] Inherent in the term *ts'e*, frequently seen in oracle bone and bronze inscriptions with the meaning "to record," was a numinous sense of "to document and hence pledge, or fix in words" (and thus ensure the successful communication of the charges recorded).[66] In Chou bronze inscriptions, "pledging" often occurs in tandem with the king's mandating (*ming*) activities.[67] The "archives of ancestral documents" thus probably contained the collection of pledges written by the founders of the early Chou dynasty.

The guardian of these archives, which are located within the environs of Multitude Jade Mountain (*ch'ün-yü shan* 羣玉山), is a figure called Jung-ch'eng 容成氏, who appears in the *Chuang tzu* as a ruler in the peaceful, more perfect past.[68] The *Shih-pen* text identifies Jung-ch'eng (written as 庸) as the Yellow Emperor's annalist and the original historian, while the bamboo slip text entitled *Ten Questions* (*Shih wen* 十問) found in the Ma-wang-tui tomb depicts him as an expert in the bedchamber art of "governing *ch'i* and accumulating semen" (*chih ch'i t'uan ching* 治氣摶精).[69] Although these texts portray Jung-ch'eng in different roles, they concur in their exposition of the symbolic purpose of the narrative of King Mu's journey. For the *Chuang tzu*, Jung-ch'eng is emblematic of unfettered rule—and thus an ideal representative of the "chaos time" from which King Mu wishes to draw creative inspiration; the Jung-ch'eng of the *Shih pen* is endowed with the talent for writing history and is able to represent the legitimacy of his political actions. Finally, as an expert on "nourishing *yang*," Jung Ch'eng controls the means to generate descendants. Multitude Jade Mountain thus provides King Mu with the tools to demarcate a new foundation for Chou rule.

There are as well other objects among those collected by King Mu that point to the symbolic significance of his trip—the "jade blossom" (*yü-jung* 玉榮), the colored stones, especially the *lang-kan* 琅玕, and feathers.[70] All of these objects figure in myths about cosmologically significant personages, and their presence on K'un-lun is related to the actions of these figures. The jade blossom probably refers to the same object tossed onto Ch'ung Mountain by the Yellow Emperor, as recorded in the *Shan-hai-ching*.[71] The *lang-kan*, which Edward Schafer identifies as malachite, figures significantly in the treasures presented to Yü in the "Yü kung" narrative and may perhaps be viewed as a remnant of Yü's flood-controlling endeavors.[72] The feathers, of course, are related to Archer I's act of shooting the nine suns, as discussed above. The rectifying roles played by Yü, Archer I, and the Yellow Emperor in early myths underscore the symbolic function of K'un-lun in the *Mu T'ien-tzu chuan*: it is a repository of all of the precious objects—the imperial regalia—needed to reestablish Chou political control and affirm its legitimacy. That King Mu appropriated these objects surely has symbolic implications.

It is apparent that there is a relationship between King Mu's penchant for hoarding and the crisis of King Chao's death. Represented initially as various objects, the *pao* are transformed into a discourse of legitimization; the connection between them and Chou legitimacy is unmistakable. If one hears "treasure" (**pog*) as "to preserve" (*pao* 保/**pog*), one can infer the real purpose of King Mu's collecting—to preserve the legitimacy of his rule. This inference is reinforced by the consistent portrayal of treasures as objects that extend, or "preserve," the dynasty's ability to survive. That this homophonic polysemy would have been understood by Chinese of the first millennium B.C. is attested by the use of the word "treasure" in the formulaic rhetoric that often closes narrative inscriptions on bronze vessels: "May sons of sons, grandsons of grandsons eternally treasure/preserve [this commemorative] bronze vessel" (子子孫孫永寶用).[73] Because commemorating a specific event is an important function of the vessel, the formula reflects both the ritualistic function of the vessel and the commemorative function of the inscription. As "prayers for genealogical endurance," to use David Keightley's apt phrase,[74] the formula reveals the goal of preservation implicit in the use of the term "treasure."

That the notion of preservation informed the ritualistic function of the vessels, and thus must have informed the context in which the vessels were made, suggests that the use of the term *pao* in the *Mu T'ien-tzu chuan* also points symbolically to the context informing its own production. This it does. Not only does the symbolism of the treasures represent the political objective—to preserve his legitimacy—of King Mu's journey, but it also points to the source of this objective, for only by keeping secret (preserving) the details surrounding his father's death, can King Mu sustain his claim to political authority. Furthermore, the use of the term *pao* for "treasure" symbolizes through allosemy with the "metal" that motivated King Chao to southern expeditions and ultimately to his watery death.[75] King Mu's ongoing search for treasures can in turn be construed as a linguistic reference to the treasures that implicitly caused his father's death. Thus, God on High's command that King Mu seek the treasures of K'un-lun serves a dual purpose: it both establishes the ostensible premise of the narrative and provides the code to decipher the narrative's role in preserving the secret responsible for its own production.

In light of the symbolic reading thus far advanced, the reader cannot help but be struck by how the personal name used by God on High to address King Mu, Man 滿, also resonates with the secret encrypted within the narrative.[76] *Man*, "to be full and overflowing," is related phonetically and graphically to words meaning "to shut the eyes," "be deluded," and "ashamed"; it is also the phonetic for the word "grief."[77] These connotations echo in an uncanny way the shameful secret that lies beyond the text yet is also inscribed within it.

While it is hard to discern the original meaning of *man* from extant sources (its earliest usage in bronze inscriptions was also as a personal name and is thus devoid of a semantic context), the graphic resemblance between *man* and the term for "double" (*liang* 兩) has led some scholars to see in *man* a pictograph of a balance.[78] It is a sense of equilibrium intimately connected to the notion of duality: two objects of equal weight in balance with each other. The name *man* may thus be understood as tacitly pointing to King Mu's symbolic function—as representing the adjustments made by the Chou to effect an equilibrium between the crisis of King Chao's death and the preservation of their claim to legitimacy.

Support for this intepretation can be found in the equivocal nuances of the word *man* itself. *Man* is homophonous and graphically similar to the word *mien* 綿 (*mjian),[79] "to draw out," and thus resonates with the Chou's desire to perpetuate (draw out) their political rule. Indeed, the title of the poem "Mien" cited above, which describes the overabundance of melons in the ancient Chou territory, may be understood as a trope of extended posterity (*yu hsien hou* 有先後) wished for at the end of the poem.

Another voice contributing to the equivocalness of *man* derives from its homophonous connection with the term *mien* "to steep," or "to be immersed in" 湎 (*mjianx). *Mien* appears early in transmitted and paleographic texts as a verb with the object "liquor" (*chiu* 酒) and is understood as referring to the drunken debauchery of the Shang, which eventually lost them Heaven's Mandate.[80] The connotations of inundation, which evoke both the manner in which King Chao died and its relation to the precarious state of the Chou, are also stressed in another context, a poem entitled "Mien shui" 沔水 where the word *mien* is glossed as "full and overflowing" (*man*).[81] And these associations do not end there: the Mien River was another name for the Han River, the location of King Chao's death.[82] That the "Mien" poem is traditionally interpreted as a lament over the prevailing state of social disorder may derive from its use of the figure of inundating waters, which we have seen is connected to cosmogonic notions of chaos.[83] Disorder is also directly linked in the poem to the loss (or absence) of parents, a connection that touches at the symbolic level of the *Mu T'ien-tzu chuan*. The parallel use of the phrase, "Alas my . . ." (*chieh wo* 嗟我), followed by references to those who aid the king in administering control in both the *Shih ching* poem and in a poem sung by King Mu, situates the implicit chaos of the poem and the more explicit conflict of the *Mu T'ien-tzu chuan* within a political context. The configuration of meaning surrounding inundation and political chaos is shared by the personal name of King Mu and the word *mien*. We should, it seems, retrace the personal name of King Mu and its textual function to a founding silence that organizes hidden principles of coherence which reflect and render intelligible the tensions in the *Mu T'ien-tzu chuan*.

The homophony that links the specific destination of King Mu's trip, Ch'ung Mountain, to the word for bell is another example of how the text cryptically reveals its symbolism. In the previous chapter I suggested that music produced by bronze bells, with its "unending" (*pu chong*) resonance of sound, was believed by the Chou to capture the essence of endurance and was thus associated with regeneration. It is a conceptual link manifested linguistically through the phonetic connection between the terms "termination" (*tung/chung*) and bell (*chung*). I now submit that the name of K'un-lun's most important mountain, Ch'ung, through its linguistic connection to "bells," and the latter's associations with the cosmogonic concepts of "termination" and "perpetuation," symbolizes with a different sense of those terms: the *termination* of Heaven's function as sanctioner of Chou rule and the consequent *perpetuation* of Chou legitimacy. In transforming King Mu, Ch'ung Mountain also symbolizes with the shift in conceptions about eternity, which ultimately allowed the Chou to transcend the crisis of King Chao's death through its emphasis on the "open-ended . . . biological" or geneaological nature of legitimacy (as opposed to the Heavenly sanctioned aspect of legitimacy).[84]

I think that we can also read into the appellation Ch'ung Mountain a tacit reference to the role played by the text in effecting, symbolically, the Chou transcendence of the same crisis. The hidden manner in which the discourse referring to the King Chao crisis is presented in the *Mu T'ien-tzu chuan* reflects the manner in which the Chou "terminated," through prohibition, the same discourse; in the *Mu T'ien-tzu chuan*, the apparent termination of the King Chao discourse is represented cryptically within the detail of the surface level of the text, King Mu's journey. Yet while the surface level of discourse hides the content concealed within the crypts, it nonetheless perpetuates its dissemination. The concepts of termination and perpetuation implied by the name Ch'ung Mountain are thus a product of the symbolic operation generated by the obstacle to being posed by King Chao's death; at the same time the mountain symbolizes with the way in which the text employs its many discursive strategies of concealing and revealing, to communicate information about the crisis.

This reading of Ch'ung Mountain as a symbol of the Chou crisis is reinforced by allusions to music buried in the *Mu T'ien-tzu chuan*. In ancient China percussion music (mostly bell and drum) was ritualistic: via music one communicated with the ancestors, and via music the ruling families reified authority—two activities not unrelated. Bells in particular, fashioned out of bronze and able to maintain the "unalterable pitch standards" essential to the performance of liturgical music, were vested with political significance, for the "preservation of correct pitches was a strategic imperative for the state that relied on ancestral support for its continuity."[85] Allusions to music then symbolize the text's hidden interest in the political legitimacy of King Mu and the Chou. The fact that bells were often used to start a musical performance and that this was considered a "powerful act of just authority" further ties the musical references to the symbolic meaning of the king's journey.[86]

The urgency of his voyage is suggested by the specific type of music that he orders performed time and again—"Expansive Music (*kuang-yüeh* 廣樂)."[87] If he needs music to reestablish his authority, it must be new music, perhaps a new pitch, something that is different from the music associated with the declining Chou court. As described in the *Shih chi*, Expansive Music clearly has qualities that meet the king's needs. Having "nine beats and 10,000 forms of accompanying dances, it is not similar to the music of the three dynasties (Hsia, Shang and Chou) and is truly moving to the heart"[88] (廣樂九奏萬舞，不類三代之樂，其聲動心). Furthermore, the music was connected to the political fate of the state of Chin: it was the object of a dream dreamt by Chao Chien-tzu 趙簡子 (the prime minister of the state of Chin 晉). A part of Heaven's repertoire, Expansive Music is invested with invigorating powers; it has a remedial effect on Chien-tzu, the sick patient who dreamt of hearing it, and it has an association with the *nine* types of heavenly music appropriated by Ch'i 啟, the son of the Great Yü.[89]

The fact of the rapport between the number nine and the underlying cosmogonic intentions of the Yü myths is suggestive of similar lines of interpretation for the number nine in related myths such as those of Ch'i. It was via the number nine that details of the Yü myths were linked to astronomy, which in turn invested the myths with cosmogonic significance. To recapitulate, the number nine—because it referred to the nine stars of the Cerulean Dragon's tail—signified the area surrounding the fork in the Milky Way and thus symbolized the transformative energies associated with the area between Scorpius and Sagittarius. The circumstances surrounding Ch'i's birth vividly anchor his emergence in the cosmogonic context of the Yü myths: Lady T'u gave birth to Ch'i after she had turned to stone in embarrassment over seeing Yü turn into a turtle (which he did so that he could pass through 以通 Hsüan-yüan).[90] In another version Lady T'u looks at Yü's transformed state because she mistakenly took the sound of Yü's pounding on a stone for that of a drum.[91] As the "product" of Yü's passing through the Hsüan-yüan, and as the result of (what was perceived as) the commencement of a musical performance, Ch'i represents a new beginning that like spring also starts after the the Cerulean Dragon passes through the Heavenly Turtle quadrant.[92]

Just what type of beginning Ch'i represents is intimated by several other details in the myths, namely, his appropriation of Heaven's Nine Songs (*Chiu ko* 九歌) and his subsequent usurpation of powers that had supposedly been "given" by Yü to his "minister," Po Yi 伯益.[93] Frequently credited with the creation of hereditary rule, Ch'i—whose name literally means "initiator"—more likely symbolizes the demarcation of a new crossroads of the ecliptic and equator. Once precession obliterated the Fire Star's function as a marker of the spring equinox, a new constellation took on that role. Just what constellation Ch'i may represent is difficult to ascertain, but in fact that is not the most important aspect of the myth. Rather, the emphasis on Ch'i's hereditary connection to Yü speaks to a need to represent the new seasonal marker as an extension—perpetuation—of the original one, Yü. (I suggest in chapter 2 above that the three asterisms Horn, Neck, and Roof represent accretions to the "original" Dragon constellation composed of Room, Heart, and Tail; these were added as precession continued to render obsolete the seasonal function of each preceding asterism). Anne Birrell draws attention to the implicit causality of these interrelated mythic elements in linking the motif of Yü's lameness, which I have suggested was related to the increasingly "late" appearance of the Fire Star at the vernal equinox, to Yü's error in pounding stone. Thus, (1) Yü's lameness is caused by his diminishing capacity to serve as a seasonal marker; (2) the lameness causes him to misstep on to a drum; (3) this in turn causes the impregnation of Lady T'u, which results in the "birth" of Ch'i.[94] Ch'i's appropriation of Heaven's Nine Songs can be construed as a symbolic rendition of the spatial connection between Ch'i's astronomical referent and the cosmogonically significant area of Yü's tail, which consists of nine stars. The songs—so ritually and politically important in ancient China—represent the new measures that must be extracted from this area, the depths of the cosmos, in order to reestablish a legitimate claim to rule. That Lady T'u gives birth to Ch'i on Sung Mountain, which is phonetically related to Ch'ung Mountain, and that the latter is homophonous with "bell" futher underscore the interconnectedness of these various myths.

Allusions to Ch'i, a true "role model," abound in the *Mu T'ien-tzu chuan*. Ch'i functions in the text both as a figured image of the genealogical imperative of political legitimacy and as a "way-opener" who perpetuated his rule by obtaining the necessary new measures. In addition to the often seen identification of Expansive Music as the music obtained by Ch'i, some of the places King Mu visits tacitly allude to the myth of Ch'i. For example, one of the first of these is Music Wilds (樂野), a place connected in the *Shan-hai-ching* to Ch'i's appropriation of nine modes of Heavenly Music.[95] The mention of a Music Capital (樂都) evokes similar images. Finally, King Mu visits the cave where Ch'i allegedly "lived."[96] It follows from my reading of the myth of Ch'i that this visit marks King Mu's entrance into the symbolic space of cosmogony, that is, origins.

There is a historical corollary to my interpretation in the "Chou-yü" passage cited above; it presents astronomical facts pertinent to the establishment of the Chou dynasty. "[A] musicological exposition of the derivation of the seven notes of the heptatonic scale and of divination by tonal resonances during the conquest campaign" of King Wu 武王, this passage "stress[es] the traditional associations between the indicated asterisms and the ancestry of the royal [C]hou line, certain numerological correspondences which define the relationship between the celestial events and their terrestrial resonances, and the seven notes which traditionally comprised the gamut or 'key' of [C]hou."[97] Joseph Needham concludes that this passage reflects the consequences of a "period of struggle between two different forms of music, an earlier one which used five regular tones, and a later one in which two auxiliary notes or semitones were used."[98] King Mu's search for a new melody thus mirrors the legitimizing activities engaged in by the early Chou; the astronomical basis of the acoustical science revealed in the "Chou-yü" passage and its relevance to issues of political legitimacy is also reflected in the *Mu T'ien-tzu chuan*.

King Mu's trip to K'un-lun is tantamount to his returning to the political and genealogical origins of the Chou dynasty. The literary conceit of undertaking a journey to "'return' and communicate with the [dynasty's] origin[s]" very much accords with Western Chou ritual objectives and even with the architectural design of their temples.[99] Wu Hung has vividly described Western Chou temples, with their multiple corridors creating a discontinuity in space, such that anyone entering must cross layers of barriers before reaching the inner chamber, where the rituals were performed. This design fostered a sense of deep secrecy that "is gradually heightened as we enter the temple yard and penetrate layers of halls leading to the shrine of the founder of the clan . . . [a] mythical world, the end of our journey where we would encounter the Origin."[100] Thus, the temple structure organizes the reenactment of the drama of the Chou's origins in a manner that parallels the symbolic mode of discourse of the *Mu T'ien-tzu chuan*. Consider Wu Hung's comment that "the visual forms [of the temple] 'conceal' the secret. These forms led people closer and closer to the center of the secret but at the same time created layers of barriers to resist such an effort. Even at the end of the ritual process, people found not a concrete image of the ancestral deity but the means to communicate with this invisible being."[101] The visual complex thus "becomes a metaphor of the ritual itself: to go back to their Origin."[102] We see that the temple, too, is a symbolic device, concealing and revealing at one and the same time.

The symbolic function of temple boundaries—to distance people from the hidden discourse of ritual—is reflected in the *Mu T'ien-tzu chuan* through the nuanced discourse of King Mu's journey. It emphasizes boundaries as a marker for the progress of the journey, and hence of the narrative, just as the Chou established discursive boundaries around the topic of King Chao's death—the very act that generated the text's production. Boundaries in the text, like their counterparts, the walls of Western Chou temples, are intended to preserve secrets.[103]

The phrase "to arrive at" (*chih yü* 至於), often repeated in the *Mu T'ien-tzu chuan*, alludes to the conceit of boundary. Ku Shih notes in his commentary that the phrase denotes having just arrived *at the border* of an area, an indication that the area has not yet been entered.[104] This repetition is meant to foreground King Mu's *transformation* of the boundaries; and indeed, the act of crossing over, expanding, and redefining boundaries is a major motif of the *Mu T'ien-tzu chuan*. The king enfeoffs five people and erects four monuments demarcating various borders.[105] Furthermore, places are frequently renamed and newly demarcated.[106] For the narrative, personal identity is attendant on the establishment of new boundaries. On the symbolic level, the text's own literary identity derives from and represents the boundary established by the Chou to redefine and render obsolete any discourse over the King Chao crisis.[107]

The text simultaneously reveals and conceals this discourse by its narratological deployment of a discursive boundary that connects yet also separates discourses pertaining to the King Chao crisis. Nowhere is this more evident than in the actual discourse of boundary itself in the *Mu T'ien-tzu chuan*, it portrays King Mu's trip in terms of how much or what type of space he crosses or occupies. These spatial markers advance the surface narrative even as they camouflage those textual elements that silently reveal the latent discourse.

Frequent references to river boundaries separate the symbolic and surface levels of the text. We have noted above that the notion of water as a boundary is connected to cosmogonic notions of destruction and creation, a sense derived from the use of water imagery to communicate a hidden astronomical discourse. River boundaries similarly suggest the cosmogonic discourse of the flood myths. And just as the myths derive from a discourse of astronomy while also hiding that discourse, so too do the references to river boundaries in the *Mu T'ien-tzu chuan* divide the literal meaning of the text from the symbolic one. So too, the use of cosmogonic symbols relating to destruction and re-creation signals a split in the narrative. Thus can this tale be construed as a symbol of the text's origins: it tells of how the text emerged from the establishment of boundaries that demarcated different strata of discourse concerning King Chao's drowning.

The text's use of the verbs "to exhaust," "to break off" (*chüeh* 絕), and "to ford," "to repair" (*chi* 濟) to narrate how King Mu traverses rivers also conveys the symbolic discourse. *Chüeh* often appears in early texts in contexts of disruption, such as the severance (*chüeh*) of ties between Heaven and Earth or in cutting short one's life (*chüeh ming* 命). The *Erh ya* defines *chüeh* in terms of uncontrolled water, stating that when "right [running water] flows *chüeh*-like (that is, it cuts off the flow), this is called disorder (正絕流曰亂)."[108] *Chüeh* is used verbally in the *Shih ching*, as it is in the *Mu T'ien-tzu chuan*, to mean surviving some mortal danger. These associations of being cut off, of termination, silently communicate the symbolic referent of the term: to the premature demise of King

Chao as he crossed a river and to the Chou fear of being cut off from Heaven as a result of this disaster, as well as to the means of overcoming the potentially fatal danger posed by the king's death. In King Mu's "exhaustion" of rivers and other spaces we see the Chou's ability to exterminate or cut off discourse about King Chao and thus transcend the threat to their political survival.

These nuances of transcendence seen in the references to river crossings are also intimated by the use of the second term mentioned above to narrate King Mu's fording of waters: *chi*. The possibility that the use of this term resonates with the trope of crossing rivers so prominent in the *Book of Changes* suggests a cosmogonic referent. Part of the name of the last two hexagrams in the transmitted version of the *Book of Changes, chi* may refer to the astronomical movements of the Cerulean Dragon as it emerges to demarcate the vernal equinox: it crosses the Heavenly River. King Mu's successful crossing of the rivers, as denoted by the term *chi* thus portends the Chou's transcendence of his father's death.[109] Similar connotations of success seem to inform the use of *chi* to mean "to rescue," which implies the transformation of a dangerous state of affairs into one of good fortune.[110]

K'un-lun Mountain—cosmological boundary and marker of transformation in the discourse of flood myths that it is—likewise symbolizes in the *Mu T'ien-tzu chuan* the means of transcending the crisis that generated the text's production. As a divide between order and chaos, K'un-lun is a temporal border as well as a spatial border. Connected with the celestial realm, where time is the dominant form of measure,[111] it seems to privilege time over space in the text. Already in the first *chüan* God on High invokes time ("pay attention to executing in a timely manner your ancestral sacrifices") in his command to King Mu to go to K'un-lun; timeliness then is the *sine qua non* of the journey.

The annalistic format, with its sense of organization and control over the (representation of the) process of the journey, also suggests the "privileged" position of time. But time is also a source of anxiety, as witnessed by the king's preoccupation with his (posthumous) fate and the motivations for his desire to travel.[112]

K'un-lun functions in the *Mu T'ien-tzu chuan* to resolve this tension. Space, or more specifically, barbarian space, is represented not only as a geographical entity but also as a temporal (chronological) one that is "younger" and "less civilized."[113] King Mu's incorporation of barbarian space (and customs) into the "older" establishment thus implies rejuvenation.[114] Consequently, the power of time as a measure of human mortality and as the source of King Mu's anxiety is mitigated by the king's ability to conquer space.[115] Like K'un-lun Mountain itself, King Mu *separates* temporal and spatial realities so that he can *transform* them. His actions symbolize in turn with the Chou efforts to transcend the crisis resulting from the death of their king. The *Mu T'ien-tzu chuan* recounts how the bewildering chaos of King Chao's death was *transformed* into order by creating a new set of discursive boundaries within which to articulate the experience. The new boundaries conceal a discourse even as they enable access to a different discourse. Embodying this new discursive landscape is the symbolic capital that K'un-lun possesses in the *Mu t'ien-tzu chuan*: the mountain demarcates the place where Kun, the symbol of blockage, died and was made inaccessible, but it is also a starting point for Yü, who creates the new (watery) boundaries within which the discourse of flood myth is expressed.

The text's representation of two distinct forms of organizing formal and rhetorical patterns—as either the calendar or as cosmogonic myths—can also be read as referring to a hidden discourse of two types of legitimacy. The form of the annal represents the genealogical claim to rule, because whenever a new dynasty emerged in ancient China, it invented a new calendar to serve as a symbol of political authority by establishing a new chronology.[116] The cosmological myths represent, by contrast, the Heavenly Mandate as source of legitimacy because of the association with astronomical phenomena. As symbols of transformation, moreover, the myths are a metaphor for Heaven's role in determining who may or may not rule.

The intermingling of the cosmological myths with the annalistic form—and their discordant views of legitimacy—reflects the contradictions implicit in these two views, one based on an external source, Heaven, and one based on human agency (in the production of descendants), genealogy. This conflict, however obscured, informs the particular representation of experience in the *Mu T'ien-tzu chuan.*

The two narrative forms operate to very different ends. Whereas the annal's linear representation of events organizes the narrative to elucidate important relationships among the events and people, the cosmological myths serve to convey nuances of King Mu's character and of the narrative—and thus symbolically reveal the source of the motivation underlying the king's desire to travel and the emergence of an identity.

Repeatedly highlighted in the king's speech is his pervasive sense of self-doubt. The relevance of this self-doubt to the underlying symbolic themes of the narrative is brought to the fore through references, both direct and indirect, to the textual fragments of myths that tacitly propel the narrative. For example, the king's expression of self-doubt follows almost immediately after God on High commands him to go to K'un-lun. About to embark on his journey, he breaks into a poetic lament:

> Alas, I the one man am not complete in virtue; but rather indulge myself in pleasure; will the later generations also make me account for my mistakes?[117]
> 於乎！予一人不盈于德，
> 而辨于樂，後世亦追數吾過乎？

The tension in this juxtaposition gives narrative voice to the dilemma of reconciling the two distinct concepts of legitimacy: the Heavenly Mandate and the genealogical. The use of the term "complete" (*ying*), a synonym for King Mu's personal name, Man, meaning "full," to describe his faults, situates his feelings of guilt squarely within the context of King Chao's demise.[118] So, too, is the rhetorical intent of the adverb "also" (*yi*) clear: King Mu fears that he, like his father, will be perceived negatively by posterity.

A similar tension is evinced in the allusion to Father Mou of Chai's recitation of the "Hao-t'ien" poem of the "Chou-sung" section of the *Shih ching* to curb King Mu's enthusiasm for excursions, and King Mu's response with the poem "Nan-shan yu t'ai." These poems reflect the different approaches to the problem of legitimacy symbolized by the *Mu T'ien-tzu chuan.*[119] The "Hao-t'ien" poem invokes precedent, Heaven's manifestation of its Mandate (*yu ch'eng ming* 有成命), and extolls the virtues of King Ch'eng 成王, as a model for King Mu. King Mu takes a completely different tack in poetic response, substituting jubilance for solemnity and genealogy for Heaven: the first five strophes close with prayers for the long life and lasting reputation of the *chün-tzu* 君子, "the ruler" who is the "founding rock for the many tribes" (邦家之基); the last strophe ends with the deontic expression, "Preserve (*pao*) and nurture your descendants." King Mu, like the late Western Chou, looks to the open-ended, biological future. This was the choice made by the Chou as they struggled to synthesize two implictly contradictory claims of legitimacy. The reference to the poems, like reference to cosmogonic myths, is a signal to read the narration of his journey as two "texts" in dialogue, mutually responding to and informing one another.[120]

The poem that King Mu sings at Yellow Bamboo in the fifth *chüan*, which on the basis of contextual clues I suggest may have been displaced from the first *chüan*,[121] is another instance in which King Mu's experience refracts two different levels of discourse. Lamenting the suffering of his freezing retinue, King Mu cries:

> I go to Yellow Bamboo, [my men] suffer obstacles of extreme cold;
> God on High has arranged the nine paths
> Alas, my marquises, hundred officials, and ministers;
> Let us make august our populace,
> Mornings and evenings we should not forget.
> I go to Yellow Bamboo, [my men] suffer obstacles of extreme cold;
> God on High has arranged the nine paths
> Alas, my marquises, hundred officials, and ministers;
> Let us make august our populace,
> Morning and evenings [we shall work] without limit.
> There is a young one, the owl
> Fluttering, fluttering, it flies
> Alas, my marquises, [hundred officials, and ministers]
> [Let us make august our populace]
> [Morning and evening] these objectives should not be altered
> As for those living amidst revelry, they are few indeed
> [Such a lifestyle] is not as worthy as altering my objectives
> [to accord with Heaven] above
> Use ritual and music as a standard for my people.

> 我徂黃竹， 負閟寒
> 帝收九行
> 嗟我公侯百辟冢卿
> 皇我萬民
> 旦夕勿忘
> 我徂黃竹， 負閟寒
> 帝收九行
> 嗟我公侯百辟冢卿
> 皇我萬民
> 旦夕勿窮
> 有皎者鴼
> 翩翩其飛

嗟我公候
勿則遷
居樂甚寡
不如遷上禮樂其民

The king concludes, "I alone am excessive; I do not make august my populace," 天子曰余一人則淫不皇萬民 whereupon "the King ascended Yellow Bamboo, and dreamed about Archer I shooting T'u Mountain."[122]

This is a symbolic matrix of several allusions that sheds light on the nature of King Mu's anxiety. First, the unexpected cold weather and the severity of its consequences hint of the political dangers faced by the Chou court, a danger also implied in the allusion to the young owl's flight. Associated with ominous events, the owl was considered "an adversary of the sun—a predatory demon who devours light . . . [it was] unfilial, and outside the normal social order."[123] Moreover, the owl's destructive forces were even believed to have an adverse affect on calendrical order and hence undermine the political authority of the ruling family. According to the *Chou-li*, so insidious was this threat that there were officials whose primary job it was to destroy owls' nests and force them to move elsewhere.[124] The connection between the owl and political instability is also drawn in early Chinese poetry, especially poetry about strife in the early Chou court.[125]

Yet in spite of these ominous associations, or perhaps because of them, the owl was also considered a protective healing agent against the very disasters it was believed to portend. Girardot states that such "structural ambiguity" was common to "chaos objects" that were consumed as a prophylactic to insure safe passage through "nodal seasonal moments" (such as the solstice) or "chaos time."[126] Thus, King Mu's sighting of the young owl may also adumbrate the potential for transcending the political crisis facing him by returning to the original chaos time symbolized by K'un-lun. The possibility of change, implied in the verb "to alter" (*ch'ien*), which occurs twice in the poem, and King Mu's invocation of God on High's arrangement of the nine provinces—itself an allusion to that portion of the sky between Scorpius and Sagittarius—emerge as twin facets of the same symbolic purpose of the king's trip. The combination reflects at once the fear of losing Heaven's mandate (Heaven "altering" its mandate to the Chou) and the Chou's response of "altering," by relocating, the focus of imperial discourse.

Immediately after composing the poem, King Mu has a dream

that recapitulates the same intentions. If dreams in traditional China were considered "to anticipate crucial events in the fortunes of certain personalities,"[127] Archer I's actions may be understood as an allusion to the transcendence King Mu is seeking in his travels. Based on a reading of Archer I's "rectifying" role in other myths, his appearance here would seem to signal a catastrophe that threatens the life of a dynasty. T'u Mountain, by contrast, evokes the regenerative associations of the space between Scorpius and Sagittarius (revealed through the sexual associations of Yü's wife, Lady T'u). Because T'u Mountain is also the site where Yü gathered all of the (feudal) lords for a meeting, presumably to solidify their fealty, Archer I's actions may perhaps be more specifically concerned with replacing Yü's venerated but inappropriate basis for dynastic power (that is, astronomical function) with a new one, such as was implied in the Ch'i myths.[128] The passing references in at least two sources to a similar gathering organized by King Mu suggests that King Mu identified with the successor of Yü, Ch'i.[129] Moreover, because Ch'i also represents the genealogical claim to legitimacy, King Mu's dream can be interpreted as representing his desire to destroy the old and re-create a new dynastic image, based primarily on genealogy.

King Mu re-creates his political image by returning to the secret source of dynastic legitimacy, the place symbolically tied to the regeneration of the cosmos. The purpose of this trip is thus not to expand the empire by conquest; rather, it is to travel *back* to his ancestors' origins. The expression "fluttering, fluttering" is suggestive of this; it is a common formula in the *Shi ching*, identified by C. H. Wang as a motif of the theme of the "bird of the Filial Return."[130]

The polysemous representation of both the narrative events (the journey) *and* the symbolic discourse encrypted within it in the *Mu T'ien-tzu chuan* sheds light on the inner experience of King Mu. The cosmological myths, that is, have a narrative function in the text, setting in relief the redefining of space on the surface level of the narrative and the tension underlying the discordant views of legitimacy on the symbolic level. Many of the place-names for the spaces transformed by King Mu have referents in the astronomical discourse of the flood myths. The duplicity implicit in this articulation signals that his actions and motives are not totally controlled by the temporal boundaries established by the annal form of the narrative. They lie deep within the symbolic realm of representation and his experience should be read on two levels. A discourse itself generated by a perpetual cosymbolizing of disparate narrative elements, the flood myths expand the historically delimiting boundaries of (narrative) representation. It is the particularity of King Mu's experience and not merely an abstract conceptual framework that makes sense of the narrative.

One can view the reworking the annal genre as analogous in structure to the Chou's modification of the old conceptual framework upon which the dynasty established its claim to rule. Pieces of the old system serve a different function in the new system. Thus, whereas Heaven is the source of legitimacy in the old framework, it is the basis of political perpetuation in the new one. As the repository of symbols of legitimacy, Heaven, it is implied, moreover, can be drawn upon for individual purposes as is represented by the narration of King Mu's actions. And dynastic order is redefined in terms of individual human agency—the underlying motivation of individuals and the role of individuals in social transformation. This mode of representation in the *Mu T'ien-tzu chuan* reveals a notion of self as a product of conflict.

K'un-lun's symbolic function in this regard reifies the individualistic nuances that characterize King Mu's reconstruction of his identity and palliates the tension implicit in the process. This literary effect is apparent in the response given to King Mu's first lament (after receiving God on High's mandate) by one of his retainers:

> That which the later generations most desire is that you do not lose sight of Heaven's constancy . . . [I]t is for this reason that there are seasons . . . [I]f you share the benefits [of your trip] with the people, your descendants will preserve them as constants.[131]
> 後世所望，無失天常 . . . 故
> 有時，與民共利，世以為常也

King Mu is assured that if he goes to K'un-lun he will no longer be in danger of displacing Heaven's regularity and hence destroying the constancy of later generations. The Heavenly Mandate, represented by the allusion to Heaven's constancy, can coexist with genealogical law (later generations) but only if both are anchored in the specific context of King Mu's journey to K'un-lun and valorized according to his particular experience.

A reference later in the text to the origins of Chou ancestral power over the realm of K'un-lun's Ch'ung Mountain reiterates the importance of revalorizing universal concepts in terms of personal experience.[132] The reference is presented as supplemental information and is preceded by the word *yüeh,* 曰 "it is said," which marks it as knowledge of oral or public provenance.[133] The literary effect of this rhetorical device is similar to the qualifications regarding the provenance of information offered by Thucydides.[134] Provided ostensibly by an implied omniscient narrator, the reference sheds light on an important dynamic of King Mu's fictional identity: a conflation of the rigidly distinct categories of private and public. Far from locating King Mu's experience within the realm of general historical truths, the narrator becomes the instrument for articulating King Mu's own individuality or subjectivity.[135] It is King Mu's personal "history" that informs and shapes the supplemental information—often of a "historical" nature—and not the other way around. The construction of an identity and the literary representation of this identity both derive from this process. The frequency with which the term *yüeh* is used attests to the importance of its function—at least thirty times in the text.[136]

The reference to the Chou ancestors in the above instance explains the connection between the Red Crow tribe and the Chou. We have already seen how allusions to a Red Crow in Chou texts have been interpreted as an imagistic rendition of an astronomical location, the Vermilion Bird quadrant, which itself was invested with the significance of demarcating the Chou's political (and cultural) identity. While the Red Crow does not belong in the Heavenly Turtle quadrant, its symbolic function nevertheless places it perfectly within the mythological geography of K'un-lun, the place where the treasures for legitimizing a political identity are found.[137]

The celebrated meeting between King Mu and Hsi-wang-mu is yet another example of how mythical elements in the *Mu T'ien-tzu chuan* communicate the symbolic context of King Mu's trip and in turn the reconstruction of King Mu's/Chou identity. As narrated in the *Mu T'ien-tzu chuan*:

> On the auspicious day *chia-tzu* (day 1 of the cycle), the Son of Heaven hosted Hsi-wang-mu, whence he upheld a black jade *kuei* and a white jade *pi* tablet to make an appearance before Hsi-wang-mu;[138] he grandly presented one hundred complete sets of embroidered brocade. Hsi-wang-mu bowed repeatedly and accepted them. . . . [O]n day *yi-ch'ou* (day 2) the Son of Heaven feasted Hsi-wang-mu atop Blue-gem Pool.[139] Hsi-wang-mu composed a song for the Son of Heaven which said:

White clouds in the sky,
Mountains and hills protrude through them.
The road [you have taken/are taking] is truly long,
Mountains and streams divide it
In sending you without death
Would that you are able to return here.

The Son of Heaven responded saying:

I return to the eastern lands,
To harmoniously order the various kingdoms.
[When] the populace is peaceful and equally [cared for],
I will be willing to see you.
[When the time elapsed since this meeting is]
approaching three years,
I will return to your wilds.[140]

吉日甲子天子賓于西王母乃執玄圭白壁以見西王母。好獻錦組百純　組三百純，西王母再拜受之。乙丑天子觴西王母于瑤池之上。西王母為天子謠曰：

白雲在天
山陵自出
道里悠遠
山川間之
將子無死
尚能復來

天子答之曰：

予歸東土
和治諸夏
萬民平均
吾顧見女
比及三年
將復爾野

Representing the apotheosis of King Mu's transforming potential, the exchange between Hsi-wang-mu and King Mu augurs the realization of the latter's objectives. As the commentator T'an Ts'ui points out, even the day on which King Mu visits Hsi-wang-mu, *chia-tzu*, symbolizes a new beginning.[141] The jade tablets presented by the King to Hsi-wang-mu likewise carry connotations of inauguration concomitant with ceremonies of political investiture. That the black *kuei* was bestowed upon Yü by God on High in commemoration of his "reestablishing" the "boundaries" of the nine provinces further links the symbolism of the jade implement to the promulgation of new measures.[142] King Mu's feasting of Hsi-wang-mu is tantamount to his performing an ancestral sacrifice: he presents gifts to her in hopes of benefiting from her symbolic function as rejuvenator of cosmic cycles. T'an Ts'ui likened their exchange to that between the Yellow Emperor and the Black Maiden when the latter presented the manifold cosmic measures to the former.[143]

The initiatory tenor of the scene is also captured in the poems exchanged by King Mu and Hsi-wang-mu. Images of peaks breaking through clouds and rivers and mountain ranges partitioning land allude to nature in a continual process of change; sky and road are not static but are a threshold that simultaneously connects and divides different dimensions of space. The similarity between Hsi-wang-mu's poetic images and the pattern of organization that informs the narrative strategies in the *Mu T'ien-tzu chuan* is instructive: it connects Hsi-wang-mu's function in the text with the Chou's transcendence of the King Chao crisis. Hsi-wang-mu hints at the symbolic nature of her role, stating that she will "send [King Mu] off without death," such that he "would be able to return." The phrase "without death," which appeared with some frequency on bronze inscriptions cast during the eighth century B.C., can refer literally to immortality, but more probably it referred figuratively to the notion of continuing life through one's descendant. Hsi-wang-mu, in other words, grants King Mu unending posterity. Indeed, that the verb used to narrate Hsi-wang-mu's composition of the poem *yao* 謠 is also etymologically related to the word for "omen" (*chou* 繇) suggests that her poem may be an oracle portending King Mu's rejuvenation and the perpetuation of his dynasty.[144]

King Mu is aware of the significance of Hsi-wang-mu's gift: with it he will "harmoniously order the various kingdoms." The verb "to order" (*chih*) is rich with symbolic significance. First, it is used to describe Yü's control of the floodwaters, by digging canals and delimiting new boundaries. By implication, King Mu must drain the "watery" chaos brought on by King Chao's drowning, and he must redefine the parameters of his own political legitimacy. Etymologically, the word is related, through the etymon *i* 以/台, to the words "beginning," "fetus," and "bequeath" and "transmit" (to later generations) such as *shih* 始, *t'ai* 胎, *i* 貽, and *i* 詒. The former two connote a sense of beginning, while the latter two indicate a sense of preservation.[145] The term "order" thus embodies King Mu's desire to reestablish his political prerogative and thereby maintain or preserve the legitimacy of his descendants. King Mu's observation that it would take *three* years to achieve this goal recalls the *three* months (in some texts *three* years) that it took Kun to "transform" himself from chaos into order—Yü. King Mu thus likens his own work to the cosmogonic process of creating order from chaos.

The intimacy of the exchange between King Mu and Hsi-wang-mu has led at least one traditional scholar, Su Shih 蘇軾 (1037–1101), to suspect a romantic connection.[146] The evidence, though scanty, is nevertheless suggestive. Our text emphasizes extending life genealogically, the implicit objective of the sexual art, and other texts document such practices "encoded in cryptic metaphors which may be understood only by one initiated in the secrets of a particular doctrine."[147] It is very possibile that references in the *Mu T'ien-tzu chuan* allude to related esoteric ideas, especially given its similarly motivated appropriation of references to cosmogonic myths. We have already seen that a reference to the alleged master of sexual arts, Jung Ch'eng, can be read as signifying the desire of King Mu to extend his genealogical claim to rule.

The location of the exchange, Blue-gem Pool (*yao-ch'ih*), has been shown to relate to the "blue-gem spring" (*ch'üan* 泉), which is a "cryptic metaphor for the reservoir of saliva under the tongue as well as the saliva stored there."[148] Saliva was considered a nourishing concentrate that could revitalize the body after extended breath cultivation. These nourishing effects were believed to emanate from female essences as well: both were called "syrupy liquid" (*li* 醴). Several texts locate a "syrupy-liquor spring" and "blue-gem pool" at K'un-lun, an understandable identification, given the mountain's associations with regeneration.[149] Not yet noted, however, is the significance of the association of these liquids with the axis of Heaven: K'un-lun is the demarcater of Heaven's axis in the astronomical/cosmogonic discourse of flood myths. Here we have an astronomical referent for the term "syrupy-liquor ford" (*chin*), which is used to describe a part of the female anatomy in sexual manuals.[150] Recall that the Heavenly Ford referred to the area spanning the fork in the Milky Way (another syrupy entity?) and was believed to facilitate the crossing of Heaven's axis, which in turn was interpreted in sexual terms as a form of regeneration. While completely veiled in metaphoric language, King Mu's feasting of Hsi-wang-mu at Blue-gem pool and his subsequent rejuvenation may thus in fact refer to procreative benefits of engaging in sexual relations with her. Marcel Granet's exposition of the role of sexual activity in the procedure for the renewal of life also seems to support this interpretation.[151]

King Mu's interaction with Hsi-wang-mu is a threshold; it connects the space defined by the hidden imperatives motivating his trip and the world of political order that must be transformed if he is to continue to exist in it. That King Mu will succeed is affirmed by the symbolism of the sophora (*huai* 槐) tree that he plants next to the stela on which he inscribes the record of his visit to Hsi-wang-mu. Known for its density and durability, the sophora tree was valued as a material for making implements and constructing buildings, (King Mu was preoccupied with the latter activity, perhaps as a manifestation of royal prerogative).[152] More significantly, the wood of the sophora tree was burned during winter to ward off epidemics, to effect the proper transition to spring, and to preserve the freshness of youth.[153] In light of this ritualistic function, the tree in the text may serve symbolically to ignite or fuel the process of transformation augured by the interaction between King Mu and Hsi-wang-mu. The juxtaposition of the inscribed record and the sophora tree points in a similar direction: both represent an attempt to reestablish a meaningful congruence between the disparate worlds symbolized by Hsi-wang-mu and King Mu.

King Mu's attempts to find congruence in his father's catastrophic death and his own (political) reality can be compared with the very features of the *Mu T'ien-tzu chuan* that mark it as a symbolic text. His endeavors, once viewed as symbolizing with an obstacle to being, lead the reader to construe the narrative as an unfolding story of transcendence in the face of an unspoken crisis. This melding of symbolic and annalistic modes of articulation represents the means used by the Chou to transcend their political trauma.

The myths in the narrative are traces whose significance emerges as they are carried back across the great silence of the Chou's unwillingness to address King Chao's death and the resultant challenge to their claim to political legitimacy. The myths, themselves products of symbolic operation, are the key to unlocking the cryptic fictional persona of King Mu. As responses to the ineffable force of precession, the myths also signify the conceptual notion of replacement (Yü replaced Kun, Ch'i replaced Yü, and so on) and transcendence of the original obstacle. And in the case of King Mu, his character *re-places* King Chao: it reflects first on the displacement of King Chao discourse and then on how the Chou were able to maintain their dynastic legitimacy. To paraphrase the *Appended Words Commentary*, "Being the fictional King Mu is a matter of providing symbols."

This hero of the *Mu T'ien-tzu chuan* attracted to his personality the manifold tradition that once had been coined for Yü.[154] The King Mu of the narrative, an undisputed historical personality, slips on Yü's equipment while at the same time slipping out of the garb of sober history; like Yü, his character is cryptically portrayed as driven by a hidden crisis (of identity). The *Mu T'ien-tzu chuan*, in dramatizing its own origins, constitutes a literary articulation of a solution to a political crisis. It consists of the revalorization of universal concepts of political legitimization, such that the Heavenly Mandate can coexist in a specific context with genealogical rule. Indeed, the narrative suggests that reality itself can only be represented or conceived of as the refraction of different perspectives in a particular, experiential context. The journey provides the background for the expression of political prerogative and then via the artful employment of contrastive modes of articulation—the annal and the myth—the narrative reexamines this political prerogative in light of the particularity of that experience.

4

Before proceeding to the larger literary implications of the *Mu T'ien-tzu chuan*, I shall pause to reconcile my interpretation with the text's date of composition, its place of composition, and its status as a tomb text. The following comments are meant to be evocative rather than conclusive.

The symbolic reading of the *Mu T'ien-tzu chuan* offered here reveals themes that, when re-historicized, find remarkable resonance with pronounced social and intellectual trends of the Warring States period. Most studies of the Warring States era, including those focusing more narrowly on intellectual, social, economic, and political trends, characterize it as a "transitional" period "between the 'feudalism' of the high Zhou state and the creation of a unified Chinese empire by the Qin state."[155] Surely the most significant transition in the political realm was the assertion by rulers of the "cosmic nature of [their] rule through systematic imitation of the Heavenly patterns."[156] As several studies have vividly portrayed, beginning with the Spring and Autumn period, political legitimacy was no longer conceived as deriving only from potent ancestors, or even from Heaven itself; rather, it was asserted through the ruler's assumption of Heaven's role by systematically connecting his rule to the patterns of the cosmos. These links were forged with rituals, calendrically organized to depict the ruler's actions as according with those of nature.[157] Such views of political authority echo the pivotal elements of the encrypted crisis of the Chou court as symbolically revealed in the *Mu T'ien-tzu chuan*, namely, that King Mu's trip to K'un-lun represents the human appropriation of Heaven's authority to grant political legitimacy.

The questions of political identity that permeate the *Mu T'ien-tzu chuan* need to be set in the context of notions of the role of human agency, especially in the political realm. Agency figures significantly in the text's depiction and resolution of the King Chao crisis. Within the early Western Chou past-oriented framework of rule legitimized by a Heavenly Mandate, the crisis of Chao's death would be imputed to his violation of Heaven's interdiction. In this vein, King Mu's journey to K'un-lun might be construed as an exploration of his own sanctity; his search ends as he redefines man's stance vis-à-vis Heaven. But the *Mu T'ien-tzu chuan* presents a different picture. The boundaries established by the king, among other things, also delimit responsibility for the death of King Chao; it resulted from his own actions and was not a case of Heaven's retribution. This distinction reflects the conceptual separation of the ethical order of doing ill from the cosmological order of faring ill. As a result, the shame of transgressing Heaven is thus transposed into the personal shame of fault.[158]

This same distinction is reflected in late Spring and Autumn and Warring States texts. Witness Confucius' difficulty accepting what to him is the inexplicable reality of unemployment: his actions, after all, are virtuous and thus faultless; his conduct is in accord with Heaven.[159] Differences in the various Kun myths also attest to a shift in conceptions of fault: whereas some texts present Kun in terms of suffering misfortune, another group of related myths presents him as a culpable deviant who deserves his sentence.[160] This notion of accountability is seen as well during the Warring States period in the use of "oaths" or "covenants" (*meng-shu* 盟書) that bound both parties to their stated intentions and in the emphasis on writing as a means of fixing people's pledges.[161] The emergence of more complex legal systems is another sign of the desire on the part of Warring States philosophers and rulers to define behavior in terms of individual agency.[162] Similarly, the proliferation of texts of "recipes" for controlling malevolent forces or for curing physical suffering is premised on assumptions of man's instrumentality.[163]

Once fault is demarcated, heavenly order reaffirms itself. It is thus man who makes it possible for Heaven to "act" and not the other way around. From legalist theories to our example of Kun, it is clear that the assignation of fault served as a means for deflecting unpleasant elements, to be done with as prescribed, for the establishment or maintenance of order, an order that was conceived of in cosmic terms. Warring States culture affirmed primordial integrity in the negative moment of destruction (that is, punishment), whether it was framed in five-phases and yin-yang rhetoric of "conquering" (*k'o* 克), expressed through acts of sanctioned violence,[164] or revealed in the myths of Yü's success deriving from the extinction of his father. I submit that the *Mu T'ien-tzu chuan* reflects an analogous treatment of King Chao: as Kun was for Yü, King Chao is the (discursively) displaced father of King Mu, and like Yü, King Mu's success in reestablishing order derives solely from the negation of his father (or more precisely his father's association with a Heavenly Mandate view of political legitimacy). By virtue of his invisibility, King Chao functions in the text as a silent portent of the displacement of Heaven's agency in the discursive practice of Warring States. A mute enunciation of the psychosocial and political conditions underlying the shift in the ideology of royal prerogative, the *Mu T'ien-tzu chuan* dramatizes the disappearance of the notion of Heaven as the agent of legitimization.[165]

Sarah Allan's incisive study of the way legends of the transference of dynastic rule functioned to mediate conflicting views of legitimacy—one based on hereditary rights and one based on "virtue"—dramatically illustrates the effects of the discursive elision of Heaven's agency in Warring States texts. While seemingly related to the issues of legitimacy surrounding the King Chao debacle, there is a crucial difference: whereas one devolved on the distinction between man and Heaven's agency, the other posits the issue exclusively in terms of man's agency. Authority to rule is decided upon by man and by man alone. While Heaven is perceived as the emodiment of a standard in both cases, it is not revealed as an active force in the latter case. "Virtue" in these legends is no longer the object of or motivation for Heaven's sanction; it is a measurable quality that is valued as a response to the demands of the larger community or state.[166] Thus, to look at a Warring States explanation of the founding of the Chou dynasty, for example, "Wen Wang, the 'cultured king,' established the virtue of the dynasty and the right of the Zhou to rule, but he did not actually overthrow his ruler. Wu Wang, the 'military king' performed the act of regicide, but in doing he also acted to avenge his father and carry on his work."[167] Regicide becomes punishment; the process of transformation of rule is represented as completely human-generated.

One point deserves elaboration. Although an oral tradition served as the source for the perspectives of political legitimacy expressed in the *Mu T'ien-tzu chuan* and other Warring States texts, the effects are completely different. The difference lies in the fact that whereas in the *Mu T'ien-tzu chuan* the manner in which myths are used has everything to do with their meaning within the system of mythical thought that they represent (astronomical/cosmogonic), myths in the latter corpus are used "in a manner which is far removed from" this meaning.[168] This disparity issues from each text's very dissimilar rhetorical intentions, intentions that may reflect on why the *Mu T'ien-tzu chuan* was found in a tomb of the state of Wei.

I have argued that the tragedy of King Chao's death and the means chosen by the Chou to deal with it propelled the fictive persona of King Mu. This implies a new way of thinking about the driving forces of the narrative itself. The connection between secrets and the actions of the fictional King Mu suggests that the generative source or "author" of the text is none other than the secret itself, which is inscribed within the work. Had there been no family trauma threatening the existence of the Chou dynasty, King Mu would not have needed to transform himself as he did. The narrative of the *Mu T'ien-tzu chuan* flows from the secret it inscribes within itself as its founding source.

Seen in this light, the probable location of the text's composition looks to be the state of Wei, because of Wei's connection to the Chou court. The state of Wei (through its filial relationship to the state of Chin, and the latter's hereditary connection to T'ang shu 唐叔 the son of King Wu and the younger brother of King Cheng) was closely related both materially and intellectualy to the Chou.[169] The familial nature of the connection provides an interesting context for Rémi Mathieu contends that the style of the *Mu T'ien-tzu chuan* reflects the interests of someone closely involved with the Wei or Chin court; the text's symbolic recapitulation of the crisis generated by King Chao's death bespeaks royal links connecting the Chin and Wei courts to that of the Chou. Presumably the familial links would have made the Chin/Wei states more privy to the source of the unstated anxiety experienced by the Chou court, and hence more susceptible to incorporating the products of symbolic operation that such an anxiety generated.

Finally, although I accept the validity of one scholar's opinion that "there was something magical and spiritual about books which made them appropriate items to be included among the burial goods,"[170] I feel that there is also a case to be made for other motives in burying texts. We have many recently excavated texts that employ discursive means for concealing the true object of discourse, especially among those associated with Taoist practices and beliefs, which suggests that they, as well as the *Mu T'ien-tzu chuan*, may have been perceived as containers of powerful illuminations that could aid the tomb master after death. Redolent of magical associations, the texts discovered at Chi in 279 and within the last three decades of the present century reveal a concern with asserting and preserving man's agency as a controller and organizer of his own destiny. They explore social, political, and even moral issues by drawing attention to the complex area in which human experience, larger historical forces, and the contingencies of circumstances overlap.

SIX

Heaven's Text and the Invention of Fictional Discourse in China

It remains finally to examine the overall literary implications of the symbolic reading of the *Mu T'ien-tzu chuan* presented herein. My interpretation is premised on the understanding that the astronomical and cosmological intentions encrypted within the myths of K'un-lun, Ho-po, and Hsi-wang-mu can explain the organization and coherence embedded in the text's linguistic elements. Having thus far delineated the symbolic significance of numerous elements and patterns, I have now to relate them to the larger issues of rhetoric and discourse. It is within this realm that the narrative artifice revealed in the *Mu T'ien-tzu chuan* makes its greatest contribution to Chinese literary history in general and to the development of fictional modes of representation more specifically.

My analysis so far extended the concept of the symbol into the literary realm in order to reread and reassess the mode of representation revealed in cosmogonic myths and their role in the *Mu T'ien-tzu chuan*. In this chapter I explore the implications of the theory of the symbol and propose that it expands the horizons of the interpretation of fiction beyond the standard notions of truth, illusion, and authorial intention.

The comments offered in this chapter are metacritical, intended to offer a new paradigm for understanding Chinese fictional discourse. The generalizations about how various genres emerged or about the development of the history of fictional representation are necessarily tentative—they do not derive from an analysis of specific texts. They are therefore open to question; indeed these remarks are planted in the hope that they will yield interpretive fruit, further reflections on the applicability of the paradigm and new research.

1

The heuristic potential for the theory of the symbol in the analysis of Chinese fictional forms lies in the congruence between these forms and the presentation of the cosmogonic myths examined above. I thus begin with an analysis of the discursive features of the cosmogonic myths; this in turn illustrates how their appropriation in the *Mu T'ien-tzu chuan* reflects a key feature of fictional representation more broadly in the Chinese narrative tradition. I first postulate that the discursive structure of the Yü flood myths has its origin in an attempt to mediate linguistically the confusing and frightening effects of the displacement of a critical seasonal marker. I then propose that the very manner in which the Yü myths were preserved reveals this purpose.

However ancient the mythic traditions may be, our only access to them is through the written record. As I have noted above, Chinese myths are recorded in what appears to be an unsystematic manner; as a result there are many competing theories about the nature of Chinese cosmogony. Indeed, for a long time the regnant argument held that the absence of "narrativized" myths signified an absence of cosmogonic theorizing.[1] Fortunately, recent work such as that of Norman Girardot has cleared the way for treating Chinese cosmogony on its own terms.[2] I would add a linguistic dimension to Girardot's conclusion that Chinese cosmogony becomes evident once one understands how China "fathomed the mythological gap of chaos." I believe, that is, that is in fact itself an important clue for piecing together the puzzle of the origins of myth's discursive form. Thus, what might otherwise be construed as lapses in the written record or perhaps a Confucian disinterest in anything supranatural begs, to the contrary, for elaboration.

Andrew Plaks has gone the farthest toward reconstructing the literary ramifications of the discursive patterns implicit in Chinese mythology, especially in his discussion of the "deemphasis of narration in the treatment of mythical lore."[3] But his assumption that "it is not the mythical materials themselves that lead to general conclusions about preference for temporal or spatial patterns in literary archetypes, but how these materials are used in shaping a cultural mainstream" restricts his discussion to the structural level, and hence precludes an exploration of the discursive origins of the mythic materials.[4] In fact, the Yü flood myths are linguistic constructions meant to alleviate the sense of disarray and confusion accompanying the displacement of a seasonal marker. They are interpretive acts that reintegrate humans into their universe by linking the old familiar elements together into a new system of relationships. The myths thus have much to reveal about reading and writing texts.

My interpretation of the Yü myths hinges on them as a response to the loss of the ability to "read" and hence control time. When the Heavenly Turtle failed to appear at its proper time, the ancient Chinese could no longer read the celestial text. But the loss was not permanent. They eventually regained this ability as is illustrated by the story of the flood and Yü's control of it—an imagistic rendition of the effects of precession on the Milky Way and Antares. At the heart of Chinese mythic language lie the mental, linguistic, and rhetorical efforts of the ancients to fathom the shift or displacement of the elements of Heaven's text—first the Heavenly Turtle and then the Milky Way.

Simply put, the ancients learned how to read a new text by turning that text into a part of the old text. What we do not have, I have noted, is a representation of the flood story based on notions of linear narrative progression from one element to another. Rather, the process is more one of backbuilding, that is, a rereading of prior fragments in terms of new narrative elements. Instead, the concept of the flood is a rereading of the Heavenly Turtle (Kun) in terms of the Milky Way; Yü's actions are a rereading of the flood—the Milky Way, itself a rereading of the Heavenly Turtle—in terms of the movements of the Fire Star. Myth then is the writing of the ancients' rewriting of the original text.

The narratological implications of this process become clearer when seen in the context of linguistic properties of the Chinese language. Most relevent to our present inquiry is the way of perceiving subject and predicate. "The grammatical meaning of subject and predicate in a Chinese sentence," asserts Chao Yüan-jen, "is topic and comment, rather than actor and action."[5] More recently, Wallace L. Chafe has qualified Chao's definition:

> What the topics appear to do is to limit the applicability of the main predication to a certain restricted domain. . . . Typically, it would seem, the topic sets a spatial, temporal, or individual framework within which the main predication holds.[6]

Charles N. Li and Sandra Thompson also expand on Chao's analysis, arguing that topic is best understood in terms of a broader discourse strategy; the topic's function cannot be defined in terms of individual sentences but rather announces the theme of the discourse.[7] Because the topic sets the parameters of discourse, it must remain in the sentence-initial position[8] and can then be left out in subsequent sentences.[9] Thus, Chafe states that a topic is one for which "I think you already know and can identify the particular referent I have in mind."[10] The topic, then, represents the known, while the comment introduces the unknown.[11]

The discursive properties of the topic-comment grammatical operation shape both the distinctive reading process reflected in the myths and the fragmented nature of their representation in writing. The Heavenly Turtle serves as the initial topic, estabishing the context within which to reread the changing elements of Heaven's text. Each succeeding fragment of the myth serves both as a comment to a previously established topic and as a topic establishing an "old" context for understanding the next element. The reading process is like a chain, with every element eventually (re)contextualized in terms of the Heavenly Turtle.

Not only the Yü myths themselves but also the corpus of written references to those myths reflect a reading process informed by topic-comment: the fragmentary, at times almost cryptic references can be understood as comments to an already established yet unstated topic—the astronomical phenomena to which the myths refer. Indeed, the sporadic and seemingly incomplete nature of the written representation of the Yü myths at once belies and points to their overdetermined, underlying astronomical meaning. The fragmentation of the myths in the written tradition can be understood as a representation of the blockage to reading, an inability to read the whole text at once without recontextualizing, while it is also a representation of the reading process that informed their eventual conceptualization.

In this vein, we can understand the source of the essentially nonnarrative nature of the Yü myths. The myths do not reflect actions that occurred within time; rather, they are comments referring to the very passage of time itself.[12] That Chinese verbs are tenseless (and were, so far as we can tell) may have contributed to the predominance of the topic-comment form of discursive representation. James Tai has shown that the principle of placing a topic—which represents "old" or "given" information—before "new" information, a comment, is consistent with the principle of temporal sequencing, which he identifies as a distinguishing feature of Chinese grammar. He states that "the given-new principle is determined by the temporal sequence in the subjective-mental-temporal axis."[13] The grammatical operation of topic-comment thus establishes a discursive temporality independent of verbs and verb tenses.

The Yü myths are a linguistic manifestation of the process of reading and rewriting a text. Myth then can be seen as a reflection on the nature of the Chinese language. Even more, it is a commentary on how to read: one must reread. Reading is only rereading, re-presenting an original text in a new context. This metamythical nature of the Yü myths can also be understood as a commentary on the origins of the myths: it re-presents the reading process from which they came.

A recent study of cognitive evolution has posited that the self-theorizing capacity of myth may also be seen as stemming from its status as a "conceptual model . . . whose function is tied to the development of integrative thought."[14] Whereas the standard analysis of myth is premised on the old notion that myths are an attempt to provide causal explanations, predictions, and controls for human experience, the cognitive approach has much new to contribute to our understanding of the discursive role of myth in the evolution of fiction in China. One of the most significant insights offered by this approach is the suggestion that myths are metaphorical; they "compare across episodes, deriving general principles and extracting thematic content" from "formerly disconnected, time-bound snippets of information." Seen in these terms, myth is "inherently a modeling device, whose primary level of representation is thematic." The conclusion that "modern humans developed language in response to pressure to improve their conceptual apparatus, not vice versa" may in fact explain the close connection between the structure of the myth and its predominant discursive strategy in the Yü flood myths. Language, accordingly, represented not an end in itself but "an adaptation that met specific cognitive and cultural needs, that is, ultimately for the formalization and unification of thought and knowledge. It was not so much a communication system as an integral by-product of a new, much more powerful method of thinking."[15]

Donald's explanation of the role of myth in the development of cognitive skills accords with the symbolic role of myth that I have elaborated throughout this study. That is, myth's function as "the prototypal, fundamental, integrative mind tool"[16] derives from the traumatic circumstances that forced their production. If these circumstances were to be overcome, new cognitive skills would be needed. Donald describes the integrative cognitive model reflected in myth as a "first attempt at coherent historical reconstruction of the past . . . [as a] reconstructive act: an attempt to piece together a large number of episodes so as to give a place and a meaning to the smaller-scale events the myth encompasses."[17] This formulation is equally appropriate for describing the symbolic means by which myths re-present the traumatic events that generated them in the first place. Indeed, one could conclude that mythic integration was contingent on symbolic production.

That the social consequences of mythic integrations were evident at the cultural level and that the myths gave contextual meaning to events can be construed as a corollary to the individualistic and experiential tendencies that we have identified as paramount features of the narrative mode of the *Mu T'ien-tzu chuan*. If we accept Donald's argument that "the entire scenario of human life gained its percieved importance from these myths," the congruence between the representative effects of Chinese fiction and cosmogonic myths becomes all the more pronounced.[18]

My argument that the production of Chinese fiction can be understood in terms of the dynamics inherent in re-presenting an original text would seem to mesh with the brilliant work of Karl S. Y. Kao, who has argued that the production of Chinese fiction consists in reworking a precursor text, a process that he calls "derivation."[19] His approach offers much of value for Chinese literary studies; indeed, the application of his theoretical framework yielded penetrating interpretations of three examples of Chinese fiction. Nonetheless, I believe that my own work goes farther. I am proposing that the heuristic potential of derivation study can be expanded by exploring the implications of the theory of the symbol. These extend the horizons of interpretation beyond a literary production and beyond the conscious intent of an author.[20] The theory of the symbol as a conceptual tool can situate certain instances of language and representation within a much broader psychoanalytic and historical perspective. It can help explain historical, social, and cultural phenomena by allowing us to trace certain literary behavior back to crises that have been collectively experienced and silently transmitted in a literary form. I will explore the implications of the symbol for the analysis of the emergence in China of a certain mode of narrative that I have termed fictional representation.

(Re-)reading Chinese fiction from the perspective of symbol formation that does not assume the conscious intent of the author as its hermeneutic maxim or heuristic baseline reveals an integrative model of linguistic operation similar to that in cosmogonic myths. I am suggesting that the integrative mode of fiction derives from the encrypting of narratives concerned with an ideology of representation—namely, in terms of the "readability" of experience—within these texts. Once revealed, this encrypted narrative can lead to a reconsideration of the status of representation in texts, and that in turn can promote a rethinking of the status of the aesthetic in fictional works. The result will be a new way of interpreting mainstays of Chinese fiction, such as orality and supernatural elements, as manifestations or extensions of symbolic operation, whereby the representational mode itself co-symbolizes with an initial collective trauma.

The identification of an encrypted, silent ideology derives from the recognition that concealed ideology is a potential response to trauma. Chinese fiction, like cosmogonic myth, is a discursive form intended to overcome a crisis; indeed, inscribed within it are traces of the sources of the trauma.

2

I believe that the trauma that generated the symbolic discourse of fiction is the same one that, in the view of most intellectual historians, inspired the different schools of thought during China's Axial Age—the sixth to third centuries B.C. According to this position, philosophical traditions—most of which articulated a model for reestablishing order—can be explained as (symbolic) "response[s] to the breakdown of the moral and political order which had claimed the authority of heaven."[21] The philosophers sought to describe but also to idealize the natural world, or more specifically, the nature of the relationship between Heaven and man. The task before them was to discover principles that could mediate between an imperfect physical/social reality and the authority and dominion of Heaven.[22] Such notions of order were integrated to the objectives of Warring States philosophy: to observe, record, and classify phenomena and to celebrate this process as an approximation of a metaphysical revelation that justified the work of Heaven.[23]

To this end philosophers related to the universe as a vast text to be plumbed for its Heavenly ordained coherence.[24] It was an epistemological quest to invent or discover an authoritative—and often self-consciously performative—semiotics.[25] These discourses were attempts to organize the discrete phenomena of the world as parts of a coherent design for the purpose of reifying that order in stable, authoritiative systems of representation.

The difficulty, of course, is that order is not a linear philosophical concept but rather is a discontinuous narrative deriving from political and cultural discourses. The various attempts to represent it ultimately destabilizied the notion of an authoritative, Heavenly written metalanguage—a single set of beliefs capable of uniting everyone.[26] Heavenly order was, in effect, ambiguous and unreadable.

With Heaven displaced as a metaphysical guarantee of authoritative meaning philosophers turned to the search for a philsophical language that would replace the unreadable experience of their reality with an idealized system of signs that ordered natural pheonomena by the simple act of naming them.[27] Correlative theories sought to do just this: their semiotic system was intended to be performative as well as descriptive.[28] These were provisional schemes of organization, to be revised as needed to accommodate changing sociopolitical needs.[29] Correlative theories demonstrated the potential of a system of representation as an ideal semiotics, as both a means to demonstrate and an unproblematic reflection of an ordered and perfect universe. They are founded on the assumption that Heaven's text can be read as a series of mutually reinforcing blueprints rather than as an infinitely problematic and ultimately undecipherable text.

The ultimate widespread appeal of correlative theories was a function of their ability to provide such a system, one that legitimated claims of a divinely ordered universe but also lent itself to practical applications with immediate economic and political payoffs. Correlative theories, then, integrated cosmological inquiry into the political and economic operations of late Warring States Chinese society and provided a manageable closed system of representation. In the process, the original inquiry into a solution for the "universal sense of an abyss between the shared norms of culture and the actuality of behavior"[30]—a problem that was inherently unsolvable—was subsumed by more pragmatic approaches.

Correlative schemes were nevertheless often at odds with the social reality they described. They simply could not really guarantee that the "order" they described really existed.[31] This is the cultural and philosophical problem that lies at the heart of attempts to construe the universe as ordered and legible, as proof of Heaven's authority. As these theories offered a symbolic means to demonstrate order, they nevertheless remained dependent on the premise that Heaven's text is ordered and that it can be read. One can appreciate the desire to read what cannot truly be read, in terms of symbolic production. Such an effort is nevertheless only an illusion, a system that represses and conceals illegible complexities. Correlative systems thus operate as symbols, born of the silencing of their traumatic origins.

What I call fictional discourse, is, I believe, the product of this same trauma of the illegibility of Heavenly order. But the philosophical (which include political) responses to the trauma provide a logocentric means of transcendence,[32] whereas fictional responses respond by discursively representing order as a complex, overlapping series of semiotic endeavors, none of which in and of itself is adequate to explain a reality that ultimately recedes toward an unreadable complexity. Each genre re-presents the traumatic source of its production in its own unique form. Thus, philosophy attempts to bridge or eliminate the gap between sign and signified by repressing it; and, fiction attempts to make it readable by refashioning it.

Just as the flood myths symbolize the chaos and incomprehension wrought by the gap in Heaven, and just as the production of the myths represents an attempt to close the gap, so too does fictional discourse symbolize with the chaotic sense of indeterminancy felt by writers in an age when the cultural verities that had once held society together no longer existed. It offers a means to make the diversity of experience readable; it uses language to reassert order, but via an integrative mode of representation rather than a totalizing, monolithic mode.[33] Chinese fictional discourse is the supreme narrative product of the mythic mode, the enactment of the operation of mythic language within a narrative context. It employs the same discursive features as myth to bridge a gap caused by existential incomprehension. This is reflected both literally and figuratively in the *Mu T'ien-tzu chuan*—the earliest extant example of what I call fiction. The unmarked appropriation of mythic elements—as opposed to the philosopher's deliberate and marked reference to mythic traditions—is discreet but nonetheless fully integrated into the overall narrative mode. Myth expands the boundaries of the annal; it also operates on the level of the topic-comment, outlined above.

The myths in the *Mu T'ien-tzu chuan* are discursive markers for the unstated topic of King Chao's death, repeated reference to which establishes the specific context. The discourse of topic-comment can shape context so that words are related with respect to a defined consciousness—that of the Chou in the aftermath of King Chao's death. The structure of the narrative, with the myths a predicate that comments on the (ostensible) topic—King Mu's westward journey—implies that it is the speaker's subjective impression being conveyed. In this case that is the narrator. A significant narrative pattern can be perceived in the use of frames (the mythic elements) supplied by the discourse notion of topic-comment to represent the context of the words contained therein as the perspective(s) of different consciousnesses. The narrative strategy of fictional representation hinges on multiple perspectives that can be distinguished from one another by virtue of the topic-comment structure. The mythic elements offer subtle hints of the different semantic systems at work. Thus, the aesthetic implications of this narrative pattern suggest that the reality of the *Mu T'ien-tzu chuan* narrative world is determined by the interactions of the various points of view.

Poetic expression, too, figures in the narrative. (Indeed, commingling of discursive forms is the most characteristic trait of fictional discourse.) The use of poetry in the *Mu T'ien-tzu chuan* is different from the explicit citation of poetry in other early texts, which identify the source of the poem. In fictional discourse, by contrast, poetic forms are simply another means of representing the polyphony of the reality.

As a mode of representation, fictional discourse signals a shift of remarkable scope—it incorporates possibilities that had previously been unthinkable. When writing had been the unique prerogative of the politically or religiously powerful, it was used by them for either of two purposes—to communicate with the spiritual world or to express ideas about the maintenance of (political) order. Still fictional discourse did not appear in revolutionary manner; its literary effects evolved within contexts that partially reinscribe the very assumptions these effects draw into question. With its characteristic multiplicity of perspectives, it serves as a crossroads for various strata and trends within the culture.

Fictional discourse did not eradicate, for example, the reliance of Chinese narrative on the specification of chronology as a marker.[34] Its rhetorical effect was drastically altered, however, by the appropriation of myth in our fourth-century-B.C. text, the *Mu T'ien-*

tzu chuan.[35] Read as the signs of the unspeakable trauma informing the production of the *Mu T'ien-tzu chuan*, the myths collapse the temporal boundaries imposed by the chronology of the surface text by calling attention to the re-presented nature of the text's origin, its unstated topic. Indeed, they are linguistic paradigms of the processes involved in rereading and rewriting texts, a model for discursive expression that operates independently of historically based chronological time. The elliptical mythic references in the *Mu T'ien-tzu chuan* drain the narrative of its literal sense and convert it into a vehicle for conveying a symbolic message.

Thus does fictional discourse stand outside the world of reified concepts, trying in effect to puncture them. It remains the necessary "chaos," the opaque turbulence, that challenges and complements the transparency of order. Experience has been historically inscribed or suppressed within a complex dynamic that connects writer, reader, and text with the culture. Chinese fictional discourse emerged from the belief that these questions deserved attention. Hence, Chinese fiction can be construed as a cultural symbol that was produced by writers seeking "to cope [i.e., read] with [their] newly perceived environment."[36] The integrative mode can be understood as a symbolic means of transcending the confusing gap between subjective experience and what was predominantly represented as an ordered reality.

Although the contextualizing background of Warring States reality is not readily apparent, it drives the linguistic patterns of Chinese fiction. The product of "pyschic mechanisms whose aim seems to be to disarray, even to annul the expressive power of language,"[37] Chinese fiction nevertheless allows readers to disinter the (psychic) disarray that led to its production.[38] Implicit in this process is a rehistoricizing of the notion of order and its relationship to narrative representation.[39] Fictional writing remaps signs; it rehistoricizes by returning to and rereading the past, excavating possibilities and potentialities that resonate with their present moment of creation.[40] So with the *Mu T'ien-tzu chuan*: only by reading it as a fiction can one glean what it has to say about historical events.

This is not to argue that every work of Chinese fiction has as its core the suppression of a secret. I am suggesting, however, that at the very least, fiction in the Chinese context takes as its representative premise the impossibility of representing order. It is particularly suited to represent reality that is "unreadable." If fictional discourse symbolically mirrors the trauma rendered by the unreadability of its historical moment, the birth of fictional genres might reflect an overall underlying context shared by numerous texts. This bears further examination.

The approach taken in this work—viewing Chinese fiction not from a bifocal lens that separates truth from fantasy but from a kalaidoscope that brings to light the commingling of a plethora of perspectives that re-present the complexity (unreadability) of reality and an obstacle to being—accords with the traditional Chinese perception of fictional discourse, *hsiao-shuo* 小說, as consisting of "public responses to the times that merited study primarily for their incidental intelligence value."[41] Fictional discourse is the public means for transcending the obstacle to being posed by an unintelligible reality. This interpretation may also account for the traces of orality that appear in even the most literary examples of fictional discourse, whether framed by the context of having been related to the implied author or mimetically represented as the content of an oral storyteller's performance. While philosophy too was perceived as orally transmitted, as Graham has noted,[42] orality had no bearing on the interpretation of the information itself, which was unambiguously demarcated as belonging to one or another philosophical context. The oral trope in Chinese fiction, itself a metonymy of the public, identifies the public as the origin of the text's content and identifies the fictional text as a retelling of this content. This gesture suggests that the trope functions as a metaphor for the way in which fiction symbolically represents its origins. Orality signals the symbolic function of fiction and thus alerts readers to the concealed nature of its traumatic origins. Specifically, then, this link between orality and a concealed origin aestheticizes the historical moment of the Warring States reality; it re-creates the inability to read or fashion order out of Heaven's inscribed text. It is through the trope of orality that the narrative of an unreadable reality is cryptically embedded in fictional discourse.

3

To probe the heuristic implications of the thesis presented thus far, I devote the rest of this chapter to a discussion of two generic examples of fictional discourse: Six Dynasties stories of the marvelous (*chih-kuai* 志怪); and the sixteenth-century vernacular novel. I focus on the strategies that mark them as genres and analyze them from the perspective of the theory of the symbol to ascertain how they reread the illegibility of the historical moment during which they were produced.

I begin with the genre of miracle tales, which "became something of a smokestack industry"[43] during the Six Dynasties period. This venerable corpus has exerted enormous influence on the development of fiction in China. Moreover, it intersects with religious tales—mostly Buddhist. We find in this regard that religious objectives and the narrative means for achieving them did not foster the production of fiction in China but rather worked in tandem with the already established symbolic function of fictional discourse.[44]

On the most superficial level, tales of the marvelous that take as their major conceit the transcendence of a crisis facilitated by the expression of devotion to a spiritual being such as Kuan-shih-yin 觀世音 or a belief in the supernatural, seem to represent a symbolic means of overcoming an obstacle to being. Indeed, as Rob Campany has eloquently argued, the narration of these tales may have served the purpose of (religious) propagation, to extend to others the experience of a similar type of transcendence.[45] But if the transcendence were their sole rhetorical objective, these tales would not qualify as examples of fiction, at least not according to the terms that I have proposed. Their fictional and symbolic status must be established, then, on other grounds.

And indeed elements of these tales alert us to the possibility that their discursive features may be read as responses to an inability to read and thus represent order. That is, an implicit recounting and dramatization of the hidden source of their production. The source can be identified most generally as the tension attendant upon the displacement of the northern Chinese court to the somwhat alien environs of southern culture. The apparent need of the literati to mediate between two distinct cultural spheres, exemplified by the appropriation and representation of southern motifs and customs, has been noted as an underlying motive for the production of tales of the marvelous.[46] While the symbolic status of a text or a corpus of texts necessarily derives from the specific linguistic structures that comprise them, something that I cannot even begin to approach in the present context, I would add that the very discursive form used to relate the tales warrants analyzing them from a psychoanalytic perspective.

For example, the seemingly ethnographic bent of the tales, which presents them as "records" of witnessed events belies the very conceit of the marvelous, which more often than not consists in the interaction of beings from different worlds or the crossing of the boundary between life and death.[47] The text is mediating between two levels of discourse, one this worldly and representable, the other unstated and hidden. The narrator seems to be addressing the unasked yet pervasive question of identity—what it means to conform to another's notion of identity. In implying that important lessons can (and should) be drawn from the tales of the marvelous,[48] the historian/narrator performs a temporal displacement by which he tacitly reads the discursive collapsing of boundaries in the texts into the context of contemporary China. The narrator as historian is displacing his discussion of recent history within the discourse of the marvelous.

Thomas Smith's incisive observation that the *chih-kuai* corpus "relates more closely to the world of myth which assumes its own truth value" is certainly important to the thesis advanced here.[49] Nevertheless, whereas Smith cites Ko Hung and Kan Pao's impassioned effort to argue for the presence of spirits in the world as the object of truth, I would suggest that the object of truth is more general in nature. Certainly the oft-cited rationale for fiction, that its value lies not in its empirically correct manner of representing events but in its ability to depict and illustrate issues of a broader nature would accord with this understanding.[50] I would push this even further, however: the truth lies in an unstated topic in the narrative. Just as myths are "true" in imagistically representing the obstacle to being that led to their production, so too are the *chih-kuai* true. Moreover, the circumstances that led to the production of *chih-kuai* narratives are intimatley related to those that gave rise to fictional discourse: problems inherent in recognizing (reading) order and their representation. Thus, in the *chih-kuai* tales, we have another encrypted dilemma.

Does the discursive form of tales of the marvelous then have a more specific function linked to the demise of the Han dynasty and the ensuing "infiltration" of other, foreign elements into the Han cultural fold? Perhaps the focus on the penetrability of experiential boundaries such as life and death may be read in that way—as a representation of the disintegration of cultural boundaries that distinguished Han culture from the surrounding (perceived to be less developed) cultures. This dissolution of boundaries, of course, raises serious questions about the nature and stability of cultural identity. The integrative mode of *chih-kuai* fictional discourse—most often described in terms of a mixing of elite and popular elements—can thus be reread as a statement of the problem of re-presenting Han identity. The collapsing of boundaries in the tales can in other words be read as a tacit assertion that the notion of Han cultural identity is in jeopardy.

That *chih-kuai* tales symbolize the unreadability of Han identity seems to be implied by the ubiquitous use of terms for the unrecognizable, different, or confusing that appear in the titles of the collections.[51] The titles suggest that the tales go beyond representing something strange for its intrinsic interest or potential shock value and that they are in fact also accounts of the unreadability of existence.

At the same time that the tales can be read as signifying the loss of the ability to recognize Han cultural identity, they can also be read as signaling a shift in the ideology of cultural imperialism. The Han imperial order sought to assert itself over alien cultures and mitigate their destructive forces.[52] Yet even the Han were forced to revalorize their perceptions in the face of changing historical circumstances. The integrative mode of fictional discourse in effect performs a reading of this process and records a moment in the history of expanding Chinese modes of acculturation. And thus the tales of the marvelous may be read as an implicit dramatization of the disappearance or restructuring of Han cultural identity.

As linguistic constructions meant to relieve as well as reflect the sense of disarray and alienation felt by subjects of the Six Dynasties period, the tales of the marvelous incorporate the same discursive features found in the cosmogonic myths and in the *Mu T'ien-tzu chuan*. This may explain the presence of many of the motifs associated with the cosmogonic intentions of the flood myths, such as the significance of the number three with regard to transformation and the significance of the motif of crossing water.[53] The appropriation of the biographical format, moreover, anchors the discourse within an individual perspective and its attendant commentarial nature. As Dennis Twitchett has shown, biography in the pre-T'ang era was linked more closely to the commentarial tradition (of the *Tso chuan*) than to historiography.[54] It is thus an appropriate genre for reflecting on a hidden (social) topic.

Vernacular fiction, like the Six Dynasties tales of the marvelous, must also be considered a rereading, but of a different order: the impossibility of representing identity is discursively deployed as a revalorization of established literary culture, including earlier examples of fiction (as opposed to the collapsing of existential boundaries). Karl S. Y. Kao's analysis of derivative forms of literature as "generated by an interaction with an existing literary tradition" seems to account for this phenomenon as well.[55]

The term "literary colloquial" may be a more appropriate label for the linguistic medium used in this mode of ficton, because it incorporates a mix of the classical and vernacular languages. It is a hybrid medium, a self-conscious combining of different levels of speech, ranging from the stylized and lofty language of the descriptive tableaus to the didactic summary of the storyteller/narrator.[56] The prose of vernacular fiction evinces fascination with particularities of expression and a sensitivity to the nuances of rhetorical and structural arrangement. More important for the present discussion, through the interplay of sameness and difference, originality and tradition, the hybrid medium represents the trauma of the impotence of traditional or paradigmatic cultural patterns to signify an "order" that can any longer adequately reflect reality.

The hybrid medium has been considered an identifying feature of the fictional mode: the major linguistic and discursive means by which the complexity of experience is represented. What then is distinct about the vernacular form? The answer lies in its representative function and the rhetorical effect of its interplay with the other modes of representation. The storyteller-narrator in vernacular fiction still retains his figural status, but it is altered by the use of the colloquial medium which locates the figure's rhetorical effect within the very discourse that it figures. Initially a figure of the fictional mode's discursive source of production, the trope of orality signified a vision of the universe as a congeries of interrelated but open possibilities; within the context of the colloquial medium, however, the rhetorical effect of the figure is rendered ironic.

The emergence of the vernacular mode may in part be read as a response to the decline of the figural value of the trope of orality. While many have rightly seen its origins as inextricably tied up with the proselytizing needs of Buddhist missionaries, to view its acceptance and eventual development only in these practical terms elides its rich symbolic significance. The eventual simplification of the storyteller figure into a predictable, almost formalized form was the result of its function as an organizing principle of fictional discourse; it inevitably become conventionalized. As the trope of orality thus lost its potency, it was unable to carry the weight of its symbolic function. In short the figure was co-opted into traditional semiotic structures; it was diffused.

Yet the symbolic function of the trope was not elided per se. It was, rather, displaced and is the absent, unstated topic in the full-length *hsiao-shuo.* The frequent disjunction between the stereotyped discourse of the storyteller-narrator and the picture presented by the careful manipulation of linguistic devices in the colloquial medium, produces a discursive gap that at once mirrors the very act of displacing the storyteller's rhetoric while also commenting on the source or reasons for the displacement.[57] The discursive gap bespeaks an implicit awareness that movement across scales is not axiomatic; one could say that the relation of "local sites" to "global conventional systems" is rendered problematic.

The transposition of the colloquial medium onto inherited literary motifs, moreover, raises the rhetorical problem of distinguishing between figural and literal meaning. We saw this enacted in the *Mu T'ien-tzu chuan,* with the unmarked appropriation of mythic elements within a narrative context. Vernacular fiction transports traditional signs of ancient culture out of their familiar habitat, just as the myths reflect the displacement of an important element from a familiar text (that is, Heaven).

Given such an overlap in function, the colloquial medium may initially have signified the figural or symbolic status of the text and hence distinguished its rhetorical intent from that of other narrative. In juxtaposing an old form and a new symbol, the colloquial medium explored not only the revelation of patterns within the precursor texts but also the mode of perceiving necessary to bring new patterns into view. The problem of local versus global systems of representation may also be read as a problem of reconciling the cultural paradigms of an "ordered" or at least recognizable cultural identity with an illegible "text" of individual identity. Vernacular fiction, in other words, is the product of the obstacle to being when cultural signs no longer functioned as demarcaters of identity.

Such an understanding of the psychoanalytic forces informing the production of the vernacular novel accords with most analyses of the intellectual dynamics of the Ming dynasty, especially for the period during which the great vernacular novels were produced.[58] This reading of vernacular fiction—as generated by its encrypted narrative of the obsolescence of meaningful cultural signs, and the problematic it poses for issues of representation—is compatible with various interpretations of the fiction produced at that time. But it also offers a new line of inquiry that probes how the embedded linguistic operations of the colloquial medium contribute to the production of meaning.

Within the commingling of levels of discourse, the loss of the ability to signify in meaninginful ways is aestheticized. Whereas the surface qualities of vernacular texts, with their seeming verbosity and rapt attention to detail, appear to conceal the nagging social questions of the day, a closer look reveals the gaps that need to be filled in.

For example, the use of linguistic patterns that project an authoritative voice and convey a sense of the speaker's authoritative status recalls the annalistic form in the *Mu T'ien-tzu chuan.* It provides a conceptual framework for identifying important relationships among people and events in the narrative. Similar to the correlative theories aimed at creating an inclusive system of thought, "a system that would embrace and explain the phenomena of the entire universe,"[59] this mode of articulation is shown to define and delimit human experience through the use of superficial and inaccurate catergorizations. It is the expressive function of the vernacular, which can be simply described as perceptually based (as opposed to conceptually based), that reveals the authoritative mode as a forced application of inappropriate classifications and thus underlines the absurdity of depicting human events fully as knowable.[60]

The perceptual representation of idenity can be construed as a discursive means to overcome the problem of representation. Perception is represented through rhetorical patterns that derive from linguistic properties embedded in grammatical operations of the colloqial language. The topic-comment grammatical operation, for example, is frequently deployed to slice the narrative according to the perspectives of the various characters, including that of the storyteller-narrator. In addition, the use of perceptually based grammatical variations, such as verb "complements," particles, and the *pa* 把 construction, subjectively nuance the deptiction of action and often bring to light the contradictory nature of the inner and outer life of the characters.[61] This contradiction evinces a skepticism about any generalized representation of experience or of another human being based on reputation or culturally formed image. The entire arsenal of colloquially based rhetorical and linguistic tools is thus used to lead the reader through alternative perceptions of characters and motives. In the end the reader is confounded by the illusory quality of perception and of representation; the illusion of the possibility of representation is thus manifested discursively.[62]

While syntax and linguistic style that accentuate form rather than content are used to illustrate a neatly conceptualized version of experience, colloquial techniques warn against such facile judgments and awaken the reader to the complexity of human motivation, to the fact that not everything is as it seems. The appearance of truth is precisely that—appearance. What a profound source of anxiety! It bespeaks the traumatic source of the fiction's production.

Thus, the colloquial medium underlines the vacuity and eventual ellipsis of cultural signifiers as meaningful signs, and signals the threat to the perpetuation of Chinese culture within Imperial China. Narrative reproduction is thus defined by the vernacular mode as a symptom generated in response to trauma, the possible obliteration of cultural, political, and social integrity.[63] Whereas established literary paradigms serve the narrative as vehicles for cryptically representing the impossibility of "copying" or reproducing classical culture such that it signifies in a meaningful way, the work of vernacular fiction becomes a symbolic mode of recounting and overcoming the impossibility of this reproduction.

The dictum on the difference between historical and fictional modes of representation made by the famous critic of the vernacular novel *Shui-hu chuan* 水滸傳, Chin Sheng-t'an 金聖歎, supports my interpretive approach, especially in light of the intepretation of the notion of *wen* 文 not only as the product of linguistic representation but also as an "instrument [used] for the re-assertion of order."[64] Chin proposes that the events represented by fictional discourse derive from the use of linguistic means to reassert order (因文為事); historiography, by contrast, "relies on events to re-assert order via linguistic means" (以事為文).[65] Chin's interpretation of what constitutes fictional discourse dovetails with the thesis argued thus far: the content of fiction is created from the attempt to represent discursively an unorderly reality. In other words, events are the product of the symbolic, mediating function of fictional discourse. Paradoxically, despite this insight into the founding source of fictional representative modes, Chin tried to subvert the rhetorical intentions of the *Shui-hu chuan* by imposing an artificial order on the text.

Emphasizing human perception as it does, fictional discourse suggests that there may be many answers to the question, What is experience? It suggests that the universe is not an objective entity to be represented in a single way; rather there are infinite ways to piece together the cosmos. The combining of various realities pulled from different time frames enabled the human imagination to weave a new, composite image out of experience. The literary effects of this mode of articulation are manifested through negotiations at multiple sites among those who interpret them and extrapolate beyond them to broader cultural, historical, and literary significances.

Thus, we have seen that the theory of the symbol can extend the theoretical parameters for evaluating and understanding the nature of fictional representation in Chinese literature. As a mode of discourse that re-presents the historical moment of its production, the act of writing can be construed as a kind of decipherment, albeit a ciphered one. Writing fiction consists in recovering and bridging the gap of existential reality. Yet, in that it constantly interrogates the language that constitutes the text and the world—reality—fiction is thus always a metafiction. Although on one level fiction is mimetic—it creates the illusion that it is transmitting information about the world—it in fact reveals the world's constructed nature. It reveals the problematic of representing "order" as it questions any cultural context that reinforces notions of order through prevailing paradigms; its mode of representation reflects how representation is never homogeneous or total. The fictional form coalesced to articulate a vision of the world, to address the anxiety over how to represent experience. It offers a new model for constructing reality, but it never pretends to escape its own self-reflexivity. Fiction's search for the multiplicity of experience is, then, a representation of eluding representation. Because the symbolic function of fictional discourse simultaneously comments upon and is a reponse to the trauma of representation, the production of fiction implies the interface of trauma, history, fiction, and a discursively encrypted ideological unconscious.

Appendix

Chüan Five and the Beginning of the *Mu T'ien-tzu chuan*

The numinous tenor of the narration of King Mu's meeting with Ho-tsung Po-yao in the first *chüan* of the *Mu T'ien-tzu chuan* marks a crucial structural and thematic juncture of the text. Up until that point the text appears to be a straight-forward narration of the places and people visited by King Mu over a period of several days. That the narrative preceding the meeting is fragmented—indeed, the first sentence of the text is actually truncated, providing no hint of a context with which to situate the object of narration—serves to highlight the structural integrity of the initial Ho-tsung scene. While the idea of a text beginning in ex-nihilo fashion accords nicely with the symbolic undertones of a universe or world age coming into being out of emptiness (that is, the cosmic gap), there are indications that King Mu's meeting with Ho-tsung Po-yao and the consequences of this meeting were perhaps more narratively determined than at first glance.

In chapter 1 of this book I suggested that parts of *chüan* five of the *Mu T'ien-tzu chuan*, may in fact represent a collection of displaced strips that are connected by having something to do with King Mu. Some of the narrative of that *chüan* resembles, in form and content, entries describing activities of early kings in the *Bamboo Annals*, while other sections resemble more closely in style the narrative of the *Mu T'ien-tzu chuan*. There is one section in particular that because of the resonance of certain phrases, which appear nowhere else in the text, with those of the first *chüan*, may perhaps be viewed as a displaced section of the narrative's beginning. Because this section also, if read as part of the first *chüan*, provides a remarkably coherent context for understanding the narrative "motivation" underlying Ho-tsung Po-yao's symbolic function within the text, it deserves at least some measure of consideration.

The section of *chüan* five that I am referring to contains the most concentrated depiction of events having to do with divination, dreams, and occurrences of strange phenomena in the entire text. The divinatory sections concern the auspiciousness of King Mu's travel plans; one dream reveals a preoccupation with the (advantages) of sacrificing to the ancestors, while the other alludes to the Archer I myth. The strange phenomena include the transformation of a "numinous drum" (*ling-ku* 靈鼓) into a yellow snake, an event that was interpreted as having portentuous significance, and an unexpected cold blast occurring during the equinox that produced dire consequences. A common denominator connecting these events is the sense of a need to justify the rationale for King Mu's journey.

The question of King Mu's motivation, or travel objective, was a topic of particular interest to recorders of the tradition of his journey. Ch'ü Yüan's famous line "What was it that [King Mu] was looking for?" captures the intriguing sense of mystery that surrounded the tradition of the king's voyage. King Mu's apparent disregard for the advice of his ministers, and an inauspicious divination, recorded in the ancient *Kuei-tsang*, further deepens the intrigue surrounding what compelled King Mu to travel westward. In the *Mu T'ien-tzu chuan*, King Mu himself is represented as feeling conflicted over his desires to travel and his sense of the needless extravagance of the trip. In *chüan* five, after some in his entourage have suffered (in one text, till their death) the bitter cold, King Mu creates a poem to lament their suffering. In the poem he invokes God on High and the latter's control of the vast lands of China, thereby connecting the object of travel with God on High's will. Because God on High in fact provides King Mu with a heavenly sanctioned motive to travel in the first *chüan*, it could be read as a response to King Mu's troubled invocation. Indeed, because King Mu's anxiety feeds into the symbolic significance of his trip, there are compelling contextual reasons to regard the section of *chüan* five as a displaced part of the beginning of the text.

In addition to these compelling contextual reasons, the similarity of place-names of both sections also seems to suggest more than a peripheral connection. For example, the similarity between the place-names where King Mu convenes his court directly after receiving God on High's order, Yellow Mountain, and the places where the events in *chüan* five take place, Yellow Pool and Yellow

Bamboo [Grove], and the Hill of the Yellow Room, invite reflection over their mutual relevance, especially since the term Yellow appears nowhere else in the text as a modifier for a place-name. Of particular interest is the possible connection between Yellow Mountain located at Yang-yü, where Ho-tsung Po-yao (and Feng-i) resides, and the Hill of the Yellow Room, which is believed (by King Mu as well as tradition) to be the place where the son of Yü and Lady T'u, Ch'i, was born. Through their association to the Yü myths both place-names share a symbolic referent.

The use of similar diction in both *chüan* one and five also invites analysis. The phrase "northern winds, rain and snow" (*pei-feng yü-hsüeh* 北風雨雪), an allusion to a poem in the *Shih ching*, appears in both *chüan*. The references to cold weather, while appearing to be merely innocuous details of a journey, nonetheless also hint at the symbolism of Ho-tsung Po-yao's residence: the wintery weather accords with the seasonal associations of the Heavenly Turtle quadrant.

Another passage in the fifth *chüan*, one which connects the dream of ancestral sacrifices to the events of the equinox, would also perform the literary function of foreshadow if it were replaced in the first *chüan*. The object of foreshadow is the symbolic function of K'un-lun as a place where regeneration is effected and its relevance to King Mu's relationship with his ancestors, which is intimated in God on High's ordering King Mu to "Pay attention to the timeliness of ancestral sacrifices" before ordering him to go to K'un-lun. The sequence of God on High's orders imply a causal connection between maintaining timeliness and the achieving of a specific objective by going to K'un-lun.

Although I can offer no concrete example of how a reconstructed first *chüan* might look with elements of *chüan* five worked into it, the strong resonance between these elements and the events narrated in the first *chüan* warrants consideration in a critical appreciation of the *Mu T'ien-tzu chuan*. The text's foregrounding of events that focus on King Mu's conscious and unconscious concerns about the legitimacy of his travel plans, and the way these events bring into relief if not set up the symbolic significance of the journey, provide an important perspective through which to analyze the major literary tenets of the narrative.

NOTES

INTRODUCTION

1. Plaks, *Archetype and Allegory in Dream of the Red Chamber* (Princeton: Princeton University Press, 1976).

2. Chatman, *Story and Discourse* (Ithaca: Cornell University Press, 1978).

3. Foucault, *The Archaeology of Knowledge and The Discourse on Language*, trans. A. M. Sheridan Smith (New York: Pantheon, 1972), 229.

4. Edmonson, *Spoken Discourse: A Model for Analysis* (London: Longman, 1981), 4.

5. Halliday, *An Introduction to Functional Grammar* (London: Edward Arnold, 1985), 290.

6. Tomlin, "The Identification of Clause Level Theme in Text and Discourse," Manuscript, University of Oregon, 38–39, cited in Yong Ho, *Aspects of Discourse Structure in Mandarin Chinese* (Lewiston, N.Y.: Edwin Mellon University Press, 1993), 17–18.

CHAPTER 1

1. For various records of the discovery, see the *Chin shu*, 10 vols. (Peking: Chung-hua, 1987), vol. 1, 3.70; vol. 2, 16.490; vol. 5, 51.1432–33. There is some discrepancy among dates reported for the year of discovery (e.g., 279, 280, 281) that may stem from confusion caused by a hiatus between the discovery of the texts and beginning of the actual editing and transcribing of it. See *Chin shu*, vol. 1, 3.85 n. 23; Chu Hsi-tsu, *Chi-chung shu k'ao* (Peking: Chung-hua, 1960), 1–3; see also Wei T'ing-sheng, *Mu T'ien-tzu chuan chin-k'ao*, 3 vols. (Taipei: Chung-hua hsüeh-shu yüan,

1970), vol. 1, 48–51, both of whom accept the 279 date. Ch'eng Meng-chia, in his "Chi-chung shu-k'ao," dates the discovery to 281, although he does not provide evidence as to why. See his *Liu-kuo chi-nien* (Shanghai: Hsüeh-hsi sheng-huo, 1955), 118.

2. The editors' belief that the vault was the tomb of King Hsiang was based on the final entry of one of the texts discovered, the *Bamboo Annals* (*Chu shu chi nien*), which uses the expression *jin wang* 今王 or "the present king," to refer to the son of King Hui-ch'eng 惠成 of Wei. The genealogical text *Shih-pen* 世本 identifies this son as Prince Hsiang; see Hsün Hsü's 荀勖 preface to the *Mu T'ien-tzu chuan*, printed in Ku Shih, *Mu T'ien-tzu chuan hsi-cheng chiang-shu* (Shanghai: Shang-wu, 1934; rpt., Taipei: Shang-wu, 1976), "*Mu-lu*," 7.

3. Private communication, 11 March 1990.

4. Actually, as Ogawa Takuji, relying on the Chi-chieh commentary of the *Shih chi*, explains it, the confusion between King Ai and King Hsiang derives from the fact that King Hui-ch'eng (according to the *Bamboo Annals*) changed his reign title in the thirty-sixth year of his reign and then ruled for another seventeen years, upon which King Hsiang assumed rule. In the *Shih chi*, however, for some reason the last seventeen years of King Hui-ch'eng's reign is counted as King Hsiang's, and hence the following period of a twenty-three-year reign was assigned to King Ai. See Ogawa, "Boku Tenshi den kō," *Kano Kyōju kanreki kinen* (Tokyo: Kōbundō, 1928); rpt. and trans. in Chiang Hsia-an, *Hsien-ch'in ching-chi k'ao*, 3 vols. (Shanghai: Shang-wu, 1929), vol. 3, 101–10.

5. *Shih chi*, 10 vols. (Peking: Chung-hua, 1959), vol. 6, 44.1849.

6. Chu Hsi-tsu, *Chi-chung shu-k'ao*, 4.

7. Cf. Li Ling's argument that since pre-Ch'in times, state archives (*tang-an* 檔案) were not regarded as constituting "ancient books" (*ku-shu* 古書). The *Bamboo Annals*, then, probably have more in common with the miscellaneous texts that were buried along with it, what Li Ling identifies as veritable ancient books, than the veritable archives of Wei. See Li Ling, "Ch'u-t'u fa-hsien yü ku-shu nien-tai ti tsai jen-shih," *Chiu-chou hsüeh-k'an* 3.1 (1988), 105–16.

8. Chu Hsi-tsu, *Chi-chung shu-k'ao*, 5.

9. For reports of the discovery of the tombs of the Marquis I of Tseng and at Ma-wang-tui, see Sui-hsien Lei-ku tun i-hao-mu k'ao-ku fa-chüeh tui, "Hu-pei Sui-hsien Tseng-hou I mu fa-chüeh chien-pao," *Wen-wu* 7 (1979), 1; and Hu-nan sheng po-wu-kuan, Chung-kuo she-hui k'o-hsüeh yüan k'ao-ku yen-chiu so, "Ch'ang-sha Ma-wang-tui erh san hao Han-mu fa-chüeh chien-pao." For a more detailed description and analysis of the artifacts discovered, see Hunan sheng po-wu-kuan, Chung-kuo k'o-hsüeh

yüan k'ao-ku yen-chiu so, *Ch'ang-sha Ma-wang-tui i-hao Han-mu*, 2 vols. (Peking: Wen-wu, 1973); and for the texts, see Ma-wang-tui Han-mu Po-shu cheng-li hsiao-tsu, *Ma-wang-tui Han-mu po-shu*, 3 vols. (Peking: Wen-wu, 1983).

10. Some of the more recent discoveries of texts in tombs include findings at the Han tomb discovered in 1972 in Lin-i 臨沂 county in Shantung (M 1, 2); in 1973 the Han tomb discovered in 1973 in Ch'ang-sha 長沙, Hunan at Ma-wang-tui 馬王堆 (M 3); also in 1973 there is the discovery of the Han tomb of Pa-chiao Lang 八角廊 in Ting county 定 of Hopei (M 40); 1975, the Ch'in tomb in Yün-meng 雲夢 county in Hupei (M 11); the Han tomb discovered in 1977 at Fu-yang 島陽 Shang-ku-tui 雙古堆 in An-hui province; the Han tomb discovered in 1983–84 at Chiang-ling 江陵 Chang-chia-shan 張家山 in Hupei. For the reports of these discoveries, see Shantung sheng po-wu-kuan, Lin-i wen-wu tsu, "Shan-tung Lin-i Hsi-Han-mu fa-hsien 'Sun-tzu pin-fa' ho 'Sun Pin pin-fa' teng chu-chien ti chien-pao," *Wen-wu* 2 (1974), 15–26; Lo Fu-i, "Lin-i Han-chien kai-shu," *Wen-wu* 2 (1974), 32–35; Ho-pei sheng wen-wu yen-chiu so, "Ho-pei Ting-hsien 40 hao Han-mu fa-chüeh chien-pao," *Wen-wu* 8 (1981), 1–10; Ting-hsien Han-mu chu-chien cheng-li tsu, "Ting-hsien 40 hao Han-mu ch'u-t'u chu-chien chien-chieh," *Wen-wu* 8 (1981), 11–12; Hu-pei Hsiao-kan ti-ch'ü ti-erh ch'i yi-kung yi-nung wen-wu k'ao-ku hsün-lian pan, "Hu-pei Yün-meng Shui-hu ti shih-i hao Ch'in-mu fa-chüeh chien-pao," *Wen-wu* 6 (1976), 1–11; and idem, "Hu-pei Yün-meng Shui-hu ti shi-i tso Ch'in-mu fa-chüeh chien-pao," *Wen-wu* 9 (1976), 51–62; Li Hsün, "Yün-meng Shui-hu ti Ch'in-chien kai-shu," *Wen-wu* 5 (1976), 1–6; An-hui sheng wen-wu kung-tso tui, "Fu-yang Shang-ku-tui Hsi-Han Ju-yin Hou mu fa-ch'üeh chien-pao," *Wen-wu* 8 (1978), 12–31; Ching-chou ti-ch'ü po-wu kuan, "Ching-ling Chang-chia-shan san-tso Han-mu ch'u-t'u ta-p'i chu-chien," *Wen-wu* 1 (1985), 1–8.

11. See Fu-yang Han-chien cheng-li tsu, "Fu-yang Han-chien chien-chieh," *Wen-wu* 2 (1983), 21–23; and Hu P'ing-sheng, "Some Notes on the Organization of the Han Dynasty Bamboo 'Annals' Found at Fuyang," *Early China* 14 (1989), 1–25.

12. The text is transcribed in Yün-meng Ch'in-mu chu-chien cheng-li hsiao-tsu, "Yün-meng Ch'in-chien shih-wen (1)," *Wen-wu* 6 (1976), 12–13. For an in-depth discussion of these *Annals*, see Shang-hai shih ch'ung-hsing chi-hsieh chih-tsao kung-ssu kung-jen li-shih yen-chiu hsiao-tsu, "Ts'ung Yün-meng Ch'in-chien 'Ta-chi-shih' k'an Ch'in t'ung-i liu-kuo ho fan-fu pi tou-cheng," *Wen-wu* 7 (1976), 12–18.

13. Wei T'ing-sheng, *Mu T'ien-tzu chuan chin-k'ao*, vol. 1, 51–57.

14. Wei T'ing-sheng, *Mu T'ien-tzu chuan chin-k'ao*, vol. 1, 54. The reference for the contents of the *Treasures of Liang Hill* text comes from Su Hsi's biography in the *Chin shu*, vol. 6, 51.1433.

15. For other studies emphasizing the importance of context for understanding the significance of objects found in tombs, see Wu Hung, "Art in a Ritual Context: Rethinking Mawangdui," *Early China* 17 (1992), 111–44; and John Major, "Will the Real Yellow Emperor Please Stand Up?," in Major, *Essays on the Huainanzi* (Albany: SUNY Press, forthcoming).

16. Wei T'ing-sheng, *Mu T'ien-tzu chuan chin-k'ao*, vol. 1, 57–66. Liang designates the name of the Wei state after King Hui-ch'eng of Wei moved his capital from An-i 安邑 in the ninth year of his reign to Ta-liang (362 B.C.). See Ch'ien Mu, *Hsien-Ch'in chu-tzu hsi-nian t'ung-piao*, 2 vols. (Hong Kong: Hong-kong University Press, 1956), "T'ung piao," vol. 2, 547. For descriptions and analyses of Tsou Yen and his contribution to early Chinese thought, see Joseph Needham, *Science and Civilization in China*, 6 vols. (Cambridge: Cambridge University Press, 1956–), vol. 2, 325ff.; and Benjamin Schwartz, *The World of Thought in Ancient China* (Cambridge: Harvard University Press, 1985), 356–69.

17. See note 1 above for the discrepancy in the year of the texts' discovery.

18. It is not clear why King An-li, the son of King Chao, who was the son of King Ai, ever became a contestant for the tomb-master position. See Chu Hsi-tsu's comments regarding the apparent absurdity of this confusion, *Chi-chung shu-k'ao*, 4.

19. These annals will be referred to as the *Bamboo Annals* throughout this study.

20. *Chin shu*, vol. 5, 51.1432–33. This excerpt is cited from the edition of the *Chin shu* that was revised by Fang Hsüan-ling 房玄齡 et al. during the T'ang 唐 dynasty. Chu Hsi-tsu cites an entry in the Yü hai 玉海 which provides an excerpt of Wang Yin's biography of Su Hsi that differs from the detailed description in the *Chin shu*. Whereas the latter describes the content and length of all of the texts discovered in the Chi vault, the former provides a description of only four texts: the *Book of Changes*, the *Bamboo Annals*, the *Fragmented Dialogues*, and a text of five *chüan* called *The Travels* of *a Chou King* (*Chou wang yu hsing* 周王游行). We will address the implications of this difference below. See Chu Hsi-tsu, *Chi-chung shu-k'ao*, 28–29.

21. For the Yin-ch'üeh shan texts, see *Yin-ch'üeh shan Han-mu chu-chien* (Peking; Wen-wu, 1985); for the Pao-shan materials, see the Hu-pei-sheng Ching-sha t'ieh-lu k'ao-ku tui, *Pao-shan Ch'u-chien* (Peking: Wen-wu, 1991).

22. Historical texts of this sort were discovered at Lin-i (*Yen-tzu* 晏子), Ma-wang-tui (*Ch'un-ch'iu Shih-yü* 春秋事語, *Chan-kuo tsung-heng chia-shu* 戰國從衡家書), and the Pa-chiao Lang tomb (*Ai kung wen wui* 哀

公問五義, *Ju-chia-che yen* 儒家者言). Cf. Li Ling's comment that books recording the ideas of a school have much in common with histories such as the *Kuo-yü* and the *Yen-tzu ch'un-ch'iu* 晏子春秋, "Ch'u-t'u fa-hsien yü ku-shu nien-tai ti tsai jen-shih," 110–11. Texts similar to the *Sheng feng*, *Chou-shih t'ien-fa*, and *Chiao-shu* are also represented in recent archaeological finds: Pa-chiao lang tomb (*Pao-fu p'ien* 保傅篇); Shui-hu ti (*Ta-shih-chi*, *Wei Li chih tao* 為吏之道); Fu-yang (*Nien-piao*, *Tso-wu yüan-ch'eng* 作務員程, *Hsing-te* 刑德).

23. Astronomical texts were part of the cache discovered at Ma-wang-tui (e.g., *Wu-hsing chan* 本行占, *T'ien-wen ch'i-hsiang tsa-chan* 天文氣象雜占); calendrical texts were discovered at the tombs of Pa-chiao Lang (*Jih-shu chan-pu* 日書占卜), Shui-hu ti (*Jih-shu*), Fu-yang (*Jih-shu*), and Chang-chia shan (*Jih-shu*, *Li-p'u* 曆譜).

24. Ch'en Meng-chia, "Chi-chung shu-k'ao," 126, divides the texts into five categories: (1) history; (2) geography; (3) divination; (4) fiction (*hsiao-shuo*); (5) miscellaneous.

25. These types of texts are also amply represented in recent finds; Ma-wang-tui (*Chou-i* 周易, *Yin-yang wu-hsing* 陰陽五行, *Mu-jen chan* 木人占, *Shen-t'u* 神圖); Fu-yang (*Chou-i*); Chang-chia shan (*Suan-shu shu* 算術書).

26. See Benjamin Schwartz, "The Age of Transcendence," *Daedalus* (1974), 1–7. See also idem, "Transcendence in Ancient China," *Daedalus* (1974), 57–68;' and idem, Introduction, in *The World of Thought in Ancient China*, 2–3. Schwartz borrows the term "axial age" from Karl Jaspers, *Vom Ursprung und Ziel der Geschichte* (Zürich: Artemis Verlag, 1949).

27. Schwartz, "The Age of Transcendence," 3.

28. A. F. P. Hulsewé, "Texts in Tombs," *Asiatische Studien* 18–19 (1965), 79–89.

29. David Hawkes "Quest of the Goddess," in Cyril Birch, ed., *Studies in Chinese Literary Genres* (Berkeley: University of California Press, 1974), 54ff. Hawkes suggests that journeys such as the one described in the *Mu T'ien-tzu chuan* were a necessary attribute of imperium; the hallmark was the inclusion of all possible forms of topography, mineral wealth, flora, and fauna. The diversity of the experiences provided the most tangible image of the emperor as a cosmic figure, an earthly simulacrum of the all-embracing Heaven.

30. The attack on Eastern Wu began just one month after the discovery of the Chi vault. See the "Annals" of Emperor Wu-ti, *Chin shu*, vol. 1, 3.70–71.

31. See Hsün Hsü's biography, *Chin shu*, vol. 4, 39.1154. Another

scholar, Ho Chiao 和嶠, Hsün Hsü's subordinate at the time, also assisted in this work. See the *Chin shu*, vol. 4, 45.1283.

32. For the first view, see *Chin shu*, vol. 1, 3.70; for the second view, see Tu Yu's 杜豫 preface to the *Tso chuan*, "Ch'un-ch'iu Tso shih ching-chuan chi-chieh hou hsü", in *Tso-shih hui-chien*, 2 vols. (Taipei: Han-ching wen-hua, 1984), vol. 2, 30.64; for the third view, see Hsün Hsü's preface to the *Mu T'ien-tzu chuan*, in Ku Shih, *Hsi-cheng chiang-shu*, "Mu-lu," 7.

33. Chu Hsi-tsu, *Chi-chung shu-k'ao k'ao*, 13–14, cites Wang Kuo-wei, who states that the term "tadpole script" was not coined until the latter part of the Han dynasty and during the Wei and Chin dynasties became a popular way of describing any script that was different from the standard clerical script. See Wang's "K'o-tou wen-tzu shuo," *Kuan-t'ang chi-lin*, 4 vols. (Peking: Chung-hua, 1984), vol. 2, 337–39. See also Ch'en Meng-chia, "Chi-chung shu-k'ao," 120; and Wei T'ing-sheng, *Mu T'ien-tzu chuan chin-k'ao*, vol. 1, 92–93. Recent discoveries of Warring States texts have allowed scholars to refine their understanding of ancient script forms. Li Xueqin, *Eastern Zhou and Qin Civilizations*, trans. K. C. Chang (New Haven: Yale University Press, 1985), 454, states that the writing system of the Chin (and Wei) states are "characterized by strokes that are fat in the middle and thin toward the end, shaped like tadpoles."

34. See Wang Kuo-wei, "Wei Shi-ching k'ao 1–5," *Kuan-t'ang chi-lin*, vol. 4, 955–75. For an informative study of the style of scripts used on the steles, see Ho Lin-i, *Chan-kuo wen-tzu t'ung-lun* (Peking: Chung-hua, 1989), 51–60.

35. Chu Hsi-tsu, *Chi-chung shu-k'ao*, 16–19. Ogawa Tokuji, "Boku tenshi den kō," 138, also points out that the names of the horses differ in the section of the *Lieh-tzu* 列子 that describes a similar journey undertaken by King Mu.

36. Chu Hsi-tsu, noting that the official title (Grand Master for Splendid Happiness 侍中中書監光祿大夫) used by Hsün Hsü in his preface to the *Mu T'ien-tzu chuan* was already superseded by the foruth month of the third year of the T'ai-k'ang reign (A.D. 282) when he was the Superior Grand Master for Splendid Happiness 左光祿大夫, concludes that Hsün Hsü must have completed his preface before this time. See his *Chi-chung shu-k'ao*, 38. Cf. Ogawa Takuji, "Boku Tenshi den kō," 119, where he claims that Hsün Hsü's preface was written in the tenth year of the T'ai-kang reign (A.D. 289), the year that Hsün Hsü died.

37. Wei was primarily responsible for the compilation of the *Bamboo Annals*; see the biography of Wang Chieh 王接, *Chin shu*, vol. 5, 51.1436; and Chu Hsi-tsu, *Chi-chung shu-k'ao*, 14.

38. Chu Hsi-tsu, *Chi-chung shu-k'ao*, 28.

39. See Hao I-hsing, ed., *Shan-hai-ching chien-shu* (Taipei: I-wen, 1974), "Chung-shan ching," 218, 219, 262. It is probably not a coincidence that Ti T'ai is associated with Ch'ung mountain in the *Shan-hai-ching*. As we shall see below, going to Ch'ung mountain is the primary objective of King Mu's visit to K'un-lun.

40. Chu Hsi-tsu, *Chi-chung shu-k'ao*, 29.

41. Chu Hsi-tsu, *Chi-chung shu-k'ao*, 29. For Yen Yen-chih's fu, see his *Ch'eng pai-ma fu* 赭白馬賦, in Hsiao T'ung, ed., *Wen hsüan*, 6 vols. (Shang-hai: Shang-hai ku-chi, 1986), vol. 2, 14.627.

42. Ch'en Meng-chia "Chi-chung shu-k'ao," 133, also argues that the present sixth *chüan* was not originally part of the text. Ogawa Tokuji, "Boku tenshi den kō," 133–35, argues that the sixth *chüan* narrating the tale of Sheng Chi's death was a part of the original "text," and that the sixth *chüan* was comprised of the *T'u-shu* text which was also found in the tomb (because he believed the illustrations contained therein were of the events and actions experienced by King Mu). He also suggests, after calculating how many strips would have comprised the longer *chüan* of the text—40 to 50—that the third and fourth *chüan* must have originally been just one, otherwise they would have been too short.

43. Chu Hsi-tsu, *Chi-chung shu-k'ao*, 28.

44. Ibid., *Chi-chung shu-k'ao*, 29.

45. See A. F. P. Hulsewé, "Notes on the Historiography of the Han Period," in W. B. Beasely, and E. G. Pulleyblank, eds., *Historians of China and Japan* (London: Oxford University Press, 1961), 41, for a discussion of this form of historiography.

46. Both Ku Shih, *Hsi-cheng chiang-shu*, 1–10, and Wei T'ing-sheng, *Mu T'ien-tzu chuan chin-k'ao*, vol. 1, 110–12, cite all bibliographic entries on the *Mu T'ien-tzu chuan* that appear in dynastic histories as well as bibliographies from private collections from the Sui dynasty down through the Ch'ing dynasty.

47. Yao Chi-heng, *Ku-chin wei-shu-k'ao* (*Chih-pu-tsu chai ts'ung-shu* ed.), 11a–12b, however, claims that this historiographical mode was invented after the Han. He thus concludes that the *Mu T'ien-tzu chuan* must have been a post-Han composition.

48. *Ssu-k'u ch'üan-shu tsung-mu*, 2 vols. (Peking: Chung-hua, 1965), vol. 2, 1205.

49. Joseph Needham, *Science and Civilization of China*, vol. 1, 151–57 discusses diffusionist theories and their relevance to Chinese studies. See also Ch'en Hsing-ts'an, "Chung-kuo shih-ch'ien wen-hua chi ch'i hsi-

lai chia-shuo ti yu-lai ho fen-hsi," *Chiu-chou hsüeh-k'an* 5.3 (1993), 71–86, for a discussion of a different aspect (archaeological) of the diffusionist theory.

50. Wei T'ing-sheng says that he was influenced in this way, *Mu T'ien-tzu chuan chin-k'ao*, vol. 1, 1.

51. Ting Ch'ien, *Mu T'ien-tzu chuan ti-li k'ao-cheng, Che-chiang t'u-shu ts'ung-shu* ed., "Fan-li," la–1b, states clearly that the *Mu T'ien-tzu chuan* shows how "Chinese" came from the West; Liu Shih-p'ei, *Mu T'ien-tzu chuan pu-shih, Liu Shen-shu hsien-sheng i-shu* ed., "Preface," 1, states that the text shows how the Chinese had always had contact and interacted with the West. See also his reading of Hsi-wang-mu as an "elongated" version of the place-name Sumer (Hsi-mo 西膜), *Mu T'ien-tzu chuan pu-shi*, 8a. Su Hsüeh-lin, *T'ien-wen cheng-chien*, rpt. (Taipei: Wen-chin, 1992), approaches the myths in the "T'ien-wen" poem from this perspective.

52. For a lucid discussion of how some of these scholastic issues were in fact inextricably mixed up with ideas of nationalistic and ethnic issues, see Laurence A. Schneider, *Ku Chieh-kang and China's New History* (Berkeley: University of California Press, 1971), 18–52 et passim.

53. Examples of anachronism include the use of the adjective "yellow" (*huang* 黃) to modify the ancient word for "metal" (*chin* 金) and thus signify gold. Wei Chü-hsien, "*Mu T'ien-tzu chuan* yen-chiu," in *Ku-shih yen-chiu* (Shanghai: I-wen, 1934), 200, claims that this implies an awareness of iron (the "other" metal) which was not discovered until Spring and Autumn period (700–500 B.C.). Noel Barnard, "Indigenous Origins of Metallurgy," in David Keightley, ed., *The Origins of Chinese Civilization* (Berkeley: University of California Press, 1983), 247–49, uses modern archaeological and scientific evidence to argue for the late discovery of cast (as opposed to that derived from meteorites) iron. Wei Chü-hsien, "*Mu T'ien-tzu chuan* yen-chiu," 196, cites the use of a royal title to refer to a living king, as is done in the first *chüan* of the text, as another example of anachronism. It is now generally accepted, however, that royal titles were used during the king's lives. See Edward Shaughnessy, *Sources of Western Zhou History* (Berkeley: University of California Press, 1991), 108, n. 4. For a dissenting view, see Sheng Dong-ling, "Hsi-Chou t'ung-ch'i ming-wen chung ti jen-ming chi ch'i tui tuan-tai ti i-i," *Wen-shih* 7 (1983), 27–64. Wei T'ing-sheng offers counterarguments for both examples of anachronism, *Mu T'ien-tzu chuan chin k'ao*, vol. 1, 163.

54. For studies that draw these conclusions, see Yao Chi-heng, *Ku-chin wei-shu-k'ao*, 11a–12b; Wei Chü-hsien, "*Mu T'ien-tzu chuan* ti yen-chiu," 196–245; Chang Hsin-ch'eng, *Wei-shu t'ung-k'ao* (Shanghai: Shang-wu, 1957; rpt. Taipei: Hung-yeh, 1979), 179–80; Ku Chieh-kang, "*Mu T'ien-tzu chuan* chi ch'i chu-tso shih-tai," *Wen shih che* 1 (1951), 63–68; Mitarai Masaru, "*Boku Tenshi den* seiritsu no haikei," *Tōhōgaku* 26 (1962),

17–30; Ch'ang Cheng, "*Mu T'ien-tzu chuan* shih wei-shu ma?," *Ho-pei ta-hsüeh hsüeh-pao* 2 (1980), 30–53.

55. For a brilliant critique of this method of dating texts and the assumptions informing this method texts, see Li Ling, "Ch'u-t'u fa-hsien yü ku-shu nien-tai ti tsai jen-shih," 105–7.

56. See Wei T'ing-sheng, *Mu T'ien-tzu chuan chin-k'ao*, vol. 1, 110–13; 209–25ff.; 423–33; and Ku Shih, *Hsi-cheng chiang-shu*, "Mu-chuan hsi-cheng nien-li," 1–14. For other scholars' assesments and discussions of this debate, see Chang Kung-liang, "Ku Shih chu *Mu T'ien-tzu chuan* hsi-cheng chiang-shu," *Yü kung* 3.4 (1935), 31–46; Rémi Mathieu, *Le Mu Tianzi Zhuan, Traduction annotée étude critique* (Paris: Institut des hautes Études Chinoises, 1978), 110ff. Cf. Edward L. Shaughnessy, *Sources of Western Zhou History*, 145, who states that the Hsia calendrical system was not used consistently during the Western Chou.

57. Wei T'ing-sheng, *Mu T'ien-tzu chuan chin-k'ao*, vol. 1, 158–59, 424–26, and Ku, *Hsi-cheng chiang-shu*, 3, both invoke the "Explanation of Months" 周月 of the *I Chou shu*, which they understand to be a Western Chou text outlining the calendrical changes they believe are reflected in the *Mu T'ien-tzu chuan*. See Chu Yu-tseng, ed., *Yi-Chou shu chiao-shih*, 2 vols., 1911 edition, vol. 2, 6.1b. Huang P'ei-jung, *Chou shu 'Chou yüeh' p'ien chu-ch'eng ti shih-tai chi yu-kuan san-cheng wen-t'i ti yen-chiu* (Taipei: Wen-shih ts'ung-k'an, 1972), argues that the content of the "Explanation of Months" does not predate the Spring and Autumn era, and he posits that the concept of a Chou calendar was not established until this time.

58. Huang P'ei-jung, *Chou shu 'Chou yüeh' p'ien chu-ch'eng shih-tai*, 8–10.

59. See David Pankenier, "Reflections of the Lunar Aspect on Western Chou Chronology," *T'oung Pao* 78 (1992), 67. Wei T'ing-sheng, *Mu T'ien-tzu chuan chin-k'ao*, vol. 1, 159, actually acknowledges that the Hsia calendrical system was used in at least one bronze inscription, the *Mao Pan kuei* 毛班簋. In this inscription King Mu dispatches Duke Pan 班 of Mao to fight the Eastern I 夷 barbarians on *chia-hsü* 甲戌 (day 11) of the eighth month. This same person is mentioned in the fourth *chüan* of the *Mu T'ien-tzu chuan* (Ku Shih, *Hsi-cheng chiang-shu*, 4.234), although there is no reference to his being dispatched to fight. In the text King Mu orders Duke Pan of Mao to return to the capital to "await [further] orders" on day *ping-yin* 丙寅 (day 3), four days after day *jen-hsü* 壬戌 (day 59) which, in the text, is described as occurring in "the beginning of winter" (*meng-tung* 孟冬). Because the cycle day in the bronze inscription falls just eight days later than the cycle day referred to in the text, Wei assumes that both the bronze inscription and the text are referring to the same events (he assumes that the bronze inscription records the "awaited" orders of King Mu), albeit via different calendrical media: the bronze inscription employs the Hsia calen-

dar while the text employs the Chou calendar, which begins two months earlier, hence the two-month discrepancy. Even if we allow for a coincidence of referents, Wei's argument that the text reflects the "official calendar" while the bronze inscription reflects the "popular calendar" is untenable. If anything, the discrepancy points to the text's anachronistic use of a calendrical system to record historical events. Unfortunately, Wei is so convinced that the *Mu T'ien-tzu chuan* is a veritable Western Chou document that he never examines fully the implications of the discrepancy. Cf. Wei Chü-hsien's argument that the use of a *Hsia* calendrical system points to a late date of composition for the text (he assumes, incorrectly with Wei T'ing-sheng, that a Chou calendrical system should have been in use during the Western Chou), "*Mu T'ien-tzu chuan* yen-chiu," 195–96. For the *Mao Pan kuei* inscription, see Ma Ch'eng-yüan, ed., *Shang Chou ch'ing-t'ung-ch'i ming-wen-hsüan*, 4 vols. (Peking: Wen-wu, 1988), vol. 3, 108–10.

60. For the use of the *Hsia* system in Chin and Wei bronzes, see Yang K'uan, *Chan-kuo shih*, rpt. (Shanghai: Jen-min, 1991), 450. The obvious connection between the *Mu T'ien-tzu chuan* and the *Bamboo Annals* makes it clear that the latter text is also a product of Chin or Wei. Textual details, such as the use of the term *ch'ing* 卿 to refer to a minister, and the successful subjugation of northern nomadic tribes, a feat ascribed to Wei Chiang 絳, also point in this direction. For the Chin use of the term *ch'ing*, see Ho Lin-i, *Chan-kuo wen-tzu t'ung-lun*, 112; for the subjugation of northern nomadic tribes, see the *Shih chi*, "Wei shih chia," vol. 6, 44.1836. Both Chang Kung-liang, "Ku Shih chu *Mu T'ien-tzu chuan* hsi-cheng chiang-shu," *Yü kung* 4 (1935), 31–46, and Ting Ch'ien, *Mu T'ien-tzu chuan ti-li k'ao-cheng*, "Fan-li," 5b, argue that the calendar used in the text is that of the *Hsia*.

61. For geographically oriented studies of the *Mu T'ien-tzu chuan*, see Paul Pelliot, "L'Etude du *Mou t'ien tseu tchouan*," *T'oung Pao* 21 (1922), 98–102; Ts'en Chung-mien, "*Mu T'ien-tzu chuan* hsi-cheng ti-li kai-ts'e," *Kuo-li Chung-shan ta-hsüeh hsüeh-pao she-hui k'o-hsüeh pan* 2 (1957), 26–48; see also Ogawa Takuji, "Boku tenshi den kō," 161–228; and "Shu Boku o no sai sei," in *Shina rekishi chiri kenkyū zokushū* (Tokyo: Kōbundō, 1929), 165ff.; Chao Li-sheng, "*Mu T'ien-tzu chuan* chung i-hsieh pu-luo ti fang-wei k'ao-shih," *Chung-hua wen-shih lun-ts'ung* 2 (1979), 287–302; Wang Fan-chih, "*Mu T'ien-tzu chuan* yü so chi ku-tai ti-ming ho pu-tsu," *Wen shih che* 6 (1963), 67, 78; Sun Chih-chung, "Mu-wang hsi-cheng yü *Mu T'ien-tzu chuan*," *Ch'i-lu hsüeh-k'an* 2 (1984), 76–82.

62. Wei T'ing-sheng is the only scholar to consider bronze inscriptions in his analysis. See his *Mu T'ien-tzu chuan chin-k'ao*, vol. 1, 193–401.

63. See Ku Chieh-kang, "*Mu T'ien-tzu chuan* chi ch'i chu-tso shih-tai," 63. See also Wang Kuo-wei, "Yü-ting-ming k'ao-shih," *Hai-ning Wang Ching-an hsien-sheng yi-shu*, 48 vols. (Shanghai: Shang-wu, 1940), vol. 16,

1a. See also Henri Maspero, "Contribution à l'étude de le société Chinoise à la fin des Chang et au début des Tcheou," *Bulletin de l'Ècole Française d'Extrême Orient* 46.2 (1954), 347–49, where he argues that the author of the *Mu T'ien-tzu chuan* must have been a citizen of the state of Cheng 鄭 in the fifth or fourth century B.C. because of the knowledge of Cheng geography exhibited by the text.

64. Wei T'ing-sheng, *Mu T'ien-tzu chuan chin-k'ao*, 1.193–401, especially, 251–92. Wang Kuo-wei places Fang (and Hao 鎬) to the "east of the [Yellow] river." See his "Chou Fang-ching k'ao," in *Kuan-t'ang chi-lin*, vol. 2, 525–28.

65. Wei T'ing-sheng, *Mu T'ien-tzu chuan chin-k'ao*, vol. 1, 288, 292.

66. For the inscriptions see Ma Ch'eng-yüan, ed., *Shang Chou ch'ing-t'ung-ch'i ming-wen hsüan*, vol. 3, 66, 69, 70, 82. For a discussion of the dates of these vessels, especially the Ling vessels, see Edward Shaughnessy, *Sources of Western Zhou History*, appendix 2, 193–216.

67. *Mu T'ien-tzu chuan chin-k'ao*, vol. 1, 379. Wei's reading of the *La ting* 剌鼎 (*Shang chou ch'ing-t'ung-ch'i ming-wen hsüan*, vol. 3, 106) is equally flawed. Whereas the graph designating the location of King (Mu) in the inscription is effaced, Wei substitutes the character "beginning" (*ch'u* 初) and then misreads the following character "seasonal indicator" (*ch'en* 辰), which precedes a cyclical date and represents a frequently seen formulaic expression in bronze inscriptions, as "government" (*fu* 服). He thus argues that the *La ting* records events that occurred "in the beginning of King Mu's reign" (*ch'u fu* 初服). Wei continues to claim that since King Chao died in the southeast of China, King Mu would have had to go eastward to claim his father's body. Rather than make the long journey back to the "Western capital Fang," Mu opted to build his father's temple and establish his new capital in Lo-yang. See Wei's *Mu T'ien-tzu chuan chin-k'ao*, vol. 1, 287.

68. For another view of some of the holes in Wei's argument, see the critique written by Hong Yeh 洪業, which appears at the end of Wei's chapter on the relocation of Tsung-chou, *Mu T'ien-tzu chuan chin-k'ao*, vol. 1, 374–402.

69. Wei Chü-hsien, "*Mu T'ien-tzu chuan* yen-chiu," 187. See also Wang Kuo-wei, "Kuei-fang K'un-i Hsien-yün k'ao," *Kuan-t'ang chi-lin*, vol. 2, 583–606.

70. Cf. the statement made by a Jung chieftain: 'We Jung are not the same as the Chinese in drink or food or clothing. Gifts or money are not exchanged; our language is mutually unintelligible," in the *Ch'un-ch'iu Tso chuan cheng-i, Shih-san-ching chu-shu*, 2 vols. (Peking: Chung-hua, 1980), Hsiang 14, vol. 2, 1956.

71. We will return to this issue in detail below in chapter 5.

72. Mathieu's study of the *Mu T'ien-tzu chuan* provides the most compelling evidence for this case. See his *Le Mu Tianzi Zhuan*, 117–18, 144–49.

73. The graph for *t'ai* "platform" in the *Mu T'ien-tzu chuan* is not conventional, but Li Xueqin, basing his analysis of the graph on similar epigraphic forms that are phonetically related to the archaic pronunciation of *t'ai*, believes it to be the same as that used in the *Shih ching*, personal communication, 16 May 1990. The reference to the poem appears in the fifth *chüan* of the *Mu T'ien-tzu chuan*; this *chüan* is stylistically inconsistent with the first four chüan in several areas. We will address this issue presently. There is also a reference in the same section of the text to another poem—*t'ien* 天, the first graph of which is unidentifiable. The commentator Kuo P'u suggests that this reference is to the poem "Hao t'ien yu ch'eng-ming" 昊天有成命, no. 271 of the "Chou Liturgies" ("Chou sung" 周頌), which is cited by King Mu's minister, Chai-kung Mou-fu 祭公謀父, as remonstration for the king's ambition.

74. Mathieu, following the *Ssu-pu pei-yao* (SPPY) recension, takes this poem as Hsi-wang-mu's response to King Mu's poem. As we shall see below, however, this poem appears later in other editions of the text and is represented not as the voice of Hsi-wang-mu but as the voice of King Mu. While I ultimately disagree with Mathieu's decision to accept without qualification the SPPY recension, his observation concerning the identity of the strophe is nonetheless significant. See *Le Mu Tianzi Zhuan*, 48–49, 117.

75. Mathieu, *Le Mu Tianzi Zhuan*, 117. The significance of this allusion goes beyond merely identifying possible literary sources of the *Mu T'ien-tzu chuan*, as we shall see in chapter 3 below; this poem not only contains phrases that resonate with details of the *Mu T'ien-tzu chuan*, but, more importantly, the general theme of the poem echoes that of the narrative.

76. For dating of the "Yü kung," see Ch'ü Wan-li, *Shang shu shih-i* (Hua-kang: Hua-kang, 1956), 27. Li Xueqin, suggests that the obvious value attributed to iron in the text suggests an earlier date of composition because by the Warring States time cast iron had become quite commonplace. He thus proposes a Spring and Autumn date of composition of the "Yü kung." See his *Eastern Zhou and Qin Civilizations*, 479.

77. Wei Chü-hsien, "*Mu T'ien-tzu chuan yen-chiu*," 197–99, 201.

78. Ibid. 197–99. See also Mathieu, *Le Mu Tianzi Zhuan*, 105ff.

79. Bernhard Karlgren, "On the Authenticity and Nature of the Tso Chuan," *Goteborgs Hogskolas Arsskrift* 32.3 (1926), 3–65.

80. Mathieu, *Le Mu Tianzi Zhuan*, 131.

81. Eric Havelock, "The Linguistic Task of the PreSocratics," in Kevin Robb, ed., *Language and Thought in Early Greek Philosophy* (La Salle, Ill.: Monist Library of Philosophy, 1983), 13.

82. The following argue that the *Mu T'ien-tzu chuan* is a product of the Warring States era: Joseph Needham, *Science and Civilization in China*, vol. 3, 404; Henri Maspero "Contribution à l'étude de la société des Chang et au début des Tcheou," 347; F. Tokei, *La naissance de l'élégie chinoise* (Paris: Gallimard, 1967), 59.

83. Some Chinese scholars, however, did point out the significance of the *Mu T'ien-tzu chuan's* literary features with regard to the evolution of fiction. See Lu Hsün, *Chung-kuo wen-hsüeh shih-lüeh* (Peking: Chung-hua, 1930; rpt., Peking: Chung-hua, 1973), 9–11, where he claims that the text is a precursor to all of Chinese fiction.

84. See, for example, F. Tokei, "À propos du genre du *Mou T'ien-tseu tchouan*," *Acta Orientalia* 9 (1958), 45–49, where he discusses the *Mu T'ien-tzu chuan* in terms of its generic resemblance to romance history. See also Hulsewé, "Texts in Tombs," 79–89; David Hawkes, "Quest of the Goddess," 54ff.; and William H. Nienhauser, "The Origins of Chinese Fiction," *Monumenta Serica* 38 (1988–89), 201, who have also discussed several literary features of the *Mu T'ien-tzu chuan*.

85. See William H. Nienhauser's incisive review of Mathieu's book in *Chinese Literature: Essays, Articles and Reviews* 4 (1982), 247–53.

86. The Yüan dynasty editions had a preface written by Wang Chien (ca. 1350) 王漸. See Ku Shih, *Hsi-cheng chiang-shu*, appendix, 12–15.

One of these printed editions is that of Fan Ch'in 范欽; Ku Shih suspects that his edition was based on a Yüan dynasty manuscript. It is this text that is preserved in the *Ssu-pu ts'ung-k'an* (SPTK) collection. Cheng Te-k'un's English translation of the *Mu T'ien-tzu chuan* was also based on this edition, see his "The Travels of Emperor Mu," *Journal of the North China Branch of the Royal Asiatic Society* 63 (1933), 125–49. Some of the Ming printed editions were printed in collectanea. One influential edition was that preserved in the *Cheng-t'ung Taoist Canon* (*Tao tsang* 道藏), which Ku Shih believes was based on a printed Yüan edition because it duplicates Wang Chien's preface. There are several extant editions of the *Taoist Canon* text. The editions preserved in the *Ku-chin yi-shih* 古今遺史 published (according to Ku Shih) by one Wu Kuan 吳琯, and the *Han-wei ts'ung-shu* 漢魏叢書 edition, which was published by Ch'eng Jung 程榮, were also influential. See Ku Shih, *Hsi-cheng chiang-shu*, appendix, 12–22.

The Ming dynasty editions are collated by Ch'en Te-wen 陳德文 and Wu Kuan, respectively. The former edition is based on Fan Ch'in's text; the latter edition is preserved in the *Ku-chin yi-shih*. See Ku Shih, *Hsi-cheng chiang-shu*, appendix, 17–18. Both are copies of editions preserved in the *Cheng-t'ung Taoist Canon*. Of the Ch'ing dynasty editions, those of Chou Meng-ling 周夢齡, Wang Ming-chi 汪明際, and Cheng Lian 鄭廉 are based on Ch'eng Jung's *Han-wei ts'ung-shu* edition. E. J. Eitel's English translation of the *Mu T'ien-tzu chuan* was based on Cheng Lian's edition. See *China Review* 17 (1888), 223–40, 247–58. Chang Kung-liang, "Chi chiu-ch'ao-pen *Mu T'ien-tzu chuan*," *Yu kung* 2.5 (1934), 31–32, and idem, "*Mu chuan* chih pan-pen chi kuan-yü *Mu chuan* chih chu-shu," *Yü kung* 2.6 (1934), 18–27, also address textual issues concerning different editions.

Both hand-copied editions are copies of editions preserved in the *Cheng-t'ung Taoist Canon*.

87. Other notable collated editions are those edited by Huang P'i-lieh 黃丕烈 and Ti Yün-sheng 翟云升.

88. The most prominent are the *T'ai-p'ing yü-lan* 太平御覽 and the *I-wen lei-chü* 藝文類聚. See Hung's preface.

89. I have used the Tao-kuang *kuei-mao* edition preserved in the Institute of Archaeology, Chinese Academy of Social Sciences, Peking, China.

90. Ku Shih, *Hsi-cheng chiang-shu*, appendix, 28.

91. I have used the *Shih-pi lin-lang kuan ts'ung-shu* edition, preserved in the Institute of History, Chinese Academy of Social Sciences, Peking, China.

92. The *T'ai-p'ing yü-lan*, 4 vols. (Peking: Chung-hua, 1985), vol. 3, 921.4086, cites an edition of the *Mu T'ien-tzu chuan* in which the poem is presented as the laments of the people themselves.

93. Here I am following the emmendation made to the text by Thomas Smith (and Rémi Mathieu, although in Smith's argument he is unacknowledged), that substitutes the first pronoun "me" (*yü* 予) for the word *tzu* 子, "you." I am convinced by Smith's argument that it not only renders the couplet comprehensible but also fits within the rhyme scheme of the poem and as a graph that resembles to a great extent that of *tzu*, could have easily been miscopied. See Smith's, "Ritual and the Shaping of Narrative: The Legend of the Han Emperor Wu," (Ph.D. diss., University of Michigan, 1992), 67. My translation of the last couplet of both poems was also influenced by Smith's excellent translation.

94. *Mu T'ien-tzu chuan*, SPPY edition, 3.1b.

95. Hao I-hsing, *Shan-hai-ching chien-shu*, "Hsi-shan-ching," 77.

96. *Mu T'ien-tzu chuan*, SPPY edition, 3.1b.

97. The word *pi* is used frequently in the *Shih ching* to refer to places that are far away, especially in the context of military expeditions.

98. See *Mu T'ien-tzu chuan*, SPPY edition, 3.1b. The third person modifier *ch'i* further underscores this perspective: why would Hsi-wang-mu refer to her own lands with this modifier?

99. Hsi-wang-mu is described as having a "leopard's tail" and "tiger's teeth" in the *Shan-hai-ching*, "Hsi-shan-ching," 76–78. Michael Loewe, *Ways to Paradise: The Chinese Quest for Immortality* (London: Allen and Unwin, 1979), 93, 114, discusses the relationship between magpie imagery and Hsi-wang-mu. The literary significance of these associations will be treated in detail in chapter 4 below.

100. See Mathieu, *Le Mu Tianzi Zhuan*, 48, and Nienhauser, "Review," 250. The character *nü* is read, as it is in several other places in the *Mu T'ien-tzu chuan*, as a loan for *ju* 汝, "you." Wei T'ing-sheng, *Mu T'ien-tzu chuan chin-k'ao*, vol. 2, 270, cites another version of this strophe: *wei-wo wei-ju* 惟我惟女, "there is I and there is you," which he claims is listed in *chüan* 961 of the *T'ai-p'ing-yü-lan*, but I have not been able to find it.

101. Ku Shih, *Hsi-cheng chiang-shu*, 3.159–63.

102. The term *ti* if not referring directly to "god on High" nonetheless referred to dead and not living rulers, the latter of whom were referred to as "king" (*wang*). See Robert Eno, "Was There a High God *Ti* in Shang Religion?," *Early China* 15 (1990), 14–26, for a discussion of Chou usages of the term.

103. See Ch'en's *Mu T'ien-tzu chuan chu pu-cheng*, 1.29a, 3.9b. For the other usage of the word "mandate" in the text, see the *Mu T'ien-tzu chuan*, SPTK edition, 2a. Cf. Thomas Smith's translation of the term as "life," which appears to me to be both anachronistic and out of context, "Ritual and the Shaping of Narrative," 66.

104. Ch'en Feng-heng, *Mu T'ien-tzu chuan chu pu-cheng*, 3.10a.

105. I will treat this aspect of the image of Hsi-wang-mu in chapter 4. For an analysis of a social movement inspired by the belief that Hsi-wang-mu could provide salvation for the populace, see Homer Dubs, "An Ancient Chinese Mystery Cult," *Harvard Theological Review* 35.4 (1942), 221–40.

106. Mathieu, *Le Mu Tianzi Zhuan*, 49. Nienhauser also notes that Mathieu did not deal adequately with the confusion caused by the apparent switch of subjects—from Hsi-wang-mu to the "common people." See his "Review," 250–51.

107. The sense of anxiety that I attribute to the expression *hsiang-hsiang* is warranted, I believe, by the definitions given to the expression in early texts, as well as its contextual use. See the *K'ang-hsi tzu-tien* (Peking: Chung-hua, 1958), 956.

108. See the *Chou-i cheng-i, Shih-san ching chu-shu* edition, vol. 1, 39. The term *wang* also figures in a poem criticizing the "wild travels" (*tang*

湯) of a young man. See the poem "Wan ch'iu" 宛丘 of the Ch'en 陳 "Airs" ("Feng" 風), *Mao shih cheng-i* 毛詩正義, *Shih-san ching chu-shu* edition, vol. 1, 376.

109. See Ku Shih, *Hsi-cheng chiang-shu*, 1.50, and the SPTK edition, 5.4a, 4b-5a.

110. That a ruler's sense of duty (especially in maintaining the propriety of rituals) should not be lost in the revelry of entertainment is also an underlying theme of the poem "Lu ming," from which the line "flutes are piping, the reeds vibrating" may have been borrowed, as noted above.

111. Thomas Smith, "Ritual and the Shaping of Narrative," 66.

112. That is, my analysis assumes the superiority of the SPTK edition. Yet, because the suite of songs is the only part of the text that differs significantly from the other recension, I will generally cite Ku Shih's text in the following analysis, for it is by far the most readable, thanks to his clear punctuation and extensive notes. Since Ku Shih treats only the first four *chüan*, however, I will refer to the SPTK edition when I cite from the fifth *chüan*, and refer to the suite of songs.

113. Mathieu, *Le Mu Tianzi Zhuan*, 194–96.

114. Ibid., 110.

115. Wei T'ing-sheng, *Mu T'ien-tzu chuan chin-k'ao*, vol. 2, 29–31; Ting Ch'ien, *Mu T'ien-tzu chuan ti-li k'ao-cheng*, 5.1b; Cheng Te-k'un, "The Travels of Emperor Mu," 133.

116. The translation is a modification of Cheng Te-k'un's.

117. See his reorganized text in *Mu T'ien-tzu chuan chin-k'ao*, vol. 2, 1–28.

118. See the *Mu T'ien-tzu chuan*, SPTK edition, 5.5a.

119. *Mu T'ien-tzu chuan*, SPTK edition, 5.4a, 5a.

120. Edward Shaughnessy, "On the Authenticity of the *Bamboo Annals*," *Harvard Journal of Asiatic Studies* 46.1 (1986), 149–80.

Chapter 2

1. Scientific thought is discussed in John Major, "Myth, Cosmology, and the Origins of Chinese Science," *Journal of Chinese Philosophy* 5.1 (1978), 1–20; the religious elements of Chinese philosophy are addressed in N. J. Girardot, "The Problem of Creation Mythology in the Study of

Chinese Religion," *Journal of History of Religions* 15.4 (1976), 289–318. Girardot argues for a reevaluation of early Taoist Philosophy that examines the mythological traces found in those texts. See Girardot, *Myth and Meaning in Early Taoism* (Berkeley: University of California Press, 1983). On models informing concepts of political legitimacy, see David Pankenier, "Mozi and the Dates of Xia, Shang, and Zhou: A Research Note," *Early China* 9–10 (1983), 175–83. Pankenier argues that certain myths contain references to astronomical phenomena that were believed to sanction political legitimacy. For a discussion of the social order, see Sarah Allan, *The Sage and the Heir: Dynastic Legend in Early China* (San Fransisco: Chinese Materials Center, 1981), which asserts that myths such as the Yü myths performed a social function of resolving tension between two forms of political legitimacy: that sanctioned by Heaven and that sanctioned by genealogical prerogative. See also Rémi Mathieu, "Yu le Grand et le mythe du déluge dans la Chine ancienne," *T'oung Pao* 78 (1992), 162–90, for a similar conclusion about the function of the Yü myth specifically.

2. Following Girardot and others, "cosmogony" in this study refers to "that kind of myth concerned primarily with the sacred history of the origins of the cosmos." See Girardot, "The Problem of Creation Mythology," 291 n. 6. Girardot draws on the work of Mircea Eliade and posits that the paradigmatic function of cosmogonic myth is such that it can imbue primitive tradition (in Girardot's case it is Taoist philosophy) with a "religious intentionality."

3. See the articles on Yü by Ku Chieh-kang in idem, ed., *Ku-shih pien*, 7 vols. (Peking: Pu-she, 1927–41); Yang K'uan, "Chung-kuo shang-ku-shih tao-lun," in *Ku-shih pien*, vol. 7; Wen I-to, *Shen-hua yü shih*, in *Wen I-to ch'üan-chi*, 4 vols. (Shanghai: K'ai-ming, 1948; rpt. Hongkong, 1972); Wei Chü-hsien, "Yü Hsia," in *Ku-shih yen-chiu*; Marcel Granet, *Danses et légendes de la Chine ancienne*, 2 vols. (Paris: Universitaires de France, 1959), vol. 2, 468–579; Henri Maspero, "Légendes mythologiques dans le Chou king," *Journal Asiatique* 205 (1924), 1–100; Wolfram Eberhard, *The Local Cultures of South and East China*, trans. Alide Eberhard (Leiden: E. J. Brill, 1968); Derk Bodde, "Myths of Ancient China," in *Mythologies of the Ancient World*, ed. S. N. Kramer (Garden City, N.Y.: Doubleday, 1961), 367–408. For the "paradigmatic work of cosmicization," see Mircea Eliade, *The Sacred and the Profane*, trans. Willard R. Trask (New York: Harcourt Brace Jovanovich, 1959), 32.

4. See, for example, Bernhard Karlgren, "Legends and Cults in Ancient China," *Bulletin of the Museum of Far Eastern Antiquities* 18 (1946), 199–365, esp. 199–206; and K. C. Chang, *Early Chinese Civilization: Anthropological Perspectives* (Cambridge, Mass.: Harvard University Press, 1976), 180ff. Chang seems to have revised his view somewhat when he argues that "the religious and cosmological concepts found in them [late Chou texts] should to some extent be continuous with those from earlier

periods"; see Change, *Art, Myth and Ritual* (Cambridge, Mass.: Harvard University Press, 1983), 68. See also Wolfram Eberhard's refutation of this argument, in "Review of Legends and Cults, by Bernhard Karlgren," *Artibus Asiae* 9.4 (1946), 355–64; and Sarah Allan, *The Shape of the Turtle: Myth, Art, an Cosmos in Early China* (Albany: SUNY Press, 1991), 23ff. Girardot provides an excellent summary and review of the polemics informing the study of Chinese mythology in the West. See Girardot, "The Problem of Creation Mythology," 296–317.

5. See Claude Lévi-Strauss, *From Honey to Ashes*, trans. John and Doreen Weightman (London: Jonathan Cape, 1973), 356; and idem, *The Raw and the Cooked*, trans. John and Doreen Weightman (New York: Harper Colophon Books, 1975), 13 et passim. I am also indebted to Chang Kuang-chih's groundbreaking treatment of creation myths. While he accepts much of Lévi-Strauss's structural approach, he also advocates paying close attention to the details of the content of each myth as well. See Chang, "Chung-kuo ch'uang-shih shen-hua chih fen-hsi yü ku-shih yen-chiu," *Bulletin of the Institute of Ethnology, Academica Sinica* 8 (1959), 47–79.

6. Giorgio de Santillana and Hertha von Dechend, *Hamlet's Mill: An Essay on Myth and the Frame of Time* (Boston: Gambit, 1969), 313. See also Moses I. Finley, "Myth, Memory, and History," *History and Theory* 4.3 (1964), 285, where the function of myth is described as "presenting concrete facts."

7. See Finley, "Myth," 283: "[Myths] make the past intelligible and meaningful by selection, by focusing on a few bits of the past which thereby acquired permanence, relevance, universal significance." Mircea Eliade, *Cosmos and History*, rpt. (New York: Harper and Brothers, 1959), especially 57, discusses how myths can be understood as presenting the origins of religious rites; Major, "Origins of Chinese Science," 7. Pankenier, "Mozi and the Dates of Xia, Shang, and Zhou," 176, argues for revising ideas about what constitutes "hard" and "soft" texts in light of the remarkable astronomical accuracy of what some may have considered spurious sources that contain remnants of ancient traditions. See also Walter Ong, *Orality and Literacy* (London: Methuen, 1982), 94, where he states that the diffusion of writing in ancient societies was not interiorized enough to affect the thought processes of the recorders of the oral tradition; orality lingered in the presence of writing. For an excellent review of the most recent scholarship on the relationship between the oral and written traditions, see Rosalind Thomas, *Oral Tradition and Written Record in Classical Athens* (Cambridge: Cambridge University Press, 1989), 1–14.

8. See Major, "Origins of Chinese Science," 7, also cited in Pankenier, "Early Chinese Astronomy and Cosmology. The 'Mandate of Heaven' as Epiphany," (Ph.D. diss., Stanford University, 1983), 9. For another study that uses a similar approach to that of de Santillana and Von Dechend, see

Harald A. T. Reiche, "The Language of Archaic Astronomy: A Clue to the Atlantis Myth?," in *Astronomy of the Ancients*, ed. Kenneth Brecher and Michael Feirtag (Cambridge, Mass.: MIT Press, 1979), 155–89.

9. Precession of the equinoxes "is due to the gravitational forces of the sun and the moon and to the fact that the earth is not perfectly spherical. As a result the axis of the earth has a conical motion, like that of a gyroscope, which slowly traces out a circle on the heavens and points to different Pole stars through the millenniums, as the observed sky changes. The precessional motion is usually described as a movement of the equator. As the point moves westward where the earth's equator cuts across the path of the sun (the ecliptic) the positions of all stars change." This exceptionally lucid description comes from Jane Sellers, *The Death of Gods in Ancient Egypt* (London: Penguin, 1993), 30, who approaches ancient Egyptian mythology from a similar perspective.

10. Pankenier has suggested that this is a major corollary of the "Grand Origin Myth" relevant to Chinese mythology; see Pankenier, "Early Chinese Cosmology and Astronomy," 6.

11. The "discovery" of precession is attributed to the astronomer Chia K'uei 賈逵 of the Han 漢 dynasty (A.D. 89). See the "Calendrical Treatise" ("Lü-li chih") of the *Hou-han shu* (Peking: Chung-hua, 1965), vol. 11, 3027. For discussions of this "discovery," see Li Ch'ang-hao, ed., *Chung-kuo t'ien-wen-hsüeh shih* (Peking: K'o-hsüeh, 1981), 91–93; and Willy Hartner, "The Obliquity of the Ecliptic according to the *Hou-han Shu* and Ptolemy," in *Oriens-Occidens* (Heldesheim: Georg Olms Verlagshuchhandulung, 1968), 208–14. Pankenier, "*Mozi* and the Dates of Xia, Shang and Zhou," 177, cites Philip Morrison, who suggested that "all one needed to notice this [the effects of precession] was an old tree and faith in the veracity of one's grandfather." Morrison's description is also cited by Harald Reiche, "Atlantis," 155. For the use of constellations as seasonal markers, see Li Ch'ang-hao, *Chung-kuo t'ien-wen-hsüeh shih*, 11–12, 16, 91–93; Ch'en Tsun-kuei, *Chung-kuo t'ien-wen-hsüeh shih* (Shanghai: Jenmin, 1980; rpt. Taipei: Ming-wen, 1984), 182.

12. Recent studies have shown the high level of observational sophistication achieved by Neolithic "astronomers." Peter Lancaster Brown, *Megaliths, Myths and Men* (New York: Taplinger, 1976), 262, asserts that the recognition and grouping of irregular configurations of stars or the invention of celestial or astral deities had likely evolved already in Upper Paleolithic times; also cited in Jane Sellers, *The Death of Ancient Gods in Egypt*, 343, n. 1. For other general accounts relating to Neolithic observations, see Alexander Thom, *Megalithic Sites in Britain and Megalithic Lunar Observatories* (Oxford: Oxford University Press, 1971), and Gerald Hawkins, *Stonehenge Decoded* (Garden City, N.Y.: Doubleday, 1973). While sites such as Stonehenge have not been discovered in China, the early

development of agricultural technology suggests a similar level of astronomical sophistication. According to Chang Kwang-chih, *The Archaeology of Ancient China*, 4th ed. (New Haven: Yale University Press, 1986), 87, agricultural experimentation began about ten thousand years ago in China. See also idem, "Concluding Remarks," in David N. Keightley, ed., *The Origins of Chinese Civilization*, 566–69, 572, where he discusses archaeological evidence of agriculture dating from the eighth and ninth millennia B.C. Ch'en Chiu-chin, "Li-fa ti kuei-yüan ho hsien Ch'in si-fen li," *K'o-chi-shih wen-chi* 1 (1978), 5ff., argues that a large part of the central plains had already been developed for agricultural use before 4000 B.C., the inhabitants of that area must have had at least a rudimentary knowledge of calendrical mechanics. See also Cheng Wen-kuang, *Chung-kuo t'ien-wen-hsüeh yüan-liu* (Peking: K'o-hsüeh, 1979), 2, for a similar argument. Certain designs and symbols on Neolithic pottery suggest a concern with astronomical phenomenon. See Chang Kwang-chih, *The Archaeology of China*, 172; Li Ch'ang-t'ao, "Ta-ho-ts'un hsin-shih-ch'i shih-tai ts'ai-t'ao shang ti t'ien-wen t'u-hsiang," *Wen-wu* 8 (1983), 53; and Cheung Kwong-yue, "Recent Archaeological Evidence Relating to the Origin of Chinese Characters," in David Keightley, ed., *The Origins of Chinese Civilization*, 366. Additional archaeological evidence was recently discovered in a Neolithic grave at P'u-yang, where forms of a [Cerulean?] dragon and [White?] tiger created from clam shells were found on the eastern and western sides, respectively, of the deceased. As these forms and their locations accord with traditional astronomical motifs, some archaeologists have pushed back the origins of ancient Chinese astronomy. See Feng Shih, "Ho-nan P'u-yang Hsi-shui-p'o 45 hao mu ti t'ien-wen-hsüeh yen-chiu," *Wen-wu* 3 (1990), 52–60, 69. Finally, David Nivison has pointed out that disks found in 1977 in Fuyang, Anhuei province, have diameter lines crossing at right angles that connect what he believes to be the points of the Big Dipper as it would have indicated the beginning of winter and of summer in pre-Shang times. See Nivison, "The Origin of the Chinese Lunar Lodge System," in A. F. Aveni, ed., *World Archaeoastronomy* (Cambridge: Cambridge University Press, 1989), 205. For the report of the discovery, see 'Fu-yang shuang-ku-tuei Hsi-Han ju-yin-hou mu fa-chüeh chien-pao," *Wen-wu* 8 (1979), 12–31.

13. Nathan Sivin, "Chinese Archaeoastronomy: Between Two Worlds," in Aveni, ed., *World Archaeoastronomy*, 59, suggests that mythology may contain the earliest allusions to an oral tradition of ancient astronomy. The effect of the precession of the equinoxes on the seasonal (spring) position of the determinative star Antares may perhaps be seen in the attibution of differing calendrical traditions to the Hsia, Shang 商, and Chou 周 dynasties. Willy Hartner, "The Earliest History of the Constellations in the Near East, and the Motif of the Lion-Bull Combat," *Journal of Near Eastern Studies* 24 (1965), 1–16, reprinted in *Oriens-Occidens*, 227–59, argues that the significance of lion and bull imagery in prehistoric art was preserved in an oral tradition that enjoyed a "pluri-millennial history."

14. Harald Reiche, "The Language of Archaic Astronomy," 160, also cited in Pankenier, "Early Chinese Astronomy and Cosmology," 7.

15. John Major, "Myth, Cosmology and the Origins of Chinese Science," 6, cited in Pankenier, "Early Chinese Cosmology and Astronomy," 9. Major suggests that Yü and Kun, his father, refer to "celestial beings, whose symbolic activities took place in the heavens even when the myths assing them a conventional terrestrial location," ibid., 4.

16. See the *Huai-nan Hung-lieh chi-chieh*, "T'ien-wen hsün" (Peking: Chung-hua, 1989), 80, for the most complete version of the myth of the butting of Pu-chou. It is translated by Major, "Myth, Cosmology and the Origins of Chinese Science," 5. See the "T'an-t'ien" chapter in *Lun-heng chu-shih*, Pei-ching li-shih hsi ed. (Peking: Chung-hua, 1979), 603.

17. Hao I-hsing, *Erh-ya i-shu*, 3 vols. (Peking: Pei-ching shu-chü, 1982), "Shih-t'ien," vol. 2, 17b.

18. De Saussure, *Les origines de l'astronomie chinoise* (Paris: Librairie Orientale et Americaine, 1930), 455.

19. *Hsing-ching* (*Han-wei ts'ung-shu* ed.), *chüan hsia*, 7a.

20. One may wonder how the "northwest" figures in this configuration of northern and eastern quadrants. I believe it refers to the location of Sagittarius and the tail of Scorpius in relation to the other asterisms that together comprise the constellations constituting the Cerulean Dragon and Heavenly Turtle. In Hsing Bing's 邢昺 commentary to the *Erh-ya*, the constellations that are associated with the eastern and western quadrants (i.e., the Cerulean Dragon and the White Tiger) are described as having their 'heads in the south and their tails in the north." The constellations comprising the southern and northern quadrants (i.e., the Vermillion Bird and the Heavenly Turtle) however, are described as "having their heads in the west and their tails in the east." The tail of Scorpius thus occupies the northernmost part of the eastern quadrant, while Sagittarius—the head of the Heavenly Turtle—occupies the westernmost part of the northern quadrant. See the *Erh-ya chu-shu*, in *Shih-san-ching chu-shu*, 2 vols. (Peking: Chung-hua, 1979), vol. 2, 2609. This is also cited in Gustav Schlegel, *Uranographie Chinoise*, 2 vols. (Leiden, 1875; rpt. Leiden: 1975), 1. Cf. the passage following the description of K'un-lun in the "T'ien-wen" chapter of the *Ch'u-tz'u*, where the poet writes, "The Northwest opens and closes, how does the air pass through there?" The "opening and closing" refers to the transition from one solar year to the next (i.e., from winter to spring); see the *Ch'u-tz'u chi-chu* (Shanghai: Shang-hai ku-chi, 1979), 57.

The issue of when the Chinese conceived of dividing the sky into quadrants is of some importance to this discussion. I believe that the system postdates the celestial events that will be our concern in the following discussion, although it undoubtedly derived from and incorporated longstanding astronomical traditions. Since the concept of a quadrant is intimately connected to the location of the solstice and equinoctial points, one could theoretically estimate the approximate time frame during which such a system could have been invented. However, because the representative function of the northern and southern quadrants is different from that of the eastern and western quadrants, the issue becomes cloudy. Whereas the former two represent the sun's position according to its conjunction with a constellation situated within those specific quadrants, the latter two clearly do not. Rather, the Cerulean Dragon in fact comprises asterisms that conjoined with the sun at the autumnal equinox, whereas asterisms that for millennia constituted the White Tiger conjoined with the sun at the vernal equinox. Yet the Cerulean Dragon and the White Tiger have traditionally been associated with spring and autumn respectively. De Saussure, *Origines de l'astronomie chinoise*, 281, citing the *Chou li*, argues that the northern and southern quadrants were determined by the location of the sun at the winter and summer solstices, while the eastern and western quadrants were determined by the location of the moon at the vernal and autumnal equinoxes. While such a rationale certainly explains away the apparent discrepancy, the obvious combination of lunisolar elements belies a late date of conception. The discrepancy may have derived from the combination of an age-old tradition of using seasonal indicators to demarcate the equinoxes, and the empirical data gleaned from the use of a gnomen to calculate the position of the sun during the solstice. We will return to the notion of seasonal indicators. My use of the appellations given to each quadrant to discuss celestial events that occurred five and six millennia ago is thus admittedly anachronistic, and it is only for convenience that I use them. Cf. theory of Chu K'o-chen, that system of quadrants was already developing during Wu Ting's 武丁 reign of the Shang, "Erh-shih-pa hsiu ch'i-yüan chih ti-tien yü shih-chien," *Ch'i-hsiang hsüeh-pao* 18 (1994), 12ff. Following Lian Shao-ming, "Pu-tz'u chung ti yüeh yü hsing," in *Ch'u-t'u wen-hsien yen-chiu hsü-chi* (Peking: Wen-wu, 1989), 122–34, I believe that the word "star" (*hsing* 星) when preceded by "bird" (*niao* 鳥) is used to mean "clear," as in "the rain cleared" and thus cannot be read as proof that the Shang had already conceived of the Vermilion Bird quadrant.

21. *Hamlet's Mill*, 205, 211, 238–39. Schlegel cites several pertinent descriptions of the Milky Way, *Uranographie*, 208. The motif of turtles serving as bridges across large bodies of water seen frequently in Chinese literature is perhaps related to this astonomical configuration: the proximity of the Corona Australis asterism to the Celestial River and especially the heavenly ford may be an astonomical source for this imagery.

22. *Huai-nan Hung-lieh chi-chieh*, "Lan-ming hsün," 207. Note that according to the commenator Liu Wen-tien, the title of this chapter, "Observing the dark and obscure," is referring to the area "where change is effected" (p. 191). This accords with my interpretation that the Heavenly

Turtle quadrant represents the starting point, that is, the source, of the problematic effects of precession.

23. These figures are based on the terrestrial coordinates of Hsi'an China, 35 degrees north latitude, 110 degrees east longitude. In calculating these figures I have taken into consideration the following factors: precession, nutation, proper motion, and parallax. Tamara Helfer, an astronomer at the University of Maryland, Department of Astronomy, has been extremely generous with her time and knowledge and has verified for me the numerical calculations. These were based on the rigorous formulae for precession presented in *The Astronomical Almanac* (Washington, D.C.: U.S. Government Printing Office, 1993), B18. According to Helfer, the accuracy of the program is about +/−2 degrees.

In using the expression "seasonal indicator," I am not suggesting that the Chinese at this early age had already determined the sun's position according to its conjunction with a star. Rather, the observation of the acronychal rising (first visible rising at twilight), heliacal rising (last visible rising before sunrise), cosmical setting (first visible setting at dawn), and heliacal setting (first setting after sunset) were taken as indicators of seasons. With this methodology a calendar can be made independently of the varying lengths of days. My estimation of what constellation the Chinese could see on the horizon is based on the premise that the sun must be a sufficient number of degrees beneath the horizon to prevent the rays from interfering with the observation. According to Willy Hartner, "The Earliest History of the Constellations of the Near East," 233, the sun must be 12 to 15 degrees below the horizon in order to observe a star of the brightest magnitude (i.e., about an hour after sunset), and it must be 18 to 20 degrees below the horizon to see stars of lesser magnitude. The magnitudes of the determinative stars—Gamma Sagittarius, Phi Sagittarius, and Corona Australis—are relatively low: 3.1, 3.3, and 3.4 respectively. Cf. Joseph Needham, *Science and Civilization in China*, vol. 3, 229–30. Needham asserts that the ancient Chinese "concentrated attention, not on heliacal risings and settings, not on the horizon, but on the pole star and on the circumpolar stars which never rise and never set." While I agree that culminations at dawn or twilight at the meridan ("the great circle of the celestial sphere passing through the pole star and the observer's zenith") played an important role in Chinese calendariography (as is evidenced by the astronomical information contained in the "Yao tien" of the *Shang shu*), this was a much later development that incorporated techniques of mathematical astronomy.

24. Nivison says that during the early Shang, the solstice month space began between the lunar stations Girl (*Nü* 女) and Cow (*Niu* 牛), which directly precede Corona Australis. See Nivison, "The Origin of the Chinese Lunar Lodge System," 213. On the appellation of the quadrant, see Pankenier, "Early Chinese Astronomy and Cosmology," 184.

25. See Jen Fang, *Shu i chi, Pai-tzu ch'üan-shu* ed., vol. 7, 2a.

26. Cf. Nivison's comment that Mound, (虛 *Hsü*, Beta Aquarri) as the location of the winter solstice "belongs to a reform on an archaic original system." The "archaic original system" may be the one in which Corona Australis served as an indicator for the vernal equinox, which would imply that the winter solstice would have been demarcated by an asterism that was further west than Hsü, for example, lunar stations 14 Wall (*pi* 壁), or even 15 Shoe (*k'uei* 奎). See Nivison, "The Origins of the Lunar Lodge System," 213.

27. Cf. the tale recorded by Yang Hsiung 楊雄 in his *Shu wang pen-chi* 蜀王本紀. In that tale a turtle spirit (*pieh-ling* 鼈靈) cuts off a mountain and controls floodwaters. The reigning emperor stepped down and allowed the turtle spirit to rule. The spirit was also known by another term: the god of K'ai-ming (*K'ai-ming ti* 開明帝). K'ai-ming, according to Hsiao Ping, is the name of the gate where the sun appears in the east. See Hsiao Ping, *Ch'u-tz'u wen-hua* (Peking: Chung-kuo she-hui k'o-hsüeh, 1990), 363.

28. See, for example, the *Ch'un-ch'iu Tso chuan cheng-i*, Hsiang 28, vol. 2, 1998. Cf. the description of Kun's aggressive behavior as *yin* in the "Chou-yü hsia" section of the *Kuo-yü*, 3 vols. (Shanghai: Shang-hai ku-chi, 1978), 103.

29. The first quote is cited by Michael Saso, "Ho-t'u," 410, and comes from the *Ho't'u chiang-hsiang* 河圖降像. The second is cited by Pankenier, "Early Chinese Astronomy and Cosmology," 315, and it comes from the text *K'ao-ling-yao* 考靈曜.

30. John Henderson, *The Development and Decline of Chinese Cosmology* (New York: Columbia University Press, 1984), 82–87 discusses how the charts came to be seen as the ultimate source of nonary cosmography although there do not seem to be any concrete clues suggesting why this was so. The interpretation I offer may contextualize this association more clearly.

See the *Lun-yü*, vol, 2, 2490. Pankenier has suggested that "the original esoteric Diagrams were in fact depictions of the configuration of the five visible planets during a conjunction," which he identifies as the astronomical event that was perceived to be the physical manifestation of the Mandate of Heaven. One such conjunction occurred in 1576 B.C. at "the ford on the Celestial River between the regions of the sky occupied by the Dragon and Turtle asterisms." See Pankenier, "Early Chinese Astronomy and Cosmology," 316. Pankenier's interpretation is brilliant and convincing. I believe, however, that the River Chart myth reflects an earlier and more general use of the imagery that concerns itself with the workings of the cosmos in general. This does not preclude the use of this imagery later (i.e., 1596 B.C.) to refer to the specific context of a conjunction. My reasons for believing that the River Chart myth referred at first to a more general conception of the workings of the universe stem from its significance for Yü's control of the flood, especially with respect to its function as a model of how the universe should work.

31. The following section on Kun has in large part been taken from my study "The Literary Significance of K'un-lun Mountain in the *Mu T'ien-tzu chuan*," *Early China* 18 (1993), 73–106.

32. For discussions of the common motif of these myths, see, for example, the references to Kun's death at Feather Mountain in Ch'ü Yüan's "Li sao" and "T'ien-wen," *Ch'u-tz'u chi-chu*, 11, 54; and the references to Feather Abyss found in the "Chin-yü" portion of the *Kuo-yü*, 478. All of these are conveniently collected in Yüan K'o, *Chung-kuo shen-hua tzu-liao ts'ui-pien* (Ch'eng-tu: Ssu-ch'uan she-hui k'o-hsüeh, 1985), 240–42. On the abyss, see the fourth hexagram line of the first hexagram (*Ch'ien* 乾) in the *Chou I cheng-i* in *Shih-san-ching chu-shu*, vol. 1, 16. See also de Saussure, *Origines de l'astronomie chinoise*, 161 n. 1; and Hsia Han-i (Edward L. Shaughnessy), "*Chou-i* Ch'ien-kua liu-lung hsin-chieh," *Wen-shih* 24 (1985), 9–14, for a discussion of the astronomical significance of *Ch'ien*'s hexagram lines. Cf. the asterism called Feather Forest (*yü-lin* 羽林), which is located in the Heavenly Turtle quadrant, Schlegel, *Uranographie*, 127.

33. Many commentators read the reference to listening to the advice of an "old turtle" as an allusion to divination by turtle shell. Perhaps, though, the allusion is to the inadequacy of the turtle (i.e., Corona Australis) in giving instructions for flood control. See the "T'ien-wen," *Ch'u-tz'u chi-chu*, 54. For a discussion of this enigmatic line, see Ho Chien-hsün, *Ch'u-tz'u shih-shen* (Ssu-ch'uan: Ssu-ch'uan jen-min, 1984), 56–57. On the relationship between Kun and Chuan Hsü, see the *Shan-hai-ching chien-shu*, "Ta-huang hsi-ching," 438, where the commentator Kuo P'u cites the *Bamboo Annals* account of Chuan Hsü's "producing" (*ch'an* 産) Kun in his thirty-first year; see the *Chu-shu chi-nien* (1877 Hsü Wen-ching edition), *chüan shang*, 1b. See also the *Shih-pen*, *Pai-pu ts'ung-shu chi-ch'eng* ed., 4.3a. For a full discussion of the relationship between Chuan Hsü and Kun, see Moriyasu Tarō, "Kei U genshi," *Kyōto joshi daigaku jinbun ronsō* 9 (1964), 1–22, rpt. in Kōtei *densetsu* (Kyoto: Kyōto Joshi Daigaku Jinbun Gakkai, 1970), 41–62. For the astrological associations of Chuan Hsü, see Pankenier, "Early Chinese Astronomy and Cosmology," 9, 180, 193 n. 30. De Saussure, *Origines de l'astronomie chinoise*, 449, cites the *Tso chuan* and the *Erh-ya* as sources pointing to the celestial association between Chuan Hsü's grave site and the lunar station *hsü*.

34. See Schlegel, *Uranographie*, 217–25. The latter quote comes from Pankenier, "Early Chinese Astronomy and Cosmology," 9.

35. On the link of Kun's failure to his strategy, see the "Yao tien" and the "Hung-fan" chapters of the *Shang shu cheng-i*, *Shi-san-ching chu-shu*, vol. 1, 122, 187; the *Kuo-yü*, 478, and the *Ch'u-tz'u chi-chu*, 54, all cited in

Yüan K'o, *Ts'ui-pien*, 241–42. The *Shan-hai-ching chien-shu*, "Hai-nei-ching," 478; also cited in Yüan K'o, *Ts'ui-pien*, 239, discusses the "swelling soil."

36. Cited from the "Yao-tien," vol. 1, 122.

37. In ancient genealogies such as the *Shih-pen*, Kun is credited with inventing the city wall—intended as much to preserve what was within the boundary as to prevent outside intrusion. See the *Shih-pen*, "Tso p'ien," 1.23a. Yang K'uan has the most detailed explication of how he arrived at this conclusion. See the section entitled "Kun Kung-kung yü Hsüan-ming Feng-i," in *Ku-shih pien*, vol. 7, 329–44.

38. See the *Kuo-yü*, 478. Cf. terminology used to describe the northern celestial quadrant: "The northern palace is the place where the numinous turtle [i.e., the Heavenly Turtle or, more specifically, Corona Australis] submerges and hides." Cited in Schlegel, *Uranographie*, 62.

39. See the *Ch'un-ch'iu Tso chuan cheng-i*, vol. 2, 2049, for the story of Kun's transformation. Akatsuka Kiyoshi identifies the drawings of tortoises on Shang dynasty bronze inscriptions as Kun; see "Kei U to Indai tōban no ki ryū zuzō," *Kodaigaku* 11.4 (1964), 273–301. Moriyasu, "Kei U genshi," 43–45, also emphasizes Kun's watery origins.

40. *Shan-hai-ching chien-shu*, "Hai-nei ching," 479; *Ch'un-ch'iu Tso chuan cheng-i*, vol. 2, 2049. Moriyasu "Kei U genshi," 48. Whalen Lai, "Symbolism of Evil in China: The K'ung-chia Myth Analyzed," *History of Religions* 24.4 (1984), 378, states that during the Three Dynasties period the terrestrial Feather Mountain was a site for the autumnal sacrifice.

41. Moriyasu, "Kei U genshi," 55, cites the *Mo tzu*, "Shang-hsien" chapter where there is a note concerning Feather Suburb. It is stated that this place is "the place where the warmth of the sun does not reach" (熱照無有及也). Shirakawa Shizuka, *Chung-kuo ti shen-hua*, trans. Wang Hsiao-lian (Taipei: Ch'ang-an, 1983), 44, argues that the transformation of Chuan Hsü's, Kun's, and Yü's appearance in myths accords with the changing of the seasons. Seasonal connotations are also implied by the binome, "turtle calculations" (*kuei-suan* 龜算), which, according to the *Shu shu chi i* written by Hsü Yüeh of the Han dynasty, refers to the function of the turtle in calculating the arrival and departure of seasons. See the *Shu shu chi i*, *Ssu-k'u ch'üan-shu chen-pen pieh-chi* ed., vol. 187, 13b. Cf. the *Li chi*, which connects the *chiao* sacrificial ritual to the winter; see "Chiao t'eh sheng," vol. 2, 1452.

42. On the "Fire Calendar," see P'ang P'u, "'Huo-li' chih ch'u t'an," *She-hui k'o-hsüeh chan-hsien* 4 (1978), 131–37.

43. About 2400 B.C., according to Joseph Needham, the equinoctial points were situated quite near the lunar stations House (*fang*) and Door

(*mao*). See Needham, *Science and Civilization*, vol. 3, 249. For the seasonal role of Antares, see David Pankenier, "Astronomical Dates in Shang and Western Zhou," *Early China* 7 (1981–82), 7, and I. Ecsedy et al., "Antares Year in Ancient China," in *World Archaeoastronomy*, ed. A. F. Aveni, 183–86. See the *Ch'un-ch'iu Tso chuan cheng-i*, Chao 17, vol. 2, 2085, for an ancient textual reference to the tradition of observing Antares after sunset. In 4500 B.C. the right ascension/declination coordinates for Antares were $10^h33.9^m/3°32'$; by 3000 B.C. the coordinates were $11^h52.8^m/-4°24'$.

44. In a compilation of passages thought originally to belong to a pre-Ch'in text, the *Shih tzu*, a passage states that "Sui jen looked above to observe the celestial mark-point (*ch'en*) [= Antares] and looked below to the five types of trees from which he made fire." See Wang Chi-p'ei, ed., *Shih tzu*, in *Erh-shih-erh tzu* (Shanghai: Shang-hai ku-chi, 1985), 374. The quotation on fires "brought out and brought in" occurs in *Ch'un-ch'iu Tso chuan cheng-i*, Hsiang 9, vol. 2, 1941. This interpretation is discussed in P'ang P'u, "'Huo-li' ch'u t'an," 132. For burning and agriculture during the Shang dynasty, see Ch'iu Hsi-kuei, "Chia-ku-wen chung so chien ti Shang tai nung-yeh," paper presented at conference entitled: Shang-shih hsüeh-shu t'ao-lun hui, Xi'an, 1985; revised and printed in his *Ku-wen-tzu lun-chi* (Peking: Chung-hun, 1992), 168. On "bringing in" fire, *Chou-li chu-shu*, "Hsia-kuan," *Shih-san-ching chu-shu*, vol. 1, 43: "The controller of fire is responsible for those orders concerning the implementation of fire . . . [w]hen Antares appears in the last month of spring, the people's [actions] are in accord; when it disappears in the last month of autumn the people do likewise." On Antares as a seasonal indicator, see the *Kuo yü*, "Chou-yü," 15; and P'ang P'u "'Huo li' ch'u t'an," 132. P'ang P'u states that although there are no written records that actually date to the period when Antares was used as a seasonal indicator, the connection between the movement of Antares and agricultural activity spanning a period of over one thousand years ensured the development of an important oral tradition that continued to be passed down and understood until a lunisolar calendar replaced the Fire Calendar.

45. See Liu Chih-hsiung and Yang Ching-jung, *Lung yü Chung-kuo wen-hua* (Peking: Jen-min, 1992), 53, and plate 5. For the discovery of the vessel, see Chung-kuo she-hui k'o-hsüeh yüan k'ao-ku yen-chiu-so, "1978–1980 nien Shan-hsi Hsiang-fen t'ao-ssu mu-ti fa-chüeh chien-pao," *K'ao-ku* 1 (1983), 30–42.

46. David Pankenier coined the latter term. See his contribution to the "Forum: Astronomical Evidence for the *Bamboo Annals'* Chronicle of Early Xia," *Early China* 15 (1990), 130. On *ch'en* as dragon's tail, see Needham, *Science and Civilization*, vol. 3, 250; L. C. Hopkins "The Dragon Terrestrial and the Dragon Celestial, Part II: Ch'en, the Dragon Celestial," *Journal of the Royal Asiatic Society* (1913), 91–97. So significant was Antares as a seasonal marker that as the science of calendrical astronomy

developed the term *ch'en* was used with specific reference to two other constellations. Orion and Ursa Major, which also demarcated the seasons (the direction in which the handle of Ursa Major points was also coordinated with specific seasons). For references identifying *ch'en* as the Fire Star (that is, *ta-huo* 大火) see *Ch'un-ch'iu Kung-yang chuan cheng-i, Shih-san ching chu-shu*, Chao 17, vol. 2, 2324; and P'ang P'u "'Huo-li' ch'u-t'an," 134. See also I. Ecsedy et al., "Antares Year in Ancient China," 183.

47. Antares' late appearance (sixth month) reflects the effect of precession on its calendrical role. See P'ang P'u, "'Huo-li' ch'u t'an," 133. For the passage in question, see the *Ch'un-ch'iu Tso chuan cheng-i*, Chao 17, vol. 2, 2082.

48. According to the *Bamboo Annals*, Yü's birth was in part inspired when his mother, a woman of the Yu-hsin 有莘 clan, named Hsiu-ssu 修巳, sighted a moving star pass through the lunar station *Mao*. This detail, an anamoly of the myths devoted to Yü, is quite similar to late forms of hagiography that suffused all accounts of births of founding emperors. See *Chu-shu chi-nien*, ch. 3, 1b. Mathieu, "Yu le Grand et le mythe du déluge," 168, treats the myths concerning Yü's mother.

Ch'ü Yüan's question regarding a *ch'iu* 虯 dragon who carries a three-legged turtle to roam (the skies?), in the "T'ien-wen," 57, may refer to a similar configuration. Cf. the top of the *Fu ju yi* 甫入匜 vessel, which is a lizard on top of a turtle, cited in Kuo Mo-jo, "Shi kan-chih," in *Kuo Mo-jo ch'üan-chi, K'ao-ku pien* (Peking: K'o-hsüeh, 1982), 260.

49. Feng Shih, "Chung-kuo tsao-ch'i hsing-hsiang t'u yan-chiu," *Tzu-jan k'o-hsüeh shih yan-chiu* 9.2 (1990), 114.

50. See the "T'ien-wen," 55, for the use of this term to describe Yü's birth.

This is precisely the graph used to describe the manner in which Yü was born in the *Shan-hai-ching chien-shu*, "Hai-nei-ching," 479. Su Hsüeh-lin cites Yü Yüeh's 俞樾 commentary to the Ch'u-tz'u (讀楚辭), in which he argues that the term *fu* refers to Yü's continuation of his father's work. See *T'ien-wen cheng-chien*, 299. On reading this as the recommencing of time, see the examples in the *Shang shu cheng-i*, "P'an keng," 168, where *fu* is used to mean "renew the former king's great achievements" (*shao fu hsien-wang chih ta yeh* 紹復先王之大業); and in the *Mao Shih cheng-i*, "Pi kung," vol. 1, 617: "He restores the domain of Chou" (*fu Chou kung chih yu* 復周公之宇). The term is used in reference to Yü's accomplishments in the *Ch'un-ch'iu Tso chuan cheng-i*, Ai 1, vol. 2, 2154.

51. "T'ien-wen," 55.

52. *Kuo-yü*, "Chou-yü," 103. *Mo tzu*, "Fei-kung hsia" 非攻下, in *Erh-shi-erh tzu*, 240.

53. That Yü was believed to have received the Lo chart—which was revealed on the back of a turtle, that is, Corona Australis—as an aid to his flood control, points to similar conclusions. See the *Shang shu cheng-i*, "Hung-fan," 187. His being bestowed with a "black jade tablet" (*hsüan-kuei* 玄圭) at the end of his work may also contain similar calendrical connotations for according to the *Chou-li*, black jade is the ritual implement associated with the northern quadrant. See the *Chou-li chu-shu*, "Ch'un-kuan ta-tsung-po," vol. 1, 762.

Yü is ordered to exterminate the San Miao 三苗. There is evidence to suggest that San Miao refers to a stellar configuration if not to Kun himself. First, San Miao is frequently described as wreaking havoc on earth in ways that resemble the kind of destruction caused by Kun's obsolescence. In other words, the destruction appears to be related to calendrical inaccuracy that results when earthly activities are not correlated correctly with celestial movements. Thus, the "sun came out at night," "it rained blood for three mornings," "the five grains were transforming [out of season]," and the "people were all shook up." The number three that appears in the name San Miao and that appears in the references to astronomical irregularities recalls the number of months of winter for which Corona Australis (i.e., Kun) serves as a seasonal marker, as well as the number of legs that the turtle associated with the celestial northwest supposedly had. Finally, the term used to refer to the type of death to which the San Miao are sentenced is the exact term, *chi* 殛, which is used (almost exclusively in pre-Ch'in texts) to describe how Kun was killed in almost every account of his execution. I am, unfortunately, not able at this time to offer any linguistic evidence for my identification of San Miao with Kun, but I believe that the structural elements alone are quite compelling. Cf. Pankenier, "*Mozi* and the Dates of Xia, Shang and Zhou," 178–79, who reads in the *Mo tzu* myth a more precise identification of the lunar lodge Mansion (*ying-shih* 營室), which is located in the northern quadrant of the heavens.

54. See the "T'ien-wen," 56; and the *Shan-hai-ching yi-wen*, collected in the *Shan-hai-ching kuang-chu*, cited by Yüan K'o, *Ts'ui-pien*, 251; For other references to the method of draining the floodwaters, see the *Kuo-yü*, "Chou-yü," 103; *Huai-nan Hung-lieh chi-chieh*, "Hsiu-wu hsün," 631, and "Yao-lüeh," 790–10; Lü Pu-wei, *Lü-shih ch'un-ch'iu*, "Shen wei" (Shanghai: Shang-hai ku-chi, 1989), 194. Cf. Su Hsüeh-lin's argument that the Responsive Dragon has no connection to the Yü myths, *T'ien-wen cheng-chien*, 123. A vivid diagram of the configuration of the Responsive Dragon's tail is contained in the Suchow planisphere, dating from 1193, and the Korean planisphere, dating from 1395, both provided by Needham, *Science and Civilization*, vol. 3, 280–81.

55. See Wang Chia, *Shih i chi*, *Pai-tzu ch'üan-shu* edition, ch. 2, 1b; also cited in Yüan K'o, *Ts'ui pien*, 251.

These myths suggest a connection between this Black Turtle and Kun. The Black Turtle is identified in the passage as "the one who carries out the orders of the River Spirit" (*ho-ching chih shih-che* 河精之使者), while in another passage of the *Shih i chi* Kun is identified as the River Spirit after he submerges into Feather Abyss and transforms into a Black Fish (*hsüan-yü* 玄魚), *Shih i chi*, ch. 2, 1a. A passage in the *Shi tzu*, 382, identifies the River Spirit as the one who presents Yü with the River Chart, which he used to control the floods. Cf. a passage in the "K'ai-shih" 開筮 chapter of the *Kuei-tsang* 歸藏, cited in the commentary to the *Shan-hai-ching chien-shu*, "Hai-nei-ching," 479, in which Kun is described as transforming into a *Yellow Dragon* after having been dead for *three* years. Both the image of the dragon and the number three tacitly point to the spatiotemporal relationship of Yü and Kun, Corona Australis, and Scorpius.

56. *Shang shu cheng-i*, "Ta hsü," vol. 1, 14.

57. For the most detailed attempt to identify the referent for the "nine regions" in terrestrial terms, see Ku Chieh-kang, "Chiu-chou chih jung yü jung Yü," in *Ku-shih pien*, vol. 7, 117.

58. *Hsing-ching, chüan hsia*, 3b.

59. Li Hsiao-ting, ed., *Chia-ku wen-tzu chi-shih* (Taipei: Academica Sinica, 1970), 3407. Lo Chen-yü describes *chou* as "a place amidst water where one can rest" (水中可居者).

60. Joseph Needham has argued that the "acceptance of a [ruler's] calendar was the demonstration of fealty, somewhat analogous to the authority of the ruler's image and the superscription on the coinage in other civilizations." See Needham's "Time and Knowledge in China and the West," in J. T. Fraser, ed., *The Voices of Time* (New York: George Braziller, 1966), 100.

Moriyasu Tarō advances an intriguing thesis about the origins of this title. In an essay on the shaman and the dragon, he suggests that the graph "shaman" (*wu* 巫) was originally a representation of two "carpenter squares" (*chü* 矩), the original form of which (according to Moriyasu) was *kung* 工. Since the carpenter squares were used to make astronomical measurements, Moriyasu argues that the title Controller of Works (written as *ssu-k'ung* in bronze inscriptions, but *ssu-kung* 司工 in later texts) was given to those whose work concerned making (heavenly) measurements, in other words, the shamans. See Moriyasu, Kōtei *densetsu*, 197.

61. *Chu-shu chi-nien*, ch. 2, 9a.

62. The king's banner is described as being embroidered with a dragon and having nine tassels in the *Li-chi cheng-i*, *Shih-san-ching chu-shu*, "Yüeh-chi," vol. 2, 1537. The "K'ao-kung-chi" section of the *Chou-li chu-shu*, vol. 1, 914, states that such a dragon banner represents the fire star.

63. Jean-Pierre Diény, *Le symbolisme du dragon dans la Chine antique* (Paris: Bibliothèque de l'Institut des Haute Études Chinoise, 1987), 205–52, illustrates the broad textual support for this connection.

64. Wei Chü-hsien, "Yü Hsia," 227–28.

65. Yang K'uan, "Yü Kou-lung yü Hsia-hou hou-t'u," *Ku-shih pien*, vol. 7, 357–59, identifies Yü as a *ch'iu-lung*. For the graph *ch'iu*, see Li Hsiao-ting, ed., *Chia-ku wen-tzu chi-shih*, 4187. *Chiu* was thought to be a pictograph of the crook of the elbow. The *ch'iu-lung* is often described in ancient dictionaries as "a dragon with horns," which would also apply to the form of the Cerulean Dragon.

66. The graph for Yü is combined with the motion radical to form the name of the caster of the vessel. See *Shang Chou ch'ing-t'ung-ch'i ming-wen hsüan*, vol. 1, 86. The vessel is dated to the reign of King Mu 穆王. For the earliest reference to the figure Yü in bronze inscriptions, see the early Ch'un-ch'iu period *Ch'in-kung kuei* 秦公簋, *Shang Chou ch'ing-t'ung-ch'i ming-wen hsüan*, vol. 2, 655. Yang K'uan, "Yü, Kou-lung yü Hsia-hou Hou-t'u," 358. Cf. Wei Chü-hsien's analysis where he reads the graph as being composed of two nines superimposed on each other, "Yü Hsia," 227.

67. See Ch'iu Hsi-kuei, "Shih hai," in his *Ku-wen-tzu lun-chi*, 13.

68. The combination of the Fire Star with the dragon motif calls to mind the Flaming Dragon (*chu-lung* 燭龍), which, according to the *Shan-hai-ching*, lives in the Northwest, on a mountain called Chang *Tail* (Chang-wei 章尾), and is red (the color of Antares). See the *Shan-hai-ching chien-shu*, "Ta-huang pei-ching," 457. Yang K'uan, "Chu-jung yü Chu-lung," *Ku-shih pien*, vol. 7, 314–16, identifies the name Chu-lung as a variation of the name of the Fire god Chu-jung 祝融, whom he then identifies as the mythic controller of fire (*huo-cheng* 火正)—the one who controlled Antares—E Po 閼伯, "E Po yü Chao-ming Chu-jung," *Ku-shih pien*, vol. 7, 312–14. (We will return to E Po presently.) P'ang P'u also argues that Chu-jung in fact is an ancient name referring to the "controller of fire"; See P'ang P'u, "'Huo-li' ch'u t'an," 136–37.

69. Cf. Feng Shih, who, on a similar line of argument, proposes that the ancient form of the graph for dragon (*lung*) is in fact a pictographic represenation of the Cerulean Dragon constellation. See Feng, "Hsing-hsiang t'u yan-chiu," 112.

70. Ku Chieh-kang, "Yü ti shen chih," *Ku-shih pien*, vol. 7, 159, cites Wei Chao's 韋昭 commentary to the "Lu-yü" of the *Kuo-yü*, where he states that sacrifices to She were conducted at the vernal equinox. For the relevant passage see the *Kuo-yü*, 153. Ku Chieh-kang, "Yü ti shen chih," 154–55, provides an excellent anlaysis of the sources that point to a connection between Yü and agriculture. See also Tōdō Akiyasu, *Kanji to bunka* (Tokyo: Tokuman shoten, 1976), 95.

71. The agricultural diety, Hou Chi 後稷, is said to have "continued the work of Yü". For the use of *tien* to describe Yü's work, see *Mao shih cheng-i*, "Han yi," 570; "Hsin Nan shan," 470. Given the epigraphic connection between the word for agriculture (*nung*) and celestial mark point (*ch'en*), it is possible that the diety Shen-nung 神農 represents another name for the Cerulean Dragon constellation. On Yü's self-disembodiment, see *Huai-nan Hung-lieh chi-chieh*, "Hsiu-wu hsün," 632; see also Granet, *Danses et légendes*, 469ff.

72. *Shan-hai-ching chien-shu*, "Hai-nei pei-ching," 366; Granet, *Danses et légendes*, 469 ff.

73. See Bernhard Karlgren, *Grammatica Serica Recensa* (Stockholm: Museum of Far Eastern Antiquities, 1972), 189, on the term *yang*. For information on *yü*, see the entries in Chou Fa-kao, *Chin-wen ku-lin* (Hong Kong: Chinese University Press, 1975), vol. 5, 292.

74. See the entry under *lung* 龍 "dragon" in the *Shuo-wen chieh-tzu* (Peking: Chung-hua, 1990), ch. 11 *hsia*, 14, which states: "At the vernal equinox the dragon ascends; at the autumnal equinox the dragon submerges into the abyss" (春分而登，秋分而入淵). See the vivid imagery of dragons without heads in the *Book of Changes* which also refers to this celestial phenomenon, *Chou-i cheng-i*, vol. 1, 14.

75. Yüan K'o provides a convenient collection of them, *Ts'ui-pien*, 269–71.

76. *Shih chi*, "T'ien-kuan shu," vol. 4, 27.1305. Stomach was known as Heaven's Granary (*t'ien-tsang* 天倉), while Bondslave was known as the masses responsible for reaping the harvest.

77. See the *Shang shu cheng-i*, "I chi," vol. 1, 143; *Ch'u tz'u*, "T'ien-wen," 59; *Lü-shih ch'un-ch'iu*, "Yin-ch'u" 音初, 48; Yüan K'o, *Ts'ui-pien*, 273–77 lists other sources. In one account Lady T'u is identified as the Nü Wa who mended the break in the sky by propping up the turtle, *Shih-pen*, 4.3a.

78. *Shih-pen*, "Ti-hsi." Wen I-to identifies Nü Wa as Yü's helper and mate, "Kao-t'ang shen-nü ch'uan-shuo fen-hsi," in *Wen I-to ch'üan-chi*, vol. 1, 116. See Hung Hsing-tsu's 洪興祖 supplementary commentary to the "T'ien-wen," in which he cites a passage from the *Huai-nan tzu* that is not included in extant editions of the text, in *Ch'u-tz'u chang-chü* (Ch'ang-sha: Yüeh-lu shu-she, 1989), 92.

79. The graph *t'u* 涂 is listed in the *Erh-ya* as a name for the last month of the year, that is, winter. See the *Erh-ya i-shu*, "Shih t'ien," 10a.

80. The antiquity of the denary calendrical system has been of great interest to historians of Chinese astronomy. For a good review of some of

the major scholarship on this issue, see de Saussure, *Origines de l'astronomie chinoise*, 294ff. De Saussure discusses the sequence of days on 294.

81. See Schlegel, *Uranographie*, 202; de Saussure, *Origines* de *l'astronomie chinoise*, 294.

82. Edward Schafer, *Pacing the Void* (Berkeley: University of California Press, 1977), 239. On relating this lameness to the flood, see *Shih tzu*, 375; and Sellers, *The Death of Gods in Ancient Egypt*, 271–73.

83. Needham, *Science and Civilization*, vol. 3, 250. The appearance of the number nine, of course, also calls to mind another stellar configuration associated with Yü, the tail of the Cerulean Dragon. For sources explaining the significance of the number of steps constituting the Dance of Yü, see Schafer, *Pacing the Void*, 239; and Kristofer Schipper and Wang Hsiu-huei, "Progressive and Regressive Time Cycles in Taoist Ritual," in J. T. Fraser, N. Lawrence, and F. C. Haber, eds., *Time, Science, and Society in China and the West* (Amherst: University of Massachusetts Press, 1986), 198–201.

Certainly, movements of the Big Dipper clearly formed the basis for cosmologies and cosmographs that were extremely popular and intellectually influential during the Warring States period. See Li Ling, "Shih-t'u yü Chung-kuo ku-tai ti yü-chou mo-shih," *Chiu-chou hsüeh-k'an* 4.1 (1992), 5–52; Christopher Cullen, "Some Further Points on the *Shih*," *Early China* 6 (1980–81), 31–46; Donald J. Harper, "The Han Cosmic Board (*Shih*)," *Early China* 4 (1978–79), 1–10, and idem, "The Han Cosmic Board: A Response to Christopher Cullen," *Early China* 6 (1980–81), 47–56.

84. See Anne Birrell, *Chinese Mythology* (Baltimore: Johns Hopkins University Press, 1993), 122.

85. *Ch'un-ch'iu Tso chuan cheng-i*, Chao 1, vol. 2, 2023. For the etiological significance of this myth, see de Saussure, *Origines de l'astronomie chinoise*, 108–10, and Cheng Wen-kuang, *Chung-kuo t'ien-wen-hsüeh yüan-liu*, 29–30.

86. Cf. de Saussure's, *Origines de l'astronomie chinoise*, 222, explanation of the significance of the term which he interprets as representing the status of plants right before the vernal equinox: "hindered" for blooming.

87. In another passage of the *Ch'un-ch'iu Tso chuan cheng-i*, Hsiang 9, vol. 2, 1941, the regulator of fire E Po is said to be responsible for "sacrificing" (*chi* 祭) to Antares, and this gave rise to the Fire Calendar. As I've noted above, some scholars have identified the mythic figure E Po as the supposed first regulator of fire, the Fire god Chu-jung.

88. Marcel Granet, "Remarques sur le Taoïsme ancien," *Asia Major* 2 (1925), 146–51. See also Donald Harper, "The 'Wu shih erh Ping Fang.' Translation and Prolegemona" (Ph.D. diss., University of California, Berkeley, 1982), 98–100.

89. Chang Kwang-chih, *Archaeology of Ancient China*, 72.

90. Cesare Emiliani et al., "Paleoclimatological Analysis of Late Quaternary Cores from the Northeastern Gulf of Mexico," *Science* 189 (1975), 1083–88; cited in Major "Origins of Chinese Science," 18 n. 3.

91. Chang Kwang-chih, *Archaeology of Ancient China*, 79. Wilfred T. Neill, *The Last of the Ruling Reptiles: Alligators, Crocodiles, and Their Kin* (New York: Columbia University Press, 1971), 123, states that the Chinese alligator is one of two alligatorine genera that have survived since the Miocene era.

92. A. A. Fauvel, "Alligators in China," *Journal of the North China Branch of the Royal Asiatic Society* 1 (1878), 3. *Shuo-wen chieh-tzu*, ch. 13 *hsia*, 285. For a discussion of *Alligator sinensis* as a numinous animal, see Chang Kwang-chih, *Archaeology of Ancient China*, 160; and Li Yu-heng, *Ta-wen-k'ou hsin-shih-ch'i shih-tai mu-tsang fa-chüeh pao-kao* (Peking: Wen-wu, 1974), 158, and plate 99. Chang Kwang-chih dates this cite to 4300–3500 B.C. (p. 165).

93. Fauvel, "Alligators in China," 3. *Mao Shih cheng-i*, "Ling t'ai," vol. 1, 525. See also Wolfram Eberhard, *Local Cultures*, 364–65, for other traditions associated with the *t'o* and the drum. *Lü-shih ch'un-ch'iu*, "Ku yüeh," 44.

94. For descriptions of the thunder god as a dragon, see the *Huai-nan Hung-lieh chi-chieh*, "Chui-hsing hsün," 150; and the *Shan-hai-ching chien-shu*, "Hai-nei tung-ching," 373. A passage in the *T'ai-p'ing kuang-chi* makes the connection between alligators and thunder explicit: "The alligator is also referred to as '[that which] calls thunder.'" See Li Fang, ed., *T'ai-p'ing kuang-chi*, 5 vols. (Taipei: Hsi-nan, 1983), vol. 5, ch. 464, 3822; cited in Ho Hsin, *Lung: Shen-hua yü chen-hsiang* (Shanghai: Jen-min, 1989), 169. Ch'iu Hsi-kuei, "Shuo pu-tz'u ti fen wu-kuang yü tso t'u-lung," in *Chia-ku-wen yü Yin-Shang shih*, Hu Hou-hsüan, ed. (Shanghai: Ku-chi, 1985), 21–35; also collected in Ch'iu's *Ku-wen-tzu lun-chi*, 224–25.

95. Ho Hsin, *Lung: Shen-hua yü chen-hsiang*, 59, cites Li Shih-chen's *Pen-ts'ao kang-mu*. L. H. Hopkins, "Dragon and Alligator: Being Notes on Some Ancient Inscribed Bone Carvings," *Journal of the Royal Asiatic Society* (1913), 545–52, provides photographs of other similar figures.

96. See the *Hsia hsiao cheng*, in the *Ta-tai Li-chi chieh-ku*, Wang P'in-chen, ed. (Peking: Chung-hua, 1989), *Li-chi cheng-i*, "Yüeh-ling," vol.

1, 1362, 1374. See also the *Huai-nan Hung-lieh chi-chieh* "T'ien-wen hsün," 99, for similar associations.

97. Neill, *The Last of the Ruling Reptiles: Alligators, Crocodiles, and Their Kin*, 271.

98. Ho Hsin, *Lung: Shen-hua yü chen-hsiang*, 174.

99. In this vein, Moriyasu Tarō has postulated an astronomical source for the connection between the Cerulean Dragon and thunder: the dragon constellation, being the home of the Fire Star Antares, was believed to give birth to fire, which in turn produced thunder. See Moriyasu, Kōtei *densetsu*, 161. Shiratori Kiyoshi, "Ryū no keitai ni tsuite no kōsatsu," Tōyō *gakuhō* 21.2, 105–32, links the dragon/rain connection to shamanistic practices.

100. Axel Schuessler, *A Dictionary of Early Zhou Chinese* (Honolulu: University of Hawaii Press, 1987), 111, 559, 493. It was T'ang Lan who first identified this graph as signifying "autumn." See his explanation in Li Hsiao-ting, ed., *Chia-ku wen-tzu chi-shih*, 3941–43. For a different interpretation of the pictographic significance of the graph, see Feng Shih, "Yin-li chi-chieh yen-chiu," *Chung-kuo K'o-hsüeh chi-shu kuo-chi hsüeh-shu t'ao-lun-hui lun-wen* (Peking, 1990), 1–11, where the author sees the graph as a representation of a locust (*huang* 蝗). Feng then argues that the graph functions in oracle bone inscriptions as a loan for the word *tung* 冬 "winter." Tōdō Akiyasu, *Kanji to bunka*, 61, suggestively identifies the graph for *hsia* (i.e., the Hsia dynasty) as the precurser for that of *ch'iu*, but offers no convincing evidence for such a reading.

101. Fauvel, "Alligators in China," 2, 7. The armor of the alligator was thought to resemble that of the turtle.

102. Besides the frequently seen phrase "this autumn" (*chin ch'iu* 今秋), which clearly marks *ch'iu* as a seasonal term, there are a number of inscriptions in which the term *ch'iu* appears to function as a noun rather than as a temporal reference. The topic of divination in these inscriptions concerns the arrival (*chih* 至) or "ascension" (*ch'eng* 稱) of *ch'iu*. The *Shuo-wen* defines the word *ch'eng* in terms of the the measurements taken of grain at the autumnal equinox; see the *Shuo-wen ch'ieh-tzu i-cheng*, 2 vols. (Peking: Chung-hua, 1987), vol. 1, 616, as well as announcements (*kao* 告) pertaining to the ascension of *ch'iu*. While one might argue that the Shang were interested in whether or not the season and the harvest associated with the season would arrive, the absence of similar divinations about other seasons, the fact that whether or not a harvest would be granted is often divined with the phrase "to receive harvest" (*shou nien* 受年), and the fact that different month notations accompany these inscriptions all diminish the likelihood of this meaning. For the relevant inscriptions, see nos. 9627, 9629, 9630, 9631, 9632, 24225, T'un 屯 no.930, Huai 懷 no. 22, no. 1600, in Yao Hsiao-sui et al., eds., *Yin-hsü chia-ku k'o-tz'u lei-tsuan*, 3 vols. (Peking:

Chung-hua, 1989), vol. 2, 695. Feng Shih, "Yin-li chi-chieh yen-chiu," 4–6, argues that the same inscriptions refer to attacks of locusts. Were this the case, one would expect the months to accord with what Feng himself identifies as the primary season of locust attacks (i.e., the ninth to the second months of the Shang calendar year). However, there are inscriptions that contain month notations for the fourth and sixth and seventh months, months that Feng identifies as the hibernating period for locusts. Cf. similar inscriptions referring to the arrival of a turtle (*kuei* 龜), nos. 30025, 30632, 30885, T'un nos. 766, 2363, 3124, *Lei-tsuan*, 693.

103. Feng Shih reads this element as a representation of the way the Shang destroyed the locusts, "Yin-li chi-chieh yen-chiu," 4.

104. Mircea Eliade, *The Sacred and the Profane*, 21.

105. Yü is actually described as the incarnation of measures (*tu* 度) in the *Shi chi*, "Hsia pen chi" 夏本紀, vol. 1, 2.51.

Chapter 3

1. See Nicolas Abraham, "Le symbole ou l'au-delà du phénomene," in Nicolas Abraham and Maria Torok, *L'Écorce et le noyau* (Paris: Flammarion, 1987), 25–76. The essay on symbol will be included in the second volume of the translation of Abraham and Torok's work cited above. The first volume, in which other significant essays relating to the concept of the symbol have been translated, has already been published. The translator and editor of the English edition, Nicholas T. Rand, provides a lucid introduction to Abraham and Torok's work, and brings out themes that are crucial to an understanding of the profound yet often unstated implications of their work. See his *The Shell and the Kernel*, vol. 1 (Chicago: University of Chicago Press, 1994). I am indebted to Professor Esther Rashkin for first introducing Abraham's work to me and for her own excellent metacritical analyses of his work. As will be evidenced from the discussion and the notes, I have greatly benefited from them. See Rashkin, "Tools for a New Psychoanalytic Literary Criticism: The Works of Abranham and Torok," in *Diacritics* 18.4 (1988), and idem, *Family Secrets and the Psychoanalysis of Narrative* (Princeton: Princeton Univesity Press, 1992), 13–48.

2. Abraham, *L'Écorce et le noyau*, 26–27; in Rashkin, *Family Secrets*, 38.

3. Rashkin, *Family Secrets*, 38. Rene Wellek and Austin Warren, *Theory of Literature* (New York: Harcourt, Brace and World, 1956), 188, allude to this original sense of the term symbol as well. There is a parallel to the Greek "symbolon" in the contemporary Chinese context: *fu* 符, "tally." The two parts of a *fu* were matched to authenticate dispatches from

the court, and eventually *fu* came to signify other associations such as auspicious portent or sign, talisman, and charm. While it functioned similarly to the symbol, in that its use implied a metaphorical correspondence between the mundane world and the supernatural, or between the hidden and the revealed, it should be distinguished from the latter because its mode of production does not imply the transcendence of a trauma, the identifying characteristic of the symbol. For the meaning of *fu*, see the *Chung-wen ta tz'u-tien*, 38 vols. (Taipei: Lien-ho, 1962), vol. 24, 462–63.

4. Rashkin, *Family Secrets*, 38–39.

5. Abraham, *Le verbier de l'homme aux loups* (Paria: Aubier-Flammarions, 1976), trans. in Nicholas Rand, *The Wolf Man's Magic Word: A Cryptonymy* (Minneapolis: University of Minnesota Press, 1986), 79; cited in Rashkin, *Family Secrets*, 39.

6. Nicholas T. Rand, *The Shell and the Kernel*, 99. Rand's "Introduction" provides a lucid account of Abraham's theory of introjection, and the psychoanalytic theories that derive from such a conception of pyschic processes.

7. Rand, *The Shell and the Kernel*, 6.

8. Rashkin, *Family Secrets*, 39.

9. Rand, *The Shell and the Kernel*, 16–17.

10. Rashkin, *Family Secrets*, 41.

11. Abraham, "Le symbole," 38, cited and trans. by Rashkin, *Family Secrets*, 41.

12. Rashkin, *Family Secrets*, 41.

13. Andrew Plaks dubbed this term; see, *Archetype and Allegory in the Dream of the Red Chamber*, 44.

14. Plaks, *Archetype and Allegory*, 59.

15. Rashkin, *Family Secrets*, 42; see also Abraham, "Le symbole," 37.

16. This derives from Plaks' distinction between symbol and allegory, *Archetype and Allegory*, 91.

17. A definition proposed by Pauline Yu, *The Reading of Imagery in the Chinese Poetic Tradition* (Princeton: Princeton University Press, 1987), 29.

18. Rashkin, *Family Secrets*, 43.

19. See the *Ch'un-ch'iu Kung-yang chuan*, Min 1, vol. 2, 2244. For a critical assessment of this form of "history," see Liu Chih-chi (661–721),

Shih-T'ung hsin-chiao-chu, Chao Lü-fu ed. (Peking: Hsin-hua, 1990), "Ch'ü-pi," 5–470. See E. G. Pulleyblank, "Chinese Historical Criticism: Liu Chih-chi and Ssu-ma Kuang," *Historians of China and Japan*, ed. Pulleyblank and Beasley, 135–67 for more on Liu Chih-chi's analysis of this form of historiography.

20. See the *Lün-yü chu-shu*, "Tzu-lu," vol. 2, 2507.

21. See the *Wen-hsin tiao-lung i-cheng*, 3 vols. (Shanghai: Shang-hai ku-chi, 1982); "Yin-hsiu," vol. 3, 1481–2525.

22. For shamans and diviners as possessors of the information preserved in myths, see John Major, "Origins of Chinese Science," 8.

23. Giorgio de Santillana and Hertha von Dechend assert that mythic languages "were from the beginning intended to be understood by initiates, as compendia of cosmological teachings." This provides a complementary angle from which to view and explain the cryptic nature of the language of myths. See de Santillana and von Dechend, *Hamlet's Mill*, 312.

24. Rashkin, *Family Secrets*, 40.

25. Ibid., 40.

26. Pauline Yu translates *hsiang* as "image" in her *Reading of Imagery*, 37; Willard Peterson translates the term as "figure," in Peterson, "Making Connections: 'Commentary on the Attached Verbalization' of the *Book of Change*," *Harvard Journal of Asiatic Studies* 42.1 (1982), 86. I will return to his justification for using the term "figure."

27. Izutsu, "Between Image and No-Image," *Eranos Lecture Series 7, On Images: Far Eastern Ways of Thinking* (Dallas: Spring Publications, 1988), 1–37.

28. In this model the higher A-stratum represents the domain of waking consciousness while the lower B-stratum corresponds to the "Storehouse Consciousness," or the unconscious. The A-stratum produces and reflects sensory images, while the B-stratum produces the "mythic, mythopoeic, archetypal or symbolic images which owe their peculiarity to their being essentially adjusted to the very structure of the B-stratum." Once produced, according to Izutsu, the symbolic images linger in between the two strata; they are a "direct reflection of reality as it is viewed at a deeper level of consciousness." See Izutsu, "Between Image and No-Image," 16–19.

29. Izutsu, "Between Image and No-Image," 17.

30. Ibid., 16.

31. Ibid., 1.

32. Major, "Origins of Chinese Science," 8. He suggests the processes contributing to the coalescence into a single civilization of the "various nuclei of civilization in the eastern mainland Asia" had the effect of harmonizing and reconciling the specifically technical (what I call symbolic) nature of early mythic language into a "newly invented vocabulary and rhetoric of philosophy by a rising new group of scholars and teachers."

33. See Girardot, *Myth and Meaning in Early Taoism*, 9.

34. My hypothesis may have some bearing on the question of the relationship between protoscience and Taoism. For the need to be justifiably cautious with any approach to this question, see Nathan Sivin, "On the Word 'Taoist' as a Source of Perplexity: With Special Reference to the Relations of Science and Religion in Traditional China," *History of Religions* 17.3–4 (1978), 303–30. Sivin's observation that "the safeguarding and perpetuation of orthodox scriptural traditions depended on esoteric rites of transmission, specifying a line of predecessors never contaminated by people uninitiated into the worship of the Tao" (p. 306), seems especially relevant, given the factors contributing to the symbolic, cryptic nature of the language representing the astronomical information discussed above.

35. See the *Lao tzu chi-shih, Hsin-pien chu-tzu chi-ch'eng* edition (Peking: Chung-hua, 1991), 42.174.

36. Girardot, *Myth and Meaning in Early Taoism*, 59.

37. Ibid., 69.

38. Ibid.

39. Thomas Worthen, *The Myth of Replacement* (Tucson: University of Arizona Press, 1991), 166.

40. David Pankenier has suggested to me (personal communication, 8 June 1994), that the actual fact that there was no star at the pole—the pole was vacant—in the Chinese skies for about "two millennia after 2000 B.C.," may better explain the interest of Taoism in the void. While his comment that "it was this 'void at the hub' that gave rise to Taoist notions of the 'utility of vacuity'" is both provocative and has the added virtue of referring to something we know the Chinese observed, the pervasiveness of water imagery in Taoist explanations of the void, coupled with the obvious linguistic resonances between terms such as *hun-tun* 混沌 and figures of the flood myths precludes me from throwing out my hypothesis. The fact that precession can also account for the cyclic interaction characteristic of Taoist notions of chaos, while the vacant pole must be viewed as a static phenomenon also suggests that the effects of precession served as the initial instigator in the symbolic construction of Taoist thought. That the vacant pole may have been viewed as another instance of chaos is quite possible.

41. For a lucidly argued analysis of Indo-European myths premised on this theory, see Worthen, *The Myth of Replacement*, 157–237.

42. Girardot, *Myth and Meaning in Early Taoism*, 59.

43. Jane Sellers, *The Death of Gods in Ancient Egypt*, and David Ulansey, *The Origins of the Mithraic Mysteries* (Oxford: Oxford University Press, 1989), 82ff. Both posit precessional movement as the source and motivation for religious traditions in ancient Egypt and Greece respectively.

44. That these boundaries were engendered by three, the number used to articulate the amount of time (in months or years) that it took for Kun to produce Yü, offers another instance of overlap between the symbolism of Taoism and the flood myths.

45. Girardot, *Myth and Meaning in Early Taoism*, 7.

46. While the first clause in the *Lao tzu chi-shih* edition is different ("the *hsiang* that derived from non-phenomena" [*wu*]), I follow almost all other editions which have *hsiang* in the place of *wu*. Stylistically, as well as semantically, this seems to make the most sense. See the notes in the *Lao tzu chiao-chih*, 14.54.

47. *Lao tzu chi-shih*, 14.54, 21.88, 35.140, 41.171. For a similar expression of ideas, see the *Chuang tzu chi-shih*, 4 vols. (Peking: Chung-hua, 1989), "Chih-lo p'ien."

48. Cf. Izutsu's argument that "Taoism symbolically reflects and reproduces—or rather, we should say, is itself a symbolic self-expression of—a metaphysical experience of Being in which the existence of all things in the so-called empirical world is actually experienced as an ontological process of their emerging out of the primordial Nothing, and establishing themselves gradually in the domain of phenomenal multiplicity"; Izutsu, "Between Image and No-Image," 7.

49. The fact that in at least one contemporaneous text the term *hsiang* is identified as part of the name of a water spirit provides further evidence linking the state of *hsiang* to that of the watery condition of the Milky Way. See the "Lu-yü hsia," in the *Kuo-yü*, 201. Kiang Chao-yuan, *Le voyage dans la Chine ancienne*, trans. Fan Jen (Shanghai: Commision Mixte des Oeuvres Franco-chinoises, 1937), Appendix III, 176, analyzes the term *wang-hsiang* 罔象 and others, and shows how it is associated with water and a sense of confusion and mystery in many texts. Donald Harper examines the common graphic variants of demon names and concludes that the "binom represented by these graphs probably resulted from the dimidiation of an initial consonant cluster in the early stages of the development of the Chinese language." "Wang Yen-shou's Nightmare Poem," *Harvard Journal of Asiatic Studies* 47.1 (1987), 258. It is not insignificant that one of the earliest appearances of these terms occurs in a passage concerning Yü's

activities while controlling the floodwaters. The demons may very well be associated with the displacement effect produced by the waters and reflected in the symbolic *hsiang*. For the said passage, see the *Ch'un-ch'iu Tso chuan cheng-i*, Hsüan 3, vol. 2, 1868. See also Wolfgang Bauer's recent study on the association between water, displacement, and themes of travel and chaos, "Voyageurs sans demeure et départs vers un monde meilleur dans la civilisation chinoise," *Diogenes* 165 (1994), 26–46.

50. This sentence opens the *Tao teh ching*. See the *Lao tzu chi-shih*, 3. Benjamin Schwartz, *The World of Thought in Ancient China*, 198, discusses the apparent paradox implicit in the statement.

51. Girardot, *Myth and Meaning in Early Taoism*, 72, cites the *Lao tzu chi-shih*, 15.58–60. The congruence of form and content contribute to what I, along with Schwartz, believe to be a mystical dimension of Taoism. My understanding of the mystical dimension is obviously anchored in a specific interpretive stance, however, and thus is more specific than Schwartz's. Cf. the discussion of the "mystification" of precessional knowledge seen in Mithraism, in Ulansey, *The Origins of the Mithraic Mysteries*, 82–84.

52. Most scholars attribute this verbal sense of the word to the early Chinese practice of harnessing the elephant to perform acts requiring great strength. With the elephant's "aid" activities that might not otherwise be possible were successfully completed. See the entries under *wei* in Chou Fa-kao, ed., *Chin-wen ku-lin*, 4.1554–68.

53. Peter Boodberg, "Some Proleptical Remarks on the Evolution of Archaic Chinese," *Harvard Journal of Asiatic Studies* 2 (1937), 937 n. 68.

54. *Chin-wen ku-lin*, vol. 4, 1554–56.

55. See Su Ling-chih's 蘇靈芝 annotation for the text based on eight stone stelae dating from the 26th year of the K'ai-yüan 開元 period (738 A.D.) of the T'ang dynasty, in *Lao tzu chi-shih*, 35.140.

56. Peterson provides a succinct analysis of the factors involved in dating the text and assessing the nature of its composition. See Peterson, "Making Connections," 67–79, esp. 77.

57. This is a somewhat modified version of Izutsu's definition, "Between Image and No-Image," 5.

58. See the *Chou-i cheng-i*, vol. 1, 76. I have benefited from Peterson's translations and employ them with some modification. Unless otherwise noted, I will cite him. For this passage, see "Making Connections," 86–87.

59. Peterson, "Making Connections," 87.

60. Ibid., 85.

61. Ibid., 80–81. Yu objects to Peterson's use of the term "figure," arguing that it "places undue emphasis on the human act of representation and interpretation"—this in contrast to her translation of the term as "image"; Yu, *The Reading of Imagery*, 39 n. 104 Cf. Charles Hartman's objections to Yu's use of the term "image," in his review of Yu's book, "Images of Allegory: A Review Article," *Early China* 14 (1989), 183–200.

62. Peterson, "Making Connections," 90.

63. Ibid., 91.

64. *Chou-i cheng-i*, vol. 89; Peterson, "Making Connections," 113.

65. Richard Kunst, "The Original 'YiJing': A Text, Phonetic Transcription, Translation, and Indexes, with Sample Glosses" (Ph.D. diss., University of California, 1985), 4ff., provides a fascinating discussion of the structure of the *Book of Changes* and its relation to primitive systematic thought.

66. Needham, *Science and Civilization in China*, vol. 2, 336. See also Arthur Waley, "The Book of Changes," *Bulletin of the Museum of Far Eastern Antiquities* 5 (1934), 5, for a similar perspective.

67. *Chou-i cheng-i*, vol. 1, 82; Peterson, "Making Connections," 99.

68. *Chou-i cheng-i*, vol. 1, 83. My translation differs in several respects from Peterson's, "Making Connections," 114. First, I do not translate the verb *chien* 見 "to see," but rather translate it as "to make manifest" (*hsien*), which is consistent with the way it is used (and translated by Peterson) throughout the text. The fact that the verb "to observe" (*kuan* 觀) follows directly after *chien* in the next passage confirms this reading. Second, I connect more directly, through the use of brackets, the context of the process of symbolization, the sages' act of penetrating the manifest mysteries of the cosmos, and the overall effect of these two acts. Without emphasizing the almost contingent relationship of symbols to mysteries, the force of the last sentence, which highlights the reason a *hsiang* is a *hsiang*, would be completely lost. Cf. Yu's translation of this passage, which completely obscures this intention; Yu, *The Reading of Imagery*, 39.

69. Peterson, "Making Connections," 108.

70. *Chou-i cheng-i*, 81; Peterson, "Making Connections," 106.

71. Peterson, "Making Connections," 107–8. *Chou-i cheng-i*, vol. 1, 82.

72. Peterson, "Making Connections," 108.

73. This is implied in the statement that "the completion of symbols is called *ch'ien* [i.e., the name of the first hexagram]," 象成謂乾, *Chou-i cheng-i*, vol. 1, 78.

74. Although he had not seen the Ma-wang-tui texts, Peterson also noted the possible watery connotation of the term *k'un*; Peterson, "Making Connections," 82. For a transcription of the Ma-wang-tui text, see "Ma-wang tui po-shu 'Liu-shih-ssu kua' shih-wen," *Wen-wu* 3 (1984), 1–8. See also Lian Shao-ming, "Po-shu 'Chou-i' kua-ming chiao shih," *Wen-shih* 36 (1992), 64. The *k'un* hexagram is placed as no. 33 in the Ma-wang-tui text.

75. Cf. Izutsu's contention that these hexagrams "are purely abstract or vacant forms having in themselves nothing to do with concrete imagery"; Izutsu, "Between Image and No-Image," 5.

76. I am indebted to David Pankenier for helping me elucidate this point. Cf. Hellmut Wilhelm, "The Interplay of Image and Concept," *Eranos Lecture Series 7, On Images: Far Eastern Ways of Thinking*, 52, where he insists that in apprehending the message of the *Book of Changes*, "the origin of the term (*ch'ien* = dry) become[s] more and more meaningless and eventually forgotten.

77. Peterson, "Making Connections," 90.

78. The graph is sometimes read as *tz'u* 賜, as in "to be given." For the reading of the expression *i-jih* 易日 (it will change to sun [from rain]), see Paul Serruys, "The Language of the Shang Oracle Inscription," *T'oung Pao* 60 (1974), 80; and Ken-ichi Takashima, "An Evaluation of the Theories Concerning the Shang Oracle-Bone Inscriptions," *Journal of Intercultural Studies* (Kansai University) 15–16 (1988–89), 14.

79. *Chou-i cheng-i*, vol. 1, 82.

80. "Change" is described as "still and unmoving," in the *Appended Words Commentary, Chou-i cheng-shu*, vol. 1, 81; Petersion, "Making Connections," 106.

81. *Chou-i cheng-i*, vol. 1, 87.

82. I am aware that the key word "being," is an artifact of the English translation. While I believe that the context of the sentence warrants the translation Peterson provides, I think that even if restated as "that which is the *change* is a matter of providing symbols," the sentence captures the essence of Abraham's theory.

Chapter 4

1. Wei T'ing-sheng, *Mu-T'ien-tzu chuan chin-k'ao*, vol. 2, 183–90, provides a convenient summary of the various locations attributed to K'un-lun and the reasons cited by several scholars. The most detailed descriptions of K'un-lun are found in the "T'ien-wen" chapter of the *Ch'u-tz'u chi-chu*, 57, and in the "Chui-hsing" chapter of the *Huai-nan Hung-lieh*

chi-chieh, 133. Yüan K'o, *Ts'ui-pien*, 83–86, provides a convenient collection of these and other excerpts focusing on K'un-lun. For an analysis of the different intellectual traditions represented in K'un-lun myths, see Ku Chieh-kang, "*Chuang tzu* ho *Ch'u-tz'u* chung K'un-lun ho P'eng-lai liang-ko shen-hua hsi-t'ung ti jung-ho," *Chung-hua wen-shih lun-ts'ung* 2 (1979), 31–57.

2. On K'un-lun as a river source, see the excerpts from the *Shan-hai-ching, T'ien-wen, Huai-nan tzu*, and *Shih chi*, collected by Yüan K'o, in *Ts'ui-pien*, 82–84. Regarding the mountain's height, see Hao I-hsing, *Shan-hai-ching chien-shu*, "Hai-nei hsi-ching," 350; also cited in Yüan K'o, *Ts'ui-pien*, 83.

3. Michael Loewe, *Ways to Paradise*, 73, 155 n. 199; N. J. Girardot, *Myth and Meaning in Early Taoism*, 173, 201, 203, passim; Eveline Porée-Maspero, *Étude sur les rites agraires des Cambodgiens*, 3 vols. (Paris: Mouton, 1952, 1964, 1969), vol. 3, 786–87, cited in Girardot, *Myth and Meaning in Early Taoism*, 173. For a discussion of the idea of an *axis mundi*, see Mircea Eliade, *Shamanism: Archaic Techniques of Ecstasy*, trans. Willard R. Trask (New York: Bollingen Foundation, 1964), 42, 71, 120, 169, passim.

4. See the *Huai-nan Hung-lieh chi-chieh*, "Pen-ching", 255. Su Hsüeh-lin argues that the Yi who can climb K'un-lun is not the same as Archer I. She claims that the former is simply a common epithet for "immortal," that is, someone who "has wings." See her *T'ien-wen cheng chien*, 364. Given the astronomical connotations associated with K'un-lun and Yi's shooting of the sun, which will be examined fully below, I am not convinced by Su's reasoning. Cf. Sun I-jang's explanation that the term *jen* 仁, which modifies I's name in the K'un-lun passage is in fact a scribal error for the character "barbarian" *i* 夷, which precedes Archer I's name in Ch'ü Yüan's "Tien-wen," and the *Tso chuan*. See Sun I-jang, *Cha-i* (Peking: Chung-hua, 1989), 92.

5. Chang Kuang-chih, "Ch'uang-shih shen-hua," 58. On the link to chaos, see Giorgio de Santillana and Hertha von Dechend, *Hamlet's Mill*, 256. For a more recent interpretation of related Hindu and Greeks sun myths, see Thomas Worthen, *The Myth of Replacement*, 157–231.

6. *Ch'u-tz'u chi chu*, 58–59.

7. Cf. the "Yü kung," in the *Shang shu cheng-i*, vol. 1, 151, where Yü "drains" Black Water into San-wei.

8. "Hai-nei pei-ching," 369; "Hai-wai hsi-ching," 306–7. See Su Hsüeh-lin, *T'ien-wen cheng-chien*, 202–3. Hung Hsing-tsu likens the Ling fish to a *t'o*, alligator/turtle, *Ch'u-tz'u chi-chu*, 58, while the *Shan-hai-ching* likens the Lung fish to a *pieh* turtle, "Hai-wai hsi-ching," 307. The

link between the fish and the turtle can be found in a commentarial note in the *Huai-nan Hung-lieh chi-chieh*, "Hsiu-wu," 667, which defines the *ch'iu* dragon as a *pieh*-like creature that nests on a hill, a *ling*, but hides in the abyss, *yüan*.

9. *Chuang tzu chi-shih*, "Hsiao-yao," vol. 1, 2. Su Hsüeh-lin, *T'ien-wen cheng-chien*, 203. For the relationship between the graphs for phoenix and dragon, see the comments made by Lo Chen-yü and Ch'en Pang-huai 陳邦懷 in Li Hsiao-ting, *Chia-ku wen-tzu chi-shih*, vol. 11, 1361, 1364. See also Ikeda Suetoshi, "Ryūjin kō," *Tōhōgaku* 6 (1953), 1–7; Su Hsüeh-lin, *T'ien-wen cheng-chien*, 203–4.

10. For an excellent discussion of the associations between Sang-lin and the sun, see Sarah Allan, *The Shape of the Turtle: Myth, Art and Cosmos in Early China*, 41–42. Cf. the suggestion of Ho Hsin that the ancient graph for the mulberry tree, *sang*, represents a pictograph of the alligator's (i.e., dragon's) underground nest with tunnels leading to the earth's surface, *Lung: Shen-hua yü chen-hsiang*, 150–54.

11. For the symbolism of shooting arrows, see Wolfram Eberhard, *The Local Cultures of South and East China*, 44–66; Girardot, *Myth and Meaning in Early Taoism*, 188. That both King Mu and Yü are credited with gathering all of the (feudal) lords at T'u Mountain, an act that traditionally symbolized the universal acknowledgment of one's legitimacy to rule, concretizes, at least textually, the implied connection between the Great Yü's achievement and King Mu's (desire). For Yü's and King Mu's congregation, see the entry under the fourth year of Duke Chao's reign, *Ch'un-ch'iu Tso chuan cheng-i*, vol. 1, 2035. The associations with political legitimacy of the congregation is implied in the *Tso chuan* passage. The importance of these political associations for our understanding of the literary significance of K'un-lun Mountain in the *Mu T'ien-tzu chuan* will be addressed below.

12. See Yüan K'o, *Ts'ui-pien*, 208. Ku Shih, *Hsi-cheng chiang-shu*, 3.172, 3.175, 4.243. In the *Shan-hai-ching chien-shu*, 347, a similar description is used to refer to a location very close to K'un-lun.

13. See Edward Schafer, "The Sky River," *Journal of the American Oriental Society* 94.4 (1974), 401–7.

14. See, for example, the *Shan-hai-ching chien-shu*, "Ta-huang hsi-ching," 433.

15. *Shan-hai-ching chien-shu*, "Ta-huang hsi-ching," 433. Allan, *The Shape of the Turtle: Myth, Art and Cosmos in Early China*, 29, regards the Jo Waters "not as an ordinary river, but as another name for the watery underworld also known as the 'Yellow Spring' (*Huang Quan*), which ran everywhere beneath the earth and which came to the surface at the feet of the Fu Sang and the Ruo Tree."

16. See T'an Ts'ui, *Mu T'ien-tzu chuan chu-shu*, 2.11a, and the *Shan-hai-ching chien-shu*, "Ta-huang pei-ching," 441.

17. Girardot, *Myth and Meaning in Early Taoism*, 5. As we saw in the preceding chapter, this gap may perhaps also be represented by the broken lines of the *k'un* (Kun) hexagram.

18. *Huai-nan Hung-lieh chi-chieh*, "Lan-ming," 207; *Shan-hai-ching chien-shu*, "Chung-shan-ching," 191. *Ch'u-tz'u chi-cheng*, 61. In her collation of the text, Su Hsüeh-lin includes these lines with others that are directly related to the Kun and Yü myths, see Su, *T'ien-wen cheng-chien*, 332 passim.

19. *T'ien-wen cheng-chien*, 330–31. John Major, *Heaven and Earth in Early Han Thought* (Albany: SUNY Press, 1993), 151.

20. In his sixty-first year, Yao orders Ch'ung-po Kun to control the floods, see *Chu-shu chi-nian t'ung-chien*, 2.5a; *Kuo-yü*, "Chou-hsia," 103. Yü is referred to as Count of Ch'ung Yü in the *I Chou shu*, see Chu Yu-tseng, *I Chou shu chi-hsün chiao-shih* (*E-kuan shu-ts'ung* ed.), 1913, 4.6b. Ku Chieh-kang follows Wang Nien-sun's 王念孫 argument that the graph *ch'ung* is the ancient epigraphic form for the graph *sung* 崧 "high." He thus equates Sung Mountain with Ch'ung. Ku's reasoning is informed by his belief that the Kun and Yü, myths are products of ethnic Jung 戎 tribes who habitated this and other nearby mountains. See Ku, "chiu-chou chih jung yü Jung-Yü," *Ku-shih pien*, vol. 7, 136–38. See Ch'ien I, *Fang-yen chien-shu*, 2 vols. (Shanghai: Shang-hai ku-chi, 1984), vol. 2, 11.11a. See the *Mao Shih cheng-i*, "Liang ssu," vol. 1, 602 for an example of *ch'ung* being used to mean "to pile on high."

21. This is how Ch'ung Mountain is described in the *Mu T'ien-tzu chuan*. See Ku Shih, *Hsi-cheng chiang-shu*, 2.87.

22. For descriptions of this mythic figure, see the *Shan-hai-ching chien-shu*, "Hai-wai pei-ching," 311, and "Ta-huang pei-ching," 457.

23. See Girardot: "Cosmologically the solar solstice marks one of the multiple yearly reversions to a cosmogonic time when the order and interaction of the dual principles were established"; Girardot, *Myth and Meaning in Early Taoism*, 31.

24. See the *Shuo-wen chieh-tzu i-cheng*, vol. 2, 1242.

25. *Shan-hai-ching chien-shu*, "Hsi-shan-ching," 65.

26. *Shuo-wen chieh-tzu i-cheng*, vol. 2, 1242.

27. This is based on Bernhard Karlgren's reconstruction of archaic Chinese pronounciation. See *Grammatica Serica Recensa*, nos. 417, 419, 470. For other analyses of linguistic implications of K'un-lun, see de

Saussure, "Étymologie," 370; and Girardot, *Myth and Meaning in Early Taoism*, 201, 203.

28. Peter Boodberg, "Some Proleptical Remarks on the Evolution of Archaic Chinese," 337, 356. At 370n. 90, Boodberg sees the name of the mountain rammed into by Kung-kung, Pu-chou (*Pəu–tsəug), as an example of "semantic individualization," whereby the (more ancient pronounciation of the) verb "to ram" *ch'u* 觸, which contained the complex glottological phoneme *BTSI^{w}OK, evolved into this compound. See his "Evolution," 404. See also William Boltz's discussion of the mythic figure Kung-kung's name in terms of the etymon *hung*, "flood"; Boltz, "Kung-kung and the Flood: Reverse Euhemerization in the Yao Tien," *T'oung Pao* 67.3–5 (1981), 141–53.

29. Chūbachi Masakazu, in his *Chūgoku no saiki to bungaku* (Tokyo: Sōbunsha, 1989), Oriental Studies Library no. 30, 19–42, provides an interesting study of the watery associations of K'un-lun and argues that K'un-lun be seen as an icon of the watery underworld where souls of the dead go to be rejuvenated. Ling Ch'un-sheng, argues that the name K'un-lun was a transliteration of the term "ziggurat" and that the "tiered" structure of K'un-lun was a motif introduced into China from Babylon during the third millennia B.C. He also argues that the "hanging garden" image of K'un-lun seen in the "T'ien-wen" poem refers to the great garden of Babylon. See Ling Ch'un-sheng, "Chung-kuo ti feng-shan yü liang-ho liu-yü ti k'un-lun wen-hua," *Bulletin of the Institute of Ethynology, Academica Sinica* 19 (1965), 1–52.

An interesting line in Ch'ü Yüan's "T'ien wen" contains the image of a turtle carrying a (sacred) mountain on its back: "The Great turtle carries a great mountain on its back [in order to] put it together [with something] to make a whole; what will the turtle use to stabilize it (the mountain)?" 鼇戴山抃, 何以安之. The resonance between this imagery and the celestial associations between Kun and K'un-lun that I have just illustrated are noteworthy. See *Ch'u-tz'u chi-chu*, 61. For other examples of turtle and mountain imagery in traditional texts, see Izushi Yoshihiko, "Kodai Chūgoku no 'kyoki fuzan' setsuwa no yurai ni tsuite," *Chūgoku shinwa densetsu no kenkyū* (Tokyo: Chuo Koronsha, 1943), 323–43. See also the engraving on a pillar at the Yi'nan tomb in Shantung, dating from the second century A. D., on which is carved a picture of a tortoise upholding a three-tiered Kun-lun Mountain in Wu Hung, *The Wu Liang Shrine: The Ideology of Early Chinese Pictorial Art* (Stanford: Stanford University Press, 1989), 131.

30. See for example, Ku Shih, *Hsi-cheng chiang-shu*, 1.24, who provides a map detailing the geography of the area.

31. Ku Shih, however, does not; *Hsi-cheng chiang-shu*, 1.24ff. The nature of the connection between Feng-i and Ho has also been questioned by one scholar, Wen Ch'ung-i, "Chiu-ko chung Ho-po chih yen-chiu,"

Bulletin of the Institute of Ethnology, Academica Sinica, 9 (1960), 148–51. Most scholars, however, understand the two names as referring to one figure, Ho-tsung or Ho-po. Cf. the *Shui-ching chu shu* (Chiang-su: Ku-chi, 1989), 1, 12, which states, "The River flows into Feng-i mountain, where *i* is written as 逸.

32. This is stated, for example, in the *Shan-hai-ching chien-shu*, "Hai-nei pei-ching," 365.

33. Masakazu Chūbachi, *Saikito bungaku*, 22, locates it in the watery underworld.

34. *Shan-hai-ching chien-shu*, "Hai-nei pei-ching," 366.

35. See the *Huai-nan Hung-lieh chi-chieh*, "Pen ching," 255; "Hsiu-wu," 631; "T'ai-tsu," 670. Dragon Gate is said to be located by the "river's abyss" in the same text, "Chui-hsing," 150. See also the "Yü kung" chapter of the *Shang shu cheng-i*, vol. 1, 150, 151, for Yü and Dragon Gate.

36. *Grammatica Serica Recensa*, pp. 44–45. The given name of Feng-i's descendant, Yao, who serves as King Mu's guide, seems to have similar connotations: the term *yao*, a pictograph of a *bending* man, was often used to refer to untimely deaths.

37. Girardot, *Myth and Meaning in Early Taoism*, 146. *Ch'u-tz'u chi-chu*, 49.

38. Wen, "Chiu-ko chung Ho-po chih yen-chiu," 148–151. Girardot, *Myth and Meaning in Early Taoism*, 9.

39. *Chuang tzu chi-shih*, "Ta-tsung," 247; *Huai-nan Hung-lieh chi-chieh*, "Ch'i-su," 362.

40. An affirmative answer is possible if we relate this to the larger context of the Sino-Tibetan language family. Paul Benedict, *Sino-Tibetan: A Conspectus* (Cambridge: Cambridge University Press, 1972), 158n. 428 (cited by Richard Kunst, "The Original 'Yijing,'" 217n. 12), treats *ch'uan* as an example of a "collective suffix" in Old Chinese. Given the collective nature of the Milky Way and its relationship to all "waters," the term *ch'uan*, in addition to reflecting an early Sino-Tibetan stage of the Chinese language, may also contain cosmogonic connotations.

41. *Huai-nan Hung-lieh chi-chieh*, "Yüan tao," 6.

42. See Ch'ü Yüan's song on Ho-po, part of the *Chiu-ko* sequence in *Ch'u-tz'u chi-chu*, 43. In the "Hsi-shan-ching" "River" (*ho*) is described anthropomorphically as submerging in the neighborhood of Pu Chou Mountain. See *Shan-hai-ching chien-shu*, "Hsi-shan-ching," 61.

43. Su Hsüeh-lin, *Ch'ü Yüan yü Chiu Ko* (Taipei: Kuang-tung, 1973), 215–50. Yang Kuan, "Kun, Kung-kung yü Hsüan-ming, Feng-i," *Ku-shih*

pien, vol. 7, 329–45. Kung-kung is said to "wreak havoc" in a passage preserved in the reconstructed *Fragmented Dialogues*, discovered at Chi-chung; see the *Ku-wen suo-yü*, Ma Kuo-han ed., *Yü-han shan-fang chi-i-shu*, 1884 Ch'ang-sha Niang-huan ed., ch. 64, 2b. In a remarkably similar passage in the *Ch'un-ch'iu Tso chuan cheng-i*, Chao 7, vol. 2, 2049, Kun is said to be the culprit; the river is described as "wreaking havoc" in the *Ch'un-ch'iu Tso chuan cheng-i*, Ai 6, vol. 2, 2162. See also Yang K'uan, "Kun, Kung-kung yü Hsüan-ming, Feng-i," 337. For examples of oracle bone inscriptions that divine whether or not the river will "wreak havoc," see nos. 557, 2415, *Ying* no. 1167, in the *Chia-ku-wen ho-chi*. Su Hsüeh-lin discusses turtle imagery in detail in *T'ien-wen cheng-chien*, 334–42.

44. Chou Fa-kao, *Chin-wen ku-lin*, vol. 7, 563–66. The term *Ho-tsung* appears in oracle bone inscriptions. See the *Chia-ku-wen ho-chi*, nos. 13532, 28207 (fragmented). Cf. Ku Chieh-kang's incorrect assertion that except for the "Chao-shih-chia" in the *Shih chi*, this term does not appear in any text besides the *Mu T'ien-tzu chuan*; Ku, "Chu-tso shih-tai," 64. In the *Chou-li* the official with the title *Tsung-po* is primarily in charge of serving the spirits to help stabilize the country. See the *Chou-li chu-shu*, vol. 1, 757, 766.

45. Sarah Allan argues that the Yellow Springs, the name for the underworld in Warring States texts, derives from the belief that everything beneath the earth was believed to be a "watery underworld." *The Shape of the Turtle: Myth, Art and Cosmos in Early China*, 29–30, 65–66, 70. Cf. a recent study on fish imagery on Neolithic pottery, which cites the Neolithic practice of burying humans with fish placed strategically under parts of the corpse to argue that fish were connected with the idea of rejuvenation from very early times. See Wang Yü-ch'eng, "Yang-shao jen-mian yü-wen yü shih-ch'ieh jen-t'ou ch'ung-pai," *Chiang-han k'ao-ku* 2 (1992), 24–35, 23.

See Izushi Yoshihiko, *Shina shinwa densetsu no kenkyu*, 115, who suggests the possibility of this being the case in China as well. See also Loewe, *Ways to Paradise*, 115. The association between the Milky Way and death may also be intimated in the function of the Southern Dipper (*nan-tou* 南斗) constellation, which lies at the extreme of the celestial river (ie., Feng-i's place of residence) and serves as the head of the Heavenly Turtle. In early Chinese astronomy this constellation was believed to "rule [and decide] the time of death of the Son of Heaven" 主天子壽命, *Hsing-ching, chüan hsia*, 7a. For a general discussion of the connection between the Milky Way and the underworld in other myths worldwide, see de Santillana and von Dechend, *Hamlet's Mill*, 406–7.

46. Allan, *The Shape of the Turtle: Myth, Art and Cosmos in Early China*, 65.

47. Ishikawa Misarō, "Soji ni okeru kyūka to kyūshō no kankei ni tsuite—sono meishō to hensū to henshō no yimi suru mono," *Tōyōgaku* 70

(1993), 1–22, provides an indepth discussion on the relation between the number nine and death. In addition to examining the "Nine Songs" from the *Ch'u-tz'u*, Ishikawa also considers the archaeological evidence from the Tseng Hou-i tomb.

48. Ch'en Meng-chia, "Shang-tai ti shen-hua yü wu-shu," *Yen-ching hsüeh-pao* 20 (1936), 323. Ch'en also mentions another name of the Yellow Emperor, *Yu Nai* (or *hsiung*) *shih* 有能, which resonates with the story of Yü changing into a *nai* as he passed through the Hsüan-yüan mountain pass.

49. For *feng-i* as crossing water without a boat, see the poem "Hsiao Min" 小旻 of the "Hsiao-ya" section of the *Mao shih cheng-i*, vol. 1, 449. There are also other elements in this poem that resonate greatly with some of the motifs in the *Mu T'ien-tzu chuan*. For example, there is mention of killing a tiger and mention of travel and the building of palaces. For *feng-i* as a dance, see the *Ch'u-tz'u chi-chu*, 111.

50. Marcel Granet, *Fêtes et chansons anciennes de la Chine*, 2nd ed. (Paris: Leroux, 1929). The exorcistic properties of Dragon boat races across rivers, relayed by Wen Ch'ung-i, may derive from the symbolic function of crossing water that I have articulated. See "Chiu-ko chung ti shui-shen yü Hua-nan ti lung-chou sai-shen," *Bulletin of Institute of Ethnology* 11 (1961), 51–124.

Ku Shih states that Ho-po is the only one capable of "transporting" (i.e., directing) King Mu on his western journey, *Hsi-cheng chiang-shu*, 1.41. Feng-i's function may be similar to that of a special animal (such as the dragon) who "carried" shamans to the other world. For a fascinating discussion of archaeological evidence that may point to the prevalence of this concept as far back as Neolithic times, see Chang Kwang-chih, "P'u-yang san-ch'iao yü Chung-kuo ku-tai mei-shu shang ti jen shou mu-t'i," *Wen-wu* 11 (1988), 36–39. Cf. the reference to the ferryman, Nibiru, in the *Enuma Elish*, the Babylonian creation epic, which states that "*Nebiru* shall hold the crossings of heaven and earth in its midst. . . . Let 'Crossing' be his name who controls the passage," cited in de Santillana and von Dechend, *Hamlet's Mill*, 432–33.

51. *Chuang tzu chi-shih* "Wai-wu," vol. 4, 933. Yü is presented with a turtle at Chiu-chiang, which transports him (yü 渝) across the water to Lo; see the "Yü kung," *Shang shu cheng-i*, vol. 1, 149; the *Chu-shu chi-nien t'ung-chien*, 8.14b, describes King Mu crossing Chiu-chiang by way of a bridge formed by large turtles (*yüan*) and alligators (*t'o*). For an example of the turtle as vehicle, see chapter 99 of the famous sixteenth-century novel, *Hsi-yu-chi*, 3 vols. (Peking: Jen-min, 1980), vol. 3, 1246–47.

52. See the *Shih tzu*, 382.

53. *Huai-nan Hung-lieh chi-chieh*, "Yüan tao," 5–6.

54. See for example, Homer H. Dubs, "An Ancient Chinese Mystery Cult," 221–40; Kominami Ichirō, "Seibo to shichi seki denshō," *Tōhō gakuhō* 46 (1974), 33–81; Yü Ying-shih, "Life and Immortality in the Mind of Han China," *Harvard Journal of Asiatic Studies* 25 (1964), 80–122; Loewe, *Ways to Paradise*, chap. 4; and Ricardo Fracasso, "Holy Mothers of Ancient China," *T'oung Pao* 74 (1988), 1–42.

55. Ch'en Meng-chia, "Ku-wen-tzu chung chih Shang Chou chi-ssu," *Yen-ching hsüeh-pao* 19 (1936), 151. See also his *Yin-hsü pu-tz'u tsung-shu* (Peking: K'o-hsüeh, 1956), 574. Fracasso, "Holy Mothers," 21n. 47. The three inscriptions referring to Hsi-mu are nos. 14335, 14344, 14345.

56. Allan discusses these myths in her *The Shape of the Turtle: Myth, Art and Cosmos in Early China*, 44–52. For associations between the sun and Tung-mu/Hsi-mu, see Akatsuka Kiyoshi, *Chūgoku kodai no shūkyō to bunka—In ōchō no saik* (Tokyo: Kadokawa Shoten, 1977), 443–54; and K. C. Chang, *Early Chinese Civilization: Anthropological Perspectives*, 157. David Keightley expresses reservations about Akatsuka's association of Tung-mu and Hsi-mu with the course of the sun's path. See "Akatsuka Kiyoshi and the Culture of Early China: A Study in Historical Method," *Harvard Journal of Asiatic Studies* 42.1 (1982), 287n. 45.

57. See Ku Shih, *Hsi-cheng chiang-shu*, 3.144. For a list of oracle bone inscriptions in which the term *pin* is used in conjunction with the sun, see the *Chia-ku-wen ho-chi*, nos. 32181, 13327, 22539. Ch'en Meng-chia has shown that the *pin* rituals for observing the sun were also used for the ancestors, *Yin-hsü pu-tz'u tsung-shu*, 578. Cf. the *Chu-shu chi-nien t'ung-chien*, 8.11b, where the term is used to describe Hsi-wang-mu's visit to the ancestral temple of King Chao 昭, King Mu's father.

58. Ku Shih, *Hsi-cheng chiang-shu*, 3.163.

59. See Ch'en Tsun-kuei, *Chung-kuo t'ien-wen-hsüeh shih*, 193–95.

60. See Kuo P'u's annotation preserved in Ch'en Feng-heng, *Mu T'ien-tzu chuan chu pu-cheng*, 3.7b.

61. Ku Shih, *Hsi-cheng chiang-shu*, 3.163.

62. See the examples collected by Kao Ming, *Ku-wen-tzu lei-pien* (Peking: Chung-hua, 1980), 205. Eliade, *The Sacred and the Profane*, 25.

63. Eliade, *The Sacred and the Profane*, 25. Chang Kwang-chih "P'u-yang san-ch'iao yü Chung-kuo ku-tai mei-shu shang ti jen shou mu-t'i," 37–39. See also idem, *Art, Myth, and Ritual*, 44–80.

64. Suzanne Cahill, *Transcendence and Divine Passion* (Palo Alto, Calif: Stanford University Press, 1993), 17, 19, 23, 26. Ch'en Feng-heng argues that the tiger imagery is related to (shamanic?) practices of western

tribes who wear tiger fur and tiger masks as props for dancing and rituals. See Ch'en, *Mu T'ien-tzu chuan chu pu-cheng*, 3.1b.

65. *Shan-hai-ching chien-shu*, "Hai-nei pei-ching," 359, also cited by Cahill, *Transcendence and Divine Passion*, 19. Her Taoist name, "Ninefold Numinous Ultimate Mystery Dark Mother of Turtle Mountain," also intimates similar associations. Cf. the iconography of the three-legged bird that often accompanies Hsi-wang-mu; it recalls the three-legged turtle (*nai*) of the Yü and Nü-kua myths. For associated images of turtles and mountains see, for example, the rubbing from the reliefs at I-nan; Wu Hung, *The Wu Liang Shrine: The Ideology of Early Chinese Pictorial Art*, 131; these are also reproduced in figure 5 of Cahill, *Transcendence and Divine Passion*.

66. See Ch'en Meng-chia, *Yin-hsü pu-tz'u tsung-shu*, 225; Ch'en Tsun-kuei, *Chung-kuo t'ien-wen-hsüeh shih*, 192–93; and Feng Shih, "Yin-li chi-chieh yen-chiu, 6–10. While I do not accept his argument that the graph *ch'iu* 龜, which I read as "autumn", signifies "winter," his conclusions regarding the bipartite division of the year into two seasons are well substantiated.

67. Kominami Ichirō, "Seibo to shichi seki denshō," 60.

68. See Girardot, *Myth and Meaning in Early Taoism*, 5.

69. The *T'ai-p'ing yü-lan*, vol. 4, 909. 4030, cites the *Wu-Yüeh ch'un-ch'iu* 吳越春秋 as stating that "a white fox with nine tails crossed with Yü," as the latter was lamenting his single status. Yü interpreted this meeting as auspicious whereupon Lady T'u sang out to him with a verse suggesting the sexual implications of Yü's meeting with the fox. For the nine-tailed fox and Hsi-wang-mu, see Loewe, *Ways to Paradise*, 108–10. Loewe also points out how the number nine is freqeuntly associated with aspects of paradise; *Ways to Paradise*, 108.

70. See the *Chou-i cheng-i*, vol. 1, 73.

71. Loewe, *Ways to Paradise*, 94–95, 103–21. For the original passage, see *Huai-nan Hung-lieh chi-chieh*, "Lan-ming," 121.

72. Loewe, *Ways to Paradise*, 120.

73. See Dieter Kuhn, *Textile and Technology*, in Joseph Needham, ed., *Science and Civilisation in China*, vol. 5, pt. II (Cambridge: Cambridge University Press, 1988), 200; Loewe, *Ways to Paradise*, 105, also touches upon the spinning connotations of the term.

74. See the *Li-chi cheng-i*, vol. 1, 1363.

75. See, for example, the depiction of a weaver above whom there is the *t'ien-ssu hsing* 天駟星 "the team of four horses," a constellation consisting of *beta*, *delta*, *pi*, and *v* Scorpii. Because the constellation reached its

highest point in the night sky of the vernal equinox, it signified the start of the silkworm season. See Kuhn, *Textile and Technology*, 260–61. The *t'ien-ssu* constellation consists of a part of the Cerulean Dragon.

76. Loewe, *Ways to Paradise*, 115–26. On early Weaving Maid myths, see Wang Hsiao-lian, "Ch'ien-niu Chih-nü ti ch'uan-shuo," in his *Chung-kuo ti shen-hua yü ch'uan-shuo* (Taipei: Lian-ming, 1977), 165–226; Hsü Ch'uan-wu, "Man-hua Niu-Nü shen-hua ti ch'i-yüan ho yen-pien," *Wen-hsüeh i-ch'an* 6 (1989), 42–47. Wang Hsiao-lian cites Wang I's "Ai sui," and the "Shu-chen" chapter of the *Huan-nan Hung-lieh chi-chieh*, 61, "Ch'ien-niu Chih-nü de ch'uan-shuo," 188. Fu-yüeh is also mentioned in the *Chuang tzu chi-shih*, "Tsung-tao," 247, as the one who obtained the Tao and then mounted the Cerulean Dragon. On the Weaving Maid's single status, see the "Ta tung" poem of *Mao shih cheng-i*, vol. 1, 461. In the poem the constellation Draught Ox is also mentioned, but there is no indication of a relationship between the two constellations. Rather, as Loewe has noted, the "poem refers to the failure of the two constellations, as personalities" (or in terms of their attributed functions). See Loewe, *Ways to Paradise*, 113.

77. Wang Hsiao-lian goes into great detail about the woman's role as weaver, see Wang, "Ch'ien-niu Chih-nü ti ch'uan-shuo," 178–85.

78. Kuhn, *Textile Technology*, 61.

79. Ibid., 89. Tōdō Akiyasu, *Kanji to bunka*, 226–28, makes similar observations.

80. Kuhn, *Textile Technology*, 113.

81. Hsü Ch'uan-wu, "Man-hua Niu-Nü shen-hua ti ch'i-yüan ho yen-pien," 43.

82. The chest was found in the tomb of Marquis Yi of Tseng. For illustrations of the chest, see Hu-pei sheng po-wu-kuan, Pei-ching kung-i mei-shu yan-chiu so ed., *Chan-kuo Tseng-hou I mu ch'u-tu wen-wu t'u-an hsüan* (Ch'ang-sha: Ch'ang-chiang, 1984), 9.

83. See Ch'iu-Hsi-kuei, "T'an-t'an Sui-hsien Tseng-hou I mu ti wen-tzu tzu-liao," *Wen-wu* 7 (1979), rpt. *Ku-wen-tzu lun-chi*, 405–17. See the *Shan-hai-ching chien-shu*, "Ta-huang pei-ching," 451, for the myth of Nü-pa and the Yellow Emperor. That the events occur near "Kung-kung's Terrace" strengthens the connection between the function of Nü-pa and Yü. In some texts Nü-pa is called Black Maiden (*hsüan-nü*) which resonates with the name of the quadrant in which the lunar lodge Girl is located, Hsüan-yüan, Black Turtle. See, for example, the *T'ai-p'ing yü-lan*, vol. 1, 15.78, which cites the *Huang-ti hsüan-nü chan-fa* 黃帝玄女戰法. Cf. the Cheng-i commentary to the "Yün-han" (Milky Way) poem, where the demon called Han-pa 旱魃 is referred to as Han-mu, 旱母 thus providing a

linguistic connection between the drought demon and Hsi-wang-mu, *Mao shih cheng-i*, vol. 1, 562.

84. Geoffry S. Kirk, *Myth: Its Meaning and Function in Ancient and Other Cultures* (Berkeley: University of California Press, 1970), 59, which cites Claude Lévi-Strauss, *Le crut et le cuit* (Paris: Librairie Plon, 1964), 346.

85. All references are conveniently collected in Yüan K'o's *Ts'ui-pien*, 208.

86. Ku Shih, *Hsi-cheng chiang-shu*, 3.172, 175; 4.243. In the *Shan-hai-ching chien-shu*, 347, a similar description refers to a location very close to K'un-lun.

87. Ku Shih, *Hsi-cheng chiang-shu*, 1.87.

88. Ibid., 3.170.

89. *Shan-hai-ching chien-shu*, "Hsi-shan-ching," 90. Ku Shih, *Hsi cheng chiang-shu*, 3.171, 172. Ju Waters are close to Feather Mountain.

90. Richard Kunst, citing Thomas Kingsmill, claims that this expression constitutes an "attached cue," which like the term *chi* 吉 "auspicious" provided important information about the nature of the prognostication. See Kunst, "The Original Yijing," 27. His concordance lists at least seven occurrences of the phrase *she ch'uan* (p. 471).

91. See the *Chou-i cheng-i*, vol. 1, 35.

92. As I noted in chapter 3 above,the graph designating the *k'un* hexagram in the Ma-wang-tui manuscript is written as *ch'uan*, "river." While phonological reasons are surely the most commonly advanced for this graphic variant, in light of the foregoing discussion, symbolically nuanced semantic reasons may perhaps also shed light on its significance.

93. Ku Shih, *Hsi-cheng chiang-shu*, 3.184. Rémi Mathieu incorrectly transcribes the name of this location as Gua-lu, Mathieu, *Le Mu Tianzi Zhuan*, 52. The first graph is a simplified rendition of the graph 瓠. On *hu-lu* as a round gourd, see Ch'en Chin-sheng, "Shih shih *Chou-i* ti 'yu t'a' yü 'pu hsia i,'" *Wen-shih* 35 (1992), 213–17, esp. 215–16. For the gourd and flood myths, see Robert G. Henricks, "On the Wherabouts and Identity of the Place Called 'K'ung-sang' (Hollow Mulberry) in Early Chinese Mythology" (Paper presented at the annual meeting of the Association for Asian Studies, Washington, D.C., 4 April 1992). For the gourd in Taoist texts, see Girardot, *Myth and Meaning in Early Taoism*, 27, 28, 29, 33 179–85, passim.

94. See the *t'ai* hexagram, *Chou-i cheng-i*, vol. 1, 28. *Chuang tzu chi-shih*, "Hsiao-yao," 37.

95. For references to three, see Ku Shih, *Hsi-cheng chiang shu*, 2.61, 76, 114, 126; 3.156, 174, 184; 4.201, 233, 250; see also the SPTK ed. 5.3a, 4b; for the number thirty, see Ku Shih 2.73, 78, 81; 4.211 (2×), 220; see also the SPTK ed., 5.4b; for the number three hundred, see Ku Shih, 1.42; 2.76, 116, 124, 125 (3X); 3.147, 182; 4.209, 211 (2×), 200, 221, 242; for the number three thousand, see Ku Shih, 2.76, 90; 3.181; 4.243, 246.

96. See Tung Fang Shuo, *Shih-chou chi, Chu-tzu pai-chia ts'ung-shu* edition (Shanghai: Shang-hai ku-chi, 1990), 7.

97. Ku Shih, *Hsi-cheng chiang-shu*, 1.68.

98. Ch'en Meng-chia, "Shang-tai ti shen-hua," 323.

99. Ku Shih, *Hsi-cheng chiang-shu*, 2.126. *Shan-hai-ching chien-shu*, "Ta-huang pei-ching," 441, 442. See T'an Ts'ui, *Mu T'ien-tzu chuan chu-shu*, 2.11a.

100. See Ku Shih, *Hsi-cheng chiang-shu*, 2.53, 115. Yü drains a body of water called Ch'ien which is near Nine Rivers, the "Yü kung," *Shang shu cheng-i*, vol. 1, 149.

101. *Shih* as it appears in the *Mu T'ien-tzu chuan* is actually a composite of the graphs for "sun" and for "to stop," or "rest," suggesting that the concept of time can be concretely expressed only in spatial terms. As we shall see below, this is relevant for understanding the narrative strategies employed in the text.

102. Kuo P'u claimed *mo-pai* refers to a form of Buddhist greeting (cited in Ku Shih, *Hsi-cheng chiang-shu*, 2.80); and T'an Ts'ui concurred (*Mu T'ien-tzu chuan chu-shu*, 3.3a). Ku Shih (p. 80) argues that the graph *mo* is a loan for the graph *p'ai* 拍. "to clap" or "to beat," and thus read the term as a reference to a Western form of ritualistic bowing. Although convincing, this reading could not appy to the other uses of the term *mo*, i.e., *mo-chi* 膜稷 (*mo*-type grain) and *mo-chin* 膜菫 (a name of a tree on K'un-lun). Cf. Ting Ch'ien's reading of Hsi-wang-mu as an 'elongated" version of the place-name Hsi-mo (Sumer); *Mu T'ien-tzu chuan ti-li k'ao-cheng*, 2.8a.

103. Ch'en Meng-chia, "Ku-wen-tzu chung chih Shang-Chou chi-ssu," 91–155; and Wen Ch'ung-i, "Chiu-ko chung Ho-po chih yen-chiu," 143, have both suggested that mention of River in oracle bone inscriptions does not necessarily refer exclusively to the Yellow River. I would extend this to suggest that the term does not refer exclusively to earthly rivers. De Santillana and von Dechend, *Hamlet's Mill*, 197ff., argue that the sacred rivers of ancient civilizations are the earthly extension of the Milky Way and that many myths confuse the heavenly rivers and those on earth.

104. See Ku Shih, *Hsi-cheng chiang-shu*, 2.59.

105. Ibid., 2.117. Wei T'ing-sheng, *Mu T'ien-tzu chuan chin-k'ao*, vol. 2, 261, identifies this placename as Terek, but it is based on the assumption that the ancient pronunciation for the first graph of the name was pronounced similarly to the modern-day *ch'i* 奇. According to Karlgren, *Grammatica Serica Recensa*, no. 1, however, the ancient pronunciation of words composed with the *ch'i* graph did not have a voiced initial.

106. *Ch'u-tz'u chih-shu*, 109.

107. Ku Shih, *Hsi-cheng chiang-shu*, 2.125. *Mao shih cheng-i*, vol. 1, 537–39.

108. The *K'ang-hsi tzu tien*, 1481, cites the *Cheng-tzu t'ung* 正字通. The official, Fu-shih 鳧氏 is described in the "K'ao-kung-chi" section of the "Winter Officials" (*tung-kuan*), in the *Chou-li cheng-i*, vol. 1, 916.

109. This phrase is used to describe why bells were associated with autumn and winter in the *Shuo-wen chieh-tzu i-cheng*, vol. 2, 1243.

110. This cosmogonic function is reflected in the large number of constellations in the Heavenly Turtle quadrant that are named for devices of measurement or "rule" (*chu* 主) activities of measuring and which exceeds those of other quardrants. See Gustav Schlegel, *Uranographie*, 171–72, 178, 185, 186–92, 227, passim.

Chapter 5

1. See Edward L. Shaughnessy, "Historical Geography and the Extent of the Earliest Chinese Kingdoms," *Asia Major* 2 (1989), 1–22; and idem, "Ts'ung Chü-fu kai ming-wen t'an Chou wang-ch'ao yü Nan Huai I ti kuan-hsi," *Han-hsüeh yen-chiu* 5 (1987), 567–73.

2. For the military, see Edward L. Shaughnessy, *Sources*, 177, passim; for political instability, see idem, "The Duke of Zhou's Retirement in the East and the Beginnings of the Minister-Monarch Debate in Chinese Political Philosophy," *Early China* 18 (1993), 41–72.

3. King Chao was not attacked, but was engaging in what was the last of several military expeditions against the Ch'u. See, Wan Ch'üan-wen, "Shang-Chou wang-ch'ao nan-chin lüeh-t'ung lun," *Chiang-han k'ao-ku* 3 (1992), 50–57. For historical records of his death, see the *Chu-shu chi-nien t'ung-chien*, vol. 2, 8.5b–5a; and the *Shih chi*, vol. 1, 4.134.

4. *Shi chi*, vol. 1, 4.134–40.

5. Ibid., vol. 6, 43.1779.

6. Ku Chieh-kang, "*Mu T'ien-tzu chuan* chu-tso shih-tai," 63. Ku argues that the association with the Chao family genealogy is more than incidental and he claims that the *Mu T'ien-tzu chuan* was written by a Chao state historian to reflect the western expansion of the king of Chao at the end of the Warring States era.

7. See the *Chu-shu chi-nien t'ung-chien*, 8.7a, 7b, 9b, 10a, 10b, 11a, where the king's activities seem to be pleasure-oriented. The last entry mentions his western journey to visit Hsi-wang-mu. Cf. the references to his building of palaces and platforms (8.6b, 7a, 9b, 10a), another indication of King Mu's fondness for pleasure. For the *Tso chuan*, see the entry in Duke Chao 12 of the *Ch'un-ch'iu Tso-chuan cheng-i*, vol. 2, 2068. The context of the "Chai-kung" 祭公 piece in the *I Chou shu* is similar to that recorded in the *Kuo-yü*; see *Chou shu chiao-shih* 8.1a–2b.

8. Anthony Yu, "History, Fiction and the Reading of Chinese History," *Chinese Literature: Essays, Articles and Reviews* 10.1–2 (1988), 1–19, discusses how both Western and Chinese historians viewed the issue of historical evidence and the role that the oral tradition played in obtaining this evidence. See also Jan Vansina, *Oral Tradition as History* (Madison: University of Wisconsin Press, 1985), and idem, "Memory and Oral Tradition," in Joseph Miller, ed., *The African Past Speaks: Essays on Oral Tradition and History* (Folkestone: Dawson and Archon, 1980), 262–76; see also the essays collected in Raphael Samuel and Paul Thompson, eds., *The Myths We Live By* (London: Routledge, 1990), for discussions on the significance of the mechanisms of memory for interpreting oral history.

9. Cf. Yang K'uan, "Shuo Hsia," in *Ku-shih pien*, vol. 7, 277–301, argues that the Hsia dynasty was a construct of the Chinese imagination; Hsia was not the name of a dynasty but a reference to "those below" in opposition to "Heaven on High." Useful in this respect is Hayden White's notion that history is itself a narrative construction. See White, *Tropics in Discourse* (Baltimore: Johns Hopkins University Press, 1978). See also Rosalind Thomas, "Ancient Greek Family Tradition and Democracy," in Samuel and Thompson, *Myths*, 204. See also Alan D. Baddeley, *The Psychology of Memory* (New York: Basic Books, 1976); and Maurice Halbwachs, *Collective Memory* (New York: Harper & Row, 1980), for memory and history.

10. For bronze inscriptions recording military activities during King Mu's reign, see Shaughnessy, *Sources*, 177–82. For King Mu's longevity, see ibid., 246–47, 254 nn. 67, 68.

11. Shaughnessy has recently tried to show how bronze texts were composed to tell a story from a particular point of view to a particular audience; see Shaughnessy, *Sources*, 177ff., where he comments on how the subjectivity of the *Tung kuei* 冬簋 text elides the actual precariousness of

the described situation. See also idem, "Chü-fu kai," 567. Cf. Clifford Geertz's discussion of how "ethnographic" narratives are sometimes "cultural fictions based on systematic and contestable exclusions"; Geertz, *The Interpretation of Cultures* (New York: SUNY Press, 1973), 6. Rémi Mathieu, *Le Mu Tianzi Zhuan*, 176–77, touches upon the ideological need for King Mu's legendary journey.

12. Sociologists too have identified ambiguous situations as the major ingredient in the generation of legends. See Tamotsu Shibutani, *Improvised News* (New York: Bobbs-Merrill, 1966), 157ff.; Gordon W. Allport and Leo Postman, *The Psychology of Rumor* (New York: Henry Holt, 1947), 160ff. Legends have been defined in this latter work as "a rumor that has become part of the verbal heritage of a people," 160.

13. *Shih chi*, vol. 1, 3.134. Ssu-ma Ch'ien posits that the perpetrators of the concealment were the infantrymen who survived but did not report the death. The *Cheng-i* commentary cites the *Ti-wang shih-chi* as saying that the Chou people were prohibited from (*hui* 諱) mentioning it. The connection between King Chao's death and the legends of King Mu's journey seems to be reinforced by literary sources having to do with Ch'u: it is someone from Ch'u who supplies information about both the death and the journey in the *Tso chuan*, Hsi 4, vol. 2, 1793; 2068; Cf. the stanza in the "T'ien wen" that combines references to a southern expedition undertaken by King Chao with references to King Mu's extensive travelling, *Ch'u-tz'u chi-chu*, 66–67.

14. The ambiguity is reflected in a passage in the *Tso chuan* in which information regarding the details of King Chao's death is solicited; see the *Ch'un-ch'iu Tso chuan cheng-i*, Hsi 4, vol. 2, 1793. Cf. Shibutani, *Improvised News*, 164, where he states that when the "demand for news in a public exceeds the supply made available through institutional channels rumor construction is likely to occur."

15. For inscriptional evidence of this insecurity, see, for example, the *Tung kuei*, which recounts a barbarian attack that came very close to the seat of Chou political control. Shaughnessy, *Sources*, 177–81, provides a translation and analysis of the historical and political significance of this inscription. See also Ch'iu Hsi-kuei, "Lun Tung kuei ti liang-ko ti-ming-Yü-lin ho Hu," *Ku-wen-tzu lun-chi, K'ao-ku yü wen-wu ts'ung-k'an* no. 2, 4–7.

16. Herlee Creel, *The Origins of Statecraft in China*, vol. 1: *The Western Chou Empire* (Chicago: University of Chicago Press, 1970), 83 passim; T'ang Chün-i, "The T'ien Ming (Heavenly Ordinance) in Pre-Ch'in China," *Philosophy East and West* 11 (1961), 195–218; 12 (1962), 29–49; Hsu Cho-yun and Katheryn M. Linduff, *Western Chou Civilization* (New Haven: Yale University Press, 1988), 101–6, 318–20, 382–83.

17. Pankenier, "Astronomical Dates," 4–5.

18. My translation and interpretation is based for the most part on the inscription annotated in the *Shang-Chou ch'ing-t'ung-ch'i ming-wen hsüan*, vol. 3, 108–10. That Mao Pan was well connected to the court is intimated by his self-reference as a direct descendant of King Wen. As the annotation states, the first feudal lord of Mao was Shu-cheng 叔鄭, one of King Wen's many sons.

19. Shaughnessy, *Sources*, 251–53. Shaughnessy's dating of the vessel is informed by his reading of two entries, separated by three years, in the chronology of King Mu's reign found in the *Bamboo Annals*. In the first reference Mao Po, whose proper name is Ch'ien 遣, leads troops to attack Jing 荊, another name for the southern state of Ch'u. Shaughnessy dates this event to 922 B.C. on the assumption that the dating of the *Mao Pan kuei* is applicable to the *Bamboo Annals*, because both contain references to Mao Ch'ien and both describe events that took place in the east (although the Jing are usually associated with the south, Hsü, the place where the Jing attacked was southeast of the Chou court). The second entry describes a battle in the east, without reference to Mao Ch'ien. Shaughnessy assumes this entry is related to the previous one because of the shared reference to the "east." However, the diction of this second entry with its reference to a place called Nine Rivers and a bridge formed by "alligators and turtles" resembles more the symbolic discourse of the flood myths than the usual straightforward accounts of the annal. I would thus not unquestioningly accept that the two entries are related contextually. Moreover, if Shaughnessy's dating were accepted, Mao kung would have to have been quite a bit older than the fifty or so years of King Mu, and it seems unreasonable to expect someone of that age to be leading troops to protect the Chou from encroaching neighbors. As we shall see, the nature of the language of King Mu and Mao kung reflects the world of a young king and his court anxious to preserve their power.

20. For the nature of the familial relationship between the duke and the king, see *Shang-Chou ch'ing-t'ung-ch'i ming-wen hsüan*, 109.

21. Ibid., 108. Shirakawa Shizuka, *Kinbun tsūshaku, Hakutsuru bijutsukanshi*, 36 vols. to date (Kobe, 1962–), vol. 15, 51, argues that the latter phrase should not be considered as remonstrating the king because the object of the duke's "report" is "those above." However, instances where pronouncements about correct or incorrect behavior are imbedded within a ritualistic context abound in the transmitted and paleographic literature. The fact that there is no account of the duke praising the king is also a noteworthy indication of the tenor of the duke's remarks.

22. David Keightley, "The Quest for Eternity in Ancient China: The Dead, Their Gifts, Their Names," in George Kuwayama, ed., *Ancient Mortuary Traditions of China* (Los Angeles: Far Eastern Art Council, Los Ange-

les Countly Museum of Art, 1991), 18–21. Keightley also suggests that this perspective is reflected in the Chao-Mu sacrificial system which included in the ancestral cult only the preceding five generations and the initial ancestor. In light of the present analysis, one may wonder whether the obvious connection between the name of the system and the temple names of King Chao and Mu reveal more about the origins of the system than has traditionally been recognized. For a recent attempt to date the inception of this system see Wang En-t'ien, "Chou-tai Chao-Mu chih-tu yüan-liu," in *Ti erh tz'u Hsi-Chou-shih hsüeh-shu t'ao-lun-hui lun-wen chiang-pien* (1992), 649–66.

23. See Shaugnessy, *Sources*, 253–54 n. 67, for a discussion of the age of King Mu when he assumed power.

24. See the *Kuo-yü*, 32.

25. One might also interpret the unduly excessive nature of the mourning rituals conducted for Sheng Chi, King Mu's concubine, in the sixth, distinct *chüan* of the text as yet another ambiguous relationship involving King Mu. The implication that this alliance was incestuous (because both king and concubine share the same surname) further complicates the possible symbolic significance of this section. Notwithstanding the obvious difference in topics between the first four *chüan* and the last of the narrative, the two may be linked via a network of symbolism that has yet to be worked out. For the incestuous nature of the relationship, see Léopold de Saussure, "Le voyage de Mou Wang," 20, where he cites M. E. H. Parker's *Ancient China Simplified*. Cf. the note to Chang P'ing-tzu's "Ssu hsüan fu" in *Wen hsüan* (Shanghai: Shang-hai ku-chi, 1992), vol. 2, 15.657, where a story regarding the mysterious birth and gruesome death of a son of King Mu is related.

26. Allan, *The Heir and the Sage*, 32–37.

27. For a survey of different studies on the dating of the "Yao tien" astronomical information, see Joseph Needham, *Science and Civilization in China*, vol. 3, 247–49.

28. *Shih chi*, "Li-shu," vol. 4, 26.1262–63, records the reform, while the "T'ien-kuan-shu," vol. 4, 27.1328, reveals how much the position had shifted.

29. These observations were shared with me by David Pankenier, personal communication. Stephen Field, "Cosmos, Cosmograph, and the Inquiring Poet: New Answers to the 'Heaven Questions,'" *Early China* 17 (1992), 103, has suggested that a reference in the "T'ien-wen" to a "Great Bird" crying as "the heavens turn, *yang* ebbs and death ensues" records the immolation of the Vermilion Bird's "body" as it set with the sun during the summer season. Field's interpretation is based on the astronomical reality

of 450 B.C. Five hundred years earlier only the bird's head, or "beak," would have disappeared. But since the planetary conjunction associated with the Heavenly Mandate took place in precisely this part of the bird constellation, the decapitation of the bird at sunset must surely have been regarded as anything but auspicious. Cf. the entry from the divination text the *Kuei-tsang* which relates an incident in which King Mu divined going on an expedition and encountered the 36th hexagram of the *Book of Changes* "Calling Pheasant" (*ming i* 明夷). The proposed journey was divined as inauspicious and a four-line poem was provided that figured imagery resembling that used to describe the ascent and descent of the dragon constellation (i.e., "rises in the sky"). Similar imagery is found in the sixth hexagram statement. There may have been some apocryphal tradition associating King Mu's expeditions with the waning force of the bird imagery as a symbol for dynastic legitmacy. See Ma Kuo-han, ed., *Yü-han shan-fang chi i-shu*, vol. 1, 9a.

30. See Pankenier, "Early Chinese Astronomy and Cosmology," 103–45, 148 n. 12. Pankenier believes the visitation of King Mu to the Red Crow tribe, whose people are hailed as descendants of the Chou royal lineage, implies that the Red Crow had a totemic siginificance for the royal lineage of Chou.

31. The *Mu T'ien-tzu chuan*, then, to use Nicolas Abraham's terminology, is the symbolic product of the "preservative repression" of events surrounding King Chao's death.

32. Cf. Allport and Postman, *Rumor*, 164, which claims that legends are interpretive tools used by people who hunger for an explanation of and/or relief from ambiguous situations when "objective evidence or knowledge does not place rational constraints upon judgment and report."

33. Shibutani, *Improvised News*, 183.

34. Ibid., 172.

35. Shaughnessy, *Sources*, 166, suggests that the death of King Chao "marked an important turning point in the fortunes of the Zhou ruling house." Cf. Ssu-ma Ch'ien's comment that "the Way had started to decline during King Chao's reign," *Shi chi*, vol. 1, 4.134. See also T'ang Lan, "Yung ch'ing-t'ung-ch'i ming-wen lai yen-chiu Hsi-Chou shih," *Wen-wu* 6 (1976), 31–37, who argues that King Mu's reign marked a transition in the development of many political and social institutions.

36. His concern with posterity, implicit in these rhetorical patterns, is made explicit in several of the verses he composes along the way. Rémi Mathieu also notes the king's preoccupation with judgment and posterity but does not draw any conclusions about it; see *Le Mu Tianzi Zhuan*, 169. The etiology of a place-name is explained five times by King Mu's actions:

he plants three commemorative trees; he orders the inscribing of three stelae, and he twice promulgates new laws. Cf. his table of King Mu's actions, 150–52

37. Shibutani, *Improvised News*, 172.

38. Allan, *The Shape of the Turtle: Myth, Art, and Cosmos in Early China*, 22. See also idem, *The Heir and the Sage.*

39. *Ch'un-ch'iu Tso chuan cheng-i*, vol. 2, 2064.

40. I want to underline that my concern is the *literary* manifestation and resolution of this conflict and not its sociohistorical ramifications. For the latter, see Allan's *The Heir and the Sage*; she provides a brilliant analysis of the social function of several myths as mediators of this inherent political tension (rule by hereditary right and rule by virtue) in five critical periods of Chinese history.

41. Rémi Mathieu, *Le Mu Tianzi Zhuan*, 189, also alludes to the initiatory function of Ho-tsung.

42. See the "Chou-yü" section of the *Kuo-yü*, 138. I am indebted to David Pankenier for pointing out the significance of this passage for my analysis. See Pankenier, "Early Chinese Astronomy and Cosmology," 179ff., esp. 186–88.

43. The story of the demise of the Chou dynasty also involves the figure of a Black Turtle: it is the Black Turtle (*hsüan-yüan*) who is responsible for impregnating the concubine who gives birth to the femme fatale Pao-ssu 褒姒. King Yu's 幽 infatuation and obsession with her is, of course, often cited as the main reason for his own death and that of the Western Chou. See the *Shih chi*, vol. 1, 4.147.

44. *Kuo-yü*, "Chou-yü," 138.

45. Ku Shih, *Hsi-cheng chiang-shu*, 1.33.

46. Ibid., 1.36, 40.

47. Michael Saso, "What is the *Ho-t'u*?," *History of Religions* 17.3–4 (1978), 411. Cf. the use of jewel terminology to refer to the positions of the planets or asterisms, discussed in Pankenier, "Early Chinese Astronomy and Cosmology," 246.

48. The first quote is cited by Michael Saso, "Ho-t'u," 410; David Pankenier, "Early Chinese Astronomy and Cosmology," 315.

49. Pankenier, "Early Chinese Astronomy and Cosmology," 316.

50. Ibid., 316. See also Gustav Schlegel, *Uranographie*, 207

51. Ch'en Feng-heng provides a list of precedents for opening up charts, *Mu T'ien-tzu chuan chu pu-cheng,* 1.24a.

52. Ku Shih, *Hsi-cheng chiang-shu,* 1.40.

53. See the *Mo tzu yin-te,* Harvard Yenching Concordance Series (Peking: Yen-ching ta-hsüeh, 1948), no. 21, "Fei-kung hsia," 33.

54. *Hsi-cheng chiang-shu,* 1.40–41. Hsi-wang-mu is also mentioned in connection with the Yellow Steed: "In the time of Shun, Hsi-wang-mu commanded an envoy to present a set of four yellow steeds to him." Cited from the *Chin-lu-tzu hsing-wang p'ien* 金樓子興王篇 in Ku Shih, 1.41.

55. See Ku Shih, *Hsi-cheng chiang-shu,* 2.82, 96.

56. *Grammatica Serica Recensa,* no. 964.

57. Peter Boodberg, "Some Proleptical Remarks," 350. Cf. de Saussure's discussion of the symbolic significance of the "heavenly branch" *tzu* 子, which he argues designates the precise instant of the winter solstice and midnight and thus symbolizes, both temporally and spatially, rebirth or regeneration; see de Saussure, *Origines de l'astronomie chinoise,* 278.

58. See the *Erh-ya i-shu,* "Shih ts'ao," vol. 3, 8a.

59. Girardot, *Myth and Meaning in Early Taoism,* 31, 33. For the *k'u-t'u* in soup, see the *Erh-ya i-shu,* vol. 3, 8a. F. Porter Smith, *Chinese Materia Medica,* rpt. (Taipei: Ku-ting, 1969), 230, writes that the *k'u* plant was believed to "preserve youth and vitality."

60. See the *Li-chi cheng-i,* vol. 2, 1446.

61. In the poem the "Chou Plains" ("Chou-yüan") are described as replete with the *chin* and the *t'u* plants, which were considered a sign of the land's fertility by the oldest ancestor of the lineage, Ku-kung 古公. As he ultimately decided that the Chou should settle there, the plants are associated with the origins of the dynasty. See the *Mao shih cheng-i,* "Ta ya," vol. 1, 510.

62. King Mu eats fish in a mulberry grove in *chüan* five; see SPTK edition, 5.1a. While there are three other references to objects of consumption, the actual act of consumption is only implied—people present the objects to the King for him to consume. We are never told explicitly whether he actually consumes the objects or not. In each case the object is blood: the blood of a horse in one instance, the blood of white cranes in the other two. See Ku Shih, *Hsi-cheng chiang-shu,* 3.186; 4.218, 237.

63. Ch'en Feng-heng, *Mu T'ien-tzu chuan chu pu-cheng,* 2.38a.

64. Ku Shih, *Hsi-cheng chiang-shu,* 2.114.

65. Ibid., 2.111.

66. For *ts'e* as written communication with the spirits, see Shirakawa Shizuka, *Kōkotsu kinbun gaku ronshū* (Kyoto: Hōyū shoten, 1974), "Shaku shi," 1–68. During the Chou the term is most often used in cases where the the king's mandates are to be recorded.

67. See, for example, the three inscriptions cited by Axel Schuessler, *A Dictionary of Early Zhou Chinese*, 55, under the entry for *ts'e*.

68. *Chuang tzu chi-shih*, "Ch'ü-ch'ia p'ien," 357.

69. *Ma-wang-tui Han-mu po-shu*, 90–93, 146. Jung Ch'eng is also mentioned in connection with the arts of the bedchamber in the *Han shu* bibliography. See the "I-wen chih" of the *Han shu*, 12 vols. (Peking: Chung-hua, 1962), vol. 6, 30.1776–80. For an excellent introduction to the Ma-wang-tui text on the arts of the bedchamber, see Li Ling and Keith McMahon, "The Content and Terminology of the Mawangdui Texts on the Arts of the Bedchamber," *Early China* 17 (1992), 145–85. See also Donald Harper, "The Sexual Arts of Ancient China as Described in a Manuscript of the Second Century B.C.," *Harvard Journal of Asiatic Studies* 47 (1987), 546, 547, who also cites post-Han sources that refer to Jung Ch'eng's mastery of sexual arts.

70. For the jade blossom, see Ku Shih, *Hsi-cheng chiang-shu*, 2.86. For King Mu's collection of colored stones and feathers, see Ku, 4.200, 203, 210, 221; 3.171, 179, respectively.

71. See the *Shan-hai-ching chien-shu*, "Hsi-shan-ching," 63.

72. Schafer, "The Transcendent Vitamin: Efflorescence of Lang-kan," *Chinese Science* 3 (1978), 27–38. See also the "Yü kung," in the *Shang shu cheng-i*, vol. 1, 150. According to the *Shan-hai-ching chien-shu*, "Ta-huang hsi-ching," 427, the *lang-kan* is also found, on "Hsi-wang-mu's Mountain."

73. Lo Chen-yü's, *San-tai chi-chin wen-ts'un*, 3 vols. (Peking: Chung-hua, 1983), vol. 2, 12.15a, contains rubbings of two bronze inscriptions in which both forms of the word *pao* are used in exactly the same context.

74. Keightley, "Quest for Eternity in Ancient China," 20.

75. Several scholars believe that these expeditions were motivated by the search for precious metals in the south; Kuo Mo-jo, *Liang-Chou chin-wen-tz'u ta-hsi t'u-lu k'ao-shih*, 2nd rev. ed. (Peking, 1958), 186; T'ang Lan, "Hsi-Chou t'ung-ch'i tuan-tai chung K'ang-kung wen-t'i," *K'ao-ku hsüeh-pao* 1 (1962), 37; and idem, "Lun Chou Chao-wang shih-tai ti ch'ing-t'ung-ch'i ming-k'o," *Ku-wen-tzu yen-chiu* 2 (1981), 3–162; Ch'iu Hsi-kuei, "Shih Ch'iang p'an ming chieh-shih," *Wen-wu* 3 (1978), 27.

76. The only pre-Ch'in reference to King Mu's personal name is found

in the *Bamboo Annals,* a text that was discovered with the *Mu T'ien-tzu chuan*; see the *Chu-shu chi-nien t'ung-chien,* vol. 2, 8.6a. Even in the unlikely case that we could historically verify that King Mu's personal name was indeed Man, my symbolic reading of the term would not be vitiated.

77. See Karlgren, *Grammatica Serica Recensa,* no. 183.

78. The inscription of the *Man kuei* 滿簋, which is dated to the "middle of the Western Chou," contains both graphs. See the *Shang-Chou ch'ing-t'ung-ch'i ming-wen hsüan,* vol. 4, 235. For interpretations of *man* as balance, see Chou Fa-kao, *Chin-wen ku-lin,* vol. 8, 7.4861–65.

79. For the reconstructions of ancient pronunciation, see Schuessler, *A Dictionary of Early Zhou Chinese,* 416, 417. The *K'ang-hsi tzu-tien,* 644, provides an "ancient form" of the graph *man,* the phonetic of which is the same as that for the word *mien,* "to draw out."

80. See the *Shang shu cheng-i,* "Chiu gao," vol. 1, 206; and the *Mao-kung ting* 毛公鼎 dated to the reign of King Hsüan (r. 827–782), in *Shang-Chou ch'ing-t-ung-ch'i ming-wen hsüan,* vol. 4, 317.

81. See the *Mao shih cheng-i,* vol. 1, 432.

82. For the identification of Mian with the Han River see the commentary to the "Yü kung," *Shang shu cheng-i,* vol. 1, 150.

83. The use of the expression *tang-tang* 湯湯 in the poem to describe the "Mien Waters" strengthens the possiblity of such a connection, for it is used to describe the floodwaters in several early texts. See, for example, the "Yao tien," *Shang shu cheng-i,* vol. 1, 122. The same expression is used in another poem in the *Shih ching,* "Chiang Han," to describe the river in which King Chao drowned. See the *Mao shih cheng-i,* vol. 1, 573.

84. Schuessler, *Dictionary of Early Zhou Chinese,* 844–45, presents two examples of the usage of the term "to end" in bronze vessels dating to the time of King Kang 康王, King Mu's grandfather. These remarkably capture the specific multivalence that I am suggesting. In one vessel the term appears in the sentence, "May God [on High] not end the mandate for the [C]hou." In another inscription the term appears in the sentence, "May my sons and grandsons [be] forever without end."

85. Kenneth J. DeWoskin, "The Power of Bronze," *Archaeology* (January–February 1994), 50. The political implications attendant upon the performance of music became even more concrete during the Warring States period, when each state had its own principal pitch standard; music was thus an identifying characteristic of statehood and political authority. Lothar von Falkenhausen, "Music in the Life of the Marquis Yi's Court," *Archaeology* (January–February 1994), 47. Haun Saussy, *The Problem of a*

Chinese Aesthetic (Palo Alto: Stanford University Press, 1993), views ancient Chinese music theory and poetry as allegories for empire building.

86. Kenneth DeWoskin, *A Song For One or Two: Music and the Concept of Art in Early China* (Ann Arbor: University of Michigan, Center for Chinese Studies, 1982), 48.

87. King Mu commands that Expansive Music be performed at least seven times; see Ku Shih, *Hsi-cheng chiang-shu*, 1.5; 2.99, 126; 3.174; 4.250; SPTK ed., 5.2b, 4a.

88. *Shih chi*, "Pien-ch'üeh Ts'ang-kung lieh-chuan," vol. 9, 105.2786–87.

89. For Ch'i and the nine types of Heavenly Music, see the "T'ien-wen," *Ch'u-tz'u chi-chu*, 59; *Shan-hai-ching chien-shu*, "Hai-wai hsi-ching," 299, "Ta-huang hsi-ching," 438.

90. See Hung Hsing-tsu's commentary to the "T'ien-wen," in which he cites a passage from the *Huai-nan tzu* that is no longer extant, *Ch'u-tz'u chi-chu*, 60. I read the graph *hsiung* 熊 as *nai* 能. To my knowledge no other commentator has suggested such a reading, but it is consistent with the way I read the same graph in the Kun myths and is more in keeping with the context—an amphibious animal would better facilitate the passage through waters than a mammal such as a bear.

91. See the note provided by Yen Shih-ku 彥師古 (581–645) in the "Annals of Emperor Wu-ti," in the *Han shu*, vol. 1, 6.190. Yen Shih-ku also cites the same nonextant passage from the *Huai-nan tzu*.

92. The term *ch'i* was used technically to mean daybreak in oracle bone inscriptions (see Ch'en Tsun-kuei, *Chung-kuo t'ien-wen-hsüeh shih*, 93), and then it evolved to mean "first month of spring" (*li ch'un* 立春); see the *Ch'un-ch'iu Tso chuan cheng-i*, Hsi 5, vol. 2, 1794.

93. For Yü's abdication in favor of Po Yi, see the *Chan-kuo ts'e*, 2 vols. (Taipei: Tung-ya, 1982), "Yen ts'e 1," vol. 2, 1059.

94. Anne Birrell, *Chinese Mythology*, 122.

95. *Shan-hai-ching chien-shu*, "Hai-wai hsi-ching," 299.

96. For Music Wilds, see Ku Shih, *Hsi-cheng chiang-shu*, 2.119; for Music Capital, see Ku Shih, 1.43. For Ch'i's residence, see *Mu T'ien-tzu chuan, SPTK* ed., 5.4a.

97. Pankenier, "Early Chinese Cosmology and Astronomy," 169.

98. Joseph Needham, *Science and Civiliation in China*, vol. 4, 156, 163; cited in Pankenier, "Early Chinese Cosmology and Astronomy," 170.

99. See Wu Hung, "From Temple to Tomb: Ancient Chinese Art and Religion in Transition," *Early China* 13 (1988), 78–115.

100. Ibid., 85.

101. Ibid., 86.

102. Ibid.

103. The "Hsiao k'ung p'ien," of the *Kuan tzu* describes King Mu's trip as an effort to return to the greatness of the dynasty's founders, Kings Wen 文 and Wu 武. See the *Kuan tzu* in the *Erh-shih-erh tzu*, 8.121.

104. *Hsi-cheng chiang-shu*, 1.21. Rémi Mathieu has counted 44 occurrences of this construction in the first four chapters of the *Mu T'ien-tzu chuan*; Mathieu, *Le Mu Tianzi Zhuan*, 269. Cf. Wei Chü-hsien's argument that the use of this construction marks the *Mu T'ien-tzu chuan* as a Warring States text; "Mu T'ien-tzu chuan yen-chiu," 199.

105. For enfeoffments, see Ku Shih, *Hsi-cheng chiang-shu*, 1.53; 2.72, 109; 4.203; SPTK ed. 5.3a; for erection of monuments see Ku Shih, 1.26; 2.72, 89; 3.163.

106. *Hsi-cheng chiang-shu*, 2.126(2×); SPTK ed., 5.3b.

107. Claude Lévi-Strauss has suggested that activities of naming and identifying—the demarcation of objective knowledge—were an essential process for ancient societies trying to establish their own identity; see Lévi-Strauss, *La pensée sauvage* (Paris: Librairie Plon, 1962), 5.

108. See the *Erh-ya i-shu*, "Shih shui," vol. 2, 11a.

109. In light of the proposed symbolic referent, namely, the disastrous finish to an expedition led by King Chao to the southern territory of Ch'u, it is noteworthy that this term is used in the "Chin-yü" section of the *Kuo-yü* to mean "destroy" (*mieh* 滅). Cited in Yang Hsiung, *Fang-yen chien-shu*, vol. 2, 13.7a.

110. See, for example, the "Ku ming" chapter of the *Shang shu cheng-i*, vol. 1, 238, where the Duke of Chou 周公 begs Heaven to "greatly rescue [the Chou] from hardship and catastrophe" (弘濟於艱難).

111. De Santillana and von Dechend, *Hamlet's Mill*, 8, 47, 49, 145, 154, 201, passim, discuss how the "dimension of Heaven is time" and how when myths speak of measures "it is always some form of Time that provides them." Cf. Schlegel, *Uranographie*, 186–92, for a long discussion on the symbolic significance of the asterism *Chien-t'ai* 漸臺, located in the Heavenly Turtle quadrant; he believes that it was the celestial measure of time and the predecessor of the water clock.

112. See Ku Shih, *Hsi-cheng chiang-shu,* 2.50, 72, 89, for the use of the term "later generations" both in King Mu's own speech and with reference to the motivations of his actions.

113. For discussions of this notion, see, Johannes Fabian, *Time and the Other* (New York: Columbia University Press, 1983); and Clifford Geertz, introduction to *The Interpretation of Culture.*

114. For example, the fiefs given to barbarian tribes, cited above, can be seen in this way. In addition, he has his feet washed in animal milk (*Hsi-cheng chiang-shu,* 4.237); and drinks the blood of a horse to *revive* himself (4.218); he also accepts two daughters presented to him by Ch'i the chief of the Red Crow tribe (2.99). Cf. Mircea Eliade's comment that "Settlement in a new, unknown, uncultivated country is equivalent to an act of Creation," Eliade, *Cosmos and History,* 10.

115. Mathieu, *Le Mu Tianzi Zhuan,* 176, discusses the political and ideological ramifications of controlling space.

116. See Yu, "History, Fiction and the Reading of Chinese History," 3ff.

117. Ku Shih, *Hsi-cheng chiang-shu,* 1.50.

118. See the *Mao shih cheng-i,* "Kua yu k'u yeh," where *ying* is used in the context of *crossing* the overflowing Chi 濟 River, and is glossed as *man.*

119. SPTK ed., 5.2a, 2b.

120. The poem following King Mu's visit to Hsi-wang-mu, expressing his dismay at the public disdain over his extravagant trip, may also be read as a sign to treat King Mu's problematic self-image and his visit to Hsi-wang-mu as two sides of the same coin. See chapter 1 above, where I discuss this poem in detail.

121. See appendix.

122. *Mu T'ien-tzu chuan,* SPTK ed., 5.4b–5a.

123. Girardot, *Myth and Meaning in Early Taoism,* 34, 37.

124. *Chou-li chu-shi,* "Che-ts'u shih," vol. 1, 889.

125. The owl seems to have functioned somewhat like a trope of political insurgency. See, for example, the poem "Chih Hsiao" (Owl) in the "Pin feng" section of the *Mao shih cheng-i,* vol. 1, 394–97, which is traditionally believed to have been written by the Duke of Chou as an allegory of the slanderous actions of people within the Chou court. See the "Chin-t'eng" chapter of the *Shang shu cheng-i,* vol. 1, 197, where the Duke of

Chou is said to have written the poem. Saussy, *The Problem of a Chinese Aesthetic*, 139–47, offers a brilliant analysis of the aesthetic implications of this attribution of authorship for the understanding of the use of allegory in ancient Chinese poetry.

126. Girardot, *Myth and Meaning in Early Taoism*, 37. Cf. the enigmatic reference to owl and turtle in the *Ch'u-tz'u chi-cheng*, 54, which occurs in the passage describing Kun.

127. Donald Harper, "Wang Yen-shou's Nightmare Poem," 255 n. 62. See also Fukatsu Tanefusa, "Kodai Chūgokujin no shisō to seikatsu—yume ni tsuite," *Uno Tetsuto sensei hakuju shukuga kinen Tōyōgaku ronsō* (Tokyo: Uno Tetsuto sensei hakuju shukuga kinenkai, 1974), 939–61, esp. 949–54, for an analysis of the relationship between dream and conscious perceptions of reality.

128. For Yü's gathering of lords at T'u Mountain, see the *Ch'un-ch'iu Tso chuan cheng-i*, Ai 7, vol. 2, 2163.

129. See the *Ch'un-ch'iu Tso chuan cheng-i*, Chao 4, vol. 2, 2035; and the entry under the 39th year of King Mu's reign as recorded in the *Chu-shu chi-nien t'ung-chien*, 8.15a.

130. Wang, *The Bell and the Drum: Shih Ching as Formulaic Poetry in an Oral Tradition* (Berkeley: University of California Press, 1974), 118ff.

131. Ku Shih, *Hsi-cheng chiang-shu*, 1.50. Ogawa Takuji, "Boku tenshi den kō," 97, believes that these two lines, which are separated in the extant text, should follow one another.

132. Ku Shih, *Hsi-cheng chiang-shu*, 1.91.

133. In ancient China, as in other ancient societies, the past was preserved almost entirely by oral transmission of traditions. See Wang, *The Bell and the Drum*; and Richard Kunst, "The Original 'Yi Jing,'" 62–82, for examples of how the Chinese classics are viewed as representing part of an oral tradition.

134. See Yu, "History, Fiction and the Reading of Chinese History," 1–19.

135. Both Mathieu, *Le Mu Tianzi Zhuan* 198; and Nienhauser, "Origins of Chinese Literature," 201, have noted that the *Mu T'ien-tzu chuan* is the earliest extant piece of Chinese narrative that deals with the experience of only a single human hero.

136. See Mathieu, *Le Mu Tianzi Zhuan*, 265–66, where he provides a concordance for the occurrence of this term. Mathieu also comments on the oral origins of the King Mu story (p. 113).

137. Providing further support for this contention is the repetition two pages later of the phrase "the origin of the Chou lineage" (literally: "that which controlled the Chou lineage" 周室之主), again in an effort to identify a location/tribe with reference to its relevance to the Chou court.

138. Although Ch'en Feng-heng's text, *Mu T'ien-tzu chuan chu pu-cheng,* 3.2a, refers to "white jade *kuei* and a black jade *pi,*" I follow Kuo P'u's annotation to the *Shan-hai-ching,* "Hsi-shan-ching," 77, which cites the *Mu T'ien-tzu chuan* as having written "black jade *kuei* and a white jade *pi* tablet." Ku Shih, *Hsi-cheng chiang-shu,* 3.147, also follows Kuo P'u.

139. This rendition of *yao-ch'ih* is borrowed from Harper, "The Sexual Arts of Ancient China," 550.

140. Ku Shih, *Hsi-cheng chiang-shu,* 3.144–58.

141. T'an Ts'ui, *Mu T'ien-tzu chuan chu-shu,* 3.1a.

142. See the "Yü kung," *Shang shu cheng-i,* vol. 1, 153.

143. T'an Ts'ui, *Mu T'ien-tzu chuan chu-shu,* 3.2a.

144. For the connection between *yao* and *chou,* see Kao Heng, *Chou-i ku-ching t'ung-shuo* (Hong Kong: Chung-hua, 1963), 11; cited in Richard Kunst, "The Original 'Yijing,'" 63, 226 n. 2.

145. See Bernhard Karlgren, *Grammatica Recensa,* no. 976, also related to the family name of the Chou court, Ssu.

146. Ch'eng Feng-heng cites Su Shih's comment that the king shares more with Hsi-wang-mu than the usual exchange of protocol observed between rulers. See the *Mu T'ien-tzu chuan chu pu-cheng,* 3.7a.

147. Harper, "The Sexual Arts of Ancient China," 543.

148. Ibid., 550. This meaning is implied in Jung Ch'eng's teaching in the *Shih-wen* text cited above; see Harper, "The Sexual Arts of Ancient China," 550.

149. Harper, "Sexual Arts in Ancient China," 576.

150. Ibid.

151. Marcel Granet, *Festivals and Songs in Ancient China,* trans. E. D. Edward (New York: E. P. Dutton, 1932).

152. See Li Shih-chen, *Pen-ts'ao kang-mu,* 4 vols. (Peking: Chung-kuo shu-tien, 1988), vol. 3, 35.25. See also F. Porter Smith, *Chinese Materia Medica,* 416.

153. See Cheng Hsüan's commentary to the *Chou-li,* "Hsia-kuan ssu-huan," *Chou-li chu-shu,* vol. 1, 843. Joseph Needham, *Science and*

Civilization in China, vol. 2, 236, cites a remnant of a lost text of Tsou Yen, the *Tsou-tzu chung-shih* 鄒子終始, in which the *huai* tree's attributes are mentioned as being best utilized during winter.

154. Mathieu, *Le Mu Tianzi Zhuan*, 173, also touches upon this point.

155. Mark Edward Lewis, *Sanctioned Violence in Early China* (Albany: SUNY Press, 1990), 5. See also Yang K'uan, *Chan-kuo shih* (Shanghai: Shang-hai jen-min, 1955), 1–4 passim.

156. Lewis, *Sanctioned Violence in Early China*, 11. The increasing valorization of tombs over ancestral temples as a sign of identity during the Eastern Chou provides an interesting angle from which to view this phenomenon. Wu Hung has shown that ritual art in this period "imitated actual things . . . to create an artificial microcosm of the universe," while ritual art in the the Shang-Chou period "aimed to visualize an intermediate stage between the human world and the world beyond it, thus linking these two separate realms. See Wu, "From Temple to Tomb," 94.

157. This can be seen in the obvious importance of the "cosmograph" (*shih* 式), an instrument of divination based on astronomy, during the Warring States era. Several scholars have pointed out that "manipulating the dial [of the cosmograph] was an esoteric art that allowed the practitioner to plumb the mysteries of the cosmos. . . . [T]he face of the *shi pan* was constructed precisely to mirror the ideal cosmos." See Field, "Cosmos, Cosmograph, and the Inquiring Poet," 96–97. See also Harper, "The Han Cosmic Board," 1–10; Cullen, "Some Further Points on the *Shih*," 31–46; Li Ling, "Shih-t'u yü Chung-kuo ku-tai ti yü-chou mo-shih," 5–52. The obvious advances and interest in astronomy, or perhaps more precisely calculative techniques, also bolstered the attempts of rulers to align their rule with heavenly principles. For calculation and calendrical astonomy, see Nathan Sivin, *Cosmos and Computation in Early Chinese Mathematical Astronomy* (Leiden: E. J. Brill, 1969) and Yang K'uan, *Chan-kuo shih*, 450–54. One may also see the proliferation of prescriptive "day books" (*jih-shu*) found in Warring States tombs as a manifestation of the same phenomenon.

158. My discussion of fault was inspired in part by the study of defilement in Paul Ricoeur, *The Symbolism of Evil*, trans. Emerson Buchanan (New York: Harper & Row, 1967) 25–46.

159. Eric Henry, "The Motif of Recognition in Early China," *Harvard Journal of Asiatic Studies* 47.1 (1987), 5–30, discusses this aspect of Confucius within the context of a "transferral of emphasis from the divine to the human dimension" (p. 17).

160. Birrell, *Chinese Mythology*, 80, notes this discrepancey in the Kun myths but does not offer an explanation for the divergence.

161. For oaths, see Lewis, *Sanctioned Violence*, 24–25, 43–50 passim; Li Xueqin, *Eastern Zhou and Qin Civilizations*, 52–58. The discovery of numerous blood covenants at Hou-ma 侯馬 in Shan-hsi has greatly expanded our understanding of the practice. It is not without significance for this present study that the convenants discovered all focus on the tumultuous political events that rocked the state of Chin and eventually led to its demise. There is no dearth of studies on these fascinating documents. For some of the basic ones see the Shan-hsi sheng wen-wu kung—tso-tui wei-yüan-hui, "Hou-ma meng-shu ti fa-hsien, fa-chüeh yü cheng-li ch'ing-k'uang," *Wen-wu* 5 (1975), 7–11; idem, "Hou-ma meng-shu chu-shih si chung," *Wen-wu* 5 (1975), 20–26; Ch'ang Kan, "Hou-ma meng-shu ts'ung-k'ao," *Wen-wu* 5 (1975), 12–19; and idem, "Hou-ma meng-shu ts'ung-shu ts'ung-k'ao hsü," *Ku-wen-tzu yen-chiu* 1 (1979), 78–102.

162. Lewis, *Sanctioned Violence*, 69ff. Cf. the two references to King Mu's promulgation of laws.

163. Donald Harper, "A Chinese Demonography of the Third Century B.C.," *Harvard Journal of Asiatic Studies* 45 (1985), 459–98, demonstrates how the "use of written testimony" figured significanctly within legal and magico-religious contexts.

164. The depiction of human and beast combat and creation of pens for keeping tigers in *chüan* five of the *Mu T'ien-tzu chuan* can perhaps be understood within the ritual context of staged violent acts that were performed during the winter months and thus calendarically in accordance with Heaven's patterns. The preceding date of the annal in the text situates this event around the winter solstice.

165. Mathieu, *Le Mu Tianzi Zhuan*, 104, suggests that King Mu's heroic stature meets people's need for stability at a time when royal power, as it was known, was in decline. Later, he also argues that the image of King Mu presented in the text reflects a Warring States perception of the king and not a Chou view (p. 166).

166. Eric Henry shows how the anomalous praise of Confucius for a statesman who served both a ruler and the ruler's assassin can be understood in terms of the Confucian esteem for public service. See Henry, "Motif of Recognition," 5–7.

167. Allan, *The Heir and the Sage*, 106.

168. Ibid., 18.

169. See, for example, the analyses of the connection between Chin/Wei culture and that of Chou in Li Xueqin in, *Eastern Zhou and Qin Civilizations*, 37 passim; Ho Lin-i, *Chan-kuo wen-tzu t'ung-lun*, 104–35.

170. Harper, "A Chinese Demonography," 470 n. 26.

CHAPTER 6

1. See, for example, Frederick Mote, "The Cosmological Gulf Between China and the West," in David C. Buxbaum and Frederick Mote, eds. *Transition and Permanence: Chinese History and Culture* (Hong Kong: Cathay Press, 1972), 3–21.

2. Girardot, *Myth and Meaning in Early Taoism*, 12.

3. Plaks, *Archetype and Allegory*, 21, 25.

4. Ibid., 26. Plaks (p. 23) acknowledges that linguistic factors may be related to the unlinear narrative treatment of Mediterranean mythology, but he does not go into any depth nor does he speculate about the linguistic "sources" of the more "spatialized" form of Chinese myth. Cf. Girardot's criticism of Plaks, *Myth and Meaning in Early Taoism*, 14.

5. Chao Yüan-jen, *A Grammar of Spoken Chinese* (Berkeley: University of California Press, 1968), 69ff., and idem, *Aspects of Chinese Sociolinguistics* (Palo Alto: Stanford University Press, 1976), 250ff. For a similar perspective on Chinese grammar, see also Chou Fa-kao, *Chung-kuo ku-tai yü-fa tsao-chü pien* (Taipei: Chung-hua, 1973), 5 passim; Charles Li and Sandra Thompson, *Mandarin Chinese: A Functional Grammar* (Berkeley: University of California Press, 1981), 85–103. Tai Lien-chang, "Ku-tai Han-yü ti yü-hsü pien-huan," *Chung-yang yen-chiu yüan kuo-chi Han-hsüeh hui-i lun-wen chi*, 10 vols. (Taipei, 1981), vol. 2, 391–420. argues that the "topic-comment" structure informed the manner in which word order changed as Chinese evolved. The earliest linguistic specimens of Chinese, the oracle bone inscriptions, evince a proclivity for expression that is better described in terms of topic and comment than subject and predicate, although this is very likely due to the contextual function of the language (i.e., divining about the appropriateness of certain actions). Ken-ichi Takashima uses the concept of topic-comment to analyze the use of copulas in oracle bone inscriptions. See Takashima "A Study of the Copulas in Shang Chinese," *Toyo Bunka Kenkyusho Kiyo* (Tokyo Daigaku) 12 (1990), 38.

6. Wallace L. Chafe, "Givenness, Contrastiveness, Definiteness: Subjects and Topics," in Charles N. Li, ed., *Symposium on Subject and Topic, University of California, Santa Barbara, March 1975* (New York: Academic Press, 1976), 50.

7. Li and Thompson, "Subject and Topic: A New Typology of Language," in Charles N. Li, ed., *Subject and Topic*, 459–89. The term "topic-prominent" was introduced by Edward Keenan, "Towards a Universal Definition of Subject," in Li, ed., *Subject and Topic*, 303–34. Kuo Shao-yü, comes to the same conclusion. See Kuo, *Han-yü yü-fa hsiu-tz'u hsin-t'an* (Peking: Shang-wu, 1979), 135ff. The issue of whether Chao Yüan-jen's

description implies a fundamental word order of object-subject-verb or subject-object-verb, as opposed to subject-verb-object, has been a source of controversy for the last fifteen years. The controversy began with James Tai's transformational treatise postulating modern Chinese to be an underlying subject-object-verb language and has continued through Sun Chao-fen and Talmy Givon's statistical study asserting a subject-verb-object ordering. See James H. Y. Tai, "Chinese as an SOV Language," in Shou-hsin Teng, ed., *Readings in Chinese Transformational Syntax* (Taipei: Crane Publishing Co., 1986), 339–54; and idem, "On the Change from SVO to SOV in Chinese," also in *Transformational Syntax*, 429–44. See also Charles N. Li and Sandra A. Thompson, "Historical Change of Word Order: A Case Study and Its Implications," in J. M. Anderson and C. Jones, eds., *Historical Linguistics* (Amsterdam: North-Holland Publishing, 1974), 199–217, idem, "The Semantic Function of Word Order: A Case Study in Mandarin," in Charles N. Li, ed., *World Order and Word Order Change* (Austin: University of Texas Press, 1975), 163–96; idem, "Subject and Topic: A New Typology of Language," 459–89. For opposing views, see Timothy Light, "Word Order and Word Order Change in Chinese," *Journal of Chinese Linguistics* 7.2 (1979), 149–80; and Sun Chao-fen and Talmy Givon, "On the So-called SOV Word Order in Mandarin Chinese: A Quantified Text Study and Its Implications," in *Language* 61.2 (1985), 329–51. Yong Ho, *Aspects of Discourse Structure in Mandarin Chinese*, 25, has more recently suggested that topic-comment structure has been grammaticalized to the "extent of becoming the unmarked way of producing sentences." Since our analysis does not depend on the universal application of Chao's definition, we need not be concerned with whether his generalizations are valid for all of Chinese syntax. Of interest are the narratological implications attendant upon such a discursive practice.

8. Li and Thompson, "Subject and Topic," pp. 465ff.

9. See also Ma Chung-chien, *Ma shih wen-t'ung* (Peking: Chung-hua, 1959), 490ff. Kuo Shao-yü, *Hsiu-tz'u*, 137ff.; Hsü Shih-ying, *Chung-kuo wen-fa chiang-hua* (Taipei: K'ai-ming, 1966), 346–50; Chu Teh-hsi, *Yü-fa chiang-i* (Peking: Shang-wu, 1984), 220–21; Wang Li, *Chung-kuo yü-fa kang-yao* (Shanghai: Hsin chih-shih, 1957), 79.

10. Chafe, "Givenness," pp. 38–43.

11. M. A. K. Halliday, *An Introduction to Functional Grammar*, 39, 54, uses the term "theme" to signify the same linguistic property.

12. This conclusion is consistent with a recent observation of a categorical difference between the functional objectives of Chinese and Indo-European grammars, namely that the latter are "more interested in finding out who does what, while Chinese is more concerned with what has happened." See James H. Y. Tai, "Toward a Cognition-based Functional Grammar of Chinese," in James H. Y. Tai and Frank F. S. Hsueh, eds.,

Functionalism and Chinese Grammar, Chinese Language Teachers Association Monograph Series, no. 1 (1989), 199.

13. James H. Y. Tai, "Toward a Cognitive-based Functional Grammar of Chinese," 211. For a fully developed discussion of the Principle of Temporal Sequence and its operative force in Chinese grammar, see Tai, "Temporal Sequence and Chinese Word Order," in John Haiman, ed., *Iconicity in Syntax* (Amsterdam: John Benjamins Publishing Company, 1985), 49–72.

14. Merlin Donald, *The Origins of the Modern Mind* (Cambridge, Mass.: Harvard University Press, 1992), 213–15.

15. Ibid., 216. See also p. 252, where Donald states that the lexicon must have been a by-product of an evolving narrative skill, "a necessary device in the formulation of commentaries upon experience."

16. Ibid., 267.

17. Ibid.

18. Ibid., 269.

19. Karl S. Y. Kao, "Aspects of Derivation in Chinese Narrative," *Chinese Literature: Essays, Articles, Reviews* 7 (1985), 1–36.

20. Ibid., 7 n. 10: "Derivation or adaptation is different from the 'recurrence of motifs' in that it is always a conscious activity."

21. See A. L. Graham, *Disputers of the Tao (La Salle: Open Court, 1989)*, 3.

22. Ibid., 107–10.

23. The Taoist's vision of the Tao as "the order of Nature that brings all into existence and governs their action" was itself originally a symbolic response to inchoate phenomena; it meshed brilliantly with the symbolic function of the philsopher's responses to the chaotic reality of the Warring States. Joseph Needham, *Science and Civilization in China*, vol. 2, 37, describes this vision as a logos.

24. This is evinced in the philosopher's interest in discovering the "origins" of their tradition; see Graham, *Disputers of the Tao*, 4. See also Benjamin Schwartz, *The World of Thought in Ancient China*, 63. Joseph Needham's description of Taoism as a theory about the "manifestations of the natural world surrounding the frail structure of society," which he believes derives from the Taoist's emphasis on observation points in a similar direction. See Needham, *Science and Civilization in China*, vol. 2, 63.

25. By semiotics I mean simply a linguistically based system of signs that reflects the thought that it is used to signify. The crucial and self-

conscious significance of language in the philosophies of early China need not be rehearsed here. See Graham, *Disputers of the Tao*, 23–25 (Confucius); 23 for philosophy as performative utterance; 138, 140, 150 passim (Mohists); 199–202 (Chuang tzu); 219–22 (Lao-tzu); 261–67 (Hsün tzu). Schwartz writes of a "language crisis," *The World of Thought in Ancient China*, 164, 169; see also his comments regarding language and Confucius, 91–93; and Taoist mysticism, 193–95; Hsün tzu, 311–13. See also Needham's assertion that the philsophy of what he calls the Naturalists (who espoused correlative theories) was "by no means mere verbal speculation" but was performative as well as descriptive; *Science and Civilization in China*, vol. 2, 234–35.

26. Graham's description of Chuang tzu's philosophy as one that wanted to prove that language was meaningful "without using it on an assumption that it is" bespeaks the futility of any search for a metalanguage, for language is always a "trap for self-reference." See Graham, *Disputers of the Tao*, 200.

27. Cf. Johh Henderson's discussion of the "epistemological space" through which correlative thought developed, Henderson, *Cosmology*, 35ff.

28. Graham, *Disputers of the Tao*, 313ff., talks of the correlative theories in transitive and performative terms, such as "incorporating" and "integrating" human morality into cosmic order. Henderson seems to address this issue as well, in his discussion of how correlative theories were expressed through the use of linguistic parallelism. The development of geometrical cosmography, also examined by Henderson, is entwined with the development of correlative thinking and constitutes another performative aspect of the theories. See Henderson, *Cosmology*, 44ff., 59–87.

29. See the discussion of "correlative cosmology," in Schwartz, *The World of Thought in Ancient China, 351–52.*

30. Ibid., 9.

31. Cf. Needham's comment that the reason the feudal lords found the correlative theories of Tsou Yen's doctrines difficult to put into practice (even though they may have been convinced of the truth of the theory which he expounded) was because it was difficult to ascertain exactly the elements by virtue of which they were ruling; Needham, *Science and Civilization in China*, vol. 2, 239.

32. Here I think Graham may not agree; see his fascinating discussion of the differences between the deconstructive theories of Jacques Derrida and Lao tzu's Taoism; Graham, *Disputers of the Tao*, 227–29.

33. Hsiao-peng Lu, "The Fictional Discourse of *Pien-wen*: The Relation of Chinese Fiction to Historiography," *Chinese Literature: Essays,*

Articles and Reviews 9 (1987), 49–70, arrives at a similar conclusion via a different interpretive road.

34. For the literary effects of this linguistic criterion, see Anthony Yu, "History, Fiction, and the Reading of Chinese History," 1–19.

35. See chapter 5 for a detailed analysis of the symbolic significance of the *Mu T'ien-tzu chuan*.

36. See the brilliant discussion on the creation of cultural symbols in Schwartz, *The World of Thought in Ancient China*, 8.

37. Nicholas T. Rand, *The Kernel and the Shell*, 17.

38. Nicolas Abraham, in an essay in which he outlines a "psychoanalytic aesthetic," argues that texts must be analyzed as if having an ego of their own, and must be viewed as a symptom of their own (psychoanalytic) problem. Abraham, "Pour une esthétique psychanalytique," in *Rythmes de l'oeuvre de la traduction et de la psychanalyse* (Paris: Flammarion, 1985), 132.

39. Thus, the fragmentary nature of early fictional representation may, like that of early cosmogonic myths, be best understood as deriving from its symbolic function.

40. Nicolas Abraham's work suggests that this newly figured temporality of representation might reflect the mode of cognition that surfaces in the face of a psychoanalytically perceived confrontation, what he calls, borrowing from Freud, "the return of the repressed." See Abraham, *Rythmes*, 120–22.

41. See Kenneth J. DeWoskin, "On Narrative Revolutions," *Chinese Literature: Essays, Articles and Reviews* 5 (1983), 38; and Yüan Hsing-p'ei, "Han-shu 'I-wen chih' hsiao-shuo-chia k'ao-pien," *Wen-shih* 7 (1979), 179–89. See also Hellmut Wilhelm, "Notes on Chou Fiction," in *Transition and Permanence: Chinese History and Culture, A Festschrift in Honor of Hsiao Kung-ch'üan* (Hong Kong: Cathay Press, 1972), 251–68.

42. Graham, *Disputers of the Tao*, 228.

43. Robert Campany, "The Real Presence," *History of Religions* 32.3 (February 1993), 236.

44. See Victor Mair, "The Narrative Revolution in Chinese Literature," *Chinese Literature: Essays, Articles and Reveiws* 5 (1983), 1–27, for the argument that the production of fictional representation in China was the direct result of the coming of Buddhism.

45. Campany, "The Real Presence," 262–68.

46. Kenneth DeWoskin, "The Six Dynasties Chih-kuai and the Brith of Fiction," in Andrew H. Plaks, ed., *Chinese Narrative: Critical and Theoretical Essays* (Princeton: Princeton University Press, 1977), 21–52.

47. For the *chih-kuai* as examples of ethnography, see DeWoskin, "The Birth of Fiction," 37–38. For an interesting analysis of the various literary techniques used to collapse boundaries, see Yeh Ch'ing-ping, "Liu-ch'ao chih T'ang-tai ti t'a-chieh chieh-kou hsiao-shuo," *T'ai-ta Chung-wen hsüeh-pao* 3 (1991), 7–28.

48. This is intimated in several prefaces of *chih-kuai* collections. See DeWoskin, "The Birth of Fiction," 29–32.

49. Smith, "Ritual and the Shaping of Narrative," 40.

50. See Andrew Plaks, "Towards a Critical Theory of Chinese Narrative," in Plaks, *Chinese Narrative*, 316–23, for a discussion of the relative meaning of truth in Chinese fiction and history. See also Hsiao-peng Lu, "The Fictional Discouse of *Pien-wen*, 49–70, for a reevaluation of Plaks's argument.

51. Kenneth DeWoskin, "Chih-kuai," in William H. Nienhauser. Jr., ed., *The Indiana Companion to Traditional Chinese Literature* (Bloomington: Indiana University Press, 1985), 280, cites four compilations that were entitled *chih-kuai*. For a reading of the term *kuai* as meaning "confused" (*huo* 惑), see *Chung-wen ta tz'u-tien*, vol. 13, 30–31.

52. Laurence Schneider, *A Madman of Ch'u: The Chinese Myth of Loyalty and Dissent* (Berkeley: University of California Press, 1980), treats the historical function of the notion of barbarian culture in a similar way.

53. For examples of the association of transformations with crossing rivers or the number three, see the *Sou-shen chi* (Ch'ang-sha: Yüeh-lu, 1989), 3.13, 24; 4.5, 31; 4.8, 32; 4.12, 33; 5.4, 38; 5.8, 41; 6.42, 41, etc. Cf. Thomas Smith's analysis of the prevalence of the number three in the *Legend of the Han Emperor Wu* and its relation to the structure of romances, Smith, "Ritual and the Shaping of Narrative," 92, 97–99.

54. Dennis Twitchett, "Chinese Biographical Writing" in W. G. Beasley and E. G. Pulleyblank, *Historians of China and Japan*, 93–114.

55. Kao, "Aspects of Derivation," 22.

56. For vernacular fiction as a hybrid medium, see Patrick Hanan, "The Early Chinese Short Story: A Critical Theory in Outline," *Harvard Journal of Asiatic Studies* 27 (1967), 168–207, reprinted in Cyril Birch, ed., *Studies in Chinese Literary Genres*; See also idem, *The Colloquial Short Story in China: A Study of the San-yen Collections*, Harvard-Yenching

Institute Studies 11 (Cambridge, Mass.: Harvard University Press, 1956), 10ff.; Jarsolov Prusek, "New Studies of the Colloquial Short Story," *Archiv Orientalni* 25 (1957), 452–99; and Andrew Plaks, "Functions of Colloquial Rhetoric in Traditional Chinese Fiction" (paper presented at the Conference of Oriental Western Literary Relations, Indiana University, June 1979), 1–3, for a discussion on the mixture of literary styles in Chinese vernacular fiction.

57. Deborah Porter (P'ei Pi-lan), "Pai-hua hsiao-shuo shuo-shu jen de yi-shu," *Chiu-chou hsüeh-k'an* (forthcoming); I analyze the aesthetic implications of the storyteller rhetoric.

58. Andrew Plaks, *The Four Masterworks of the Ming Novel* (Princeton: Princeton University Press, 1987), 3–52, 497–512; Wai-yee Li, *Enchantment and Disenchantment: Love and Illusion in Chinese Literature* (Princeton: Princeton University Press, 1993), 47–88.

59. Feng Yu-lan, *A History of Chinese Philosophy*, trans. Derk Bodde (Princeton: Princeton University Press, 1973), 131.

60. For the perceptual basis of the colloquial medium, see Deborah Porter, "*Shui-hu chuan* yü-fa hsiu-tz'u shen-mei hsiao-ying hsi li," *Chung-kuo wen-hsüeh yen-chiu* 21 (1991), 32–40; and idem, "Toward an Aesthetic of Chinese Vernacular Fiction: Colloquial Style in the *Shui-hu chuan*," *T'oung Pao* 79 (1993), 113–53.

61. For an analysis of the representation of character from this discursive perspective, see Deborah Porter, "The Formation of an Image: An Analysis of the Linguistic Patterns that form the Character of Sung Chiang," *Journal of the American Oriental Society* 12.12 (1992), 233–53.

62. The following discuss the significance of the illusory quality of perception in the vernacular novel: Anthony Yu, "History, Fiction, and the Reading of Chinese History," 10–19; Plaks, *The Four Masterworks*, 497–512; Wai-yee Li, *Enchantment and Disenchantment*, 257–68.

63. Wai-yee Li's conclusion that the Ch'ing text, the *Liao-chai chih-i*, represents "in some ways the solutions to the problem posed by the late-Ming legacy: how to valorize subjective projection without undermining socio-political order and equilibrium of the self," seems to accord with my argument, although it should be noted that the text was written in the classical not the vernacular medium. That the *Liao-chai* is viewed as a Ch'ing representation of *chih-kuai* fiction, however, suggests that it is the form, not the medium itself that reveals the tension underlying the text's production. See Li, *Enchantment and Disenchantment*, 264.

64. See the comments of Anthony Yu for the panel "Wen: The Nature

of Chinese Language and Literature" (presented at the conference of the annual Association for Asian Studies, Boston, 1994), 4.

65. See the "Tu-fa," *Shui-hu chuan hui-p'ing-pen* (Peking: Pei-ching ta-hsüeh, 1981). Cf. interpretation of this passage of Plaks, "Critical Theory," 317; and Karl S. Y. Kao, "Aspects of Derivation," 31 n. 54.

Bibliography

Chinese and Japanese Sources

Akatsuka Kiyoshi 赤冢忠. "Kei U to Indai tōban no ki ryū zuzō" 鯀禹と殷代銅盤の鼉龍圖像. *Kodaigaku* 古代學 11.4 (1964), 273–301.

———. *Chūgoku kodai no shūkyō to bunka—In ōchō no saiki* 中國古代宗教の文化—殷王朝の祭祀. Tokyo: Kadokawa Shoten, 1977.

An-hui sheng wen-wu kung-tso tui 安徽省文物工作隊. "Fu-yang Shuang-ku-tui Hsi-Han Ju-yin Hou mu fa-ch'üeh chien-pao" 阜陽雙古堆西漢汝陰侯墓發掘簡報. *Wen-wu* 8 (1978), 12–31.

Chan-kuo ts'e 戰國策. 2 vols. Taipei: Tung-ya, 1982.

Ch'ang Cheng 常征. "*Mu T'ien-tzu chuan* shih wei-shu ma?" 穆天子傳是偽書嗎. *Ho-pei ta-hsüeh hsüeh-pao* 河北大學學報 2 (1980), 30–53.

Chang Hsin-ch'eng 張心徵. *Wei-shu t'ung-k'ao* 偽書通考續. Shanghai: Shang-wu, 1957. Rpt. Taipei: Hung-yeh, 1979.

Ch'ang Kan 長甘. "Hou-ma meng-shu ts'ung-k'ao" 侯馬盟書叢考 *Wen-wu* 5 (1975), 12–19.

———. "Hou-ma meng-shu ts'ung-k'ao hsü" 侯馬盟書叢考續. *Ku-wen-tzu yen-chiu* 古文字研究 1 (1979), 78–102.

Chang Kuang-chih 張光直. "Chung-kuo ch'uang-shih shen-hua chih fen-hsi yü ku-shih yen-chiu" 中國創世神話之分析與古史研究. *Bulletin of the Institute of Ethnology, Academica Sinica* 8 (1959), 47–79.

———. "P'u-yang san-ch'iao yü Chung-kuo ku-tai mei-shu shang ti jen shou mu-t'i" 濮陽三蹻與中國古代美術上的人獸母題. *Wen-wu* 文物 11 (1988), 36–39.

Chang Kung-liang 張公量. "Ku Shih chu *Mu T'ien-tzu chuan hsi-cheng chiang-shu*" 顧實著穆天子傳西征講疏. *Yü kung* 禹貢 3.4 (1935), 31–46.

———. "*Mu chuan* chih pan-pen chi kuan-yü *Mu chuan* chih chu-shu" 穆傳之板本及關於穆傳之著述. *Yü kung* 2.6 (1934), 18–27.

———. "Chi chiu ch'ao-pen *Mu T'ien-tzu chuan*" 記舊抄本穆天子傳. *Yü kung* 2.5 (1934), 31–32.

Chao Li-sheng 趙儷生. "*Mu T'ien-tzu chuan* chung i-hsieh pu-luo ti fang-wei k'ao-shih" 穆天子傳中一些部落的方位考識. *Chung-hua wen-shih lun-ts'ung* 中華文史論叢 2 (1979), 287–90.

Ch'en Chiang-feng 陳江風. *T'ien-wen yü jen-wen* 天文與人文. Peking: Hsin-hua, 1988.

Ch'en Chin-sheng 陳金生. "Shih shih *Chou-i* ti 'yu t'a yü pu hsia i'" 試釋周易的"有它與不遐遺". *Wen-shih* 文史 35 (1992), 213–217.

Ch'en Chiu-chin 陳久金. "Li-fa ti kuei-yüan ho hsien-Ch'in si-fen li" 曆法的起源和先秦四分曆. *K'o-chi-shih wen-chi* 科技史文集 1 (1978).

Ch'en Feng-heng 陳逢衡. *Mu T'ien-tzu chuan chu pu-cheng* 穆天子傳注補正. Tao-kuang kuei-mao 道光癸卯 edition.

Ch'en Hsing-ts'an, 陳星燦, "Chung-kuo shih-ch'ien wen-hua chi ch'i hsi-lai chia-shuo ti yu-lai ho fen-hsi" 中國史前文化及其西來假說的由來和分析. *Chiu-chou hsüeh-k'an* 九州學刊 5.3 (1993), 71–86.

Ch'en Meng-chia 陳夢家. "Ku-wen-tzu chung chih Shang Chou chi-ssu" 古文字中的商周祭祀. *Yen-ching hsüeh-pao* 燕京學報 19 (1936).

———. "Shang-tai ti shen-hua yü wu-shu" 商代的神話與巫術. *Yen-ching hsüeh-pao* 20 (1936), 485–576.

———. "Chi-chung shu-k'ao" 汲冢書考. *Liu-kuo chi-nien* 六國紀年. Shanghai: Hsüeh-hsi sheng-huo, 1955.

———. *Yin-hsü pu-tz'u tsung-shu* 殷虛卜辭總述. Peking: K'o-hsüeh, 1956.

Ch'en Tsun-kuei 陳遵媯. *Chung-kuo t'ien-wen-hsüeh shih* 中國天文學史. Shanghai: Jen-min, 1980. Rpt. Taipei: Ming-wen, 1984.

Cheng Wen-kuang 鄭文光. *Chung-kuo t'ien-wen-hsüeh yüan-liu* 中國天文學源流. Peking: K'o-hsüeh, 1979.

Chia-ku-wen he-chi 甲骨文合集. Hu Hou-hsüan 胡厚宣 ed. 13 vols. N.p.: Chung-hua, 1978–82.

Ch'ien I 錢繹. *Fang-yen chien-shu* 方言箋疏. 2 vols. Shanghai: Shang-hai ku-chi, 1984.

Ch'ien Mu 錢穆. *Hsien-Ch'in chu-tzu hsi-nian t'ung-piao* 先秦諸子繫年通表. 2 vols. Hong Kong: Hong Kong University Press, 1956.

Chin shu 晉書. 10 vols. Peking: Chung-hua, 1987.

Ching-chou ti-ch'ü po-wu kuan 荊州地區博物館. Ching-ling Chang-chia-shan san-tso Han-mu ch'u-t'u ta-p'i chu-chien" 江陵張家山三座漢墓出土大批竹簡. *Wen-wu* 1 (1985), 1–8.

Ch'iu Hsi-kuei 裘錫圭. "Chia-ku-wen chung so chien ti Shang tai nung-yeh" 甲骨文所見的商代農業. *Ku-wen-tzu lun-chi* 古文字論集. Peking: Chung-hua, 1992.

———. "Shih hai" 釋害.˙ *Ku-wen-tzu lun-chi*, 11–16.

———. "T'an-t'an Sui-hsien Tseng-hou I mu ti wen-tzu tzu-liao" 談談隋縣曾侯乙墓的文字資料. *Ku-wen-tzu lun-chi.*, 418–28.

———. "Lun Tung kuei ti liang-ko ti-ming—Yü-lin ho Hu" 論冬簋的兩個地名—域林和誻. *K'ao-ku yü wen-wu ts'ung-k'an* 考古文物叢刊. No. 2, 4–7.

———. "Shih Ch'iang p'an ming chieh-shih" 史牆盤銘解釋. *Wen-wu* 3 (1978), 25–32.

———. "Shuo pu-tz'u ti fen wu-wang yü tso t'u-lung" 説卜辭的焚巫尪與作土龍. *Chia-ku-wen yü Yin-Shang shih* 甲骨文與殷商史. Hu Hou-hsüan ed. Shanghai: Ku-chi, 1985, 21–35.

Chou Fa-kao 周法高, ed. *Chin-wen ku-lin* 金文詁林. 19 vols. Hong Kong: Chinese University Press, 1975.

———. *Chung-kuo ku-tai yü-fa tsao-chü pien* 中國古代語法造句編. Taipei: Chung-hua, 1973.

Chou-i cheng-i 周易正義. *Shih-san-ching chu-shu* edition.

Chou-li chu-shu 周禮注疏. *Shih-san-ching chu-shu* edition.

Chu Hsi-tsu 朱希祖. *Chi-chung shu-k'ao* 汲冢書考. Peking: Chung-hua, 1960.

Chu K'o-chen 竺可楨. "Erh-shih-pa hsiu ch'i-yüan chih ti-tien yü shih-chien" 二十八宿起源之地點與時間. *Ch'i-hsiang hsüeh-pao* 氣象學報 18 (1944).

Chu-shu chi-nien t'ung-chien 竹書紀年統箋. 1878 Hsü Wen-ching 徐文靖 edition.

Chu Teh-hsi 朱德熙. *Yü-fa chiang-i* 語法講義. Peking: Shang-wu, 1984.

Ch'u-tz'u chi-chu 楚辭集注. Shanghai: Shang-hai ku-chi, 1979.

Ch'u-tz'u chang-chü 楚辭章句. Ch'ang-sha: Yüeh-lu shu-she, 1989.

Ch'ü Wan-li 屈萬里. *Shang shu shih-i* 尚書釋義. Hua-kang: Hua-kang, 1956.

Chu Yu-tseng 朱右曾. *I Chou shu chi-hsün chiao-shih* 逸周書集訓校釋. *E-kuan shu-ts'ung* 鄂官書叢 edition, 1913.

Chuang tzu chi-shih 莊子集釋. 4 vols. Peking: Chung-hua, 1989.

Chūbachi Masakazu 中鉢雅量. *Chūgoku no saiki to bungaku* 中國の祭祀と文學. Tokyo: Sōbunsha, 1984.

Ch'un-ch'iu Tso chuan cheng-i 春秋左傳正義. *Shih-san-ching chu-shu* edition.

Ch'un-ch'iu Kung-yang chuan cheng-i 春秋公羊傳正義. *Shih-san ching chu-shu* edition.

Chung-kuo she-hui k'o-hsüeh yüan k'ao-ku yen-chiu-so 中國社會科學院考古研究所. "1978–1980 nien Shan-hsi Hsiang-fen t'ao-ssu mu-ti fa-chüeh chien-pao" 1978–1980 年山西襄汾陶寺墓地發掘簡報. *K'ao-ku* 考古 1 (1983), 30–42.

Erh-ya chu-shu 爾雅注疏. *Shih-san-ching chu-shu* edition.

Feng Shih 馮時. "Ho-nan P'u-yang Hsi-shui-p'o 45 hao mu ti t'ien-wen-hsüeh yen-chiu" 河南濮陽西水坡45號的天文學研究. *Wen-wu* 3 (1990), 52–60, 69.

———. "Yin-li chi-chieh yen-chiu" 殷曆季節研究. *Chung-kuo k'o-hsüeh chi-shu kuo-chi hsüeh-shu t'ao-lun-hui lun-wen* 中國科學技術國際學術討論會論文. Peking, 1990, 1–11.

———. "Chung-kuo tsao-ch'i hsing-hsiang t'u yen-chiu" 中國早時星象圖研究. *Tzu-jan k'o-hsüeh shih yan-chiu* 自然科學史研究, 9.2 (1990), 114.

Fukatsu Tanefusa 深津胤房. "Kodai Chūgokujin no shisō to seikatsu—yume ni tsuite" 古代中國人の思想と生活—夢について. *Uno Tetsuto sensei hakuju shukuga kinen Tōyōgaku ronsō* 宇野哲人先生白壽祝賀記念,東洋學論叢. Tokyo: Uno Tetsuto sensei hakuju shukuga kinenkai Tōyōgaku ronsō, 1974.

Fu-yang Han-chien cheng-li tsu 阜陽漢簡整理組. "Fu-yang Han-chien chien-chieh" 阜陽漢簡簡介. *Wen-wu* 2 (1983), 21–23.

Han shu 漢書. 12 vols. Peking: Chung-hua, 1962.

Hao I-hsing 郝懿行. *Erh-ya i-shu* 爾雅義疏. 3 vols. Peking: Pei-ching shu-chü, 1982.

———. *Shan-hai-ching chien-shu* 山海經箋疏. Taipei: Yi-wen, 1974.

Ho Hsin 何新. *Lung: Shen-hua yü chen-hsiang*: 龍: 神話與真相. Shanghai: Jen-min, 1989.

Ho Lin-i 何琳儀. *Chan-kuo wen-tzu t'ung-lun* 戰國文字通論. Peking: Chung-hua, 1989.

Ho-pei sheng wen-wu yen-chiu so 河北省文物研究所. "Ho-pei Ting-hsien 40 hao Han-mu fa-chüeh chien-pao" 河北定縣40號漢墓發掘簡報. *Wen-wu* 8 (1981), 1–10.

Hou-Han shu 後漢書. 12 vols. Peking: Chung-hua, 1965.

Hsia Han-i 夏含夷 (Edward L. Shaughnessy). *Chou-i* Ch'ien-kua liu-lung hsin-chieh" 周易乾卦六龍新解. *Wen-shih* 文史 24 (1985), 9–14.

———. "Ts'ung Chü-fu kai ming-wen t'an Chou wang-ch'ao yü Nan Huai-i ti kuan-hsi" 從駒父蓋銘文談周王朝與南淮夷的關係. *Han-hsüeh yen-chiu* 漢學研究 5 (1987), 567–73.

Hsiao Ping 蕭兵. *Ch'u-tz'u wen-hua* 楚辭文化. Peking: Chung-kuo she-hui k'o-hsüeh, 1990.

Hsiao T'ung 蕭統, ed. *Wen hsüan* 文選. 6 vols. Shanghai: Shang-hai ku-chi, 1986.

Hsing-ching 星經. *Han-wei ts'ung-shu* 漢魏叢書 edition.

Hsü Ch'uan-wu 徐傳武. "Man-hua Niu-Nü shen-hua ti ch'i-yüan ho yen-pien" 漫話牛女神話的起源和演變. *Wen-hsüeh i-ch'an* 文學遺產 6 (1989), 42–47.

Hsü Shih-ying 許世英. *Chung-kuo wen-fa chiang-hua* 中國文法講話. Taipei: K'ai-ming, 1966.

Hsü Yüeh 徐越. *Shu shu chi i* 述數記遺. *Ssu-k'u ch'üan-shu chen-pen pieh-chi* 四庫全書珍本別輯 edition.

Hu-nan sheng po-wu-kuan, Chung-kuo k'o-hsüeh yüan k'ao-ku yen-chiu so 湖南省博物館，中國科學院考古研究所. "Ch'ang-sha Ma-wang-tui erh-san hao Han-mu fa-chüeh chien-pao" 長沙馬王堆二三號漢墓發掘簡報. *Wen-wu* (1974), 39–48.

———. *Ch'ang-sha Ma-wang-tui i-hao Han-mu* 長沙馬王堆一號漢墓. 2 vols. Peking: Wen-wu, 1974.

Hu-pei Hsiao-kan ti-ch'ü ti-erh ch'i yi-kung yi-nung wen-wu k'ao-ku hsün-lian pan 湖北孝感地區第二期亦工亦農文物考古訓練班. "Hu-pei Yün-meng Shui-hu ti shih-i tso Ch'in-mu fa-chüeh chien-pao" 湖北雲夢睡虎地十一座秦墓發掘簡. *Wen-wu* 6 (1976), 1–11.

———. "Hu-pei Yün-meng Shui-hu ti shi-i tso Ch'in-mu fa-chüeh chien-pao." *Wen-wu* 9 (1976), 51–62.

Hu-pei sheng Ching-sha t'ieh-lu k'ao-ku tui 湖北省荊沙鐵路考古隊. *Pao-shan Ch'u-chien* 包山楚簡. Peking: Wen-wu, 1991.

Hu-pei sheng po-wu-kuan 湖北省博物館. Pei-ching kung-i mei-shu yan-chiu so 北京工藝美術研究所 ed. *Chan-kuo Tseng-hou I mu ch'u-tu wen-wu t'u-an hsüan* 戰國增侯乙墓出土文物圖案選. Ch'ang-sha: Ch'ang-chiang, 1984.

Huai-nan Hung-lieh chi-chieh 淮南鴻烈集解. Peking: Chung-hua, 1989.

Huang P'ei-jung 黃培容. *Chou shu 'Chou yüeh' p'ien chu-ch'eng ti shih-tai chi yu-kuan san-cheng wen-t'i ti yen-chiu* 周書"周月"篇著成的時代及有關三正問題的研究. Taipei: Wen-shih tsu'ung-k'an, 1972.

Ikeda Suetoshi 池田末利. "Ryūjin kō" 龍神考. *Tōhōgaku* 東方學 6 (1953), 1–7.

Ishikawa Misarō 石川三佐郎. "Soji ni okeru kyūka to kyūshō no kankei ni tsuite—sono meishō to hensū to henshō no yimi suru mono" 楚辭にすける九歌と九章の關係について—その名稱と篇數と併稱の意味するもの. *Tōyōgaku* 東洋學 70 (1993), 1–22.

Izushi Yoshihiko 出石誠彥. *Chūgoku shinwa densetsu no kenkyū* 中國神話傳説の研究. Tokyo: Chuo Koronsha, 1943.

Jen Fang 任昉. *Shu i chi* 述異記. *Pai-tzu ch'üan-shu* 百子全書 edition.

Kan Pao 干寶. *Sou-shen chi* 搜神記. Ch'an-sha: Yüeh-lu, 1989.

K'ang-hsi tzu tien 康熙字典. Peking: Chung-hua, 1989.

Kao Heng 高亨. *Chou-i ku-ching t'ung-shuo* 周易古經通説. Hong Kong: Chung-hua, 1963.

Kao Ming 高明. *Ku-wen-tzu lei-pien* 古文字類編. Peking: Chung-hua, 1980.

Kominami Ichirō 小南一郎. "Seibo to shichi seki denshō" 西母と七夕傳承. *Tōyō gakuhō* 東洋學報 46 (1974), 33–81.

Ku Chieh-kang 顧頡剛, ed. *Ku-shih pien* 古史編. 7 vols. Peking: Pu-she, 1927–41.

———. "Chiu-chou chih jung yü jung Yü" 九州之戎與戎禹. *Ku-shih pien*. vol. 7, *hsia-pien*, 117–39.

———. "Yü ti shen chih" 禹的神職. *Ku-shih pien*. Vol. 7, *hsia-pien*, 152–59.

———. "*Mu T'ien-tzu chuan* chi ch'i chu-tso shih-tai" 穆天子傳及其著作時代. *Wen shih che* 文史哲 1 (1951), 63–68.

———. "*Chuang tzu* ho *Ch'u-tz'u* chung K'un-lun ho P'eng-lai liang-ko shen-hua hsi-t'ung ti jung-ho" 莊子和楚辭中崑崙和蓬來兩個神話系統的融合. *Chung-hua wen-shih lun-ts'ung* 中華文史論叢 2 (1979), 31–57.

Ku Shih 顧實. *Mu T'ien-tzu chuan hsi-cheng chiang-shu* 穆天子傳西征講疏. Shanghai: Shang-wu, 1934. Rpt. Taipei: Shang-wu, 1976.

Ku-wen so-yü 古文瑣語. Ma Kuo-han 馬國翰, ed. *Yü-han shan-fang chi-i-shu* 玉函山房輯佚書 1884 edition.

Kuei-tsang 歸臧. Ma Kuo-han, ed. *Yü-han shan-fang chi i-shu* edition.

Kuo Mo-jo 郭末若. "Shi kan-chih" 釋干支 in *Kuo Mo-jo ch'üan-chi* 郭末若全集. *K'ao-ku pien* 考古編. Peking: K'o-hsüeh, 1982.

———. *Liang-Chou chin-wen-tz'u ta-hsi t'u-lu k'ao-shih* 兩周金文辭大系圖錄考釋. 2nd rev. ed. Peking, 1958.

Kuo Shao-yü 郭紹虞. *Han-yü yü-fa hsiu-tz'u hsin-t'an* 漢語語法修辭新探. Peking: Shang-wu, 1979.

Kuo-yü 國語. 2 vols. Shanghai: Shang-hai ku-chi, 1978.

Lao tzu chi-shih 老子集釋. *Hsin-pien chu-tzu chi-ch'eng* 新編諸子集成 edition. Peking: Chung-hua, 1991.

Li Ch'ang-hao 黎昌顥, ed. *Chung-kuo t'ien-wen-hsüeh shih* 中國天文學史. Peking: K'o-hsüeh, 1981.

———. "Ta-ho-ts'un hsin-shih-ch'i shih-tai ts'ai-t'ao shang ti t'ien-wen t'u-hsiang" 大河村新石器時代彩陶上的天文圖像. *Wen-wu* 文物 8 (1983), 52–54.

Li-chi cheng-i 禮記正義. *Shih-san-ching chu-shu* edition.

Li Fang 李昉, ed. *T'ai-p'ing kuang-chi* 太平廣記. 5 vols. Taipei: Hsi-nan, 1983.

Li Hsiao-ting 李孝定, ed. *Chia-ku wen-tzu chi-shih* 甲骨文字集釋. 14 vols. Taipei: Academica Sinica, 1970.

Li Hsün 李勛. "Yün-meng Shui-hu ti Ch'in-chien kai-shu" 雲夢睡虎地秦簡概述. *Wen-wu* 5 (1976), 1–6.

Li Ling 李零. "Shih-t'u yü Chung-kuo ku-tai ti yü-chou mo-shih" 式圖與中國古代的宇宙模式. *Chiu-chou hsüeh-k'an* 九州學刊 4.1 (1992), 5–52.

———. "Ch'u-t'u fa-hsien yü ku-shu nien-tai ti tsai jen-shih" 出土發現與古書年代的再認識. *Chiu-chou hsüeh-k'an* 3.1 (1988), 105–36.

Li Shih-chen 李時珍. *Pen-ts'ao kang-mu* 本草綱目. 4 vols. Rpt. Peking: Chung-kuo shu-tien, 1988.

Li Yu-heng 李有恆. *Ta-wen-k'ou hsin-shih-ch'i shih-tai mu-tsang fa-chüeh pao-kao* 大文口新石器時代墓葬發掘報告. Peking: Wen-wu, 1974.

Lian Shao-ming 連邵明. "Po-shu 'Chou-i' kua-ming chiao-shih" 帛書"周易"卦名校釋. *Wen-shih* 36 (1992), 51–76.

———. "Pu-tz'u chung ti yüeh yü hsing" 卜辭中的月與星. *Ch'u-t'u wen-hsien yen-chiu hsü-chi* 出土文獻研究續集. Peking: Wen-wu, 1989, 122–34.

Ling Ch'un-sheng 凌純聲. "Chung-kuo ti feng-shan yü liang-ho liu-yü ti k'un-lun wen-hua" 中國的封禪與兩河流域的崑崙文化. *Bulletin of the Institute of Ethnology,* Academica Sinica, 19 (1965), 1–52.

Liu Chih-hsiung 劉志雄 and Yang Ching-jung 楊靜榮. *Lung yü Chung-kuo wen-hua* 龍與中國文化. Peking: Jen-min, 1992.

Liu Shih-p'ei 劉師培. *Mu T'ien-tzu chuan pu-shih* 穆天子傳補釋. Liu Shen-shu hsien-sheng i-shu 劉申叔先生遺書 edition.

Lo Chen-yü 羅振玉. *San-tai chi-chin wen-ts'un* 三代吉金文存. 3 vols. Peking: Chung-hua, 1983.

Lo Fu-i 羅福頤. "Lin-i Han-chien kai-shu" 臨沂漢簡概述. *Wen-wu* 2 (1974), 32–35.

Lu Hsün 魯迅. *Chung-kuo wen-hsüeh shih-lüeh* 中國文學史略. Peking: Chung-hua, 1930. Rpt. Peking: Chung-hua, 1973.

Lü Pu-wei 呂不韋. *Lü-shih ch'un-ch'iu* 呂氏春秋. Shanghai: Shang-hai ku-chi, 1989.

Lun-heng chu-shih 論衡注釋. Pei-ching li-shih hsi ed. Peking: Chung-hua, 1979.

Ma Ch'eng-yüan 馬承源, ed. *Shang Chou ch'ing-t'ung-ch'i ming-wen-hsüan* 商周青銅器銘文選. 4 vols. Peking: Wen-wu, 1988.

Ma Chung-chien 馬忠建. *Ma shih wen-t'ung* 馬氏文通. Peking: Chung-hua, 1959.

Ma-wang-tui Han-mu Po-shu cheng-li hsiao-tsu 馬王堆帛書整理小組. *Ma-wang-tui Han-mu po-shu* 馬王堆漢墓帛書. 3 vols. Peking: Wen-wu, 1983.

———. "Ma-wang-tui po-shu 'Liu-shih-ssu kua' shih-wen" 馬王堆帛書"六十四卦"釋文. *Wen-wu* 3 (1984), 1–8.

Mao shih cheng-i 毛詩正義. *Shih-san-ching chu-shu* edition.

Mitarai Masaru 御手洗勝. "*Boku Tenshi den* seiritsu no haikei" 穆天子傳成立の背景. *Tōhōgaku* 東方學 26 (1962), 17–30.

Mori Mikisaburō 森三樹三郎. *Shina kodai shinwa* 支那古代神話. Tokyo, 1944.

Moriyasu Tarō 森安太郎. "Kei U genshi" 鯀禹源始. *Kyōto joshi daigaku jinbun ronsō* 京都女子大學人文論叢. 9 (1964), 1–22. Rpt. *Kōtei densetsu* 黄帝傳説. Kyoto: Kyōto Joshi Daigaku Jinbun Gakkai, 1970.

Ogawa Takuji 小川琢治. "Boku Tenshi den kō" 穆天子傳攷. *Kano Kyōju kanreki kinen* 狩野教授還歷記念. Tokyo: Kōbundō, 1928. Rpt. Trans. Chiang Hsia-an 江俠庵. *Hsien-Ch'in ching-chi k'ao* 先秦經籍考. 3 vols. Shanghai: Shang-wu, 1929.

———. *Shina rekishi chiri kenkyū zokushū* 支那歷史地理研究續集. Tokyo: Kobundo, 1929.

P'ang P'u 龐樸. "'Huo-li' chih ch'u t'an" 火曆初探. *She-hui k'o-hsüeh chan-hsien* 社會科學戰線 4 (1978), 131–37.

P'ei Pi-lan 裴碧蘭 (Deborah Porter). "*Shui-hu chuan* yü-fa hsiu-tz'u shen-mei hsiao-ying hsi li" 水滸傳語法修辭審美效應析例. *Chung-kuo wen-hsüeh yen-chiu* 中國文學研究 21 (1991), 32–40.

———. "Pai-hua hsiao-shuo shuo-shu jen de yi-shu" 白話小說說書人的藝朮. *Chiu-chou hsüeh-k'an*, forthcoming.

Shan-hsi sheng wen-wu kung–tso-tui wei-yüan-hui 山西省文物工作隊委員會. "Hou-ma meng-shu ti fa-hsien, fa-chüeh yü cheng-li ch'ing-k'uang" 侯馬盟書的發現發掘與整理情況. *Wen-wu* 5 (1975), 7–11.

———. "Hou-ma meng-shu chu-shih si chung" 侯馬盟書注釋四種. *Wen-wu* 5 (1975), 20–26.

Shan-tung sheng po-wu-kuan, Lin-i wen-wu tsu 山東省博物館, 臨沂文物組. "Shan-tung Lin-i Hsi-Han-mu fa-hsien 'Sun-tzu pin-fa' ho 'Sun Pin pin-fa' teng chu-chien ti chien-pao" 山東臨沂西漢墓發現, 〝孫子兵法〞和〝孫臏兵法〞等竹簡的簡報. *Wen-wu* 2 (1974), 15–26.

Shang-hai shih ch'ung-hsing chi-hsieh chih-tsao kung-ssu kung-jen li-shih yen-chiu hsiao-tsu 上海市重型機械制造公司工人歷史研究小組. "Ts'ung Yün-meng Ch'in-chien 'Ta-chi-shih' k'an Ch'in t'ung-i liu-kuo ho fan-fu pi tou-cheng" 從雲夢秦簡〝大紀事〞看秦統一六國和反複辟斗爭. *Wen-wu* 7 (1976), 12–18.

Shang shu cheng-i 尚書正義. *Shih-san-ching chu-shu* edition.

Sheng Dong-ling 盛冬玲. "Hsi-Chou t'ung-ch'i ming-wen chung ti jen-ming chi ch'i tui tuan-tai ti i-i" 西周銅器銘文中的人名及其對斷代的意義. *Wen-shih* 7 (1983), 27–64.

Shih chi 史記. 10 vols. Peking: Chung-hua, 1959.

Shih-pen 世本. *Pai-pu ts'ung-shu chi-ch'eng* 百部叢書集成 edition.

Shih-san-ching chu-shu 十三經注疏. 2 vols. Peking: Chung-hua, 1980.

Shirakawa Shizuka 白川靜. *Chung-kuo ti shen-hua* 中國的神話. Trans. Wang Hsiao-lian 王孝廉. Taipei: Ch'ang-an, 1983.

———. *Kinbun tsūshaku* 金文通釋. *Hakutsuru bijutsukanshi* 白鶴美術館誌. 36 vols. to date. Kobe, 1962.

———. *Kōkotsu kimbungaku ronshū* 甲骨金文學論集. Kyoto: Hōyū shoten, 1974.

Shiratori Kiyoshi 白鳥清. "Ryū no keitai ni tsuite no kōsatsu" 龍の形態に就いての考察. *Tōyō gakuhō* 21.2 (1934), 105–34.

Shui-ching chu-shu 水經注疏. 2 vols. Chiang-su: Ku-chi, 1989.

Shui-hu chuan hui-p'ing-pen 水滸傳會評本. Peking: Pei-ching ta-hsüeh, 1981.

Shuo-wen chieh-tzu 說文解字. Peking: Chung-hua, 1990.

Shuo-wen chieh-tzu i-cheng 說文解字義証. 2 vols. Peking: Chung-hua, 1987.

Ssu-k'u ch'üan-shu tsung-mu 四庫全書總目. 2 vols. Peking: Chung-hua, 1965.

Su Hsüeh-lin 蘇雪林. *Ch'ü Yüan yü Chiu Ko* 屈原與九歌. Taipei: Kuang-tung, 1973.

———. *T'ien-wen cheng-chien* 天問正簡. Rpt. Taipei: Wen-chin, 1992.

Sui-hsien Lei-ku tun i-hao-mu k'ao-ku fa-chüeh tui 隨縣擂鼓墩一號考古發掘隊. "Hu-pei Sui-hsien Tseng-hou I mu fa-chüeh chien-pao" 湖北隨縣曾侯乙墓發掘簡報. *Wen-wu* 7 (1979), 1–13.

Sun Chih-chung 孫致中. "Mu-wang hsi-cheng yü *Mu T'ien-tzu chuan*" 穆王西征與穆天子傳. *Ch'i-lu hsüeh-k'an* 齊魯學刊 2 (1984), 76–82.

Sun I-jang 孫詒讓. *Cha-i* 札迻. Peking: Chung-hua, 1989.

Ta-tai Li-chi chieh-ku 大載禮記解詁. Wang P'in-chen 王聘珍 ed. Peking: Chung-hua, 1989.

Tai Lien-chang 戴璉璋. "Ku-tai Han-yü ti yü-hsü pien-huan" 古代漢語的語序變換. *Chung-yang yen-chiu yüan kuo-chi Han-hsüeh hui-i lun-wen chi* 中央研究院國際漢學會議論文集. 10 vols. Taipei, 1981.

T'ai-p'ing yü-lan 太平御覽. 4 vols. Peking: Chung-hua, 1985.

T'an Ts'ui 檀萃. *Mu T'ien-tzu chuan chu-shu* 穆天子傳註疏. Shih-pi lin-lang kuan ts'ung-shu edition.

T'ang Lan 唐蘭. "Hsi-Chou t'ung-ch'i tuan-tai chung K'ang-kung wen-t'i" 西周銅器斷代中的康宮問題. *K'ao-ku hsüeh-pao* 考古學報 1 (1962), 15–48.

———. "Yung ch'ing-t'ung-ch'i ming-wen lai yen-chiu Hsi-Chou shih" 用青銅器銘文來研究西周史. *Wen-wu* 6 (1976), 31–37.

———. "Lun Chou Chao-wang shih-tai ti ch'ing-t'ung-ch'i ming-k'o" 論周昭王時代的青銅器銘刻. *Ku-wen-tzu yen-chiu* 2 (1981), 3–162.

Ting Ch'ien 丁謙. *Mu T'ien-tzu chuan ti-li k'ao-cheng* 穆天子傳地理考証. Che-chiang t'u-shu ts'ung-shu 浙江圖書叢書 edition.

Ting-hsien Han-mu chu-chien cheng-li tsu 定縣漢墓竹簡整理組. "Ting-hsien 40 hao Han-mu ch'u-t'u chu-chien chien-chieh" 定縣40號漢墓出土竹簡簡介. *Wen-wu* 8 (1981), 11–12.

Tōdō Akiyasu 藤堂明保. *Kanji to bunka* 漢字と文化. Tokyo: Tokuma shoten, 1976.

Ts'en Chung-mien 岑仲勉. "*Mu T'ien-tzu chuan* hsi-cheng ti-li kai-ts'e" 穆天子傳西征地理概測. *Kuo-li Chung-shan ta-hsüeh hsüeh-pao she-hui k'o-hsüeh pan* 國立中山大學學報社會科學班 2 (1957), 26–48.

Tso-shih hui-chien 左氏會箋. 2 vols. Taipei: Han-ching wen-hua, 1984.

Tsou Heng 鄒衡. *Hsia Shang Chou k'ao-ku-hsüeh lun-wen chi* 夏商周考古學論文集. Peking: Wen-wu, 1980.

Tung Fang Shuo 東方朔. *Shih-chou chi* 十洲記. *Chu-tzu pai-chia ts'ung-shu* 諸子百家叢書 edition. Shanghai: Shang-hai ku-chi, 1990.

Wan Ch'üan-wen 萬全文. "Shang-Chou wang-ch'ao nan-chin lüeh-t'ung lun" 商周王朝南進掠銅論. *Chiang-han k'ao-ku* 江漢考古 3 (1992), 50–57.

Wang Chi-p'ei 汪繼培, ed. *Shih tzu* 尸子. *Erh-shih-erh tzu* 二十二子. Shanghai: Shang-hai ku-chi, 1985.

Wang Chia 王嘉. *Shih i chi* 拾遺記. *Pai-tzu ch'üan-shu* edition

Wang Chien-ming 王健民, Liang Chu 梁柱, and Wang Sheng-li 王勝利. "Tseng-hou I mu ch'u-t'u ti erh-shih pa hsiu ch'ing-lung pai-hu t'u-hsiang" 曾侯乙墓出土的十八宿清龍白虎圖像. *Wen-wu* 7 (1979), 40–45.

Wang En-t'ien 王恩田. "Chou-tai Chao-Mu chih-tu yüan-liu" 周代昭穆制度原流. Paper presented at the *Ti erh tz'u Hsi-Chou-shih hsüeh-shu t'ao-lun-hui* 第二次西周史學術討論會, 1992.

Wang Fan-chih 王范之. "*Mu T'ien-tzu chuan* yü suo chi ku-tai ti-ming ho pu-tsu" 穆天子傳與所記古代地名和部族. *Wen shih che* 文史哲 6 (1963), 61–67, 78.

Wang Hsiao-lian 王孝廉. *Chung-kuo ti shen-hua yü ch'uan-shuo* 中國的神話與傳説. Taipei: Lian-ming, 1977.

Wang Kuo-wei 王國維. *Kuan-t'ang chi-lin* 觀堂集林. 4 vols. Peking: Chung-hua, 1984.

———. *Hai-ning Wang Ching-an hsien-sheng i-shu* 海寧王靜安先生遺書. 16 vols. Shanghai: Shang-wu, 1940.

Wang Li 王力. *Chung-kuo yü-fa kang-yao* 中國語法剛要. Shanghai: Hsin chih-shih, 1957.

———. *Han-yü shi-kao* 漢語史稿. 3 vols. Peking: K'o-hsüeh, 1957.

Wang Yü-ch'eng 王育成. "Yang-shao jen-mian yü-wen yü shih-ch'ien jen-t'ou ch'ung-pai" 仰劭人面魚紋與史前人頭崇拜. *Chiang-han k'ao-ku* 2 (1992), 24–35, 23.

Wei Chü-hsien 衛聚賢. "*Mu T'ien-tzu chuan* yen-chiu" 穆天子傳研究. *Ku-shih yen-chiu* 古史研究. Shanghai: I-wen, 1934.

———. "Yü Hsia" 虞夏. In *Ku-shih yen-chiu*.

Wei T'ing-sheng 衛挺生. *Mu T'ien-tzu chuan chin-k'ao* 穆天子傳今考. 3 vols. Taipei: Chung-hua hsüeh-shu yüan, 1970.

Wen Ch'ung-i 文崇一. "Chiu-ko chung Ho-po chih yen-chiu" 九歌中河伯之研究. *Bulletin of the Institute of Ethnology*, Academica Sinica, 9 (1960) 148–51.

———. "Chiu-ko chung ti shui-shen yü Hua-nan ti lung-chou sai-shen" 九歌中的水神與華南的龍舟賽神. *Bulletin of the Institute of Ethnology*, Academica Sinica, 11 (1961), 51–124.

Wen I-to 聞一多. *Shen-hua yü shih* 神話與詩. *Wen I-to ch'üan-chi* 聞一多全集. 4 vols. Shanghai: K'ai-ming, 1948. Rpt. Hong Kong, 1972.

Wu Ch'eng-en 吳承恩. *Hsi-yu-chi* 西遊記. 3 vols. Peking: Jen-min, 1980.

Yang K'uan 楊寬. "Chung-kuo shang-ku-shih tao-lun" 中國尚古史導論. In Ku Chieh-kang, ed. *Ku-shih pien* 古史編. 7 vols. Peking: Pu-she, 1927–41. Vol. 7.

———. "Chu-jung yü Chu-lung" 祝融與燭龍. *Ku-shih pien*. Vol. 7, 314–316.

———. "E Po yü Chao-ming Chu-jung" 閼伯與照明祝融. *Ku-shih pien*. Vol. 7, 311–14.

———. "Yü, Kou-lung yü Hsia-hou Hou-t'u" 禹句龍與夏后后土. *Ku-shih pien*. vol. 7, 353–65.

———. *Chan-kuo shih* 戰國史. Rpt. Shanghai: Jen-min, 1991.

Yao Chi-heng 姚祭恆. *Ku-chin wei-shu k'ao* 古今偽書考. *Chih-pu-tsu chai ts'ung-shu* 知不足齊叢書 edition.

Yao Hsiao-sui 姚孝遂, et al., ed. *Yin-hsü chia-ku k'o-tz'u lei-tsuan* 殷墟甲骨刻辭類纂. 3 vols. Peking: Chung-hua, 1989.

Yeh Ch'ing-ping 葉慶炳. "Liu-ch'ao chih T'ang-tai ti t'a-chieh chieh-kou hsiao-shuo" 六朝至唐代的他界結構小說. *T'ai-ta Chung-wen hsüeh-pao* 臺大中文學報 3 (1991), 7–28.

Yin-ch'üeh shan Han-mu chu-chien cheng-li hsiao-tsu 銀雀山漢墓竹簡整理小組. *Yin-ch'üeh shan Han-mu chu-chien* 銀雀山漢墓竹簡. Peking: Wen-wu, 1985.

Yu Jen-teh 尤仁德. "Liang-Chou yü tiao lung-wen ti tsao-hsing yü wen-shih yen-chiu" 兩周玉雕龍的造型與紋飾研究. *Wen-wu* 7 (1982), 70–75.

Yüan Hsing-p'ei 袁行霈. "Han-shu 'I-wen chih' hsiao-shuo k'ao-pien" 漢書藝文志小說考辨. *Wen-shih* 7 (1979), 179–89.

Yüan K'o 袁柯. *Chung-kuo shen-hua tzu-liao ts'ui-pien* 中國神話資料萃編. Ch'eng-tu: Ssu-ch'uan she-hui k'o-hsüeh, 1985.

Yün-meng Ch'in-mu chu-chien cheng-li hsiao-tsu 雲夢秦墓竹簡整理小組. "Yün-meng Ch'in-chien shih-wen (1)" 雲夢秦簡釋文(一). *Wen-wu* 6 (1976), 12–13.

Western Sources

Abraham, Nicolas. "Le symbole ou l'au-delà du phénomene." In Nicolas Abraham and Maria Torok, *L'Écorce et le noyau*. Paris: Flammarion, 1987.

———. *Le verbier de l'homme aux loups*. Paris: Aubier-Flammarions, 1976.

———. *Rythmes de l'oeuvre de la traduction et de la psychanalyse*. Paris: Flammarion, 1985.

Allan, Sarah. *The Sage and the Heir: Dynastic Legend in Early China*. San Fransisco: Chinese Materials Center, 1981.

———. *The Shape of the Turtle: Myth, Art, and Cosmos in Early China*. Albany: SUNY Press, 1991.

Allport, Gordon W. and Leo Postman. *The Psychology of Rumor*. New York: Henry Holt and Co., 1947.

Baddeley, Allan D. *The Psychology of Memory*. New York: Basic Books, 1976.

Barnard, Noel. "Indigenous Origins of Metallurgy." In David Keightley, ed.

The Origins of Chinese Civilization. Berkeley: University of California Press, 1983.

Bauer, Wolfgang. "Voyageurs sans demeure et départs vers un monde meilleur dans la civilisation chinoise." *Diogenes* 165 (1994), 26–46.

Benedict, Paul. *Sino-Tibetan: A Conspectus*. Cambridge: Cambridge University Press, 1972.

Birrell, Anne. *Chinese Mythology*. Baltimore: Johns Hopkins University Press, 1993.

Bishop, John L. *The Colloquial Short Story in China: A Study of the San-yen Collections*. Harvard-Yenching Institute Studies 11. Cambridge, Mass.: Harvard University Press, 1956.

Bodde, Derk. "Myths of Ancient China." In S. N. Kramer, ed., *Mythologies of the Ancient World*. Garden City, N.Y.: Doubleday & Co., 1961.

Boltz, William. "Kung-kung and the Flood: Reverse Euhemerization in the Yao Tien." *T'oung Pao* 67.3–5 (1981), 141–53.

Boodberg, Peter. "Some Proleptical Remarks on the Evolution of Archaic Chinese." *Harvard Journal of Asiatic Studies* 2 (1937), 330–370.

Brown, Peter Lancaster. *Megaliths, Myths and Men*. New York: Taplinger, 1976.

Cahill, Suzanne. *Transcendence and Divine Passion*. Stanford: Stanford University Press, 1993.

Campany, Robert. "The Real Presence." *History of Religions* 32.3 (1993), 233–72.

Chafe, Wallace L. "Givenness, Contrastiveness, Definiteness: Subjects and Topics." In Charles N. Li, ed., *Symposium on Subject and Topic, University of California, Santa Barbara, March 1975*. New York: Academic Press, 1976.

Chang, K. C. *Early Chinese Civilization: Anthropological Perspectives*. Cambridge, Mass.: Harvard University Press, 1976.

———. *Art, Myth and Ritual*. Cambridge, Mass.: Harvard University Press, 1983.

———. *The Archaeology of Ancient China*. 4th ed. New Haven: Yale University Press, 1986.

Chao Yüan-jen. *A Grammar of Spoken Chinese*. Berkeley: University of California Press, 1968.

———. *Aspects of Chinese Sociolinguistics.* Palo Alto: Stanford University Press, 1976.

Chatman, Seymour. *Story and Discourse.* Ithaca: Cornell University Press, 1978.

Cheng Te-k'un. "The Travels of Emperor Mu." *Journal of the North China Branch of the Royal Asiatic Society* 43 (1933), 125–49.

Cheung Kwong-yue. "Recent Archaeological Evidence Relating to the Origin of Chinese Characters." In David Keightley, ed., *The Origins of Chinese Civilization.* Berkeley: University of California Press, 1983.

Creel, Herlee. *The Origins of Statecraft in China.* Volume 1: *The Western Chou Empire.* Chicago: University of Chicago Press, 1970.

Cullen, Christopher. "Some Further Points on the *Shih.*" *Early China* 6 (1980–81), 31–46.

de Santillana, Giorgio and Hertha von Dechend. *Hamlet's Mill: An Essay on Myth and the Frame of Time.* Boston: Gambit Inc., 1969.

de Sausure, Léopold. *Les Origines de l'Astronomie Chinoise.* Paris: Librairie Orientale et Americaine, 1930.

———. "Le Voyage de roi Mou et le hypothese d'E. Chavannes." *T'oung Pao* 20 (1920–21), 19–31.

DeWoskin, Kenneth J. "The Six Dynasties Chih-kuai and the Birth of Fiction." In Andrew H. Plaks, ed., *Chinese Narrative: Critical and Theoretical Essays.* Princeton: Princeton University Press, 1977.

———. *A Song for One or Two: Music and the Concept of Art in Early China.* Ann Arbor: Center for Chinese Studies, 1982.

———. "On Narrative Revolutions." *Chinese Literature: Essays, Articles and Reviews* 5 (1983), 29–45.

———. "Chih-kuai." In William H. Nienhauser, Jr., ed., *The Indiana Companion to Traditional Chinese Literature.* Bloomington: Indiana University Press, 1985.

———. "The Power of Bronze." *Archaeology* (January/February 1994), 50.

Diény, Jean Pierre. *Le symbolisme du dragon dans la Chine antique.* Paris: Collège de France, 1987.

Dubs, Homer, H. "An Ancient Chinese Mystery Cult." *Harvard Theological Review* 35 (1941), 221–40.

Eberhard, Wolfram. *The Local Cultures of South and East China.* Trans. Alide Eberhard. Leiden: E. J. Brill, 1968.

———. "Review of Legends and Cults, by Bernhard Karlgren." *Artibus Asiae* 9.4 (1946), 355–64.

Ecsedy, I. K. Barlai, R. Dvorak, and R. Schult. "Antares Year in Ancient China." In A. F. Aveni, ed., *World Archaeoastronomy*. Cambridge: Cambridge University Press, 1989.

Edmondson, Willis. *Spoken Discourse: A Model for Analysis*. London: Longman, 1981.

Eitel, E. J., trans. *Mu T'ien-tzu chuan. China Review* 27 (1888), 223–40, 247–58.

Eliade, Mircea. *The Sacred and the Profane*. Trans. Willard R. Trask. New York: Harcourt Brace Jovanovich, 1987.

———. *Cosmos and History*. Rpt. New York: Harper & Brothers, 1959.

———. *Shamanism: Archaic Techniques of Ecstasy*. Trans. Willard R. Trask. New York: Bollingen Foundation, 1964.

Emiliani, Cesare et al. "Paleoclimatological Analysis of Late Quaternary Cores from the Northeastern Gulf of Mexico." *Science* 189 (1975), 1083–88.

Eno, Robert. "Was There a High God *Ti* in Shang Religion?" *Early China* 15 (1990), 14–26.

Fabian, Johannes. *Time and the Other*. New York: Columbia University Press, 1983.

Fauvel, A. A. "Alligators in China." *Journal of the North China Branch of the Royal Asiatic Society* 1 (1878).

Feng Yu-lan. *A History of Chinese Philosophy*. Trans. Derk Bodde. Princeton: Princeton University Press, 1973.

Field, Stephen. "Cosmos, Cosmograph, and the Inquiring Poet: New Answers to the 'Heaven Questions.'" *Early China* 17 (1992), 83–110.

Finley, Moses I. "Myth, Memory, and History." *History and Theory* 4.3 (1964).

Foucault, Michel. *The Archaeology of Knowledge and the Discourse on Language*. Trans. A. M. Sheridan. New York: Pantheon, 1972.

Fracasso, Ricardo. "Holy Mothers of Ancient China." *T'oung Pao* 74 (1988), 1–42.

Geertz, Clifford. *The Interpretation of Cultures*. Albany: SUNY Press, 1973.

Girardot, Norman. *Myth and Meaning in Early Taoism*. Berkeley: University of California Press, 1983.

———. "The Problem of Creation Mythology in the Study of Chinese Religion." *Journal of History of Religions* 15.4 (1976), 289–318.

Graham, A. C. *Disputers of the Tao.* La Salle, Ill.: Open Court, 1989.

———, trans. *The Book of Lieh tzu.* London: John Murray, 1960.

———. "The Date and Composition of the *Lieh tzu.*" *Asia Major* 8 (1961), 139–98.

Granet, Marcel. *Danses et légendes de la Chine ancienne.* 2 vols. Paris: Presses Universitaires de France, 1959.

———. "Remarques sur le Taoisme." *Asia Major* 2 (1925), 146–51.

———. *Fêtes et chansons anciennes de la Chine.* 2nd ed. Paris: Leroux, 1929.

———. *Festivals and Songs in Ancient China.* Trans. E. D. Edward. New York: E. P. Dutton, 1932.

Halbwachs, Maurice. *Collective Memory.* New York: Harper & Row, 1980.

Halliday, M. A. K. *An Introduction to Functional Grammar.* London: Edward Arnold, 1985.

Hanan, Patrick. "The Early Chinese Short Story: A Critical Theory in Outline." *Harvard Journal of Asiatic Studies* 27 (1967), 168–207. Rpt. Cyril Birch, ed., *Studies in Chinese Literary Genres.*

———. *The Chinese Vernacular Story.* Cambridge, Mass.: Harvard University Press, 1981.

Harper, Donald. "The Wu shih erh Ping fang: Translation and Prologemena." Ph.D. Diss., University of California, Berkeley, 1982.

———. "The Han Cosmic Board (*Shih*)." *Early China* 4 (1978–79), 1–10.

———. "The Han Cosmic Board: A Response to Christopher Cullen." *Early China* 6 (1980–81), 47–56.

———. "A Chinese Demonography of the Third Century B.C." *Harvard Journal of Asiatic Studies* 45 (1985), 459–98.

———. "Wang Yen-shou's Nightmare Poem." *Harvard Journal of Asiatic Studies* 47.1 (1987), 239–84.

———. "The Sexual Arts of Ancient China as Described in a Manuscript of the Second Century B.C." *Harvard Journal of Asiatic Studies* 47.2 (1987), 539–94.

Hartner, Willy. "The Obliquity of the Ecliptic According to the *Hou-han Shu* and Ptolemy." *Oriens-Occidens.* Heldesheim. Georg Olms Verlagshuchhandulung, 1968.

———. "The Earliest History of the Constellations in the Near East, and the Motif of the Lion-Bull Combat." *Journal of Near Eastern Studies* 24 (1965), 1–16.

Havelock, Eric. "The Linguistic Task of the PreSocratics." In Kevin Robb, ed., *Language and Thought in Early Greek Philosophy.* La Salle, Ill.: Monist Library of Philosophy, 1983.

Hawkes, David. "Quest of the Goddess." In Cyril Birch, ed., *Studies in Chinese Literary Genres.* Berkeley: University of California Press, 1974.

Hawkins, Gerald. *Stonehenge Decoded.* Garden City, N.Y.: Doubleday, 1973.

Henderson, John B. *The Development and Decline of Chinese Cosmology.* New York: Columbia University Press, 1984.

Henricks, Robert G. "On the Wherabouts and Identity of the Place Called 'K'ung-sang' (Hollow Mulberry) in Early Chinese Mythology." Paper presented at the annual meeting of the Association for Asian Studies, Washington, D.C., 4 April 1992.

Henry, Eric. "The Motif of Recognition in Early China." *Harvard Journal of Asiatic Studies* 47 (1987), 5–30.

Ho, Yong. *Aspects of Discourse Structure in Mandarin Chinese.* Lewiston, N.Y.: Edwin Mellen University Press, 1993.

Hopkins, L. C. "The Dragon Terrestrial and the Dragon Celestial, Part II: Ch'en, the Dragon Celestial." *Journal of the Royal Asiatic Society* (1913), 91–97.

———. "Dragon and Alligator: Being Notes on Some Ancient Inscribed Bone Carvings." *Journal of the Royal Asiatic Society* (1913), 545–52.

Hsu Cho-yun and Katheryn M. Linduff. *Western Chou Civilization.* New Haven: Yale University Press, 1988.

Hu P'ing-sheng. "Some Notes on the Organization of the Han Dynasty Bamboo 'Annals' Found at Fuyang." *Early China* 14 (1989), 1–25.

Hulsewé, A. F. P. "Notes on the Historiography of the Han Period." In W. B. Beasley and E. G. Pulleyblank, eds., *Historians of China and Japan.* London: Oxford University Press, 1961.

———. "Texts in Tombs." *Asiatische Studien* 18–19 (1965), 79–89.

Izutsu, Toshihiko. "Between Image and No-Image." *Eranos Lecture Series 7, On Images: Far Eastern Ways of Thinking.* Dallas: Spring Publications, 1988.

Kao, Karl S. Y. "Aspects of Derivation in Chinese Narrative." *Chinese Literature: Essays, Articles, Reviews* 7 (1985), 1–36.

———. ed., *Classical Chinese Tales of the Supernatural and the Fantastic: Selections from the Third to the Tenth Century*. Bloomington: Indiana University Press, 1985.

Karlgren, Bernhard. "Legends and Cults in Ancient China." *Bulletin of the Museum of Far Eastern Antiquities* 18 (1946), 199–365.

———. *Grammatica Serica Recensa*. Stockholm: Museum of Far Eastern Antiquities, 1972.

———. "On the Authenticity and Nature of the *Tso Chuan*." *Goteborgs Hogskolas Arsskrift* 32.3 (1926), 3–65.

Keenan, Edward. "Towards a Universal Definition of Subject." Charles N. Li, ed. *Symposium on Subject and Topic, University of California, Santa Barbara, March 1975*. New York: Academic Press, 1976, 303–34.

Keightley, David N. ed. *The Origins of Chinese Civilization*. Berkeley: University of California Press, 1983.

———. "Akatsuka Kiyoshi and the Culture of Early China: A Study in Historical Method." *Harvard Journal of Asiatic Studies* 42.1 (1982).

———. "The Quest for Eternity in Ancient China: The Dead, Their Gifts, Their Names." In George Kuwayama, ed., *Ancient Mortuary Traditions of China*. Los Angeles: Far Eastern Art Council, Los Angeles County Museum of Art, 1991.

Kirk, Geoffrey S. *Myth: Its Meaning and Function in Ancient and Other Cultures*. Berkeley: University of California Press, 1970.

Kuhn, Dieter. *Textile and Technology*. Vol. 5, part 2 in Joseph Needham, ed., *Science and Civilisation in China*. Cambridge: Cambridge University Press, 1988.

Kunst, Richard. "The Original 'YiJing': A Text, Phonetic Transcription, Translation, and Indexes, with Sample Glosses." Ph.D. diss., University of California, Berkeley 1985.

Lai, Whalen. "Symbolism of Evil in China: The K'ung-chia Myth Analyzed." *History of Religions* 23.4 (1984), 316–343.

Lewis, Mark Edward. *Sanctioned Violence in Early China*. Albany: SUNY Press, 1990.

Lévi-Strauss, Claude. *From Honey to Ashes*. Trans. John and Doreen Weightman. London: Jonathan Cape, 1973.

———. *The Raw and the Cooked.* trans. John and Doreen Weightman. New York: Harper Colophon Books, 1975.

———. *La pensée sauvage.* Paris: Librairie Plon, 1962.

Li, Charles N. "The Semantic Function of Word Order: A Case Study in Mandarin." In Charles N. Li, ed., *Word Order and Word Order Change.* Austin: University of Texas Press, 1975, 163–96.

———. "Subject and Topic: A New Typology of Language," in Charles N. Li, ed., *Word Order and Word Order Change* , 459–89.

———. *Mandarin Chinese: A Functional Grammar.* Berkeley: University of California Press, 1981.

Li, Charles N. and Sandra A. Thompson. "Historical Change of Word Order: A Case Study and Its Implications." In J. M. Anderson and C. Jones, eds., *Historical Linguistics.* Amsterdam: North-Holland Publishing Co., 1974, 199–217.

Li Ling and Keith McMahon. "The Content and Terminology of the Mawangdui Texts on the Arts of the Bedchamber." *Early China* 17 (1992), 145–85.

Li, Wai-yee. *Enchantment and Disenchantment.* Princeton: Princeton University Press, 1993.

Li Xuequin. *Eastern Zhou and Qin Civilizations.* Trans. K. C. Chang. New Haven: Yale University Press, 1985.

Light, Timothy. "Word Order and Word Order Change in Chinese." *Journal of Chinese Linguistics* 7.2 (1979), 149–80.

Loewe, Michael. *Ways to Paradise: The Chinese Quest for Immortality.* London: Allen and Unwin, 1979.

Lu, Hsiao-peng. "The Fictional Discourse of *Pien-wen*: The Relation of Chinese Fiction to Historiography." *Chinese Literature: Essays, Articles and Reviews* 9 (1987), 49–70.

Mair, Victor. "The Narrative Revolution in Chinese Literature." *Chinese Literature: Essays, Articles and Reveiws* 5 (1983), 1–27.

Major, John. "Myth, Cosmology, and the Origins of Chinese Science." *Journal of Chinese Philosophy* 5.1 (1978), 1–20.

———. *Heaven and Earth in Early Han Thought.* Albany: SUNY Press, 1993.

———. "Will the Real Yellow Emperor Please Stand Up?" *Essays on the Huainanzi.* Albany: SUNY Press, forthcoming.

Maspero, Henri. "Légendes mythologiques dans le Chou king." *Journal Asiatique* 205 (1924), 1–100.

———. "Contribution a l'étude de le société chinoise à la fin des Chang et au début des Tcheou." *Bulletin de l'École Francaise d'Extreme Orient* 46.2 (1954), 347–49.

Mathieu, Rémi. *Le Mu Tianzi Zhuan: Traduction annotée, Étude critique.* Paris: Collège de France, 1978.

———. "Yu le Grand et le mythe du déluge dans la Chine ancienne." *T'oung Pao* 78 (1992), 162–90.

Mote, Frederick. "The Cosmological Gulf between China and the West." in David C. Buxbaum and Frederick W. Mote, eds., *Transition and Permanence: Chinese History and Culture.* Hong Kong: Cathay Press, 1973, 3–21.

Needham, Joseph. *Science and Civilization in China.* 6 vols. Cambridge: Cambridge University Press, 1956.

———. "Time and Knowledge in China and the West." In J. T. Fraser, ed., *The Voices of Time.* New York: George Braziller, 1966.

Neill, Wilfred., T. *The Last of the Ruling Reptiles: Alligators, Crocodiles, and Their Kin.* New York: Columbia University Press, 1971.

Nienhauser, William H. Jr. "The Origins of Chinese Fiction." *Monumenta Serica* 38 (1988–89), 191–219.

———. "Review of Rémi Mathieu's *Le Mu Tianzi Zhuan, Traduction annotée, Étude critique.*" *Chinese Literature: Essays, Articles and Reviews* 4 (1982), 247–53.

Nivison, David. "The Origin of the Chinese Lunar Lodge System." In A. F. Aveni, ed., *World Archaeoastronomy.* Cambridge: Cambridge University Press, 1989.

Ong, Walter. *Orality and Literacy.* London: Methuen, 1982.

Pankenier, David W. "Astronomical Dates in Shang and Western Zhou." *Early China* 7 (1981–82), 2–37.

———. "Mozi and the Dates of Xia, Shang, and Zhou: A Research Note." *Early China* 9–10 (1983), 175–83.

———. "Early Chinese Astronomy and Cosmology: The 'Mandate of Heaven' as Epiphany." Ph.D. Diss., Stanford University, 1983.

———. "Forum: Astronomical Evidence for the *Bamboo Annals'* Chronicle of Early Xia." *Early China* 15 (1990), 117–32.

———. "The *Bamboo Annals* Revisited: Problems of Method in Using the Chronicle as a Source for the Chronology of Early Zhou, Part 1." *Bulletin of the School of Oriental and African Studies* 55, part 2 (1992), 272–97.

———. "The *Bamboo Annals* Revisited: Problems of Method in Using the Chronicle as a Source for the Chronology of Early Zhou, Part 2: The Congruent Mandate Chronology in *Yi Zhou shu*." *Bulletin of the School of Oriental and African Studies*, 55, part 3 (1992), 498–510.

———. "Reflections of the Lunar Aspect on Western Chou Chronology." *T'oung Pao* 78 (1992), 33–76.

Pelliot, Paul. "L'Étude du *Mou t'ien tseu tchouan*." *T'oung Pao* 21 (1922), 98–102.

Peterson, Willard. "Making Connections: 'Commentary on the Attached Verbalizations' of the *Book of Change*." *Harvard Journal of Asiatic Studies* 42.1 (1982), 67–116.

Plaks, Andrew. *Archetype and Allegory in the Dream of the Red Chamber*. Princeton: Princeton University Press, 1976.

———. "Towards a Critical Theory of Chinese Narrative." In Andrew Plaks, ed., *Chinese Narrative: Critical and Theoretical Essays*. Princeton: Princeton University Press, 1976.

———. "Functions of Colloquial Rhetoric in Traditional Chinese Fiction." Paper presented at the Conference of Oriental Western Literary Relations, Indiana University, June 1979.

———. *The Four Masterworks of the Ming Novel*. Princeton: Princeton University Press, 1987.

Porée-Maspero, Evilene. *Étude sur les rites agraires des Cambodgiens*. 3 vols. Paris: Mouton and Co., 1952, 1964, 1969.

Porter, Deborah. "Toward an Aesthetic of Chinese Vernacular Fiction: Colloquial Style in the *Shui-hu chuan*." *T'oung Pao* 79 (1993), 113–53.

———. "The Formation of an Image: An Analysis of the Linguistic Patterns that Form the Character of Sung Chiang." *Journal of the American Oriental Society* 12.12 (1992), 233–53.

———. "The Literary Significance of K'un-lun Mountain in the *Mu T'ien-tzu chuan*." *Early China* 18 (1993), 75–106.

Prusek, Jarsolov. "New Studies of the Colloquial Short Story." *Archiv Orientalni* 25 (1957), 452–99.

Pulleyblank, E. G. "Chinese Historical Criticism: Liu Chih-chi and Ssu-ma Kuang." In W. G. Beasley and E. G. Pulleyblank, eds., *Historians of China and Japan.* Oxford: Oxford University Press, 1961.

Rand, Nicholas, trans. *The Wolf Man's Magic Word: A Cryptonymy.* Minneapolis: University of Minnesota Press, 1986.

———, trans. *The Shell and the Kernel.* Vol. 1. Chicago: University of Chicago Press, 1994.

Rashkin, Esther. "Tools for a New Psychoanalytic Literary Criticism: The Works of Abraham and Torok." *Diacritics* 18.4 (1988).

———. *Family Secrets and the Psychoanalysis of Narrative.* Princeton: Princeton University Press, 1992.

Reiche, Harald A. T. "The Language of Archaic Astronomy: A Clue to the Atlantis Myth?" In Kenneth Brecher and Michael Feirtag, eds., *Astronomy of the Ancients.* Cambridge, Mass.: MIT Press, 1979.

Ricoeur, Paul. *The Symbolism of Evil.* Trans. Emerson Buchanan. New York: Harper & Row, 1967.

Ronan, Colin. *The Shorter Science and Civilization in China.* Cambridge: Cambridge University Press, 1981.

Samuel, Raphael and Paul Thompson, eds. *The Myths We Live By.* London: Routledge, 1990.

Saso, Michael. "What is the *Ho-t'u?*" *History of Religions* 17.3–4 (1978), 399–416.

Saussy, Haun. *The Problem of a Chinese Aesthetic.* Stanford: Stanford University Press, 1993.

Schafer, Edward. *Pacing the Void.* Berkeley: University of California Press, 1977.

———. "The Sky River." *Journal of the American Oriental Society* 94.4 (1974), 401–7.

———. "The Transcendent Vitamin: Efflorescence of Lang-kan." *Chinese Science* 3 (1978), 27–38.

Schipper, Kristoffer and Wang Hsiu-huei. "Progressive and Regressive Time Cycles in Taoist Ritual." In J. T. Fraser, N. Lawrence, and F. C. Haber, eds., *Time, Science, and Society in China and the West.* Amherst: University of Massachusetts Press, 1986.

Schlegel, Gustav. *Uranographie Chinoise.* 2 vols. Leiden, 1875. Rpt. Leiden: 1975.

Schneider, Laurence A. *Ku Chieh-kang and China's New History*. Berkeley: University of California Press, 1971.

———. *A Madman of Ch'u: The Chinese Myth of Loyalty and Dissent*. Berkeley: University of California Press, 1980.

Schuessler, Axel. *A Dictionary of Early Zhou Chinese*. Honolulu: University of Hawaii Press, 1987.

Schwartz, Benjamin. *The World of Thought in Ancient China*. Cambridge, Mass.: Harvard University Press, 1985.

———. "The Age of Transcendence." *Daedalus* (Spring 1974), 1–7.

———. "Transcendence in Ancient China." *Daedalus* (Spring 1974), 57–68.

Sellers, Jane. *The Death of Gods in Ancient Egypt*. London: Penguin, 1993.

Serruys, Paul. "The Language of the Shang Oracle Inscriptions." *T'oung Pao* 60 (1974), 12–120.

Shaughnessy, Edward. *Sources of Western Zhou History*. Berkeley: University of California Press, 1991.

———. "On the Authenticity of the *Bamboo Annals*." *Harvard Journal of Asiatic Studies* 46.1 (1986), 149–80.

———. "Historical Geography and the Extent of the Earliest Chinese Kingdoms." *Asia Major* 2.2 (1989), 1–22.

———. "The Duke of Zhou's Retirement in the East and the Beginnings of the Minister-Monarch Debate in Chinese Political Philosophy." *Early China* 18 (1993), 41–72.

Shibutani, Tamotsu. *Improvised News*. New York: Bobbs-Merrill Co., 1966.

Sivin, Nathan. "On the Word 'Taoist' as a Source of Perplexity: With Special Reference to the Relations of Science and Religion in Traditional China." *History of Religions* 17.3–4 (1978).

———. "Chinese Archaeoastronomy: Between Two Worlds." In A. F. Aveni, ed., *World Archaeoastronomy*. Cambridge: Cambridge University Press, 1989.

———. *Cosmos and Computation in Early Chinese Mathematical Astronomy*. Leiden: E. J. Brill, 1969.

Smith, Thomas. "Ritual and the Shaping of Narrative: The Legend of the Han Emperor Wu." Ph.D. Diss., University of Michigan, 1992.

Sun Chao-fen and Talmy Givon. "On the So-called SOV Word Order in

Mandarin Chinese: A Quantified Text Study and Its Implications." *Language* 61.2 (1985), 329–51.

Tai, James H. Y. "Chinese as an SOV Language." In Shou-hsin Teng, ed., *Readings in Chinese Transformational Syntax.* Taipei: Crane Publishing Co., 1986, 339–54.

———. "On the Change from SVO to SOV in Chinese." *Transformational Syntax* 429–44.

———. "Toward a Cognition-Based Functional Grammar of Chinese." In James H-Y. Tai and Frank F. S. Hsüeh eds., *Functionalism and Chinese Grammar.* Chinese Language Teachers Association Monograph Series, no. 1, 1989, 187–226.

———. "Temporal Sequence and Chinese Word Order." In John Haiman ed., *Iconicity.* Amsterdam: John Benjamins, 1985.

Takishima, Ken-ichi. "An Evaluation of the Theories Concerning the Shang Oracle-Bone Inscriptions." *The Journal of Intercultural Studies* (Kansai University) 15–16 (1988–89).

———. "A Study of the Copulas in Shang Chinese." *Toyo Bunka Kenkyusho Kiyo* (Tokyo Daigaku) 1.12 (1990).

T'ang Chün-i. "The T'ien Ming (Heavenly Ordinance) in Pre-Ch'in China." *Philosophy East and West* 11 (1961), 195–218; 12 (1962), 29–49.

Thom, Alexander. *Megalithic Sites in Britain and Megalithic Lunar Observatories.* Oxford: Oxford University Press, 1971.

Thomas, Rosalind. *Oral Tradition and Written Record in Classical Athens.* Cambridge: Cambridge University Press, 1989.

———. "Ancient Greek Family Tradition and Democracy." In Raphael Samuel and Paul Thompson, eds., *The Myths We Live By.* London: Routledge, 1990.

Tokei, Ferenc. *La naissance de l'élégie chinoise.* Paris: Gallimard, 1967.

———. "À propos du genre du *Mou T'ien-tseu tchouan.*" *Acta Orientalia* 9 (1958), 45–49.

Twitchett, Dennis. "Chinese Biographical Writing." In W. G. Beasley and E. G. Pulleyblank, eds., *Historians of China and Japan.* Oxford: Oxford University Press, 1961.

Ulansey, David. *The Origins of the Mithraic Mysteries.* Oxford: Oxford University Press, 1989.

van der Loon, P. "The Ancient Chinese Chronicles and the Growth of Historical Ideals." In W. G. Beasley and E. G. Pulleyblank, eds., *Historians of China and Japan.* Oxford: Oxford University Press, 1961.

Vansina, Jan. *Oral Tradition as History.* Madison: University of Wisconsin Press, 1985.

———. "Memory and Oral Tradition." In Joseph Miller, ed., *The African Past Speaks: Essays on Oral Tradition and History.* Folkestone: Dawson and Archon, 1980.

von Falkenhausen, Lothar. "Music in the Life of the Marquis Yi's Court." *Archaeology* (January/February 1994), 47.

———. *Suspended Music.* Berkeley: University of California Press, 1993.

Wang Ching-hsien. *The Bell and the Drum: Shih Ching as Formulaic Poetry in an Oral Tradition.* Berkeley: University of California Press, 1974.

Wellek, René and Austin Warren. *Theory of Literature.* New York: Harcourt, Brace & World, 1956.

White, Hayden. *Tropics in Discourse.* Baltimore: Johns Hopkins University Press, 1978.

Wilhelm, Hellmut. "The Interplay of Image and Concept." *Eranos Lecture Series* 7, *On Images: Far Eastern Ways of Thinking* , 41–67.

———. "Notes on Chou Fiction." In David C. Buxbaum and Frederick W. Mote eds., *Transition and Permanence: Chinese History and Culture.* Hong Kong: Cathay Press, 1972.

Worthen, Thomas. *The Myth of Replacement.* Tucson: University of Arizona Press, 1991.

Wu Hung. "Xiwangmu, The Queen Mother of the West." *Orientations* 18.4 (1987), 24–33.

———. "From Temple to Tomb: Ancient Chinese Art and Religion in Transition." *Early China* 13 (1988), 78–115.

———. *The Wu Liang Shrine: The Ideology of Early Chinese Pictorial Art.* Stanford: Stanford University Press, 1989.

———. "Art in a Ritual Context: Rethinking Mawangdui." *Early China* 17 (1992), 111–44.

Yang Lien-sheng. "The Organization of Chinese Official Historiography." In W. G. Beasley and E. G. Pulleyblank, eds., *Historians of China and Japan.* Oxford: Oxford University Press, 1961.

Yu, Anthony. "History, Fiction and the Reading of Chinese History." *Chinese Literature: Essays, Articles and Reviews* 10.1–2 (1988), 1–19.

Yu, Pauline. *The Reading of Imagery in the Chinese Poetic Tradition.* Princeton: Princeton University Press, 1987.

Yü Ying-shih. "Life and Immortality in the Mind of Han China." *Harvard Journal of Asiatic Studies* 25 (1964), 80–122.

Index

D

E

F

L

M

N

O

P

R

S

T

U

V